Latin American Collection Concepts

Latin American Collection Concepts

Essays on Libraries, Collaborations and New Approaches

Edited by
GAYLE ANN WILLIAMS and
JANA LEE KRENTZ

McFarland & Company, Inc., Publishers
Jefferson, North Carolina

LIBRARY OF CONGRESS CATALOGUING-IN-PUBLICATION DATA

Names: Williams, Gayle Ann, 1954– editor. | Krentz, Jana Lee, editor.
Title: Latin American collection concepts : essays on libraries,
collaborations and new approaches / edited by Gayle Ann Williams
and Jana Lee Krentz.
Description: Jefferson, North Carolina : McFarland & Company, Inc.,
Publishers, 2019 | Includes bibliographical references and index.
Identifiers: LCCN 2018053937 | ISBN 9781476667591
(paperback : acid free paper) ∞
Subjects: LCSH: Acquisition of Latin American publications. |
Libraries—Special collections—Latin America. |
Collection development (Libraries)—United States.
Classification: LCC Z688.L4 L38 2019 | DDC 025.2/98—dc23
LC record available at https://lccn.loc.gov/2018053937

BRITISH LIBRARY CATALOGUING DATA ARE AVAILABLE

ISBN (print) 978-1-4766-6759-1
ISBN (ebook) 978-1-4766-3471-5

Front cover images © 2019 DNY59/Connel_Design/iStock

Printed in the United States of America

*McFarland & Company, Inc., Publishers
Box 611, Jefferson, North Carolina 28640
www.mcfarlandpub.com*

To all SALALM members,
Past, Present, Future

Acknowledgments

I owe a special debt of gratitude to my mentors, Suzanne Hodgman (retired, University of Wisconsin, Madison) and Glenn Read (retired, Indiana University, Bloomington). Suzanne set me on my career path and introduced me to SALALM. Glenn gave me tools to secure my first library job. How can I ever thank you?—Jana Lee Krentz

I want to recognize two important role models, Ann Hartness (retired, University of Texas at Austin), and Laura Gutiérrez Witt (retired, University of Texas at Austin). Both of you welcomed me to the Benson Latin American Collection when I worked there as a clerk. Ann was a great boss who encouraged my career goals. Laura let me know about a grant that led to my first librarian position as a cataloger at the Benson collection. You're both always in my heart!—Gayle Ann Williams

Table of Contents

Preface

GAYLE ANN WILLIAMS *and* JANA LEE KRENTZ

Latin American Collection Concepts: Essays on Libraries, Collaborations and New Approaches intends to be a bold argument for the importance of Latin American and Caribbean studies subject specialist librarians for libraries now and in the future. Collecting workflows for Latin Americana and Caribbeana are in transition between traditional purchasing (firm orders, approval plans, etc.), the creation of digital collections, and digital scholarship applications in research and publication. Contributed essays on various approaches to collection development highlight the need to maintain the status quo in the face of compelling technological changes in libraries along with innovative and pioneering techniques to create a hybrid collecting methodology.

A discussion at the Committee on Interlibrary Cooperation during the 2010 annual meeting of the Seminar on the Acquisition of Latin American Library Materials (SALALM) in Philadelphia brought up the possibility of creating a book of collected essays on how Latin American and Caribbean studies selectors build and maintain print (and other format) collections as academic libraries move toward an increasingly digital/virtual environment. The group acknowledged that within their respective institutions, their work may be viewed as anachronistic and out of step when viewed against academic library practices bent on streamlining collection development practices. Yet paradoxically there are aspects of Latin American librarianship that are ground-breaking and have been used as models for other branches of information science, especially other area studies disciplines.

Our purpose in compiling this work is to demonstrate that Latin American studies librarians are indeed still ordering print materials from the region as they would have done twenty or thirty years ago due to the fact that there is little or no digital equivalent for materials needed to advance critical research.[1] In addition, locating and purchasing materials from Latin America is still problematic and may present obstacles to libraries as well as modern business offices. Building print collections now takes place in an environment in which many of us also contend with funding shortages. At the same time, librarians are challenged to meet user demands to address gaps in a certain discipline or region. Librarians are also urged to create digital resources as well as assist in digital scholarship applications, and to incorporate best practices for information literacy to assist users in locating and using our subject-specific sources. These challenges, in terms of both time and funding, have obliged Latin American librarians to pioneer resource-sharing networks, and have compelled us to search out methods to exploit open access resources, while formulating ways to make traditional collecting more efficacious.

1

The essays that follow are the response to the Call for Papers issued to SALALM members in September 2015. The editors, Gayle Ann Williams and Jana Lee Krentz, arranged them according to the overall story they could tell with regard to current practices of collection building of Latin American books and other materials. Sarah A. Buck Kachaluba opens this exploration of our particular bibliographic world with a useful history of the acquisition of Latin American materials. Her approach provides an overview of the different organizational players that are referenced throughout other contributions and weaves in and out of the acronyms that are not so obvious to some of our readers. Judith Eckoff Alspach's history of the Latin American Materials Project (LAMP) then provides a jumping off point to one of the aforementioned acronyms and provides the first encounter to the concept of resource sharing that has long been a mainstay in the collection of Latin Americana. The change in the M in LAMP from "Microfilm" to "Materials" chronicles the shift in institutional collaboration's recognition of the need to move out of an old technology into one (digitization) that holds new promise for making materials available beyond one locale.

Other mainstays for most area studies librarians are strong, dynamic, working relationships with book dealers located in the region that are critical to supplying readily available and hard to find materials. S. Lief Adleson, long-time owner of Books from Mexico, provides the book dealer's point of view of how supplying books to the U.S. academic library market has changed over the years of his involvement. His essay points to how much things have changed for area studies specialists and where their concerns meld with the book dealers with whom they work.

The buying trip also allows individual librarians the opportunity not to duplicate the book dealer's task but the opportunity to gain hands-on experience with the local publishing market and to also pursue acquisition of more arcane items or ephemera outside of the book dealer's purview. Non-area studies librarians sometimes view book buying trips as boondoggles used by their area studies colleagues as a relaxing vacation in a pleasant, exotic clime. Authors Peter Altekrueger and Ricarda Musser dispel such notions with their essay on how to utilize a buying trip to best advantage. Their description of having two librarians from the same institution travel together differs from the U.S. model in which an area studies librarian usually fends for his or herself. Nonetheless, they demonstrate the potential for a book buying trip as another means of rooting out hard-to-find noncommercial or gray material that engenders uniqueness within a university library collection and which is so prized by scholars.

While the scope of this volume is meant to go beyond the institutional histories, it does include descriptions of leading Latin American collections in the U.S. Many prominent institutions have built strong collections but those at the University of Texas at Austin, the University of Florida, and Tulane University receive special attention as the three stand-alone collections devoted to Latin American holdings in the United States. Their individual descriptions do not merely rest upon their laurels as critical collections. Essential to their mission is the necessity for long-term planning tied into new innovations that continue to make their holdings critical and significant to users.

Hortensia Calvo and Guillermo Náñez Falcón paint a rich and fascinating account of how the Latin American Library (LAL) at Tulane University emerged from its origins within the Library of the Department of Middle American Research. While still known for its valuable collections of monographs and archives focusing on Central America, the authors take into account how the LAL has expanded its collections in other regions and formats. The LAL has more recently begun to share its riches to scholars who may not be able to travel to New Orleans by digitizing its formidable collections.

In their description of the Benson Latin American Collection at the University of Texas at Austin, Julianne Gilliland, Melissa Guy, and Theresa E. Polk move quickly from its beginnings in 1921 with the acquisition of a significant collection of Mexicana to examining new initiatives developed since the library's 2011 consolidation with the UT Teresa Lozano Long Institute of Latin American Studies from which emerged LILLAS Benson. They describe their commitment to incorporate values of diversity and social justice in building and sharing materials through a variety of digital projects. Their engagement sharing institutional expertise with partners in the region through post-custodial archival practices will build new digital resources available to the scholarly community.

Lara Lookabaugh, Paul S. Losch and Richard F. Phillips chronicle the development of the Latin American and Caribbean Collection (LACC) at the University of Florida as part of that institution's growth in building a robust academic Latin American and Caribbean studies program. Their focus on the collection as a physical space and emphasis on the human factor that contributed to LACC also highlights its efforts to share its resources beyond Gainesville. For example, LACC's dedication to microfilming Caribbean archival resources and newspapers demonstrates a natural evolution by transcending the physical library and becoming a critical partner of the Digital Library of the Caribbean, a cooperative digital library for resources from and about the Caribbean.

It is not a surprise to find five contributions regarding collaborative collection development within this volume. Resource-sharing has long been a topic of interest in SALALM given its members' long-standing participation in LAMP, along with the realization of the danger of our collections becoming highly duplicative due to the use of the same book suppliers. The increasing issue of dwindling materials budgets adds weight to the former concern to pave the way to institutional collaboration that somewhat creates a "national collection" of Latin American materials. Holly Ackerman and Teresa Chapa's opening essay in this section chronicles the longest-standing formal institutional collaborative agreement in which the libraries at Duke University and the University of North Carolina (UNC) work together to divide up collecting responsibilities and provide a dynamic courier service that makes it easy for respective Duke and UNC users to quickly request and receive materials from the two different collections. The essay by Sean Patrick Knowlton and Sócrates Silva indicates a different and unique resource sharing model in which the *librarian* is the shared resource. The 2CUL model managed between the universities of Columbia and Cornell leverages the joint acquisitions budgets being managed by one librarian who takes the individual collection needs of each institution into account. The expectation that the public services responsibilities (instruction and specialized reference) for the non-home institution in the arrangement (Cornell) can be managed with periodic site visits, face to face technology, and backup by the general reference staff can be viewed with skepticism but the account from the previous and current librarians in the arrangement indicate it is possible. It remains to be seen if other institutions might court this model.

Jana Lee Krentz's essay on using the BorrowDirect Program of the Ivy Plus Consortium as a way to better supply a wider variety of Brazilian imprints indicates that the challenges and opportunities of collaboration with many more institutional partners can be achieved through exhaustive analysis and commitment to a memorandum of understanding.

The model of dual institutional collaboration is employed at different scales of funding as related in the essay by coauthors Philip S. MacLeod and Laura D. Shedenhelm and the essay by Lynn M. Shirey. MacLeod and Shedenhelm demonstrate that collaborative collecting does not require massive funding and can indeed be effective for a project in which a smaller haul of returns is expected. Shirey's account of collaboration between Yale and Harvard takes on the bigger scale of collecting but also brings in the complexities of trying to assess effectiveness in multidisciplinary returns that do not lend themselves to analysis tools for large, discrete disciplines or highly inclusive call number ranges.

Though most Latin American Studies librarians develop collections with a primary focus in the humanities and social science, there is awareness that other disciplines and/or subject specialties come into play and may need to follow different collecting strategies. Daisy Domínguez advocates for building Latin American music collections as another resource that informs on the region. She describes some of the specialized collections held in U.S. academic libraries but encourages non-music librarians to add a new element to their collection building. Julienne E. Grant and Teresa M. Miguel-Stearns' chronicle of collecting Latin American legal materials in the U.S. offers a textbook case on the topic. The essay provides a useful framework to both the neophyte law librarian who needs to take on collecting Latin Americana and for general Latin American studies librarians who must occasionally provide legal materials for non–law school users. Sarah Aponte and Nelson Santana's history of the Dominican Studies Institute Library at CUNY emphasizes the community engagement tied to the academic setting that made it possible to grow and build the library. Their essay is a reminder that collecting efforts can impact users outside of the scholarly environment.

The final section of the book offers a look at how Latin American collection development can use and is using technological/digital tools to enhance resource sharing. Fernando Acosta-Rodríguez and Luis A. González outline several outstanding digitization projects in the Latin American realm as part of a deeper discussion about successful implementation of what may be new or unfamiliar workflows. Pamela M. Graham and Kent Norsworthy make a strong argument for taking Latin American collection building beyond print resources by dynamic archiving of web pages that can disappear all too quickly. Jennifer Osorio points to the region's successes with Open Access initiatives with the journal portals of *Scielo* and *Redalyc*. Her summary indicates what has been achieved so far but remains to be developed. Denis Lacroix's essay on digitization of a local television program combines factors from essays in earlier sections of this collection. He blends the development of a digitization project to preserve the program *Nosotros* with the background of its importance in one Canadian community with new arrivals from Latin America. Virtual resource building with ties to the local community allows that diaspora to be viewed in the home countries. This has the potential of providing new research possibilities.

Readers may wonder if other topics could have been included here with regard to collection assessment, citation analysis, information literacy, working with Special Collections or Cataloging, etc. This collection represents what its contributors wanted to stress in terms of working with collection building and management that must still take print-based resources into account. We point to Manuel Ostos' publication on citation analysis of holdings at Pennsylvania State University. It would have been welcome in this collection but is no less valuable as a stand-alone article.[2]

We are grateful to our contributors for their hard work, illuminating observations in their individual essays, and willingness to take our editorial direction to heart. Reviewing the essays for publication allowed us to better hone expectations for this book. We value all of the essayists as friends and colleagues. You can learn more about them in the "About the Contributors" section. Gayle also wants to express her appreciation for the Professional Development Leave granted by the Office of the Provost of Florida International University during Spring 2016. Having the time over one semester to be fully dedicated to setting up the review structure was invaluable support.

NOTES

1. Given that many Latin Americanist subject librarians have a variety of germane subject assignments in terms of Caribbean, Iberian, and U.S. Latinx Studies, we employ "Latin American Studies librarian" here as a generic description that may include some of the aforementioned assignments.

2. Manuel Ostos, "What Do They Use? Where Do They Get It?: An Interdisciplinary Citation Analysis of Latin American Studies Faculty Monographs, 2004–2013." *College & Research Libraries* 78:5 (2017) 567–577.

From the Print to the Digital, Networked Era

Transformations in Latin American Studies, Scholarly Communication and Latin American Library Collecting and Collections

SARAH A. BUCK KACHALUBA

Librarianship, and particularly collection development (the selection and acquisition of information materials to support study and research), have been central to the emergence and evolution of area (including Latin American) studies programs in the United States. The earliest area studies programs in the United States were created before the Cold War, but they proliferated after World War II in particular, as a way to train specialists to combat the influence of the Eastern, Communist bloc in the "non-aligned" third world.

Since the fall of the Iron Curtain in 1989, which brought consequent changes in global geo-political forces and structures, collection development goals and strategies have continued to adapt to and help define the shifting place of area studies in a world acknowledging the realities of political-economic globalization and producing scholarship embracing macro-global approaches alongside those following more traditional regional, communal, or other micro foci. This essay traces historical changes in area studies collection development, as a way to discuss the current and future status and roles of Latin American studies especially (and area studies more generally) as they continue to evolve in connection to a global landscape once defined by the Cold War and an information explosion and shifts in scholarly communication transformed by the rise of the internet and digital age.

Before World War II, Latin American studies programs were rare at U.S. universities and few faculty even focused on researching or teaching the non-western world. The first exception to this general rule was the University of Florida, whose president John Tigert established an Institute for Inter-American Affairs (IIAA) at commencement on June 2, 1930. Tigert's decision to do so is attributed to his experience as U.S. Commissioner of Education (1922–28), his related awareness of a "growing interest in foreign affairs in the nation's political, commercial and academic circles" and his desire to "promote the 'Good Neighbor Policy' of the Hoover and Roosevelt administrations."[1] The School of

Inter-American Studies was renamed the Center for Latin American Studies in September 1963.[2]

Tulane University created its Middle American Institute even earlier than Florida's Institute for Inter-American Affairs, in 1924, but because the Middle American Institute focused on "advanced research into the archaeology, history, tropical botany, and natural resources and products of countries facing New Orleans across the waters of the south," it has not been recognized as a true center for Latin American studies.[3] Nevertheless, Tulane later broadened its Latin American offerings after World War II, through the Stone Center for Latin American Studies, while maintaining its historical strengths in Mesoamerica. Consequently, since the mid–1960s, over 300 students have graduated with interdisciplinary M.A. degrees in Latin American Studies and almost 40 have earned interdisciplinary Ph.Ds. in Latin American Studies since the late 1970s. Tulane's academic programs and research institutes focusing on Latin America in general, and Central America and Mexico in particular, are also significant because they are tied to the "turn-of-the-century gift of a large Mesoamerican library" which maintains its status today as one of the strongest U.S. (and indeed international) library collections in Latin Americana.[4]

Another early, pre–World War II center for Latin American studies: the University of Texas Austin's Institute for Latin American Studies, created in 1940, was also tied to the creation of a key repository for Latin American Studies: the University's Nettie Lee Benson Latin American Collection, which began with the acquisition of the private library of Mexican historian Genaro García in 1921.[5] The creation of the Benson Collection illustrates the typical trajectory for the emergence of early Latin American collections, which generally constituted purchases or gifts of scholars' entire, specialized libraries. Systematic selection to build and expand Latin American collections did not occur until after World War II.[6]

The University of North Carolina Chapel Hill (UNC) also established its Institute of Latin American Studies (ILAS) in 1940, which was renamed the Institute for the Study of the Americas (ISA) in 2007.[7] The last pre–World War II Center for Latin American Studies (CLAS) was created at San Diego State University in 1942 as part of the History Department.[8]

The existence of all of these early academic centers for Latin American studies can be attributed largely to the presence of faculty specializing in Latin America at the institutions at which they were created. At the University of Texas these included Herbert E. Bolton, who taught a history course on Spanish colonization from 1904 to 1905; Spanish professor and librarian Carlos E. Castañeda who was instrumental in building the Latin American collection; and historian Charles Hackett who helped lead the drive to establish a Latin American studies institute.[9] At UNC, Latin American courses were coordinated in a special curriculum as early as 1915.[10] Several other institutions also attribute their eventual creation of Latin American studies institutes to the presence of faculty. For example, Columbia University suggests that Professor Frank Tannenbaum, a preeminent Latin Americanist in the United States since the 1930s, was instrumental in founding the Institute of Latin American Studies (ILAS) in 1962. Tannenbaum was the institute's initial director, and he conceived of it as a response to the need for knowledge about an area of central importance to U.S. foreign policy.[11]

In addition to driving the foundation of the country's first centers of Latin American studies, Latin Americanist academics and librarians active before World War II also fostered the emergence of Latin American studies as a field in other ways. In 1918 a group of historians within the American Historical Association focusing on Latin America founded the *Hispanic American Historical Review* (*HAHR*), which maintains its status today as a leading scholarly journal in Latin American studies and history. In 1926, the group that founded the *HAHR* also formed the Conference of Latin American History (CLAH), which continues to coordinate its annual meetings with the American Historical Association (AHA). The Hispanic Division of the Library of Congress began publishing its *Handbook of Latin American Studies* (*HLAS*) in 1936, which to the present day constitutes a "premier reference" tool for Latin American studies scholars by selecting and highlighting recently published materials in Latin American Studies in the form of annotated bibliographies.[12]

The American Library Association and the Pan American Union also launched early collaborative acquisitions initiatives focusing on Latin American in the 1930s, with the creation of the Committee for Library Cooperation with Latin America (now the International Relations Committee) and the Inter-American Bibliographical and Library Association, respectively.

At the same time that librarians and library organizations recognized the need to commit to adequate collecting in Latin Americana (presumably with the goal of ensuring that foreign diplomats were adequately prepared for their exchanges with their Latin American counterparts), academic philanthropist organizations such as the Rockefeller, Carnegie, and Ford Foundations sought ways to expand the numbers of trained Latin Americanist subject specialists. To this end, in addition to "financing ... the Council on Foreign Relations from 1921 onwards" as well as the "War and Peace Studies group between the CFR and the U.S. State Department, ... between 1927 and 1945 the Rockefeller Foundation ... provided the [CFR] with over $443,000 specifically for 'study group' research which 'resulted in authoritative publications which could be and often were used in policy implementation.'"[13] During and following World War II, such organizations became even more committed to the goal of training subject experts in Latin America, as well as Africa and Asia, who would help the United States compete effectively with the USSR and China for the sympathies of recently decolonized, "non-aligned" (in terms of the cold war poles of communist vs. capitalist), newly labeled "third-world" countries (something that was a concern and goal for liberal and conservative academics and policy-makers alike). Consequently, "[b]etween 1934 and 1942 the Rockefeller Foundation contributed $1 million to the establishment of area studies at major American universities. The Carnegie Foundation followed up with $2.5 million between 1947 and 1951"[14] and between 1951 and 1966, the "Ford Foundation invested more than $270 million in Area Studies training, research, and related programs."[15] Ford Foundation support came in the form of the prestigious "Foreign Area Fellowship Program (FAFP)" which provided "two years of inter-disciplinary and language training on a selected country or region of the world, plus two years of funding for in-depth overseas dissertation research and write-up" and was taken over by the interdisciplinary (humanities and social sciences) Area Studies Committees jointly sponsored by the Social Science Research Council (SSRC) and the American Council of Learned Societies (ACLS) in 1972.[16]

In 1957, in response to the USSR's October launching of Sputnik, the U.S. government called for additional funding for area studies programs in the National Defense Act of 1957, renamed the Higher Education Act in 1965, which allocated funding for some 125 U.S. university-based area studies units (National Resource Centers, or NRCs) in the form of Title VI grants (referring to Title VI, Part A, § 602 of Higher Ed Act of 1965) and Foreign Language and Area Studies (FLAS) fellowships for graduate students affiliated with such study centers. Thus, NRCs and FLASs, which were directly funded by the U.S. government, illustrate the institutional legitimacy that the Cold War brought to Latin American studies as a field in general, and to Latin American studies subject specialists and institutes more specifically.

Alongside interwar and World War II philanthropic and U.S. state-supported initiatives to develop area studies experts, libraries began to develop systematic, collaborative strategies to build strong area collections. The first of these came in the form of the Farmington Plan, proposed in 1942. Initially, this proposal was driven by a commitment on the part of academic libraries to acquire and preserve European publications whose existence was threatened by the war. U.S. research libraries took responsibility for collecting in specific European regions and subjects, and soon expanded to other global areas as well, including Latin America (whose regional plan was well-established by the 1960s). At the same time, several complementary collaborative agreements focusing on Latin American collecting emerged. The Duke and University of North Carolina Chapel Hill collaborative collecting agreement, still in existence today, is an example of one of these initiatives. The year World War II ended (1945) the Library of Congress began publishing the *Guide to the Official Publications of the Other American Republics*.[17]

After World War II, librarians continued to work on developing more effective collaborative systems to build Latin American collections. This was, however, challenging, largely because of the "incipient" nature of "Latin American systems of publishing, distribution and bibliographic control…: local book audiences were generally small, commercial publishers scarce, and libraries were limited in ambition and scale. Most publishing originated from small presses, which often produced authors' self-published materials."[18] And although governments and quasi-governmental agencies and research institutions produced increasing numbers of materials (including annual reports, congressional debates, development plans, and statistical yearbooks), such materials often evaded commercial distribution networks and were "difficult to acquire locally, and much more so from abroad."[19] Such acquisition challenges were compounded by "[m]inimal print runs, recurrent civil and military strife, economic crises, and censorship in many [Latin American] countries" and by the fact that national bibliographies remained rare in Latin America due to "economic constraints" and "widespread evasion of law for legal deposit."[20]

In the 1950s, two important initiatives in the United States sought to address the challenges of "identifying, obtaining, processing, and preserving [Latin American] publications." In 1956 the Pan American Union and University of Florida brought together thirty librarians and professors and one international bookseller to meet at Chinsegut Hill, Florida and "discuss and try to solve problems 'concerned with the selection, acquisition, and processing of library materials from the Latin American nations and the dependent territories of the Caribbean.'"[21] This initial meeting gave rise to the Seminar on the Acquisition of Latin American Library Materials (SALALM), an international organization that continues to meet annually, counting over two-hundred librarians, archivists, and booksellers as members. In 1959, motivated by the same issues, the firm of Stechert-Hafner created the Latin American Cooperative Acquisitions Program (LACAP), which sent agents (including UT Austin's Latin American Collection bibliographer, Dr. Nettie Lee Benson) on trips to Latin America to select, purchase, and ship back library materials, and also to identify in-country book vendors. New bookselling companies arose out of this initiative and a bookselling service to which some 38 libraries subscribed resulted. Some of the participating libraries had early approval plans with LACAP that authorized it to select and ship materials on specific topics, countries, and regions, whereas other libraries selected and firm ordered from prepared lists of in-stock materials.[22]

Together, the Farmington Plan and LACAP constituted the major collaborative approaches to Latin American collection development for some two decades, and then, in the early 1970s, the Farmington Plan collapsed and the Stechert-Hafner's support of LACAP ended. The demise of both projects is attributed to two factors. First, ironically, both initiatives made themselves obsolete, by "creating vendor and distribution structures upon which libraries could rely without intermediaries or programmatic superstructures."[23] At the same time, the numbers and quality of Latin American publications materials specifically, and the production of information materials more generally, increased dramatically in the post-war period in which the Farmington Plan and LACAP emerged and evolved.

A new project, the Research Library Group (RLG)'s Conspectus was designed to fill the void left by the decline of the Farmington Plan and LACAP. In describing the rise of the Conspectus, Dr. Mary C. Bushing writes of the "so called 'information explosion' [that] threatened to bury libraries in unreasonable amounts of information and publications" in the 1970's, making it "harder and harder" for a "librarian to 'know'" his or her collection and select new materials accordingly.[24] In Latin America, this information explosion took the form not only of more information, but of information in previously under-represented (and studied) subject areas (including agriculture, business, science, and technology) as well as information in new formats, such as statistics.[25] Since the 1970s, Latin American publishing has grown significantly, characterized by the existence of strong national commercial and university presses as well as the presence of international publishing conglomerates such as Planeta, Alfaguara, and Santillana.

At this moment of information and publishing proliferation in the mid–1970s (circa 1975), U.S. librarians focusing on collections in many areas (not just Latin America) came together to formulate a new approach to assessing collections that would lead to more comprehensive and less duplicative collecting. Earlier collaborative collection development agreements such as the Farmington Plan and LACAP aimed to ensure that U.S. libraries were acquiring important materials without a concern for duplication. In other words, any number of libraries might purchase the same book, which was fine, as long as at least one library did so. Online Computer Library Center (OCLC) researcher Lorcan Dempsey attributes this largely to the fact that in the immediate post–World War II decades (the 1950s and 1960s), library collections were strongly shaped by a "print logic … requir[ing] the distribution of print copies to multiple local destinations." In this way, materials could be closer to the user, to allow immediate access. This had two consequences. First, collections were assembled on a 'just in case' basis" and owned by individual libraries. "And second, the size of the collection was strongly associated with the goodness of the collection."[26]

In the midst of the 1970s information explosion, librarians began to shift away from the construction of duplicative collections based on a print logic. Instead, they began to assess their collections with the goal of each acquiring unique materials based on their historic strengths, so that together, through borrowing consortia, they could share a larger, unique collection, rather than create a number of separate, duplicative collections to rely on locally. Using worksheets organized by the Library of Congress classification system, librarians adopted a scheme developed by members of the Research Libraries Group (RLG): the Conspectus, which involved taking surveys of their collection patterns and strengths (identifying the materials that they historically held the most of, as well as those they were emphasizing in their current collection strategies). In 1982, RLG launched the Conspectus Online (as an electronic file made searchable through the RLIN system interface). And in 1983, the Association of Research Libraries (ARL) adopted the Conspectus to keep statistics of ARL member holdings. Although the online[27] tool is no longer used as it once was, many libraries still rely on Conspectus categories of collection strength and terminology for assessment and collection purposes. For example, approval plans (agreements with vendors to provide materials based on previously agreed regional, subject, or other parameters) often follow language defined by the Conspectus.

In the same years that the Conspectus emerged, the Center for Research Libraries (CRL) launched another similarly-conceived, collaborative, yet specifically Latin American project: the Latin American Microform Project[28] (LAMP), which had the goal of "acquir[ing], preserving, and maintain[ing] … collections of unique, rare and bulky or voluminous Latin American research materials for its members. LAMP emphasizes original preservation, either through microfilming or digitization, though it may also purchase existing microfilm."[29]

Between the 1970s and the 1990s, the "information explosion" continued and reached a new moment of crisis/transformation. In 1991 Lynne Reiner, representing a leading publisher of Latin American scholarly studies, lamented in a SALALM conference presentation that the publishing industry and all who were connected to it were in, or were "approaching, a state of crisis" resulting, "simply stated," from the fact that there were "too many books" being published. The publication of too many books—which was driven by the nature of scholarly communication itself (scholars want to share their work and findings) and by the nature of promotion and tenure in the modern university (university professors need to publish books in order to advance in their profession), meant publishers could not sell as many copies of each book as they or book authors wanted. As a result, publishers increased book prices, which meant that people bought even less copies, and/or took on more titles make up the losses resulting from declining book sales.[30] Rienner also observed that libraries' tendency to discourage duplication in their collections, relying on inter-library loan to supplement their collections, compounds the problem because it also results in the purchase of less books.[31]

The mid–1990s publishing crisis also occurred in a time of general economic recession, which meant that libraries (important purchasers of books) faced budget constraints. In Latin American librarianship, this crisis resulted in yet another experiment in collaborative collection development: The Latin Americanist Research Resources Project (LARRP), sponsored by the Association of American Universities, Association of Research Libraries, and SALALM, and benefitting from funding from the Andrew W. Mellon foundation.[32] The initiative launched in 1995, when thirty-five libraries committed to participating in the Distributed Resources Project, in which each institution pledged to dedicate a previously-defined base amount plus 7 percent of its monographic allocation for Latin American resources to acquiring Latin American collections in specific areas (regional, national, subject-specific, or a combination thereof); maintaining statistics on their spending and acquisitions for the project; and achieving timely bibliographic control that would ensure that users throughout library networks would know about the new acquisitions.[33]

Alongside the mid–1990s crisis in publishing and scholarly communication that helped give rise to LARRP, area studies faced a crisis initiated with the fall of the Berlin Wall and the Iron Curtain. Without a Cold War and a bipolar world order, would there be a need to train experts on what was once called the "non-aligned" third world? As Peter H. Smith explains, an "awful term, 'the New World Order,' a phrase that contains at least two oxymorons and probably three, in a fictional statement of an order that does not now exist" had dominated discussions since the beginning of the end of the Cold War, and yet, "[a]s we look around and ponder the significance of the end of the Cold War, we are actually witnessing the end of the Cold War." In other words, the end of the Cold War and the resulting new post-war order were on-going developments.[34] Smith goes on to propose three possible scenarios for Latin America in the "new world order": one in which the "First World … promote[s] development in the Third World, including in Latin America[,]" a second in which a "restoration of rather traditional spheres of influence by great powers, rather than a world in which everything flows freely"[35] occurs, and a third, in which a "series of free market economies" draw "capital …[to] … where the opportunities are" (the North), creating a North-North axis, basically leaving out the South and the Third World, with the exception of a very small number of players."[36]

Thus, as LARRP committed to ensuring the collection of Latin American resources through a new collaborative agreement similar in many ways to its precursor, the Farmington Plan, Latin American scholars specifically and area studies specialists more broadly watched to see what the "new world order" might look like and what this would mean for the future of area studies as a discipline.

LARRP's Distributed Resources Project thrives today, and its 2012–2013 report indicates that in this fiscal year, the total budget for the Distributive Resource Project collections among respondents who could provide dollar amounts constituted $548,862.[37] In the past two decades, SALALM members have also created a series of regional consortium bringing together SALALM members from libraries collecting Latin Americana in various regions (these include LANE: Latin America North East Libraries Consortium; LASER: Latin American Studies Southeast Region; MOLLAS: Midwest Organization for Libraries for Latin American Studies; and CALAFIA: California Cooperative Latin American Collection Development Group). All of these groups interact within and with LARRP, as do larger and smaller consortia, such as the Center for Research Libraries (CRL) and the Greater Western Library Alliance (GWLA); and smaller, university-specific partnerships such as the agreements between UNC-Chapel Hill/Duke, UC Berkeley/Stanford, and Harvard/Yale. Several libraries in the northeast ("Borrow Direct" institutions) are planning a collaborative collecting effort for Brazilian materials.[38]

At the same time, the "New World Order" continues to evolve. Free trade agreements have proliferated and they have generally resulted in the concentration of capital in the global north. Production, however, often occurs in the global south, where lower wages and more lax or absent human rights and environmental standards mean lower costs for manufacturers. Communism and capitalism continue as one ideological axis, but terrorism, autocracy, and nuclear capabilities make actors of various ideological colors threats to world peace.

A third development in the 1990s compounded the scholarly communication/publishing crisis and possibilities regarding the emergence of a "New World Order." This originated in the emergence of the Internet and consequent developments in digital technologies. The Internet produced an "information explosion" unimaginable in the 1970s and the related conversion from analog to digital information production has brought an "unprecedented level of mobility of capital and information" which has transformed global communication, political-economic, and even social and cultural systems.[39] Consequently, national and international security is more challenging, scholarly communication relies on multiple communication channels (informal and formal, published and open access) and libraries are more committed than ever to building unique, non-duplicative collections that are supplemented with the sharing of print and digital materials through unmediated and electronic borrowing.

In contrast to earlier collections whose construction followed a print logic, today's collection, Lorcan Dempsey explains, is "organized according to a network logic." Instead of a print model of "scarcity, requiring distribution to local nodes[, t]he network model is one of abundance, encouraging aggregation at central hubs." Instead of a print model facilitating local discovery in the library stacks, "a variety of network-level discovery venues exist … often … far beyond the collection" itself. The network environment encourages creativity and collaboration. "We see a blurring between content, workflow and identity" and a "growing interest in sharing research and learning outputs from the institution with external users." Local collections now form part of shared, collective collections from which all member institutions can borrow, identifying material through various discovery points. In such an environment, duplication is discouraged, so that the collective collection can be a large collection of unique and diverse materials which are shared by all member institutions rather than separate, small collections of duplicative materials.[40]

David Block explains that in library speak, this means that instead of owning materials "just in case" they are needed, libraries now privilege ensuring "just in time" access to materials through on-demand purchase and borrowing.[41] Library collection usage statistics, the rise of the e-book, and ongoing financial problems in the publishing industry have only reaffirmed this orientation to building unique, non-duplicative collections. Block explains that although "[f]or forty years prevailing opinion held that bibliographers in close consultation with faculty would be in the best position to predict use," of library materials, usage statistics have not proven this. Many of the materials selected by bibliographers in consultation with faculty have circulated little, if at all.[42] Libraries have welcomed e-books for several reasons: they don't require the space or shelf-maintenance of print and they can be purchased (or even rented) "just in time" through subscription-based on-demand programs. Publishers continue to produce "more and more books while average book sales steadily decline"[43] and have also turned to e-books as a way to save production costs, only to find such "savings … dissipated by the discounted sale price charged for the e-book"[44] and the need to "re-commercialize their backlists by bundling them in electronic format and selling them to libraries" at further discounts."[45]

The declining ability of U.S. libraries to purchase print books (and move towards a subscription-based model for e-book access instead) is related to a transformation in journal publishing and access from print to digital. Although "[t]raditional journal subscriptions have fallen drastically," leading journals have remained financially solvent because "payments from search engines and savings in printing and mailing costs have compensated for lost revenues."[46] But libraries pay increasing amounts for access to such search engines, and this cuts dramatically into print and electronic monograph budgets.

Thus, online journal publication and paid and open electronic access is transforming scholarly communication and driving down book sales and book use in the process. Lyman Johnson speculates that the dominance of the e-journal will transform scholarship in other ways as well. He asks how "minimal peer review[,]" the increasing tendency to measure "the influence of our articles ... in online 'hits,'" "uncompensated authors, peer reviewers, and editorial board members," and the ability to keyword search instead of reading an article in its entirety will change our reading, thinking and writing.[47] Johnson confesses that his own reading has changed with online search capabilities; "[r]ather than reading entire articles, ... [he] ... disassemble[s] them via key word searches, stripping out the material of direct use to [him] and read[s] the entire article only if it turns out to be closely focused on [his] own topic of the moment."[48] He warns that if and when "this pattern attaches itself to the book, the effect will be devastating" as authorial and reading skills will both be lost.[49] Johnson similarly attributes declining book sales to increasingly narrow research topics and monograph topics and suggests that all academics respond to this trend by making an effort to read more widely and assign publications addressing broader topics in their courses.[50]

The Association of American University Presses (AAUP) affirms many of Johnson's observations, explaining that the "technological and cultural shifts of the last decade—the transformation from a print-based system of content scarcity and centralization to a digital, decentralized system of content abundance, easy access to expertise, attention as the coin of the realm, handheld connections, and distraction as a big business—challenge not just publishers' business models, but may even threaten many of the intellectual characteristics most valued by the scholarly enterprise itself: concentration, analysis, and deep expertise."[51] Publishers have been displaced by new norms of scholarly communication; in the "pre-web age" scholars depended on publishers to communicate their work in the form of publication.[52] Nonetheless, the AAUP explains, publishers provide many services besides dissemination which are as relevant—and perhaps even more needed and relevant—in the digital age than the print-dominated age that preceded it. These include the ability to select quality works to promote, editorial services, marketing and presentational expertise, metadata authority and enhancement, and rights authority and licensing.[53] Thus, although "[t]he dominant business model for scholarly publishing over the past several decades—sales of print books and journals to institutional, retail, and text markets, supplemented by modest amounts of institutional support—is no longer sustainable," scholarly publishers are exploring new ways to participate in scholarly communication, including "publishing digital editions of books in various formats; distributing digital books on an open access basis, usually combined with sales of print editions and digital-only publications that go beyond the standard book and journal formats" as well as new strategies to "fund these experiments, including print sales as a means of supporting open access digital publications; subscription sales for digital book collections and digital-only projects; foundation support, usually as investment capital for new projects; and parent institution support."[54]

As professionals supporting scholars by helping them to identify and access materials to produce their scholarship, academic librarians and libraries share some of the roles and skills claimed by publishers, including the expertise to select quality primary and secondary source materials for the collection, skilled metadata and licensing abilities, and technical and legal infrastructures to promote open access. The availability and distribution of digital publications of Latin American imprints and journals within and beyond the region depends on developments in digital publishing and distribution within Latin America as well as non–Latin American vendors who make Latin American content available in digital formats to U.S. and European markets.

As in the U.S., the first digital libraries and sales platforms for e-books appeared in the Latin American-Caribbean region in the 1990s. Nonetheless, "in the early 2000s, in almost every Latin American country, traditional publishing showed signs of great dynamism" and this, combined with relatively low rates of computer and internet access at that time to hamper the development of digital publishing.[55] In 2010, the UN's Economic Commission on Latin America and the Caribbean (ECLAC)/Comisión Económica para América Latina y el Caribe (CEPAL) estimated the population of Latin America and the Caribbean to be 588,649,000 people.[56] Of these only about a third (34.5 percent) used the internet.[57] A much higher number, however (90 percent)) had access to cell phones.[58]

A 2009 poll administered by UNESCO's Centro Regional para el Fomento del Libro en América Latina y el Caribe (CERLALC) in a 2009 poll indicated that 20 percent) of publishers surveyed used print-on-demand (POD) technology, a number that increased to 32 percent) in 2010, so that by 2012, POD terminals existed in most Latin American capital cities and had POD had "begun to displace the traditional Offset system, in a context of decreasing average print runs."[59] Simultaneously, "traditional bookstores … discovered successful formulas for selling paper books via the Web" and the Latin American-Caribbean region also "witnessed the emergence of purely digital bookshops, … stores that only sell electronic books…."[60] Latin American entrepreneurs have also created some local e-book aggregators, who distribute digital publications produced by various publishers; examples of ones that are still in existence today include Xeriph and Ventara. However, the vast majority of e-books published in the languages spoken and read in Latin America (Spanish, Portuguese, other Romance languages, and creole and indigenous languages) are produced by external aggregators, in particular from Spain, the U.S. and the UK.[61]

There are at least two obvious reasons for the lower interest in e-books in Latin America than the United States. First, the high cost of e-readers (especially Ipads) has inhibited the development of a mass market for e-books in Latin America and the Caribbean. And second, even as late as 2007, "70% of Internet users in the region claimed never to have made a purchase through the web." Reasons for this included low per capita access to credit cards (32.6 percent)), wariness of making online purchases (31.6 percent)), fear that items ordered would not be delivered (25.5 percent)), familiarity with and preference for in-store selection and purchase (24.5 percent)), the absence of personal of attention (15.4 percent)) and high shipping costs (9.3 percent)).[62] Lower e-book production in Latin America can also be attributed to the fact that most Latin American publishers lack expertise with ePub, relying instead on PDF or outsourcing ePub conversion at the high cost of $50–100 per title.

Although rates of Latin American–Caribbean e-book production are relatively low in a comparative context, online periodical and article-length distribution in repositories is much higher. The region supports "countless online literary journals and blogs" and in general, academic articles published in Latin America is openly accessible on the internet because research institutions are generally funded publicly (that, is, by Latin American governments) and researchers working at such institutions are required to make the fruits of such funding (their research) openly available through digital repositories. In other words, academic publishing in Latin America constitutes part of the publicly financed cost of academic research, and this contrasts with strong North American and European traditions of commercial academic publishing and scholarly communication. Major networks providing open-access repositories of article-length Latin American material include the Consejo Latinoamericano de Ciencias Sociales (CLACSO)'s virtual library; the Scientific Electronic Library Online (SciELO), REDALYC (scholarly journals from Latin America, Spain, and Portugal), CSIC (Spain's Consejo Superior de Investigaciones Científicas)'s e-Revist@s platform, Spain's Dialnet, the Consejo Español de Estudios Iberoamericano (CEEIB) and the Red Europea de Documentación de Información (Redial).

In addition to public and private initiatives and infrastructures promoting digital publication from within Latin America, there are a number of North American and European aggregators producing and distributing Latin American e-books through packages and/or title-by-title. These include *Digitalia*, *ebrary*, the Spanish division of Casalini's Torrosa Full-text platform, ediciónespañolaonline, and *JSTOR*.

Collection development and information management are not the only areas of academic librarianship affected by the rise of the internet and digitization. As the Association of Research Libraries (ARL) explains, in academic libraries the Internet has brought a "shift in responsibility from purchasing print materials for a local constituency to managing a proliferation of formats, business models, and ownership and licensing arrangements," and "bibliographers previously dedicated almost exclusively to collection development [have] assumed reference and instruction responsibilities to help students and faculty find and use these resources."[63] Such changes are also articulated as a shift in focus in libraries "from collections to services" or, Lorcan Dempsey suggests, "to move towards thinking about collections as a service."[64]

In summary, scholarly publishing, the roles of librarians and their approaches to building library collections, and the place for area studies within "the new world order" continue to evolve in an information landscape that has been transformed by the digital age. In the new digital environment, the authors, formats, and business and legal models defining access to information resources have proliferated, yet despite dire predictions of their demise, print books, libraries, and area studies programs survive.

Academic institutions have offered different models for promoting global, international, and/or area studies programs and curricula. Philanthropic foundations and nonacademic institutional bureaucracies have increasingly emphasized interregional themes such as "Development and Democracy" as a way to incorporate both. One reason that it is possible to simultaneously embrace global and area studies approaches to education and analysis is that both are interdisciplinary. An effective approach to designing global studies courses in virtually any subject (history, political science, economics, and sociology, for example) is to rely on community (whether local, state, or national) case studies. Use of such case studies allows professors to illustrate and students to examine and understand how macro trends take on particularly micro characteristics due to local cultural, social, and political-economic traits. And the understanding of the micro manifestations of broader trends points to the need to continue studying the regional processes that produce unique, local social, political-economic, and cultural features and processes. Hopefully academic institutions and libraries with strong Latin American programs and collections can continue to build upon their historic strengths, through such flexible curricula and selective collection development following such approaches as LARRP's

Distributed Resources Project. Hopefully scholars, for their part, can produce materials that provide macro and micro perspectives and can therefore appeal to a wide enough audience to support sufficient book sales and selective duplication among these libraries. And hopefully publishers and libraries can create flexible distribution methods relying on combinations of print and digital technologies that are affordable to readers and libraries and meet publishers' production costs.

NOTES

1. http://www.latam.ufl.edu/home/history/.
2. http://www.latam.ufl.edu/home/history/.
3. https://stonecenter.tulane.edu/pages/detail/6/History.
4. https://stonecenter.tulane.edu/pages/detail/6/History.
5. http://www.utexas.edu/cola/llilas/about/history.php.
6. Lynn Shirey, "Latin American Collections," in Dan Hazen and James Henry Spohrer, eds., *Building Area Studies Collections* (Wiesbaden: Harrassowitz Verlag, 2007) 112.
7. http://isa.unc.edu/about/.
8. http://latinamericanstudies.sdsu.edu.
9. http://www.utexas.edu/cola/llilas/about/history.php.
10. http://isa.unc.edu/about/.
11. http://ilas.columbia.edu/about-ilas/.
12. In his 1994 study, "The Bibliographic Control and Preservation of Latin Americanist Library Resources: A Status Report with Suggestions," Dan C. Hazen characterized HLAS as "the premier reference source for Latin Americanist scholarship" (Washington, D.C.: Association of Research Libraries, April 1994. Editor Jutta Reed-Scott, Sr. Program Officer for Preservation and Collections Services. Accessed: http://files.eric.ed.gov/fulltext/ED374827.pdf).
13. Andrew Gavin Marshall, "An Education for Empire: The Rockefeller, Carnegie, and Ford Foundations in the Construction of Knowledge": http://andrewgavinmarshall.com/2011/10/18/an-education-for-empire-the-rockefeller-carnegie-and-ford-foundations-in-the-construction-of-knowledge/. Marshall cites Inderjeet Parmar, "To Relate Knowledge and Action: The Impact of the Rockefeller Foundation on Foreign Policy Thinking During America's Rise to Globalism, 1939–1945," *Minerva* Vol. 40 (2002): 235, 241.
14. Marshall, "An Education for Empire": http://andrewgavinmarshall.com/2011/10/18/an-education-for-empire-the-rockefeller-carnegie-and-ford-foundations-in-the-construction-of-knowledge/.
15. David L. Szanton, "Introduction: The Origin, Nature, and Challenges of Area Studies in the United States," in *The Politics of Knowledge: Area Studies and the Disciplines*, Gaia Books, 2002. Accessed: http://escholarship.org/uc/item/59n2d2n1.
16. Szanton, "Introduction."
17. Shirey, "Latin American Collections," 114.
18. Shirey, "Latin American Collections," 112.
19. Shirey, "Latin American Collections," 112.
20. Shirey, "Latin American Collections," 112.
21. http://www.ala.org/groups/affiliates/affiliates/salalm.
22. Shirey, "Latin American Collections," 114.
23. Shirey, "Latin American Collections," 114.
24. Mary C. Bushing, "The Evolution of Conspectus Practice in Libraries: The Beginnings and the Present Applications," paper delivered at CASLIN 2001, the 8th international seminar of the Czech and Slovak Library Information Network: http://klement.nkp.cz/caslin/caslin01/sbornik/conspectus.html.
25. Shirey, "Latin American Collections," 115.
26. "The Facilitated Collection," Lorcan Dempsey's Weblog on Libraries, Services, and Networks: orweblog.oclc.org.
27. http://www.oclc.org/research/activities/conspectus.html.
28. LAMP has been recently renamed the Latin American Materials Project, in recognition of a shift from microfilming to digitization (https://www.crl.edu/programs/lamp).
29. https://www.crl.edu/programs/lamp.
30. Lynne Rienner, "Is the Sky Falling? Scholarly Publishing in the 1990s," in *Latin American Studies in the Twenty-First Century: New Focus, New Formats, New Challenges: Papers of the Thirty-Sixth Annual Meeting of the Seminar on the Acquisition of Latin American Library Materials, San Diego, CA, June 1991* (General Library, University of New Mexico: SALALM Secretariat, 1993), 159.
31. Rienner, "Is the Sky Falling?" 161.
32. Dan Hazen, "The Latin Americanist Research Resources Project: A New Direction for Monographic Cooperation?" *ARL: A Bimonthly Newsletter of Research Library Issues and Actions* No. 191 (April 1997), 1.

33. Hazen, "The Latin Americanist Research Resources Project," 2.

34. Peter H. Smith, "Latin America and the New World Order," in *Latin American Studies in the Twenty-First Century: New Focus, New Formats, New Challenges: Papers of the Thirty-Sixth Annual Meeting of the Seminar on the Acquisition of Latin American Library Materials, San Diego, CA, June 1991* (General Library, University of New Mexico: SALALM Secretariat, 1993), 3.

35. Smith, "Latin America and the New World Order," 5.

36. Smith, "Latin America and the New World Order," 5–7.

37. Latin Americanist Research Resources Project Distributed Resources Project (DRP). "Participants Progress Reports for Fiscal Year 2012/2013": http://www.crl.edu/sites/default/files/d6/attachments/pages/Distributed%20Resources%20report%202013.pdf.

38. Latin Americanist Research Resources Project Distributed Resources Project (DRP). "Participants Progress Reports for Fiscal Year 2012/2013."

39. Neil L. Waters, "Introduction," in *Beyond the Area Studies Wars: Toward a New International Studies*, Neil L. Waters, editor (Hanover: Middlebury College Press and the University Press of New England, 2000).

40. "The Facilitated Collection," Lorcan Dempsey's Weblog on Libraries, Services, and Networks: orweblog.oclc.org.

41. David Block, "Where Are We; Where We May Be Going; What Will We Do There?," presentation on panel "What Do Libraries Want Now?," at SALALM LIII, New Orleans, LA, 2008: https://ecommons.cornell.edu/bitstream/handle/1813/10827/Where%20are%20we.doc?sequence=4.

42. Block, "Where Are We...?"

43. Johnson, "CLAH Lecture: Have We Loved the Book to Death?" *The Americas* 72:3 (July 2015): 365.

44. Johnson, "CLAH Lecture," 367.

45. Johnson, "CLAH Lecture," 368.

46. Johnson, "CLAH Lecture," 366–367.

47. Johnson, "CLAH Lecture," 366–367, 371–372.

48. Johnson, "CLAH Lecture," 372.

49. Johnson, "CLAH Lecture," 372.

50. Johnson, "CLAH Lecture," 365, 373.

51. Association of American University Presses (AAUP), "Sustaining Scholarly Publishing: New Business Models for University Presses." *A Report of the AAUP Task Force on Economic Models for Scholarly Publishing* (New York: Association of American University Presses, 2011) 3: http://www.aaupnet.org/images/stories/documents/aaupbusinessmodels2011.pdf.

52. AAUP, "Sustaining Scholarly Publishing," 6.

53. AAUP, "Sustaining Scholarly Publishing," 7–8.

54. AAUP, "Sustaining Scholarly Publishing," 32.

55. Kulesz.

56. Comisión Económica para América Latina y el Caribe (CEPAL), *Anuario estadístico de América Latina y el Caribe*, December 2010, cited in Octavio Kulesz, "The History of Digital Publishing in Latin America," International Alliance of Independent Publishers, 2010: http://alliance-lab.org/etude/archives/17?lang=en. This year, the estimate has risen to 641,029 (Comisión Económica para América Latina y el Caribe [CEPAL], *Anuario estadístico de América Latina y el Caribe*, December 2015: http://repositorio.cepal.org/bitstream/handle/11362/39867/S1500739_mu.pdf?sequence=1).

57. Internet World Stats, "Internet Usage Statistics," 2010, cited in Kulesz. Today, 61.5 percent use the internet (Internet World Stats, "World Internet Usage and Population Statistics," June 30, 2016: http://www.internetworldstats.com/stats.htm).

58. David Cuen, "Latinoamérica es el segundo mercado de celulares más grande del mundo," *BBC Mundo*, 7 October, 2010: http://www.bbc.com/mundo/noticias/2010/10/101006_1046_telefonos_celulares_america_latina_dc.shtml, cited in Kulesz.

59. Richard Uribe Schroeder and Sandra Villamizar Mantilla, CERLALC, "Percepción sobre el clima epresarial editorial y tendencias a corto plazo," *Boletín 9*, October 2010, 8: http://www.cerlalc.org/secciones/libro_desarrollo/Boletin_9.pdf, cited in Kulesz.

60. Uribe Schroeder and Villamizar Mantilla, CERLALC, "Percepción sobre el clima empresarial editorial"; América EconomiaIntelligence, "Estudio de comercio electrónico en América Latina," June 2010: http://especiales.americaeconomia.com/2010/comercio_electronico/files/Estudio_comercio_electronico_LA.pdf, cited in Kulesz.

61. *Conexión Publildisa*, October 2010: http://www.publidisa.com/conexion/Octubre-2010.html, cited in Kulesz.

62. Tendencias Digitales, "70% de los usuarios latinos aseguran no haber comprador por internet," *Internet en latinoamérica*, 19 November 2007: http://internet-latinoamerica.blogspot.com/2007/11/70-de-los-usuarios-latinos-asguran-no.html.

63. Association of Research Libraries (ARL), "Association of Research Libraries/Columbia University/

Cornell University/University of Toronto Pilot Library Liaison Institute: Final Report, Held at Cornell University, Ithaca, New York, June 2015": http://www.arl.org/storage/documents/publications/library-liaison-institute-final-report-dec2015.pdf.

64. Lorcan Dempsey, "The Facilitated Collection," In Lorcan Dempsey, *Weblog On libraries, services, and networks*: http://orweblog.oclc.org/towards-the-facilitated-collection/.

Latin American Materials Project

Forty Years of Preserving Unique
Latin American Research Material

JUDITH ECKOFF ALSPACH

The Latin American Materials Project (LAMP) has contributed in unique ways to the North American collection of research material from and about Latin America. Since its founding in 1975, LAMP has worked with organizations throughout the Americas to preserve rare but vital Latin American research materials and make them available to scholars at member institutions. LAMP's consistent goal has been the preservation of unique materials to create a shared collection, but the means by which LAMP has worked toward this goal have shown great flexibility on the part of its membership.

Librarians specializing in Latin American materials at LAMP member institutions are the intellectual leaders and driving force of LAMP's work. Through contacts they have made in their own work and on behalf of their libraries and scholars, LAMP librarians uncover collections in need of preservation in a variety of disciplines and housed in libraries and archives in a wide range of locations. Research interests of LAMP librarians and the scholars they serve lead them to discover collections held in Latin American institutions that would benefit from preservation and broader accessibility. Collections and projects proposed to LAMP may also come from the holdings at member institutions, which librarians may discover to be unique and desirable to be added to LAMP's shared collection. This collaborative approach to increasing the size of the North American research collection on Latin America has resulted in LAMP's amassing a unique shared collection of rare but important primary source material valuable to the study of Latin America.

LAMP held its first meeting in 1975 with sixteen member libraries. Its current membership includes forty-nine academic libraries from across North America. These institutional members create a financial pool as well as an aggregation of expert library professionals who convene annually at the meeting of the Seminar on the Acquisition of Latin American Library Materials (SALALM) under the direction of LAMP's Executive Committee. At these meetings, LAMP considers and prioritizes preservation proposals, often concentrated on safeguarding newspapers and archival materials from Latin America. LAMP has preserved a variety of types of materials with research value in many fields of study, including political archives, newspapers, serials, and government documents.

21

Recent projects include the preservation of newspapers from Bolivia, Brazil, Colombia and Mexico as well as archival materials from Puerto Rico, Argentina, Brazil and Mexico.

LAMP is well-positioned to provide access to the shared collection for its members, as it is based at the Center for Research Libraries (CRL), which acts as the fiscal and legal agent for the program. CRL was founded as the Midwest Inter-Library Corporation (MILC) in 1949 by ten major U.S. universities. The purposes of the Center for Research Libraries, as outlined in its founding documents, included "To establish and maintain an educational, literary, scientific, charitable and research interlibrary center; to provide and promote cooperative, auxiliary services for one or more non-profit educational, charitable and scientific institutions; to establish, conduct and maintain a place or places for the deposit, storage, care, delivery and exchange of books … and other articles containing written, printed, or recorded matter."[1]

CRL's long history in supporting collaborative collection development, as well as its capability in storing and serving shared collections, made it a natural home for programs that aggregate librarians' expertise, collection and store rare material, and make this shared material accessible to participating institutions. Beginning in 1963 with the founding of the Cooperative Africana Microform Project (CAMP), CRL has become the administrative home of six cooperative projects that focus on different world regions: the South Asia Microform Project (SAMP) (founded in 1967); the Southeast Asia Microform Project (SEAM) (1970); the Latin American Microform Project (LAMP) (1975); the Middle East Microform Project (MEMP) (1987); and the Slavic & East European Microform Project (SEEMP) (1995). All six "AMPs" acquire, preserve and maintain collections of rare and hard to obtain research materials from or about their respective world regions. They each collect annual fees from their institutional members that are for the acquisition and reformatting of important collections identified by the members. CRL houses these items and makes them available to members on generous terms through interlibrary loan or digital access.

LAMP's organizational structure has allowed a great deal of flexibility in the methods of acquiring new material and in the variety of formats and subject areas included in its collection. While LAMP's earliest acquisitions were on microfilm, in recent years many LAMP projects have been accomplished through digitization. Over the years, microfilm had been considered the most cost effective and stable technology for LAMP's preservation goals, but members of LAMP have been submitting increasing number of digital proposals in the early years of the twenty-first century. In fact, in recent years, all six projects have changed their names to include the word "Materials" rather than "Microform." This modification reflects the changing collections landscape, which now features more digital collections.

A recent example of a LAMP project illustrates how preservation can play an important role in digital projects. Beginning in 2012, LAMP provided funding to the University of Florida to digitize and make freely available its holdings of *O diário de Pernambuco* (Recife, Brazil) from November 1825–September 1922. The University of Florida was the only library in North America that held this title, and its copy of the microfilm became increasingly at risk because of the frequency with which scholars were using it. In order to ensure the longevity of the content on microfilm, and to enable broader access, Florida proposed that this title be digitized. *O diário de Pernambuco* is critical for research, as it covers early Brazilian commerce, social affairs, politics, family life, slavery, and other topics. It contains numerous announcements of maritime movements, crop production, legal affairs, and cultural matters.

LAMP's enduring mission to preserve "materials in danger of being lost or becoming inaccessible"[2] helps guide selection and standards in much the same way it informed the consortium's early challenges and accomplishments. In "The Latin American Microform Project: The First Decade," Carl Deal recounts the first years of LAMP's work.[3] Efforts to evaluate the strengths and weaknesses in Latin American collections throughout the United States and to identify prospects for collaboration led to strong emphases on materials from Mexico and Brazil. Projects built on professional connections between LAMP members and individuals at institutions in these countries. For example, LAMP representatives negotiated directly with directors of the Biblioteca Nacional and the Arquivo Nacional in Rio de Janeiro in order to ensure the cooperation of these institutions in some of LAMP's early projects to acquire microfilm copies of Brazilian local government materials.

The collaborative spirit of these first archival filming projects expanded later to incorporate other documents from Brazil including the reports of the First Brazilian Republic, twentieth-century ministerial reports (1825–1890) and the *Almanak Laemmert* (1884–89). James Simon[4] addresses the expansive nature of this first Brazilian documents project in his commemorative thirty-year retrospective "Treinta Años de LAMP—A Brief Look Back." As he notes "the collection of reports from Latin American ministries is one of LAMP's 'crown jewels.'" Today this collection, which began with reports from Brazil, includes ministerial materials from eighteen additional Latin American countries.

Simon also outlines an invitation from the Andrew W. Mellon Foundation in 1994 to digitize the Brazilian Government Publications, further emphasizing the success of LAMP's early efforts to select and preserve these documents in microfilm. This $225,000 grant started LAMP's transition to digital projects as a means to continue its work in supporting scholarship on Latin America. Scott Van Jacob's writing on the CRL/LAMP Brazilian Government Serials Digitization Project[5] provides insight into how LAMP's successful work on this early digital project was instructive for future projects. The Brazilian Government Serials Digitization Project sought to provide access to this specific set of historical documents and worked through international collaboration. As Van Jacob notes, the project team included collaboration across institutions including the University of Notre Dame, Cornell University, the University of Texas at Austin, Harvard College Library, CRL and the Fundação Biblioteca Nacional (National Library Foundation) (FBN) and the Arquivo Nacional (National Archive) (AN) in Rio de Janeiro. The project endeavored to facilitate scholarly access, expand the corpus digitally, implement mechanisms for bibliographic and structured access and indexing (discovery), explore levels of demand and patterns of use and refine process for creating digital image files from preservation microfilm. It was an early manifestation of articulating tools, operations, standards and policies for digital collecting with attention to processes for selecting and integrating digital representations with appropriate metadata. Most importantly, it relied heavily on deep collaboration.

Based on the success of the Brazilian Government Serials Digitization Project and the interest of scholars in working with digital materials, LAMP members have brought more digital proposals for consideration. LAMP has responded by implementing rigorous guidelines and additional requirements for digital proposals. For a digital proposal to be approved, it must contain provisions for long-term sustainability and preservation, either at the institution digitizing the material, or the agreement that the digital files will be deposited at CRL. LAMP digital projects must include metadata created in accordance with best practices that facilitate access to specific images or text files as well as interoperability with the OAI-PMH (Open Archives Initiative Protocol for Metadata Harvesting). This requirement for enhanced discoverability and access expands the opportunity for scholars to find and use this material. Beginning in 2013, LAMP added an additional layer to its evaluation process for digital proposals. All proposals for digital projects are evaluated first by a committee from among the membership with demonstrable knowledge of best practices in digital preservation for archiving.

In the early years of the twenty-first century, LAMP's continued efforts in collecting research materials from and about Latin America have resulted in new collections in a variety of formats and subject areas. While digitization has become a more frequent method for accessing LAMP's collection, many LAMP collections have continued to be preserved on microfilm, as the debate continues over whether digitization should be considered stable enough to be a viable preservation medium. Depending on the specifics of each LAMP proposal, as well as the inclinations of the person or institution proposing the project, currently LAMP may pursue either digitization or microfilming for new projects. Several recent projects highlight the variety of LAMP materials and project strategies used by LAMP.

Newspapers make up a large portion of LAMP's collection, as many researchers from a variety of academic disciplines find important information in these publications. Recently, LAMP microfilmed seven newspaper titles from late nineteenth and early twentieth century Bolivia from the collection at the University of Connecticut, a long-time member of LAMP. These newspapers represent a cross-section of opinion from Bolivia during a period of political instability and conflict. These issues, which had not been preserved on microfilm, cover 1877–1908, and include titles such as *El heraldo* (Cochabamba) (1877–1908), *La industria* (Sucre) (1881–1908), and *El trabajo* (Tarija) (1882–1892). These titles were identified as a potential LAMP project when a member librarian noticed a dearth of Bolivian newspapers for this era in an accessible format and realized that the University of Connecticut owned materials that might fill this gap. LAMP's microfilm of this set of materials has made this content available to a much larger pool of researchers than previously had easy access to it. As a matter of policy, LAMP provides a copy of the microfilm to the institution that provided the materials for preservation. It this case, the University of Connecticut now holds a copy of the microfilm in addition to the print, so that patrons may consult the microfilm rather than risk additional damage to the paper copies.

LAMP also played a key role in the preservation and eventual digitization of the collection *Brasil: Nunca Mais*, which contains one million pages from the cases of more than 7,000 persons arrested, convicted, and/or executed by the Supremo Tribunal Militar (Military Supreme Court) (STM) of Brazil between 1964 and 1979. In 1979, a group of religious officials and lawyers began an extremely ambitious project: to access records of the STM containing information and evidence of human rights violations committed by agents of the state during the military dictatorship, then still in power. The project's founders took the *processos* off site for reproduction, taking advantage of a 24-hour period permitted by the Court to remand the cases. Reverend James Wright of the United Presbyterian Church of Brazil and Cardinal Dom Paulo Evaristo Arns, archbishop of the Roman Catholic Archdiocese of São Paulo, coordinated the activities in Brazil. After nearly six years of working in secrecy, the organizers completed the reproduction of the 707 lawsuits consulted, which totaled about one million copies on paper and 543 reels of microfilm. The project team also created a twelve volume index that contained, among other data: (i) how many prisoners passed through the military courts, (ii) how many were formally charged, (iii) how many were arrested, (iv) how many people reported having been tortured, (v) how many people disappeared, (vi) what methods of torture were practiced, and (vii) where prisoners were detained. In 1987, Wright arranged for LAMP to take in the collection, so that it would be widely accessible to researchers from academic and research institutions throughout North America. In 2011, an official from the Ministério Público Federal (Public Federal Ministry) (MPF) contacted CRL to explore an opportunity to digitize the full collection of reels. LAMP readily agreed to contribute duplicate negatives of the reels for scanning in Brazil, so that the files may be accessible openly on the Internet. LAMP's copy of this collection was the most complete and in the best condition of these materials still in existence for the 2011 digitization project in Brazil. LAMP's stewardship of these materials for several decades made it possible for the material to be returned to Brazil for further research into this important period of its history.

LAMP has added significant content to its collection in the past decade by building on the preservation work of the Nettie Lee Benson Latin American Collection at the University of Texas at Austin (UT). In the early 1980s, the Benson Collection received funding from the U.S. Department of Education to microfilm approximately 600 serial titles from Latin America. These rarely held serials were deteriorating, due to the acidic-based paper on which they were printed. The best possible image was taken in the 1980s, resulting in high quality microfilm, which conforms to contemporary standards for archival microfilm. The U.S. Department of Education grant had paid for the creation of the master negative microfilm and one positive service microfilm copy of each reel. By policy, however, UT could not complete OCLC cataloging, as they lacked a negative printing master copy of the microfilm. In the first decade of the twenty-first century, LAMP supported the costs of creating a negative printing master copy of the microfilm for UT's collection and a duplicate positive service copy of the microfilm for LAMP, which is now stored at CRL and available for members to borrow. While the 1980s project funded by the Department of Education had preserved the material, the resulting microfilm had been neither discoverable through OCLC records, nor accessible to researchers outside of Austin, Texas. The longest running title in this set of material is the Colombian weekly popular interest serial publication *Cromos*, which was duplicated for LAMP's collection for the period January 1916–December 1966 on 117 reels of microfilm. In addition to *Cromos*, many other commercially published and government serials from across all regions of Latin America were microfilmed by LAMP on approximately 900 reels. Some titles in this collection include: *Revista universitaria: órgano de los Centros de Estudios de la Universidad Católica* (Santiago, Chile) (1916–1968); *Revista de los Archivos Nacionales* (San José, Costa Rica) (1936–1965); *El hijo del Ahuizote* (Mexico City, Mexico) (1885–1902); and *Boletín de la Cámara de Comercio de Caracas* (Caracas, Venezuela) (1945–1980).

The Arquivo do Estado de São Paulo requested LAMP funding to microfilm its holdings of *Correio paulistano* in order to preserve the content, as the Arquivo's fairly complete run of this important title had become fragile due to frequent use. The LAMP-funded project preserved the Arquivo's holdings of *Correio paulistano* from January 1929 to July 1963 on 179 reels of microfilm. Once the Arquivo received the microfilm copy, users were able to have access to the microfilm instead of the fragile paper copies. LAMP also receives a positive service copy of the microfilm produced from its projects, and this copy can be borrowed by LAMP and CRL members. *Correio paulistano*, founded in 1854, was a leading newspaper in the Brazilian city of São Paulo and represented the viewpoint of the city's elite. Coverage of political, economic and cultural topics of the day were well-represented in this newspaper.

LAMP has acquired the collection *Encuesta de Folklore de 1921*, which is preserved on 109 reels of microfilm containing approximately 88,000 manuscript pages of songs, legends, nursery rhymes, and traditional stories from rural Argentina. The original project to collect this material was directed beginning in 1921 by Ricardo Rojas and implemented by the Ministry of Education to collect folklore material from across Argentina. Primary school teachers from all parts of Argentina were given strict guidelines to collect this material in a consistent and unbiased manner so that it could be documented for future generations. LAMP acquired this collection from Argentina's Centro de Estudios Histíoricos e Informacíon Parque de Espãna (CEHIPE).

In the 2010s, LAMP microfilmed New Mexico State University's (NMSU) holdings of the Mexican newspaper *El diario de Juárez* for the period January 2008–December 2010 on seventy-eight reels of microfilm. 2008 began an extraordinary period of extreme violence relating to drug-trafficking and government actions that included the deployment of the Mexican military and Federal police into the city. During this time period, Juárez experienced some of the highest murder rates in the world. LAMP member NMSU proposed this microfilming project in order to preserve the publication's full content, including advertisements and *condolencias* (personal notices on deaths of city residents), which do not appear in commercial databases that include this newspaper. Molly Molloy, Border & Latin American Studies Librarian at New Mexico State University, worked with the Universidad Autónoma at Ciudad Juárez in Mexico to secure additional issues of the newspaper to make the microfilm run as complete as possible.

In a project that was carried out over about fifteen years, LAMP supported the microfilming of Latin American religion periodicals held by the Princeton Theological Seminary. This project included 134 titles that focus on Protestant and Catholic religious literature, with an emphasis on post–Vatican II material and the emergence of liberation theology. Princeton Theological Seminary's collection includes materials from the early twentieth century forward, but it began research-level collection of Latin American materials in religion and theology with intensity in the 1970s. LAMP member librarians saw this to be an important collection with wide research interest. While the titles focus on religion and theology, researchers from many disciplines may find the content valuable, as it contains a wealth of information about social conditions and customs. Sample titles include: *Revista teológica limense* (Lima, Peru) (1973–1991); *La unión valdense* (Colonia Valdense, Uruguay) (1905–1919); *Estudios teológicos* (Guatemala) (1974–1989) and *Ciencia y fe* (San Miguel, Argentina) (1944–1964).

LAMP has supported the preservation of the archive of Abdias do Nascimento (1914–2011), an influential Afro-Brazilian artist, activist, scholar and politician. The archive is held by the Instituto de Pesquisas e Estudos Afro-Brasileiros (IPEAFRO) in Rio de Janeiro, Brazil. With support from LAMP, the Fundação Biblioteca Nacional (National Library Foundation) (FBN) of Brazil, the Arquivo Nacional (National Archive) (AN), and the Library of Congress Field Office in Rio de Janeiro, IPEAFRO organized and microfilmed the documents in the archive. LAMP has received the microfilm produced by this project, and, with separate funding, IPEAFRO has digitized and hosted selections of the material on its website. Nascimento's archive is a rich source for scholars interested in twentieth century Brazil as it documents artistic expression, race relations and political activities over several decades. Nascimento founded the Teatro Experimental do Negro (Black Experimental Theater) (TEN) in 1944 and played many roles in the theater's productions. A leader in the campaign for Afro-Brazilian rights, Nascimento was forced into exile in 1968. While in exile, he was active in the Pan-African movement and became a visiting professor at several U.S. universities. He returned to Brazil in 1983 and was elected as the first Afro-Brazilian Senator in 1994.

In administering LAMP-funded projects, CRL has the flexibility to carry project funds across fiscal years, thereby allowing projects to be carried out over a number of years if projects run into unexpected delays. LAMP had a long-running goal to preserve the Argentine anarchist newspaper *La protesta*, but the difficulty in locating a sufficiently complete run of this newspaper that was in good condition delayed the project for several years. Finally, after trying unsuccessfully to piece together a relatively complete run of issues of *La protesta* from the holdings of North American libraries, LAMP member librarians found that the Centro de Documentación e Investigación de la Cultura de Izquierdas en Argentina (CeDInCI) could digitize from hard copy the issues of *La protesta* from 1935 to 2012 from the collections of three libraries in Buenos Aires: CeDInCI, the Biblioteca José Ingenieros, and the Federación Libertaria Argentina. The project included more than 400 issues of this title and the digitized issues are now hosted at CRL. The earliest years of this title had been preserved elsewhere, but the holdings included in this LAMP project had proved difficult to access by North American researchers.

LAMP is uniquely positioned in the landscape of North American institutions that collect research materials on Latin America. LAMP has for forty years focused on preserving at-risk materials, especially those that are rare and have value to current and future scholars. LAMP's model of collaborative collection relies on the aggregated expertise and professional networks of its member librarians, many of whom are accomplished scholars with decades of experience in identifying research materials for themselves and scholars at their home institutions. LAMP's funding is also an aggregation that allows the acquisition of highly specialized research material that might be too expensive and too narrowly focused for any one institution to purchase. The materials owned by LAMP are available for borrowing through interlibrary loan to members of the project, expanding the buying power of all member libraries.

LAMP's collection is the result of the tenacity of its member librarians in identifying and pursuing opportunities to acquire collections to support scholarship in Latin American studies. Using varied methods of acquisition, LAMP has amassed an impressive collection over its forty years. LAMP has commissioned original microfilming, digitization from microfilm, digitization from print, the duplication of microfilm that was previously inaccessible, and has stored at-risk human rights documentation until its country of origin was ready to take custody of it. By employing a variety of methods to taking in new collections, LAMP has been able to complete projects that an individual library, working on its own, might not be able to fund or manage. LAMP's collection is not narrowly focused by subject, but rather useful to scholars in a wide array of academic disciplines. The LAMP collection has served scholars well for the last forty years, and is positioned to be of great use to future researchers for decades to come.

NOTES

1. "History of CRL," Center for Research Libraries, http://www.crl.edu/about/history.

2. Carl W. Deal, "The Latin American Microform Project: The First Decade," *Microform & Imaging Review* 15, No. 1 (1986): 22–27. http://www.crl.edu/area-studies/lamp/membership-information/project-history.

3. Deal, "The Latin American Microform Project."

4. James Simon, "Treinta Años de LAMP—A Brief Look Back," *FOCUS on Global Resources*, 24, No. 2 (2004): https://www.crl.edu/focus/article/518.

5. Scott Van Jacob, "CRL/LAMP Brazilian Government Serials Digitization Project Report," last modified December 2001: www-apps.crl.edu/sites/default/files/attachments/pages/FinalReport.pdf.

Changes and Continuities in the Mexican Academic Publishing Industry, 1980–2015

Reflections of a Book Vendor

S. Lief Adleson

This essay deals with the changes and constants that I have observed in the Mexican academic book market from 1980 to 2015. I have been a specialized book dealer concentrating on Mexican publications since 1978. During this period of almost four decades, Mexico has undergone changes which have altered the face of the country and which have reorganized the production and distribution of academic books and serials.

I define academic publications as books and serials in the social sciences and humanities which are appropriate for collection by university and research libraries intent on building and preserving content that reveals multiple facets of Mexican society, culture and history. These include publications produced not only by entities directly associated with educational endeavors (universities and research centers), but also those produced by diverse agencies of government, commercial and independent presses, non-governmental organizations (NGOs), and assorted representatives of civil society (religious, professional and cultural groups). In addition, I include in this essay commentary about the changes and constants I have observed in academic libraries that acquire these types of Mexican publications.

Finding and Obtaining Mexican Publications

When I first started offering Mexican books to academic libraries in the U.S. and Europe, I was intrigued by the absence in Mexico of an efficient book distribution system. I arrived in Mexico City in September 1975 to study for a doctorate in history at El Colegio de México, after having traveled extensively around the country and having conducted historical research there during the previous three years. Two years later, while still studying and researching, I signed on as the Mexican purchasing agent for a book vendor based in Los Angeles, California.

At that time most of the academic publishing industry pivoted around the historical center of the country, Mexico City. The Universidad Nacional Autónoma de México (National Autonomous University of Mexico) (UNAM) dominated the national higher educational panorama with more than 165,000 students in its Mexico City campus.[1] Only a few state universities, such as those in Guadalajara, Jalisco; Puebla, Puebla; Monterrey, Nuevo León; Xalapa, Veracruz; and Mérida, Yucatán offered an educational alternative to students unable or unwilling to move to the nation's capital. Because of these and other factors, I estimate almost 90 percent of academic publishing emanated from the country's traditional economic, political and administrative center.

As I travelled to state capitals and large cities in Mexico in search of regional publications appropriate for export to university and research libraries, I realized that very few books produced in the nation's capital could be found outside of the Federal District. Conversely, few, if any, non–Mexico City publications were available in the nation's commercial and educational epicenter. In the "provinces," I discovered that there were three kinds of establishments that handled the kinds of books I was looking for.

First, there were shops affiliated with or serving as university book stores. These stocked titles that were published by their sponsoring institution—not infrequently books written by academic staff and intended as text books or as required reading for specific courses. Additionally, they often contained a varied assortment of titles ranging from academic to popular, from cookbooks to inspirational testimonials. Such titles, I discovered, were what a few adventuresome Mexican book distributors and publishers had trucked to the provinces to sell on a cash basis to even more adventuresome book store owners who hoped they could sell them in their local market.

From my experience with publishers in Mexico City, I understood the kind of risks such book store operators were undertaking. In those days commercial publishers and book distributors only sold their products to book stores on a non-returnable, cash basis, generally with a 35 percent discount. Hence, the store owners were carrying a disproportionate portion of the industry's commercial burden on their shoulders. If they were unsuccessful in their attempts to sell copies of a title, the losses were all theirs. They had already paid for the publications, which could gather dust for years on the shelves. Hence, I encountered a structural hesitancy to sell academic books far from the main market, Mexico City.

The second kind of book-selling establishment I encountered in the Mexican provinces were little more than stationery outlets that offered a few printed titles and perhaps an assortment of back issues of popular magazines among a bewildering array of wrapping paper, ribbons and bows, writing paper sold by the sheet, envelopes, glues, scissors and other miscellaneous objects associated with paper products' manual arts.

A chain of book stores, Librerías de Cristal, was the third type of book selling outfit I discovered in the provinces. In addition to its dozen or so outlets in the nation's capital, the Librerías de Cristal enterprise ran a series of book shops in regional cities. Unfortunately, this once glorious chain of book stores was slowly unraveling and stocked little more than self-help titles, translations of U.S. best-seller titles, and the front and back list of Mexico's eight major commercial publishing houses (all located in Mexico City).[2]

My initial impressions, then, in the late 1970s and early 1980s regarding the Mexican academic book publishing activity led me to perceive a marketplace full of distorted commercial practices, limited selection and a truncated distribution system.

Why did the Mexican academic book production, distribution and sales system have such an odd configuration? The answer had to do with three factors: (1) the market for scholarly publications, (2) the mission and purpose of Mexican academic publishers and (3) the financial context in which they operated.

Academic Monographs for a Closed Market

Mexican academic publishing in the late 1970s and early 1980s was to a great extent reduced in scope. With a few exceptions, Mexican scholars, literary personages, playwrights, social scientists and other intellectuals produced for limited audiences. Topics of research and discussion frequently centered on important local, regional and national concerns, and they focused on reaching a quantifiable circle of scholars, politicians and policy makers, literate elite and educated public. Even after fifty years of intense educational effort following the violent phases of the Mexican revolution, in the 1970s the Mexican national median educational level was still a bit less than fourth grade. The educated middle class was generously estimated to comprise approximately 10 percent of the population.[3] Even so, wherever I looked about me, I did not perceive much of a book-reading tradition among the populace. While it is hard to calculate its precise dimensions in the early 1980s, it is safe to say that the market for Mexican academic publications was relatively small.[4]

The Mission of University Publishing Departments

In the 1970s and 1980s Mexico was still an agrarian country with a high national fecundity rate. Even though most of the population resided in rural areas, the trend toward rural to urban migration was clear. In this context, the nation's higher educational system gravitated toward the UNAM model of "education for the masses."[5] Teaching was the primary emphasis, while research and scholarly publication took a back seat.

The resulting blueprint for university education emphasized state subsidized, free public education. The institutional structure of the nation's university system developed with this focus in mind. Universities' publishing branches followed suit. For example, many editorial departments of state-operated schools were frequently instructed to price their books and serials at or below nominal production costs in order to make them more accessible to students and professors. Some universities granted a 50 percent discount off the list price of publications to students, faculty and staff. Each institution of higher education was focused internally on itself and its own academic community. Few administrators were concerned with extending the distribution reach of their publishing departments beyond the confines of their professional members.

Financial Context of Academic Book Production

Almost without exception, university editorial departments were assigned an annual operating budget within which they had to carry out their mission of publishing the academic monographs produced by affiliated scholars. Income generated through the sale of publications reverted to the institution's general fund, and was not seen by the department that had created the texts. There were few economic incentives to distribute and sell books beyond the confines of the immediate academic context.

These, then, were some of the structural parameters I observed in the Mexican academic book marketplace in the late 1970s and early 1980s. Nonetheless, by then the country had launched initiatives that would alter its relationship to the rest of the world, and would modify the availability of university education for the populace.

Beginning with the presidential administration of Miguel de la Madrid Hurtado (1982–1988), Mexico accelerated the process of opening its economy to global markets. Previously the country had maintained a relatively closed economy, using high import tariffs to back an import substitution model for promoting growth of Mexican industry.[6] The relatively scarce presence of foreign industry and commerce was accompanied by the dissemination of a political ideology called "nacionalismo revolucionario" which espoused nativism and fueled among the population a love/hate relationship the USA.[7] As an American citizen studying history in Mexico City and searching for academic publications to export, I was a relative oddity in the country. More than once, I was naïvely accused of working for the Central Intelligence Agency and on one occasion was requested to pay in U.S. dollars the Mexican peso price of books. Notwithstanding the evidence from the sometimes parochial reception I received, the country was already on the road to substantial and significant changes. Expansion and revitalization of the nation's educational policy led the way in many respects.

National Educational Expansion

In part as a reaction to the 1968 student movement, the Mexican government embarked on an ambitious program to develop higher education beginning in the 1970s. The national population had increased from 38.68 million inhabitants in 1960 to 86.08 million in 1980.[8] Institutions of higher learning were gearing up to the challenge of the Mexican baby boom. For example, the Universidad Autónoma Metropolitana was established in 1974 with three strategically located campuses in the Federal District.[9] In 1979 El Colegio de Michoacán was inaugurated in Zamora, Michoacán.[10] Both the Centro de Estudios Fronterizos del Norte de México (later to be renamed El Colegio de la Frontera Norte) and El Colegio de Sonora were born in 1982. The National Institute of Anthropology and History (INAH) pushed the development of its regional centers in Merida, Oaxaca, Hermosillo, Chihuahua, and other cities. Later the Centro de Investigaciones y Estudios Superiores en Antropología Social (CIESAS) established satellite operations in Guadalajara, Jalisco; Xalapa, Veracruz; San Cristóbal de las Casas, Chiapas; Mérida, Yucatán; Oaxaca, Oaxaca; and Monterrey, Nuevo León.

Growth of Publishing in Social Sciences

In conjunction with the push to expand academic opportunities in higher education, the Secretaría de Educación Pública (Secretariat of Public Education) (SEP) promoted several initiatives to bring printed academic content to the reading populace. The Consejo Nacional de Fomento Educativo (National Council for Educational Development)

(CONAFE), created in 1971, provided financial support to private and public entities to publish titles in the social sciences and humanities. The following year, with the participation of Gustavo Sáinz, SEP launched the *SepSetentas* series. This was an ambitious project to publish one new title in the social sciences each week. More than 300 titles were eventually released. Moreover, the print run of each title consisted of 10,000 copies and the federal government subsidized the price of these pocket books (ten pesos) to make them more accessible to the general public. During the following decade, SEP, in conjunction with the para-state publisher, Fondo de Cultura Económica, continued the precedent set by *SepSetentas* by publishing more than 150 low-priced titles on historical and cultural themes in its *SEP/80* series.[11]

National Decentralization and Publishing Output without Distribution

After the devastating 1985 earthquake in Mexico City the federal government promoted a national development plan that emphasized decentralization. State governments were granted increasing political, economic, and financial authority. State universities, many of which had long existed, began to receive significant subsidy increases. They enhanced their educational offerings, grew in size, hired more staff, and expanded the number of titles published under their institutional seal.

I observed, nonetheless, that inside many public universities—both in Mexico City and in the Mexican states—it looked as though their academic editorial units lived in closed spheres. On the one hand, there was little centralized publishing which could have led to uniform editorial guidelines and to peer reviews. Each department, research center, *facultad*, and institute strove to maintain its freedom from external control, even if this meant publishing without regard to what other academic entities in the same or different institutions were producing. Publishing calendars did not exist. Similarly, thoughts of dissemination continued to be few and far between. I customarily encountered storerooms on university campuses full of entire print runs. The few copies of a particular title that might have seen the light of day were frequently the work of the authors themselves. Often they received copies of the printed product as payment for their intellectual contribution. These they gave to friends and colleagues and/or dropped off a few copies at a local book store or two.

Academic Diversification

Over time research activities in universities increased and became more specialized. Centers of higher learning and research institutes grew in size and in the number of faculty they employed. Within these institutions, the departmental publishing entities multiplied for two reasons. First, many separate academic units grew out of increased intellectual specialization and out of the division of more basic structures. For example, at UNAM, the Instituto de Investigaciones Sociológicas (Institute of Sociological Research) grew out of the Factultad de Ciencias Políticas (Department of Political Science); the respective research institutes of psychology, esthetics and philosophy emerged from the Facultad de Filosofía y Letras (Department of Philosophy and Literature); the

Instituto de Investigaciones Jurídicas (Institute of Judicial Research) was spawned from the Facultad de Derecho (Department of Law); etc. Many of the newly created research centers, specialized institutes and departments sought to define separate academic and administrative identities by, among other things, setting up organizational units charged with publishing the intellectual products of their collegial members.

Second, some departmental publishing units arose from the contractual need to ensure that affiliated scholars would publish the fruits of their research under the editorial seal of the host institution. Many contracts between university departments and research branches and their scholars stipulated that the academicians give preference to their institutional press when seeking to publish their works. In the arcane setting of a quickly expanding system of public higher education, the publishing branches of many universities soon took on the role of offering what appeared to be automatic publishing services for content provided by their members.

At the institutional level, the Mexican educational expansion phenomena initially appeared like the workings of an amoeba: divide, separate, proliferate. However, close up, I perceived a reiterated pattern of differentiation, autonomy and an attempt to establish unique academic identities. Translated to the realm of editorial output, this explained why only rarely and in exceptional circumstances did publishing centralization and cooperation exist among departments, research centers, *facultades*, programs and schools in the same institution. As a result, for example, I had to identify and acquire publications from more than thirty-five distinct UNAM units in Mexico City alone, most of which were unaware of the editorial production of their colleagues across campus or down the hall. Similarly, the personnel in many university book stores, such as those in the Librería Universitaria of the Universidad de Guadalajara, knew that they did not stock all the new titles from the major academic departments of their university. However, few of the people who worked in the book store, for example, were knowledgeable about the existence of many more titles published by smaller, newer or more remote branches of the Universidad de Guadalajara. I learned that in order to find out about new Mexican academic publications, I had to establish direct contact with each separate production unit.

Sistema Nacional de Investigadores

Meanwhile, the Consejo Nacional de Ciencia y Tecnología (National Council of Science and Technology) (CONACYT) implemented a system of incentives to increase the productivity of Mexico's scholarly research personnel. Through the Sistema Nacional de Investigadores (National Research System) (SNI)—created in 1984—it established a tiered framework of monetary rewards for increased academic output. Publication of scholarly monographs was high on the list of proof of productivity. The economic benefits of jumping through the hoops and barrels, achieving status, and maintaining presence in the SNI, combined with those of other institutional incentive programs, at times represented an increase from three to five times the researcher's base salary.[12]

In retrospect, some authors have alleged that the SNI incentives distorted the nature of academic production in Mexico.[13] Especially in the social sciences and humanities, monograph publishing became the objective of academic research, at times supplanting other lofty ideals such as the creation of new knowledge or contributing to scholarly discussion on a particular theme. Academic content providers increasingly pressured their publishing departments to hasten publishing turnaround, because SNI rules stipulated that only a physical copy of a published work would suffice as proof of publication. In an environment of weak editorial oversight, and with the supposed added justification that more is better, the production of academic monographs continued apace.

As a result of these efforts to expand university educational offerings and to promote academic research in Mexico, the number and quality of suitable university-level books and serials increased. Moreover, their publishing venues multiplied as state and regional academic and research institutions produced new content. Notwithstanding the increase in the volume of academic publishing, distribution networks did not grow or mature correspondingly. Impediments to the distribution of individual titles continued to be the order of the day, and economic incentives for increased sales did not take hold as the norm in many university publishing departments.

The structural framework of the Mexican academic publishing industry, characterized by increased output without regard to distribution and commercialization, continued into the 1980s and 1990s. To cope with the growing number of new titles in more distant areas, I traveled more often to remote regions of the country. My mission on each trip was to identify and acquire appropriate new publications, and to establish and renew commercial relations with diverse academic and for-profit publishing outfits. Additionally, on my acquisitions trips I approached the state governor's offices to obtain copies of recent annual state of the state reports (*informe anual*), as well as those of regional development commissions, state secretariats, etc. Although limited in demand, these local and regional government publications provided testimony to the kind of changes many Mexicans were experiencing in their daily life. Similarly, as the states received greater funding and autonomy from the federal government, many promoted local cultural projects and established state cultural secretariats. Soon the regional *casas de cultura* (cultural centers) began publishing the works of local poets, historians, playwrights, novelists, political commentators, art critics, etc.

Federal Government Publications and National Politics

A peculiar aspect of the Mexican publishing market that I witnessed beginning in the 1980s revolved around the printed output of secretariats of state at the federal level and their subordinate agencies. In addition to the annual reports, departmental studies and secretariat political messages, the production of monographs played a unique part in the arcane and complicated dance of Mexican presidential politics. Both lavish monographs and mundane technical publications served to enhance the stature and political presence of possible candidates. Additionally, the research and production support teams assembled for such projects often yielded contacts and information for participating in future political undertakings. For example, the Secretaría de Programación y Presupuesto (Secretariat of Programming and Budget) (SPP) during the López Portillo administration (1976–1982) invested hundreds of thousands of dollars in research trips for scholars and political operatives to produce the *Atlas cartográfico histórico*.[14] Similarly, an insider commented to me that the preparation and publication of Miguel de la Madrid Hurtado's *Planeación para el desarrollo* in 1981 was important in the configuration of certain high level working groups that operated during his subsequent presidential administration.[15]

In the same vein Carlos Salinas de Gortari promoted a virtual avalanche of publications through the Instituto Nacional de Estadística, Geografía e Informática (National Institute of Statistics, Geography, and History) (INEGI) when he was the Secretary of Programming and Budget.[16] This, in turn, enhanced the credibility of INEGI, which, in turn, contributed to Salinas de Gortari being selected by the outgoing president as the candidate of the Partido Revolucionario Institucional (Institutional Revolutionary Party) (PRI) for the next presidential term. During Salinas de Gotari's administration, SPP continued to publish such series as the *Antología de la planeación en México* as well as to perpetuate INEGI's tradition as a source of statistical information about the nation's economy, demographics and natural and human resources.

I discovered, unfortunately, that the political value of many government publications frequently usurped their scholarly distribution. The producing agencies routinely dedicated prime resources to ensuring that copies of their publications reached the offices of federal senators and deputies, secretaries of state, governors and other high level politicians, before thinking about the public at large. As a result, and especially during times of economic austerity, few if any copies were left over for commercial distribution. Often times, I resorted to writing formal petitions and to using personal contacts to procure even a single copy of many government-sponsored publications. Other times, my personal political resources yielded unexpected results.[17] In summary, to be effective in my trade, I had to cultivate contacts in the public relations departments of many state and federal government offices. Notwithstanding, like the never ending spiral of Mexican politics, I would have to start the process anew when personnel changed or when key public officials left office. Mexico was and continues to be a country where personal contacts and who you know count more than institutional representation.

What I Learned from Bibliographers and Librarians

When I started selling Mexican books to American university and research libraries, I began dealing with very capable and well-educated people such as Carl Deal, Pauline Collins, Nelly González, Lee Williams, Larry Lauerhauss,[18] and others. Much of their work consisted of activities related to area studies collection development. They had spent much of their professional life perusing specialized journals from and about Latin America in history, sociology, anthropology, art history, economics, theater, literary analysis, etc., as well as examining newly published subject bibliographies and literary supplements of Latin American cultural newspapers and magazines. Part of their arsenal of tools also included book catalogs offered by book vendors. Traditionally, these collection development area specialists identified titles necessary for their libraries and ordered them from trusted book dealers with whom they had cultivated commercial and professional relationships. Initially I was surprised by the detailed nature of some of their requests. However, in time I realized that many of their orders were the result of referencing bibliographies in professional journals. I quickly recognized that I could stay a step ahead of them by systematically offering new publications from academic presses in my periodic book catalogues.

Over time I grew to understand more about the single-mindedness of these professionals. They worked to ensure that their library collections contained the most appropriate titles and tried to not miss any important publications from the geographic areas of their jurisdiction. They were respected academicians in their own right, and were consulted frequently by scholars and students. I was surprised to learn that many of them had worked for many years, if not for decades, in the same institution. They labored with a quiet passion, focused on their main objective with few distractions. For these librarians, this was a full-time endeavor in which they maintained a certain degree of autonomy and freedom to carry out their mission.

Another concept I learned from my contact with librarians and bibliographers dealt with the notion of fair play in the market place. Some Latin American book dealers sought to aggressively dominate their respective areas of influence, at times employing non-economic and coercive methods to achieve their ends. I observed how some used their political influence and close ties with police and government agencies to intimidate and restrain competing book vendors in the area. Others engaged in physical altercations with their competitors. Still others attempted to acquire market advantage by covertly entering into monopolistic combinations, while others attempted to obtain confidential customer information from competing book vendors through the use of spies and plants. The reaction of librarians upon learning of such unprincipled activities was enlightening. For the most part, my personal values were vindicated, and the response to my attempts to build a company that would endure beyond my personal presence, were positive. However, some librarians seemed to be enchanted by the unique, idiosyncratic human qualities embodied in Latin American culture and preferred a more personal approach. It seemed as though they viewed the more questionable ethical attitudes and undignified actions of some book dealers as either personal foibles or as something to be expected and the natural result of competition in an undisciplined environment that they conceived Latin America to be.

Libraries and Market Forces

The growth in higher education in Mexico beginning in the 1980s resulted in an increase in the number of new scholarly monographs published there each year. Simultaneously, in libraries in the U.S., Canada and Europe new technologies and their implementation spurred changes. The transition from card catalogs to computers demanded more time and new commitments from professional bibliographers. For instance, administrators in libraries of the University of California system[19] requested their Latin American bibliographers, among others, to dedicate varying percentages of their acquisitions budgets to cover the cost of installing computers in their departments. With increased frequency, I heard commentary from bibliographers about new assignments to the much-maligned "reference desk" and about having to work even more closely with students and faculty to aid them in the efficient use of the library. One consequence of the pressures of time and technology was an increase in the number of academic libraries that began implementing approval plans. The change from bibliographer selection to vendor-initiated acquisitions was a major conceptual switch for many inveterate professionals.

I resisted the use of the term "blanket order" and preferred the terminology of "approval plan." The former seems to have been the creation of U.S. and/or European book vendors who supplied publications from other geographic areas, and offered to fulfill the needs of their academic library customers in a one-way service. They promised to provide suitable publications without the possibility of returning unwanted or inappropriate titles, sometimes citing cross-border and customs limitations as reasons for their policies. I preferred to defer to bibliographers. Any book I supplied on an approval plan basis was subject to librarian approval and could be returned for full credit for any reason. I learned much about the idiosyncrasies and specific collection needs of many libraries by paying attention to the nature of returned books.

I grouped early adopters of Mexican approval plan publications into two types. One was comprised of well-financed institutional libraries with specialized Latin American area bibliographers. In the 1980s, the Latin American bibliographers of such organizations as the Library of Congress, Harvard University, University of California–Los Angeles, Yale University, Tulane University, University of Chicago, University of Texas at Austin, New York Public Library, Stanford University, et al. commanded acquisitions budgets commensurate to their collection interests. The characteristics of their acquisitions profiles suggested that in the 1980s and 1990s they conceived the approval plan as a method of implementing programs for acquiring Mexican publications in a comprehensive fashion. Their overriding interest at the time could be summarized as emphasizing quantity over quality, that is, with less regard for the variability of the publications they acquired and a greater focus on the scope.

A second type of academic library in the U.S., Canada and Europe taught me other lessons about the nature of collecting patterns. These approval plan institutions were characterized by more restrictive budgetary limitations. Their selection profiles enumerated specific subject areas and suggested levels of collection intensity for each. To fulfill the requirements of these types of approval plans, I evaluated each title and compared it against the universe of monographs in the same subject area published during the then-current and previous imprint year. At the same time, I had to take into account the relative importance of that monograph's subject with respect to all of the library's approval plan subject interests. If I judged a particular title to be of sufficient importance to pass through these conceptual filters, I then had to appraise each library's overall approval plan purchasing power and contemporary budgetary cycle.[20]* If a particular title withstood all these tests, I would select it for inclusion in an institution's upcoming approval plan shipment.

Crises as Motors of Change

Over time, and as institutional libraries experienced successive economic crises, the job of specialized book vendors changed. In the best of circumstances, yearly library budget allocations remained flat while the dollar cost of Mexican publications continued stable or dropped as a result of monetary devaluations of the Mexican peso. In the worst case scenarios, library budgets were trimmed and reduced as the dollar cost of books increased. Meanwhile, the number of appropriate Mexican academic publications grew each year. This meant that fewer libraries could afford to purchase all of the appropriate publications in their areas of interest. We approval plan book vendors increasingly had to make decisions about which books were germane to library collections and which books to refrain from sending to specific libraries due to budget considerations.

For their part, librarians sought to deal creatively with these new realities by establishing cooperative acquisitions programs among various institutions. One popular methodology involved assigning territorial responsibilities among several participating institutions. Thus, for example, one university library would dedicate a special collection emphasis to one or more Mexican states, while another partner institution would make a commitment to obtain the publications from other states.[21] Thus, in principle, several libraries would jointly cover all the bases. From a book vendor point of view, this marked an important change in the nature and style by which academic libraries collected Mexican publications. On the one hand, subject categories were now dissected by territorial considerations. On the other, notwithstanding librarian assurances at the time to the contrary, the number of Mexican publications being sold to academic libraries outside of Mexico was slowly being reduced.

Moreover, those early collaborative acquisitions projects lacked adequate flexibility and vision. They were conceived as innovative measures to resolve novel problems in specific circumstances. However, some participating libraries suffered from additional, unexpected financial difficulties, and trimmed their allocations for area-specific acquisitions without notifying other participants in the program. Some libraries experienced staffing and/or responsibility changes, which left holes in their monitoring processes. Review and supervision of these experimental programs dropped in importance as other issues assumed greater priority. As a collaborative acquisitions exercise, I believe that the long term effectiveness of such programs left much to be desired.

Over the years I witnessed different attempts by which librarians tried to resolve particular acquisitions problems, most of which originated from diminishing acquisitions budgets. One creative bibliographer suggested that I no longer include in approval plan shipments monographs that were part of numbered series. Instead, I was to quote such titles separately so he could pay for them from a discrete funding code (as if they were serial titles). Unfortunately, as his job incorporated more new professional responsibilities, he had less time to respond to the quotes and his library received fewer Mexican monographs in numbered series. In another private university a change in institutional leadership precipitated, among other things, a reorganization of library priorities and, consequently, of funding availability. In response, the Latin American bibliographer decided in a rather unbibliographic approach to problem solving that I was to refrain from sending publications that emanated from the Mexican provinces and to remit approval plan books originating only from Mexico City.

One innovative collaborative acquisitions program cut through the traditional rivalries between Harvard and Yale universities. The Latin American bibliographers in these institutions still maintained sufficient professional authority and independence so that they could design and implement a novel acquisitions scheme that not only affected existing work flows, but that also strived to creatively resolve structural problems in the collection development process. They devised a procedure by which I, as approval plan supplier of Mexican publications for both libraries, sent non-core selections from distinct geographic areas to the bibliographer in the other institution. That is, I dispatched non-core collection books destined for Yale to the bibliographer in Harvard, and I submitted to Yale's Latin American bibliographer non-core collection books I had selected for Harvard. When the specially marked boxes arrived at their initial destinations, the respective bibliographer examined the titles in each package, firm ordered any publication he or she specifically wanted to incorporate in his or her collection and then sent the entire batch to the library for which it was originally destined.

This novel program allowed the libraries at Harvard and Yale to acquire between them a wider scope of publications than either could have procured alone. The bibliographers reduced duplication of books by reviewing the selections I had sent to their institutional counterpart and they selected for immediate acquisition titles that corresponded to particular interests and needs of faculty and students. Moreover, I learned that the notion of a library's "core collection" varied from institution to institution. By paying attention to these two librarians' selections I could discern differences in the relative academic idiosyncrasies of each library.

These and other instances of bibliographer maneuvers were, for the most part, valiant attempts to adapt to unexpected circumstances, mostly of the economic kind. They originated from operational levels of academic library management. A far as I could perceive, such adjustments were responses to unforeseen variations. Soon structural changes began to modify the form and function of university libraries, as well as the panorama of acquisitions of Latin American library materials.

What Has Changed, What Is Changing and What Has Stayed the Same

When I began to distribute Mexican academic books in the mid–1970s, Mexico boasted three cities whose population exceeded one million inhabitants. In 2015, thirteen urban conglomerations claimed that dubious distinction.[22] Not only has the overall population grown, but it also has converged in urban areas. In the realm of education, successive Mexican government administrations have attempted to keep up with the expansion and flow of the populace by funneling money into the public primary, secondary and university school systems, both in the nation's capital and in the "provinces." On a national scale the number of higher education institutions and the number of students served has escalated.[23] Just as important, enhanced educational opportunities have attracted a more diverse and international academic staff, particularly in the states. Such institutions as the Universidad de Quintana Roo (University of Quintana Roo), the regional centers of the Centro de Investigaciones y Estudios Superiores en Antropología Social (Center of Research and Higher Studies in Social Anthropology), the Centro de Investigaciones y Docencia Económicas (Center of Economic Research and Teaching), the Benemérita Universidad Autónoma de Puebla (Distinguished Autonomous University of Puebla), the Universidad Autónoma de Chihuahua (Autonomous University of Chihuahua), etc., have opened their doors to researchers from the rest of North America, South America, Europe and Asia. The volume of academic publications has accompanied these advances. Moreover, the pattern of publication has changed. Thirty-five years ago approximately 90 percent of Mexico's academic content emanated from the Mexico City valley. In 2015, approximately only 50 percent of Mexican academic books were published by entities located in the nation's capital.[24]

The scope and breadth of content has also bloomed. Local and regional studies have matured in substance, argument, and methodology.[25] In addition, scholars in Mexico have gone farther afield, studying and analyzing topics beyond the confines of domestic jurisdictions. El Colegio de la Frontera Norte (College of the Northern Frontier), a prestigious institution of higher learning, has led the field in dealing with subjects related to international migrations and in studying the construction of culture on both sides of the U.S.-Mexican border.[26] Mexican academics now scrutinize such topics as references to

Mexico in the U.S. discourse on economic, social, and political issues; conflicts and the arms race during and after the Cold War; the nature and achievements of the Arab Spring; relations between Syria and Iraq; immigration policies of the European Union; politics and the press in the Caribbean basin; politics and power of the World Bank and the International Monetary Fund; economic and financial development in the Asia-Pacific basin, etc.[27]

Unfortunately, the physical distribution and commercialization of such publications has not kept pace. Even though the country has undergone important economic transformations by opening its markets to international trade, by embracing economic globalization as a development strategy and by adopting neo-liberal economic reforms, the basic conceptual underpinnings of higher education have remained the same. University education continues fundamentally to be a state sponsored program for national social, cultural and economic development. Notwithstanding the expansion in the number of private universities that have opened in Mexico during the last twenty years, in terms of published academic output, government sponsored institutions easily produce 90 percent of them. The trickle-down effect of depending on public funding means, among other things, that university and research institute publishing departments do not necessarily operate from a bottom-line economic mentality. Most continue to receive fixed annual budgets from which they are charged with publishing (in print format) the content created by members of their institution. Revenues generated by the sale of books and serials revert back to the institutional general fund and are seldom seen by the publishing entity. Consequently, distribution and commercialization of their products is weak, at best.

In recent years many academic presses in Mexico have responded in two ways to the pressures of constant or falling budgets and to the increasing number of manuscripts they must publish. On the one hand they have reduced the size of print runs by using print-on-demand technology. Typical print runs have plummeted to around 500 copies for many academic books; some are released with as few as 125 copies and others appear with between 750 and 1000 copies. Most are never reprinted. The second strategy for remaining within budget has been the use of co-publishing arrangements.

Several commercial vendors have negotiated contracts on a title-by-title basis to co-publish academic monographs of participating institutions. Important among the commercial players are Miguel Angel Porrúa, Bontilla Artigas Editores, Juan Pablos Editores, Plaza y Valdéz (in its various incarnations), Porrúa Hermanos, and Siglo XXI Editores, all located in the nation's capital. Typical arrangements call for the university institution to provide the content and to pay the commercial press for publishing the work. In exchange, the commercial publisher produces a finished product according to the contract stipulations, includes the institution's logo and credit on the title page, and may or may not have the right to distribute and sell a certain number of copies of the publication. This latter arrangement has alleviated only slightly the publish-and-store syndrome, which affected many Mexican academic presses for years. Nonetheless, the willingness of commercial publishers to receive a percentage of the print run as a form of payment waxes and wanes depending on their track record in selling previous titles. Given the nature of the market for Mexican academic content in the social sciences and humanities, no clear tendency has emerged. While co-publishing with private concerns seems to be on the rise, it accounts for only a minuscule percentage of the academic monographs appearing annually in Mexico.

In the final analysis, the publishing of Mexican academic content is a low volume, low rent commercial activity. The market is small and geographically disperse. Academic publishing in Mexico can hardly be considered a financially viable, stand-alone enterprise. Directly or indirectly it is dependent on government subsidies. Commercial enterprises that offer to co-publish with research institutes and university presses do so with the idea of recovering their costs and generating a modest profit from the printing and binding aspects of the projects. It is worth noting that very few of the new private universities which have appeared on the scene during the last two decades—most of whom are exceedingly conscious of their for-profit mission—publish books under their institutional imprints (except for captive-audience, required reading textbooks). Presumably, they are aware of the low economic return of academic publishing. One notable exception is the Universidad Iberoamericana (a private Jesuit university).

Changes in Libraries

Fast disappearing are the days of the semi-autonomous, professional area studies bibliographer in academic libraries in the so-called First World, especially in the United States. New generations of young librarians are replacing the old guard. They bring with them novel concepts regarding the profession. The "old timers" studied librarianship. The next cohort specialized in library science. Recent generations are steeped in information science. The knowledge stored in libraries has transmutated from *publications* to *content* to *objects*. Changes in world economies as well as technological innovation have affected the management and operation of university libraries.

Twenty-five years ago university libraries eschewed the notion of utilizing vendor produced cataloging records. Driven by economic necessity, these days such off-shore services are increasingly common.[28] Indeed, the form and function of university libraries are being reshaped as they strive to redefine their mission in a rapidly changing world. Reinterpretation and reassignment of librarian activities, among other transformations, are a common theme. Most veteran library specialists are now responsible for a variety of duties that play down the importance of their particular professional expertise and require them to labor as generalists and/or to hastily learn new "capacities."[29] One librarian at a major institution in California, in addition to performing as the Team Leader in Humanities and Social Sciences, was saddled with six different job titles: Librarian for English Literature, Librarian for American Literature, Librarian for Comparative Literature, Librarian for Ethnic Studies, Librarian for Latin American Studies, and Librarian for Spanish and Portuguese.[30] While such a dramatic proliferation of responsibilities is uncommon, two or more job assignments are not.

The assignation of additional and diverse professional functions to librarians is a harbinger of greater changes. Indeed, the October 2013 "Area and International Studies Librarianship Workshop" sponsored by the Indiana University, Bloomington[31] brought together area study librarians and library administrators in a setting that provided insights on the nature of current changes and foreshadowed future transformations. From that experience I concluded[32] such things as:

- Area studies librarians in many institutions and from many areas of specialization, not just Latin American and Iberian studies librarians, are experiencing the unsettled waters of change.

- There is a dissonance between the discourse of librarians and administrators. The former are generally more conservative and defensive of their roles and activities; the latter advocate changes, renewal, new approaches, and search for new ideas.
- The responses of area studies librarians to the exigencies of change can be summarized as processes of adaptation, implementation, resistance, and coping.
- Individual university and research libraries are likely to strive for increased specialization and differentiation of their collections. In the U.S. there will be much less duplication of non–English language publications among libraries.
- There will be fewer copies of non–English language publications in academic libraries in the U.S. Some (many?) printed publications will not be held by any institution in the U.S.
- If present trends and tendencies continue, one generalist, likely to be known as a global studies librarian, will gradually fulfill many area studies librarian roles.

The Digital Hinterland

Mexico has not been exempt from the influence of the digital revolution. People using smart phones are omnipresent. Students of all ages search the Internet for answers to their homework and research assignments. Private companies and government agencies employ electronic resources in the conduct of daily activities.[33] In academia scholars increasingly turn to electronic resources for communication, investigation and teaching. Many publishing department heads receive requests from academic content creators to make their publications available in digital format. Nonetheless, among Latin American countries especially, Mexico has been notoriously slow in adopting digital format for academic monographs. Why is this?

Tradition, structure, and experience weigh heavily on the reluctance of Mexican academic publishers to leap into the digital arena. First, the publishing departments of Mexican universities traditionally function as vital components of their departmental administrative structures. The director or departmental head apportions their budgets annually. This leaves little room for maneuver, experimentation and innovation and promotes a sense of hesitancy among staff, especially when the costs of new ventures are difficult to ponder. Similarly, publishing departments engage the content-creating members of their community as their prime natural clientele. As a result, many academic publishers focus their attention principally inward and not toward the potential external reading audience. Fixed budget considerations reinforce these attitudes and predispose editorial administrators to underestimate the potential value of digital formats, especially for scholarly monographs.

Second, attempts to commercially produce and offer digital content—especially scholarly monographs—in Mexico have yielded unexpectedly meager results. The electronic store of the Librería Gandhi chain of book stores[34] has been unable to gain much traction. Similarly, the Fondo de Cultura Económica platform for selling digital content has underperformed.[35] Juan Luis Bonilla, co-founder of Bonilla-Artigas Editores, which specializes in producing Mexican academic content and has released more than eighty titles, recently commented that his foray into offering all his published content in digital format through the *Digitalia* database, left him unconvinced that he can recover even his electronic production costs from the sale of digital content. The low number of sales his titles have garnered dismayed him.[36]

More tellingly, Sayri Karp Mitastein, director of the Universidad de Guadalajara publishing department, surveyed several of her South American university press counterparts to assess their experience with publishing digital monographs. She found that most of the university presses reported insignificant sales of the publications they offered in digital format. According to her, the editorial directors of South American academic institutions despaired at the promise of digital format. As a result, the Universidad de Guadalajara has scaled back its plans to produce and distribute monographs in digital format.[37]

Third, the advent of digital platforms for academic content has reorganized the structure of the market. More than a simple change of information delivery systems, electronic format has brought new actors to the table. Such players as Proquest, Baker and Taylor, Amazon, Ingram, Google, Apple, JSTOR and others are organized to provide access to content, and to compete on a scale that shares little commonality with the realities of Mexican academic publishing. Rather, these enterprises vie for market share, interface supremacy, content discoverability, inter-operability with existing library systems, collection curatorship, etc. Frequently their business models are premised on the strategy of earning modest income either from each of many transactions or from a revenue stream based on charging annual subscription fees for curatorial services for building thematic collections.

These models lack affinity to the low-use, disperse, and heterogeneous nature of Mexican academic publications. Indeed, many of these modern companies are unaware of the difficulties involved in identifying and acquiring Mexican academic content and they are uninformed about the disparate, divergent and varied forms and methods of negotiating digital rights licensing from myriad Mexican academic publishers. Thus, they are unwilling or unprepared to pay the steep acquisition costs of offering Mexican academic content in digital format.

The current structure of the digital marketplace for Mexican academic publications offers little solace to us specialized book vendors who supply research libraries with printed content. Currently, we seem to be the only agents with the experience, contacts, and wherewithal to bring together the scattered elements—geographic, legal (copyright negotiation), and conceptual—necessary to transform the precarious state of digitization of Mexican academic monographs. We may be the key to the source of supply. However, platform operators and their interface developers guard the doors to market demand. Nonetheless, the current potential economic benefits of channeling digital content through them do not compare favorably to the return we currently receive from selling printed versions of academic content to library end-users.

The government directly or indirectly subsidizes most of Mexican academic publishing. It is associated only loosely to the economic markets in which commercial digital content vendors operate. I believe, therefore, that the growth of Mexican digital monographs will depend on altering the bonds that tether them conceptually to the marketplace. This may happen in a variety of ways. Three occur to me as being potentially feasible in the short term. One, perhaps an agency of the Mexican government such as the Secretaría de Educación Pública or the Asociación Nacional de Universidades e Institutos de Educación Superior, would provide the context or develop the incentives necessary to compel academic publishers associated with universities and research institutions to venture into the waters of electronic publishing. This might happen by mandating the use of a common digital format; and/or by providing financial assistance for publishing new, prize-winning or scholarly acclaimed monographs in digital format; and/or by offering attractive national server/software/platform infrastructure to induce a significant number of academic presses to publish in digital format.

Two, an enterprising, well-capitalized private company might endeavor to "mature the market" by investing sufficient time, energy and resources to license the right to sell in digital format enough monographic titles to reach the critical mass necessary to offer curated collections or packages of thematic digital collections. Such collections might be versed on themes similar to "Mexican revolution" (history and literature); "contemporary Mexican politics," "society and gender studies in Mexico," "the impact of the North American Free Trade Agreement (NAFTA) in Mexico" (economics, sociology, anthropology, migration studies), "new trends in contemporary Mexican literature," etc.

Three, the future of digital monographs publishing in Mexico might veer in the direction of Open Access (OA). A combination of two of the above scenarios—private enterprise and public initiative—may converge to establish and maintain the hardware and software infrastructure necessary to establish an attractive OA platform for Mexican digital monographs. Many masters' theses and doctoral dissertations produced in Mexican universities are available through OA.[38] Perhaps a quasi-governmental consortium of stakeholders could convince the multitude of academic publishers that they could better serve their content creators by loading it to a well-managed, national, digital platform than by printing it on paper and storing the texts for years.

In summary, much has changed and much as stayed the same during the almost forty years I have participated in the Mexican academic publishing world. The quantity and quality of content has increased. Books of interest to research libraries are being produced in a dizzying array of cities throughout the country. However, distribution, dissemination, and circulation of new titles continue to be an important backwater with little sign of improvement, given the origins and objectives of academic publishing in Mexico. For similar reasons, propagation of digital content has been slow to take off and appears to be headed for an equally long trial.

NOTES

1. Hugo Aboites, "Matricula, selección de estudiantes y financiamiento en la UNAM," in *Anuario de Investigacioïn, 2009* (México, D.F.: Universidad Autónoma Metropolitana, Unidad Xochimilco, 2010), 643–668.

2. The history of the Librerías de Cristal saga has been hard to document. One limited version can be found in Serafín Vázquez, "Gregorio, la Librería de Cristal y la Lagunilla," http://svazquez.blogspot.mx/2004/05/gregorio-la-librera-de-cristal-y-la.html (accessed February 2, 2016). Additionally, I was told by one informant close to the source at the time that the chain was in virtual "technical bankruptcy" in the middle 1980s. Instead of closing up shop entirely, the eight principal creditors—Mexico's top commercial publishers—took over receivership of the organization and have run it since, using the book store chain to sell their product lines and to try to recoup their investment. Unfortunately, the Librería de Cristal chain looks like a slowly sinking ship in comparison to the recent efforts of such enterprises as Librería Gandhi, Librería de Porrúa Hermanos y Compañía, and Librería El Sótano, which now have branches in many cities around Mexico.

3. Gladys Lopez-Acevedo, and Angel Salinas, "Earnings Inequality, Educational Attainment and Rates of Returns to Education after Mexico's Economic Reforms," 14, figure 2, in http://siteresources.worldbank.org/INTPGI/Resources/342674–1206111890151/13233_EarningsInequality_Mexico. pdf (accessed February 2, 2016).

4. Gabriel Zaid, *Los demasiados libros* (México, D.F.: Océano, 1996). Guillermo Sheridan wrote a sardonic commentary about the 2007 OECD and UNESCO annual report concerning "hábitos de lectura" in Mexico: http://www.letraslibres.com/revista/columnas/la-lectura-en-mexico1 (accessed December 28, 2015).

5. Gilberto Guevara Niebla, "Masificación y Profesión Académica en la Universidad Nacional Autónoma de México," *Revista de la Educación Superior*, Vol. 15, No. 58 (April–June 1986): 31–44.

6. Leopoldo Solís M., *Medio siglo en la vida económica de México* (México, D.F.: El Colegio Nacional, 1994).

7. Alan Riding, *Distant Neighbors: A Portrait of the Mexicans* (New York: Knopf, 1984); Jorge G. Castañeda, *Mañana Forever?: Mexico and the Mexicans* (New York: Alfred A. Knopf, 2011).

8. https://en.wikipedia.org/wiki/Demographics_of_Mexico#cite_ref-14 (accessed December 27, 2015).

9. https://es.wikipedia.org/wiki/Universidad_Autónoma_Metropolitana (accessed December 28, 2015).

10. http://www.colmich.edu.mx/index.php/presentacion/9-presentacion/340-fundacion-e-historia (accessed December 28, 2015).

11. Gabriel Zaid, "Tirar millones," *Letras libres*, No. 163 (July 2012): 34–36.

12. Manuel Gil Antón, "La monetarizacioïn de la profesiún acadèmica en Mèxico: Un cuarto de siglo de transferencias monetarias condicionadasî en *Espacios en Blanco*." *Revista de Educación*, No. 23 (June 2013): 157–186 (accessed March 18, 2016, in http://www.redalyc.org/articulo.oa?id=384539805008).

13. Adrián Acosta Silva, "El poder de los estímulos," *BoCES, Boletín de Ciencia, Educación y Sociedad*, 6 March 2014 (accessed March 18, 2016, https://boletinboces.wordpress.com/2014/03/06/el-poder-de-los-estimulos/); Salvador Vega y León, coord., *Sistema nacional de investigadores: retos y perspectivas de la ciencia en México* (México, D.F.: Universidad Autónoma Metropolitana, Unidad Xochimilco, 2012).

14. *Atlas cartográfico histórico*. ([México, D.F.]: Secretaría de Programación y Presupuesto, Programación y Presupuesto, Instituto Nacional de Estadística, Geografía e Informática, 1982).

15. Comment by Flor Hurtado, 1983(?).

16. *México: información sobre aspectos geográficos, sociales y económicos* (México, D.F.: SPP, Programación y Presupuesto, Coordinación General de los Servicios Nacionales de Estadística, Geografía e Informática, 1981). *Sistema de cuentas nacionales de México* (México, D.F.: Secretaría de Programación y Presupuesto, Coordinación General de los Servicios Nacionales de Estadística, Geografía e Informática, [1981–]). *Nomenclátor de Baja California* (México, D.F.: Secretaría de Programación y Presupuesto, Coordinación General de los Servicios Nacionales de Estadística, Geografía e Informática, 1981). *Características del empleo y desempleo en las áreas metropolitanas de México, Monterrey y Guadalajara* (México, D.F.: Secretaría de Programación y Presupuesto, Coordinación General del Sistema Nacional de Información, 1979). *Manual de estadísticas básicas del sector comunicaciones y transportes* (México: Secretaría de Programación y Presupuesto, Coordinación General de los Servicios Nacionales de Estadística, Geografía e Informática, [1981]). *Encuesta mexicana de fecundidad* (México, D.F.: Secretaría de Programación y Presupuesto, Coordinación General del Sistema Nacional de Información, 1979).

17. One year, much to my surprise, two army trucks delivered 25 copies of President Miguel de la Madrid's annual state of the nation report to my offices. Each copy consisted of the main volume containing the "political message," plus eight thick, oversized tomes of statistical data, all packed in solid white cardboard boxes weighing nearly 25 kilograms each. Fidel Herrera Beltrán, governor of the state of Veracruz (2004–2010), had hand-delivered to me multiple copies his periodic publication, *Crónica de Veracruz* (Xalapa-Veracruz: Gobierno del Estado de Veracruz de Ignacio de la Llave, [2007–]) which summarized his recent political activities, so that I would send them to university and research libraries in the U.S. and Europe.

18. Carl Deal last worked at the University of Illinois, Urbana-Champaign; Pauline Collins served at University of Massachusetts, Amherst; Nelly González dedicated many years to the University of Illinois, Urbana-Champaign; Lee Williams was the Latin American Curator at Yale University; and Larry Lauerhauss served many years at the University of California, Los Angeles.

19. Campuses located in Riverside, Los Angeles, Irvine and Berkeley.

20. The period during a library's budget year when we attempted to acquire publications also played a part in our considerations. In order to avoid over spending a library's budget, toward the end of the fiscal year we had modify our usual acquisitions procedures due to the habitual unpredictability of book delivery in Mexico. Publications that arrived at our offices after the library's fiscal year closed, remained in a holding pattern, which could last as long as three months, until the beginning of the next budget period. Sometimes we had to forego selecting certain titles due to the difficulty of obtaining copies opportunely.

21. Several regional collection development consortia for Latin American publications sprang up over the years. The Latin America North East Libraries Consortium (LANE) was established in 1993, see http://salalm.org/lane/statement/. The Latin American Studies Southeast Regional Libraries (LASER) appeared in 1996, see http://salalm.org/laser/laser-mission/. For information on the Midwest Organization of Libraries for Latin American Studies (MOLLAS), see http://salalm.org/mollas/. Specific collaborative collection projects among institutions are spelled out in the CALAFIA web site. See http://library.stanford.edu/areas/latin-american-iberian-collections/calafia/mission.

22. I have updated the list of Mexico's most populous cities found in https://en.wikipedia.org/wiki/Metropolitan_areas_of_Mexico (accessed February 2, 2016) to include Mérida, Yucatán; Aguascalientes; and Cuernavaca, Morelos on the list of urban areas with a population exceeding one million inhabitants. These cities have experienced explosive growth since the 2010 census.

23. Adriana Olvera, "Las últimas cinco décadas del sistema educativo mexicano," *Revista Latinoamericana de Estudios Educativos (México)* XLIII (2013): 73–97.

24. This assertion is based on a manual count of monographic titles identified in recent years. The following chart illustrates the trend in number of titles identified each year (hatched line) with an indication of the percentage of titles that were published outside the Mexico City valley (solid line).

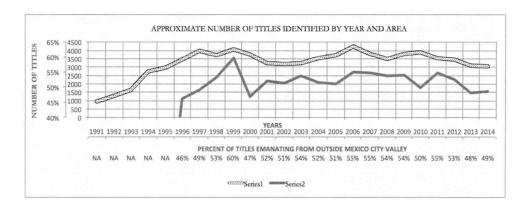

25. Luis Gonzalez y Gonzalez' classic historical study of a small town in Michoacan led the way to a proliferation of local and regional studies by professional historians and scholars. Luis González y González, *Pueblo en vilo: microhistoria de San José de Gracia* (México, D.F.: El Colegio de México, Centro de Estudios Históricos, 1968). See for examples of other regional studies: Ramón Kuri Camacho, *Chignahuapan: sierra norte de Puebla: voces y miradas de su historia*, 2 tomos (Puebla, México & Chignahuapan, Puebla: Benemérita Universidad Autónoma de Puebla, Dirección de Fomento Editorial; Ayuntamiento de Chignahuapan, 2006). J. Jesús López García, *Aguascalientes [1920–1944]: la transición arquitectónica* (Aguascalientes, México: Universidad Autónoma de Aguascalientes, 2008). Carlos Alonso T. Aguilar et al., *Jalisco artesanal: Guadalajara, Sayula, Tlajomulco de Zúñiga, Tlaquepaque, Tonalá, Tuxpan, Cajititlán, San Juan Evangelista, Tizatirla* (Guadalajara, México: Instituto Jalisciense de Antropología e Historia: Editorial Conexión Gráfica, 2004). Francisco López Bárcenas, *La diversidad mutilada: los derechos de los pueblos indígenas en el estado de Oaxaca* (México: Universidad Nacional Autónoma de México, 2009). Jesús Gómez Serrano, *Haciendas y ranchos de Aguascalientes: estudio regional sobre la tenencia de la tierra y el desarrollo agricola en el siglo XIX* (Aguascalientes, México/México, D.F.: Universidad Autónoma de Aguascalientes: Fomento Cultural Banamex, 2000). Guadalupe Margarita González Hernández, *Centralidad y distribución espacial del ingreso: cambios en la estructura de la ciudad Zacatecas-Guadalupe (1990–2004)* (Zacatecas, México: Universidad Autónoma de Zacatecas, 2009). Jesús Gómez Serrano, *Eslabones de la historia regional de Aguascalientes* (Aguascalientes, México: Universidad Autónoma de Aguascalientes, 2013). Alejandro Palma Castro, *Eslabones para una historia literaria de Puebla durante el siglo XIX* (México: Educación y Cultura; Benemérita Universidad Autónoma de Puebla, 2010).

26. On migration see, for examples, *Frontera y migraciones* (Tijuana, Baja California, and Ciudad Juárez, Chihuahua: El Colegio de la Frontera Norte; Universidad Autónoma de Ciudad Juárez, 1992); René M. Zenteno Quintero, *Migración hacia la frontera norte de México* (Tijuana, Baja California: Colegio de la Frontera Norte, Departamento de Estudios de Población, 1993); Soledad González Montes, et al., compilers, *Mujeres, migración y maquila en la frontera norte* (México, D.F. & Tijuana, Baja California: El Colegio de México, Programa Interdisciplinario de Estudios de la Mujer; El Colegio de la Frontera Norte, 1995); Norma Ojeda de la Peña, and Silvia López, *Familias transfronterizas en Tijuana: dos estudios complementarios* (Tijuana, Baja California: El Colegio de la Frontera Norte, Departamento de Estudios de Población, 1994); María Eugenia Anguiano Téllez, *Agricultura y migración en el Valle de Mexicali* (Tijuana, Baja California, México: El Colegio de la Frontera Norte, 1995); María Eugenia Anguiano Téllez, Daniel Villafuerte Solís, coordinators, *Cruces de fronteras: movilidad humana y políticas migratorias* (Tijuana, Baja California, México and Tuxtla Gutiérrez, Chiapas, México: El Colegio de la Frontera Norte; Universidad de Ciencias y Artes de Chiapas, Centro de Estudios Superiores de México y Centroamérica, 2015); Rodolfo Cruz Piñeiro, Cirila Quintero Ramírez, coordinators, *Ires y venires: movimientos migratorios en la frontera norte de México* (Tijuana, Baja California and San Luis Potosí, México: El Colegio de la Frontera Norte; El Colegio de San Luis, 2011); Jorge Eduardo Mendoza Cota, *Cambios en los flujos migratorios de México: un enfoque económico* (Tijuana, Baja California, México: El Colegio de la Frontera Norte, 2014).

Concerning the development and nature of border culture and the influence of foreign societies on national and regional populations, see, for examples, Aralia López-González, Amelia Malagamba and Elena

Urrutia, editors, *Mujer y literatura mexicana y chicana: culturas en contacto* ([Mexico City, Mexico] and Tijuana, Baja California, México: El Colegio de México, Programa Interdisciplinario de Estudios de la Mujer; Colegio de la Frontera Norte, 1988); José Manuel Valenzuela Arce, *El color de las sombras: Chicanos, identidad y racismo* (Tijuana, Baja California, México, and México, D.F.: El Colegio de la Frontera Norte; Universidad Iberoamericana; Plaza y Valdes Editores, 1998); Lawrence Douglas Taylor, *El nuevo norteamericano: integración continental, cultura e identidad nacional* (México, D.F. & Tijuana, Baja California: Universidad Nacional Autónoma de México, Coordinación de Humanidades, Centro de Investigaciones sobre América del Norte; El Colegio de la Frontera Norte, 2001); Manuel Ceballos Ramírez, coordinator, *Encuentro en la frontera: mexicanos y norteamericanos en un espacio común* (México, D.F.; Tijuana, Baja California; Ciudad Victoria, Tamaulipas: El Colegio de México, Centro de Estudios Históricos; El Colegio de la Frontera Norte; Universidad Autónoma de Tamaulipas, 2001); Manuel Ceballos Ramírez, et al., *Fenómenos sociales y urbanos transfronterizos entre México y Estados Unidos* (Tijuana: El Colegio de la Frontera Norte, Dirección General Regional Noreste, 2009); Rafael Alarcón Acosta, Luis Escala Rabadán and Olga Odgers Ortiz, *Mudando el hogar al norte: trayectorias de integración de los inmigrantes mexicanos en Los Ángeles.* Preface by Roger Waldinger (Tijuana, Baja California, México: El Colegio de la Frontera Norte, 2012); Gustavo Córdova Bojórquez, Justin Dutram Hansen, Blanca Esthela Lara Enríquez, José Guadalupe Rodríguez Gutiérrez, coordinators, *Desarrollo humano transfronterizo: retos y oportunidades en la region Sonora-Arizona* (Hermosillo, Sonora, México, and Tijuana Baja California, México: El Colegio de Sonora; Universidad de Sonora; Universidad Estatal de Sonora; El Colegio de la Frontera Norte, 2013); Rodolfo Cruz Piñeiro and Rogelio Zapata-Garibay, coordinators, *¡Vivir en el norte!: condiciones de vida de los mexicanos en Chicago* (Tijuana, Baja California, México: El Colegio de la Frontera Norte, 2013).

    27. See, for examples, María Eugenia Anguiano Téllez and Rodolfo Corona Vázquez, coordinators, *Flujos migratorios en la frontera Guatemala-México* (México, D.F. & Tijuana, Baja California: Secretaría de Gobernación, Instituto Nacional de Migración, Centro de Estudios Migratorios; DGE Ediciones; El Colegio de la Frontera Norte, 2009); Adolfo Aguilar Zínser and Silvia Núñez García, compilers, *México en el pensamiento económico, político y social de los Estados Unidos* (Ciudad Universitaria, México, D.F.: Universidad Nacional Autónoma de México, Centro de Investigaciones Interdisciplinarias en Ciencias y Humanidades, 1995); Arturo Bonilla and Margot Sotomayor, coordinators, *Conflicto geoestratégico y armamentismo en la posguerra fría* (México, D.F.: Universidad Nacional Autónoma de México, Instituto de Investigaciones Económicas; Ediciones El Caballito, 1999); César Cansino and Servando Pineda, coordinators, *La modernidad exhausta: posiciones sobre nuestro tiempo veinte años después de la caída del muro de Berlín* (Ciudad Juárez, Chihuahua, México: Universidad Autónoma de Ciudad Juárez, 2012); César Cansino, Samuel Schmidt and Guillermo Nares Rodríguez, editors, *¿Democratizando la democracia?: de la Primavera Árabe a los indignados* (Puebla de Zaragoza, México, and México, D.F.: Benemérita Universidad Autónoma de Puebla; Juan Pablos Editor, 2014); Gilberto Conde, *Turquía, Siria e Iraq: entre amistad y geopolítica* (México, D.F.: El Colegio de México, 2013); Ileana Cid Capetillo, Beatriz Nadia Pérez Rodríguez and Cuauhtémoc V. Pérez Llanas, coordinators, *Las políticas de migración de la Unión Europea* (México, D.F.: Universidad Nacional Autónoma de México, 2012); Leticia Bodadilla González and Martín López Ávalos, coordinators, *Independencias y revoluciones en el Caribe: prensa, vanguardias y nación en Puerto Rico y Cuba, siglos XIX y XX* ([Morelia, Michoacán, México] and Madrid, Spain: Universidad Michoacana de San Nicolás de Hidalgo, Facultad de Historia, Instituto de Investigaciones Históricas; El Colegio de Michoacán; Red de Estudios Comparados del Caribe y Mundo Atlántico [RecCMa], [2012]); Samuel Lichtensztejn, *Fondo Monetario Internacional y Banco Mundial: instrumentos del poder financiero* (Xalapa, Veracruz, México: Universidad Veracruzana, 2010); Geneviève Marchini W., *Crecimiento económico y desarrollo financiero en Asia-Pacífico* (Guadalajara, México: Universidad de Guadalajara, Centro Universitario de Ciencias Sociales y Humanidades, 2012); Geneviève Marchini W., *Las economías primario exportadoras de Oceanía y América Latina: Australia, Nueva Zelanda, Chile y Perú* (Guadalajara, México: Universidad de Guadalajara, Centro Universitario de Ciencias Sociales y Humanidades, 2012).

    28. Books from Mexico currently supplies cataloging records to nine major university libraries in the United States.

    29. Jesús Alonso-Regalado Mary K. Van Ullen, "Librarian for Latin American and Caribbean Studies in U.S. Academic and Research Libraries: A Content Analysis of Position Announcements, 1970–2007," *Library Resources & Technical Services* 53.3 (2009): 139–158.

    30. Jennifer Osorio identified her library functions in an e-mail communication to the author, 23 September 2014.

    31. For additional information, please see http://www.indiana.edu/~libarea/workshop.html (accessed June 1, 2016) [One editor respectfully disagrees with the observation from the 2013 Area Studies and International Studies Librarianship Workshop held at Indiana University that one speaker prophesied the imminent disappearance of distinct area studies librarians into global studies librarians. She attended the meeting while Mr. Adleson heard its streaming presentation, and may have misunderstood the speaker's comments.].

    32. S. Lief Adleson, "Commentary About University of Indiana Area Studies Librarians Conference, October 2013," personal notes, 8 November 2013.

    33. Since 2013, the Mexican government has required businesses and individuals to conduct all legal commercial transactions through electronic invoicing.

34. http://www.gandhi.com.mx.
35. https://www.fondodeculturaeconomica.com.
36. Commentary by Juan Luis Bonilla to author, Mexico City, 24 February 2016.
37. Observations offered by Sayri Karp Manstein to author during interview at the Feria Internacional del Libro in Guadalajara, 4 December 2015.
38. They are locatable by institution at: http://www.remeri.org.mx/tesis/.

The Librarian's Treasure Hunt

Acquisition Trips to Latin America and the Caribbean

PETER ALTEKRUEGER *and*
RICARDA MUSSER

Beginnings

Ever since people first began to collect knowledge, information and artifacts in special places such as archives, libraries and museums, the acquisition trip has been a favored strategy for extending and systematically building a collection.

In Europe's Middle Ages, the acquisition trip was one of the very few opportunities available for collectors to complete their libraries. They would travel to a distant monastery, copy the coveted text, and carry it away to add to their own collection. With the advent of the printed book and in the age of humanism, books primarily circulated in scholarly networks. Alongside the private libraries that came into being at this time, universities, too, began to show a stronger interest in acquiring printed volumes. The acquisition trip continued to play a vital role, especially when there was a need for foreign publications that could spread the latest scientific findings among a university's professors and students. In this context, the statutes of the University of Coimbra in Portugal first proclaimed the intention of systematically building a library in 1591, allocating the sum of 100 cruzados every three years for new acquisitions and appointing the Rector to oversee that the money was properly spent.[1] The results of such industrious collecting—also due in no small part to acquisition trips—appear to be most gratifying:

> From the beginning of the 17th century, accounting records show evidence of the extensive acquisitions of books from abroad. Shortly after the university was reopened following the devastation of the plague, an acquisition contract (…) was signed with the Scholar of Canon Law, Pedro de Mariz, proof-reader at the university printing press and library supervisor, on 19th May 1601. So as not to lose touch with scientific developments in Europe, he was charged with acquiring books in Italy—Venice is explicitly mentioned. Expenditure was set at a total of 500 Milréis.[2]

Yet the gradual professionalization of the retail bookseller's trade, and the evolution of book fairs as major hubs for the trade in books of whole countries and regions, also brought with it a sharp decline in the importance of acquisition trips within Europe. Booksellers' networks steadily gained in importance and in the nineteenth century also took in the regular transatlantic book trade, as illustrated, for instance, by the network established by the French publishing house Garnier between Paris and Latin America.[3]

In the twentieth, and certainly twenty-first centuries, in a time that has seen the rise of the online book trade with guaranteed delivery of just a few days between continents, an almost bewildering array of antiquarian book portals, and the huge and ongoing expansion of Open Access digitally born publications, the acquisition trip might finally be considered as an anachronistic relic of the past.

Nonetheless, for libraries specialized in particular regions of the world, the acquisition trip still remains a major plank in their acquisition strategies, and an essential means of systematically extending their holdings, one that meaningfully complements their orders from booksellers and over the Internet, their approval plans, exchanges, gifts and bequests.

This essay's purpose is to show how acquisition trips in the twenty-first century can contribute to the enrichment of Latin American and Caribbean collections, and what the special challenges are during preparation and realization of such trips. This account draws on the experiences made by the Ibero-Amerikanisches Institut, Stiftung Preußischer Kulturbesitz (Ibero-American Institute) (IAI) over the past ten years. Although the IAI has been engaged in acquisition trips for a much longer period of time, these past ten years have seen a radical reshaping of the practices of the acquisition trip to bring them into line with new technical and human resources openings. Trips are usually undertaken by bibliographers specialized in the respective country and accompanied by a member of the respective regional working group. Yet in the context of special projects, it is also common practice for an acquisition trip to be undertaken by two of the Institute's five bibliographers. The length of the trip can vary from a few days to three weeks.

Finding the Best Time, Place and Person

The importance of preparing for such an acquisition trip down to the last detail cannot be overestimated. As soon as it is known that funding for the trip has been secured, other questions need to be clarified, including who will go, when will they go, and where will they go. Sometimes the first two questions take care of themselves. If you have received funding to visit a book fair or attend a conference and decide to use the occasion as an opportunity for acquisitions, the place and time, and sometimes even the specific flight, hotel and evening program, are all preordained. But what do you need to be mindful of when this is not the case? For the IAI, a large number of factors come into play in the choice of the right country and place. The IAI has a certain focus on Argentina which may be traced back to the core of its founding collection from the private library of Ernesto and Vicente Quesada. Furthermore, countries with the biggest or most lively book trade such as Brazil, Colombia, and Mexico are regularly included in travel plans. Specific forms of partnerships, and the need to include literature and other media in ongoing projects in Latin American research in Germany, are two of the reasons that speak for regular trips to Chile and Cuba.

At first glance, finding the right cities to visit, once the countries have been chosen, might seem pretty straightforward as only a handful of places have established themselves as true centers of book publishing and selling. Yet, especially when the trip is concerned with materials with a regional bearing, and those from smaller publishing houses, careful consideration needs to be given to which places outside the urban centers are really worth a visit. In the three week trips that have taken place over the past ten years, it has become a best practice to visit at least one of the country's main publishing centers together with an additional visit to a place where work mainly concentrates on researching and acquiring local and regional materials. For instance, regular acquisition trips to Brazil, at least once every two years, are taken to São Paulo and one other place. In the past few years we have alternated among Salvador, Porto Alegre, Belo Horizonte, Curitiba and, of course, Rio de Janeiro (which comes a very close second to São Paulo as a major publishing center). Any trip to Mexico inevitably involves a visit to Mexico City. Previous acquisition trips have also made a point of visiting Puebla and Chihuahua. And on each occasion the question posed sardonically by booksellers and publishers, and librarians and academics who operate in the metropolitan centers is what on earth one hoped to find in the depths of the provinces. This question can be countered by producing a corpus of publications singularly absent from the distribution and sales systems of the urban centers. Support in the search for suitable places to buy books can also be found in the directories of the chambers of booksellers and publishing, which list bookshops and some antiquarian bookshops, as well as in the directories of regional antiquarian booksellers, while insight into vital academic publishing can be gained from the publishing houses of local universities.

In terms of the best time to travel, it is rather obvious that the summer holiday break in January and February is not the most rewarding period. Nor is it advisable to take a trip to Brazil when Carnival is in full swing. Trips during international political or sporting events such as the UN Climate Change Conference in Lima 2014 or the Olympic Games 2016 in Rio de Janeiro are equally unconducive to a successful outcome. Quite apart from the fact that travel and accommodation expenses tend to skyrocket at these times, it is also much more difficult to find a decent hotel or grab a taxi. On the other hand, elections, as a national political event, are a much more promising time for the acquisition of grey literature.

The immediate stock-in-trade answer to the question of who should actually go on the trip is that this should be the respective bibliographer supported by a colleague. Yet if somebody has been invited to a book fair or asked to give a paper at a conference who is not a specialist in the particular country, this is the person who will be responsible for acquisitions. As such, he or she will need to be in touch with the relevant bibliographer and familiarize themselves with the ways and means of acquisitions common to that country.

The advantages of having the expert bibliographer organize and carry out the trip are plain to see. These are the people who best know the country and its book market, and they are familiar with the dos and don'ts of traveling in the region. Over time, repeated trips to a country and repeated visits to the same bookshops and antiquarian booksellers build up bonds of trust and confidence that facilitate and accelerate the stages of the acquisition process. Sometimes a bibliographer who has a good working relationship with an antiquarian bookseller has the opportunity of inspecting and buying warehouse-stored material that has not yet been priced and posted on the Internet. And if business partners in Latin America and the Caribbean know your fields of special interest, they will communicate with you via email offering specific titles. Otherwise, they may just post what they have to offer only on portals such as *Mercado Libre / Mercado Livre*. Bibliographers are just as likely to miss them as stumble across them by chance.

Familiarity with a country and its customs and written and unwritten codes is another criteria which predestines the expert bibliographer to bring the acquisition trip to a successful outcome. Such knowhow shapes and colors a great many aspects of business relationships and can even be decisive in the acquisition of a long sought after item. If you know, for instance, that in Chile punctuality is considered "the politesse of kings," you will take care not to be late for the appointment you've made with the antiquarian bookseller. Or if you're aware that in Argentina—unlike Brazil, say—it is nearly impossible to find a taxi driver who's prepared to take you plus the three boxes of material you have just bought, you might plan alternative transport arrangements well ahead of time.

The IAI has found that it pays dividends to always send two people on longer acquisition trips. Ideally, a member of the respective regional working group in the Acquisitions and Cataloguing Department[4] should accompany the expert bibliographer. Such colleagues are well acquainted with the material coming from the respective country either by approval plan or in exchanges, and are in email contact with the vendor bookseller with whom they also place further orders. Since it is critical that the close working partnership maintained by the two colleagues traveling together for a period of several weeks should run without a hitch, the bibliographers who organize the trips and are responsible for their successful outcome, should have the right to propose or select their travel companions. Over the course of time quite a number of successful teams have been formed who repeatedly come together and join forces on acquisition trips.

In terms of practical on the ground work in Latin America and the Caribbean, one form of division of labor consists of the bibliographer making contact with the booksellers, antiquarian booksellers, and institutions to be visited, and in selecting the type of material worth the effort to acquire. The second colleague is responsible for searching the offline version of the catalog brought in a laptop computer to avoid duplication of titles already held at the IAI. At the same time he or she also keeps an inventory list of all material media purchased on the trip. Such day to day work calls for almost boundless creativity, especially since the ways, means, and indeed, opportunities for acquisitions can vary enormously from country to country, and from trip to trip.

How Do We Really Know What We Need?

Sometimes the vast amount of books offered at book fairs or larger antiquarian booksellers can make you scratch your head in bewilderment. This is where the preparatory work described above can come to your aid, because it should have familiarized you with a sense of the types of material lacking in your library, and the areas of specialization that need expansion. In 2006 the IAI introduced a constantly updated offline version of the online catalog that can be loaded on a laptop and taken on field trips. This means that travelers are no longer dependent on WLAN or Internet connectivity should they wish to check books offered at a trade fair or in an antiquarian bookshop against the offline catalog. The first version of this application from 2006 gave you the feeling of directly working with MS-DOS; now the app generally looks and feels like the user version of the online catalog, and also offers most of its functionalities. What is more, we can now use a hand scanner to read the barcodes of books and check them much more quickly against the offline version of the catalog which represents an enormous increase of efficiency in terms of new publications.

Colleagues from other libraries on acquisition trips work with other technical aids but with equal success. One widespread current method is to photograph theoretically interesting materials with a smartphone and then check back at the hotel to determine if the item is already owned by your library or not. The downside to this method is that the librarian may have to visit the same vendor more than once if he extends or changes his offerings during the trip. There is also no guarantee that the publications the library is interested in will still be for sale the following day. That can happen as well in the case of current publications as with a rare item that the bookdealer might not hold while the librarian makes his or her decision and checks the catalog in the hotel. For countries with a smaller publishing output (for example, some of the smaller Caribbean islands or those countries outside of your own library's main areas of interest), there is the possibility of taking printed lists of library holdings with you, arranged by authors and titles, and comparing them directly with what is available on the spot.

The Very Special Cases: Cruising the Caribbean and Cuban Bureaucracy

Acquisition trips in the smaller Caribbean islands pose a challenge. The book market might be straightforward enough yet the majority of books are self-published. Distribution structures are practically non-existent, and often there are no bookshops, just a few shelves in general stores, souvenir shops or museum shops, and, of course, government publications alongside those of various state institutions. Generally speaking, each of the smaller islands only produces a few dozen publications and magazines each year.

At first sight the relatively high costs for flights, hotels, travel expenses and the large amount of time and effort invested hardly seem justified for the relatively sparse number of publications obtained. On the other hand, despite all the best efforts of our vendors, a significant number of such publications which are absolutely essential for research into regional history, literature and culture, are not found in the *WorldCat* database.

Island hopping as an acquisition trip is an expensive proposition; two overnight stays must be planned for each island, transport for acquired material must be organized as baggage allowance on the next flight is limited. If you wish to visit seven to ten islands, costs quickly mount up. The logistics of air travel within the Caribbean islands is challenging. It is not unusual to rely on Miami as the travel hub for getting to and from various jurisdictions. With any luck, there might be fifty titles from Tortola and Antigua, or there might be some one hundred items per island from Grenada and Barbados. At best, trips to small islands are worthwhile once every five years because at least then you can be sure to bring back a sizable amount of purchases.

However, there is a relatively low cost alternative—cruising the Caribbean! Rather than flying from island to island, the floating hotel travels from island to island by night, and transport only becomes problematic when the ship docks at harbor. Eight hours of concentrated shopping is usually enough for the small and medium-sized islands, provided, of course, that you have done your homework. Our own experiences on two such trips together with those made by one of our intrepid vendors who tried out this model on his own initiative have shown that in all likelihood this is the most economical way to make acquisitions. The IAI must be the only library to boast a nearly complete set of *Bay Island Voice: A Community Magazine* of the English-speaking island Roatán, the largest of the Bay Islands of Honduras. The average cost of an inside cabin on a cruise liner in the early or late season is as much as a single flight from island to island and full catering on the ship is already included in the price. All this substantially reduces the acquisition costs per title and justifies the effort.

Even so, this model does have its weak points. For one thing, the ship only calls on certain islands which means that several trips with various shipping lines are needed to ensure more or less adequate coverage. It may be difficult to justify to your own accounts department and the Bundesrechnungshof (Federal Audit Office) exactly why a Caribbean cruise is the most economical form an acquisition trip can take. But on the other hand a business trip through the Caribbean—how wonderful a librarian's job can be!

Another possibility is to ask friends, colleagues, and library users to pick up publications for the library on their own travels through the smaller Caribbean islands. Even a few duplicate copies would be justification enough and much cheaper than undertaking the trip yourself. Acquisition trips to the larger islands, the Dominican Republic, Jamaica, and Haiti, for example, might bring their own sets of challenges but, in general, these tend to be comparable to those of other Latin American countries. There is one notable exception—Cuba.

Cuba is an island in constant change, and the recent loosening of travel restrictions certainly makes acquisition trips to the island a much more tempting prospect. On the last such trip undertaken by the IAI, the sought-after material was acquired within two days, however, it took a further four days to obtain the requisite export license. All materials published between 1900 and the Revolution require purchase of a *sello de exportación* (export stamp). Some items even need a special permit issued by the Ministerio de Cultura (Ministry of Culture).[5] Anything published before 1900 is subject to a general export ban.

Any in-depth travel preparations are hardly possible because there are so few addresses to be found on the Internet and those there are aren't always trustworthy. Addresses and hours change, the official you need to speak to may or may not be there, the cashier's office where you have to pay is closed. The responses vary from "*No es fácil,*" to "*Sí, se puede ... mañana.*" The various currencies used on Cuba are another idiosyncrasy. Some bookshops sell books for the *peso nacional* (national peso) while others deal exclusively in the p*eso convertible CUC* (convertible CUC peso). The difference is not in the books but in a dual rate in which one price is twenty-three times of the rate of other. Having good local knowledge is of immense benefit here. However, it seems that plans are in the pipeline to do away with this double currency situation in the foreseeable future. An antiquarian book market is now beginning to take root with the appearance of the first true antiquarian booksellers that rise above the level of a thrift store. Cuba has always had an extensive and very lively publishing sector. Many of the recently acquired antiquarian magazines do not yet appear in the *WorldCat* database. An acquisition trip always pays dividends beyond the acquisition of current publications. There is still one more major problem to grapple with—shipment of the materials from the island. The postal service has a reputation of being exorbitantly expensive and notoriously unreliable—quite apart from the amount of time needed to spend just organizing a shipment. The remaining options are either to take a second suitcase, or perhaps use your national embassy and its courier services. Cuba, a land where bureaucracy rules the roost, is the antithesis of an acquisition trip made easy.

Financing the Trip

Undisputedly, acquisition trips are a highly cost-intensive pursuit; this is a characteristic they have in common with all other such ventures across the course of history. The biggest money-guzzling items to consider are flights, hotel accommodations, financing the stay, and funding acquisitions. Financing a three week acquisitions trip from the travel funds of the IAI is an impossible venture which means we are dependent on the acquisition of third party funding. One excellent source for ongoing travel activities comes in the shape of the regular travel funding provided by institutions for the advancement of academic research. From 2016 to 2018, for instance, the Deutsche Forschungsgemeinschaft (German Research Foundation) (DFG) provided the IAI with €21,000 from which three to four acquisition trips can be funded. However, as experience has shown, regular visits to a country intensify contact with the country's antiquarian booksellers and bookshops and thus facilitate acquisitions. Therefore, such a limited number of trips is not really enough for satisfactory acquisition work covering the whole of the subcontinent. Further travel funding is thus needed. This is where projects come in that also include acquisition components. For instance, and once more with support from the DFG's Excellence in Research Libraries program, between 2013–2016 the IAI carried out the project Kulturzeitschriften Lateinamerikas (Cultural Periodicals of Latin America) which, among other things, sought to complete and extend sets of periodicals on modernism and the avant-garde from Argentina, Chile, Ecuador, Peru, Cuba, and Puerto Rico. Two acquisition trips were included on the project agenda.

Other third-party projects that include trips to Latin America and the Caribbean can, under certain circumstances, be extended by a few days to allow for acquisitions or for raising donations to the library in the respective countries. This is currently the case at the IAI with the recent Mobile Objekte (Mobil Objects) cooperation project. Funded by the DFG's Exzellenzcluster (Clusters of Excellence), the Bild Wissen Gestaltung: Ein Interisziplinäres Labor (Image Knowledge Gestaltung: An Interdisciplinary Laboratory) is an alliance of humanities, natural sciences, engineering, medicine, design, and architecture which focuses on cultural and natural objects investigating their contents of emergence, their movements, and their transformations. Through the project's strategy of internationalization, workshops will be held in Latin America. Attendance at conferences in Latin America or the Caribbean financed by our own or third-party funding also offers opportunities and synergies for acquisitions, either by extending travel time to cover visits to booksellers and antiquarian dealers, or by purchase of materials from exhibitors and authors during the academic gathering.

Invitations to Latin American book fairs are yet another excellent window of opportunity for such travels. Along with the primary opportunity to visit the country and the book fair, there generally come a host of opportunities from the event organizers to meet publishers, editors, and authors. These opportunities can prove extraordinarily beneficial for creating further fruitful collaborations and partnerships, and have particularly proven so in building up the collection of popular literature at the IAI, one of its main acquisition focal areas.

Unlike travel funding, the acquisitions budget for new publications, and their shipment, comes directly as a rule from IAI's own funds, and must be factored into annual budget planning. Here, too, third party funding for acquisitions opens up further leeway for acquisition work. At the IAI experience has shown that for a three week acquisition trip involving the purchase of between 3,000 and 4,000 items about €10,000 to €15,000 is needed for acquisition, and an additional €5,000 for shipment to Berlin.

Bringing the Treasure Trove Home

After several days or weeks of hard acquisitions work, ways and means must be found to bring the materials cheaply, quickly, and safely to the home library. First, the materials acquired have to be clearly marked in order to be assigned to the invoice by which they were first purchased. Before shipment, we need to check which material needs special protection or stabilization. This applies particularly to those fragile materials whose paper is already brittle and crumbly. Generally, wrapping them in household plastic wrap is enough to ensure transport safety.

The easiest shipment situation is when an approval plan has already been set up with a bookseller. The IAI Approval Plan contains a clause which obliges the bookseller to ship all the material acquired locally by employees of the contracting partner. The bookseller will probably choose the same tried and tested way with which he sends his procurement deliveries. However, it can prove necessary here to give him a list of the goods to be shipped together with copies of their invoices to avoid hitches in shipment; after all, the bookseller is running a book export business, not a logistics company.

In other places within Latin America where you cannot count on the support of an approval plan supplier, you may have the chance to have your shipment organized by a bookseller with whom you have a solid, long-standing business relationship. Such a move should be discussed with your vendor well in advance during the preparatory phase.

However, in the majority of Latin American towns and cities, acquisition travelers are left very much to their own devices when it comes to shipping materials, and the librarian has to decide between DHL, FedEx, UPS and the local postal service or follow up on other ingenious ideas like container shipment with a logistics agency.[6] Here it is wise to make a preliminary price check between the rates offered by the various providers, and also to get information about the exact kind of documentation needed for shipment. You also should consider the amount of time needed to bring the materials to the selected logistics provider, and what their terms and conditions are. Who would not be frustrated to learn in a Brazilian post office to which you have just brought a hefty 150 kilograms of books and periodicals for shipment that, "Sorry, we don't accept credit cards," when in Brazil every *cafezinho* on the corner can be paid with plastic money?

If the next stage of your journey is to a place where a contractual bookseller has his business, you can consider taking the material acquired with you. This is easily done, for instance, on the long-haul coach services in Chile which usually don't charge supplements for an extra piece of luggage. In this way it was possible for us to transport sixty kilograms of books, periodicals, and DVDs from Valdivia to Santiago.

If you have only collected a small amount of material, you might consider checking in a second suitcase on your return flight. Although this also causes extra costs, time and again we have found that not only is this less expensive than shipping with a logistics company, but also has the considerable advantage that the material arrives at the home destination at the same time you do. Some air carriers offer the option of ordering and paying for this on your flight out of Latin America. You can also reserve room in the overhead carry-one bins for particularly precious treasures such as rare periodicals.

In exceptional cases, and if you already have good relations with them, you can also call on the embassy in your particular country to help you out with shipment. Instances of such cases are when the material for shipment is acquired in the context of bi-national cultural projects or when shipment, as in Cuba, is especially problematic. Be aware, however, that embassies of different countries may have different policies or practices regarding the level of service they are willing to provide.

Providing Outreach and Publicity

Once the treasure trove has been delivered, unpacked, and extensively admired in the library, once its cataloging is complete, and all the acquired material has been placed at the disposal of scholarly research, it is time to think about how to present the new materials. Publicity can have positive effects on planning and fundraising for the next acquisition trip. Modern libraries have a broad range of means and channels at their disposal in order to publicize new acquisitions. Social media such as Facebook, Twitter, and thematic blogs are the main means of spreading news quickly to a wide audience. There is always the good old-fashioned print newsletter sent to users and friends of the library. A small and easy to assemble exhibition on display in the library can familiarize library users with the new acquisitions. If the artifacts to be exhibited are rarities that need restoration or should be digitized, it might be a good idea to combine the exhibition with a call for sponsorship and an appeal for donations. If one or more acquisition trips have succeeded in assembling a truly unique collection, it would be worthwhile to direct a little extra effort to draw attention to that fact. In a period of about ten years, the IAI has succeeded, for instance, in compiling a vast majority of Argentine theater and literary periodicals up to 1940, thus possessing a collection unrivaled anywhere in the world. At the time of its publication, such material was scorned by academic and national libraries because of its seemingly "inferior status" as the kind of popular escapist pulp fiction to be found in railway kiosks, and thus was confined to public libraries which eventually discarded it. Nowadays, however, such material is an invaluable resource for literary and linguistic research, media and cultural studies and social history. The 6,500 issues that make up the collection were indexed and digitized in a third-party funded project, and are now online where they can be consulted by scholars from all over the world. A special exhibition and catalog raised the profile of the collection in both Germany and Argentina. The plays featured in the collection are now being used as primary source material by a number of research projects, and the scholars involved with them and the librarians at the IAI both share a keen interest in extending and completing the collection's holdings. Another way of bringing particular collections and artifacts to the attention of the academic community is to act on your own initiative and submit conference papers, or indeed, whole panels drawing on the newly acquired materials.

The End of One Trip Is the Start of Another

Whenever possible, acquisition trips should be conducted at regular intervals and cover the whole spectrum, both in terms of geography—countries, cities and regions—and format—books, periodicals, films, photographs, posters, etc. Yet even with the best intentions and the best possible funding, there will still be countries that can only be visited at irregular intervals or that are repeatedly visited by a variety of colleagues from the same institution who travel there with different purpose in mind, such as attending a conference, and not primarily for making new acquisitions. For such reasons, documentation of the single stages of the preparations and execution of an acquisition trip is of immense importance. Ideally, each stage should be mirrored and matched by documentation as it unfolds, to ensure that no information is overlooked that could be of value to a future acquisition trip. This includes obvious practical matters such as details of a well-situated, low cost hotel as well as listings of antiquarian bookshops with Internet access, and which documents need to be filled in for shipment of material. This documentation is centrally stored and each prospective traveler is given access to it. The IAI now has its first best practices handbook which is continually updated and expanded.

Far Away, Time-Consuming, Expensive ... and Well Worthwhile!

Everybody who has conducted acquisition trips knows that such an expedition is no three week sun and fun beach holiday. Traveling from Europe, after anything from fifteen to thirty hours travel time, you finally arrive at your destination and have to contend with giant cockroaches and rampant mold, unwilling taxi drivers, overcrowded streets and nonfunctioning ATMs—all in heat of around 95°F and humidity of 90 percent. So, in an age of digital networks, online shopping, and globalization, why bother with acquisition trips in the first place?

The national bibliographic situation in all Latin American countries leaves a great deal to be desired. In other words, you cannot get an overview of the literature produced by any individual country from your desk. This can only be achieved by visiting the country, and ideally by having solid contacts with its national library. The IAI has such relationships with the Biblioteca Nacional de Chile (National Library of Chile), the Biblioteca Nacional de Colombia (National Library of Colombia), and the Biblioteca Nacional José Martí (José Martí National Library) in Cuba. Between 2007 and 2015, the IAI had contracts with these national libraries for the exchange of materials.[7] The IAI bought for them, with funds from the DFG, German publications about the respective country. In exchange, we received duplicate copies from the legal deposit not needed in the national libraries. Here we had the advantage of selecting materials directly from the stacks and, in doing so, got a good overview on the countries media production as well.

Visiting book fairs in Latin American and Caribbean countries is an excellent way of assessing publications sent by booksellers fulfilling approval plans, as well as of evaluating their relevance and price structure. Such fairs generally attract not just publishing houses from the major publishing centers but also regional and provincial publishers who are usually embedded only in local or regional distribution networks. Furthermore, book fairs are wonderful places to get to know new publishing houses and perhaps have them integrated in the spectrum of publishers covered by approval plans.

Outside of the book trade, there are also numerous government institutions, NGOs, and private foundations who publish highly interesting and topical material on politics, the economy and culture which are exclusively distributed to a country's libraries and other collecting institutions, often in the form of donations.

The jornadas profesionales (professional conferences) which are frequently held in tandem with book fairs in places like Guadalajara, Buenos Aires and Santiago de Chile offer a forum for dialogue and exchange of ideas with a country's librarians out of which ideally new projects can grow. Nor should the importance of regular personal contact with booksellers contracted under approval plans be underestimated. Some of these relationships stretch back several decades and conversations with such seasoned partners can help clarify the finer points of acquisition and even lead to cooperation in evolving and testing new acquisition strategies. Participation in conferences and congresses in Latin America and the Caribbean makes it possible to build up and extend academic networks which can prove crucial for the acquisition of physical and digital artifacts.

Since nearly all libraries in the United States and Europe specialized in Latin America and the Caribbean are supplied by the same booksellers, they also receive the same publications—allowance being made, of course, for the constituencies served by their approval plans—even though there are still many other important publications. In the long term this results in a certain uniformity in current library holdings as well as the singular lack of any works from certain publishing houses. Regular acquisition trips with clear set priorities are an effective means of addressing such insufficiencies.

The systematic building and extension of special themed and regional collections, such as the collection of Argentine theater and literary periodicals mentioned above, is only possible when visiting and combing the country. Visits to antiquarian bookshops are of undoubted importance here, especially when your library has made a priority of collecting missing historical material. Despite the existence of Amazon-like portals such as IberLibro.com, and the *Mercado Libre/Mercado Livre* in various Latin American countries, there are still a great number of antiquarian booksellers who do not have any form of Internet presence. Examining their holdings in person is worth the effort when it yields unique and hard to find titles. A further problem is that many of the antiquarian bookshops which are online will not sell books directly to foreign countries which means that a direct visit is the only way to acquire them. Since their inventory is not listed or only partially listed on the Internet, visits to antiquarian bookshops frequently start out as a kind of fumbling in the dark black box experiment. Time and again, experience has shown that sudden joyous discoveries can be made, especially for titles whose existence was totally unsuspected until they were stumbled upon in this or that antiquarian bookshop. Such revelations are the highpoints of the librarian's treasure hunt. For instance, the visit to the Cultura Peruana antiquarian bookshop in Lima in 2009 led to a well-hidden corner, covered in dust, and long forgotten, where there were whole stacks of issues of the periodicals *El Perù ilustrado* (1887–1892), *Prisma* (1906–1907), and *Actualidades* (1903–1908). This treasure trove eventually formed the basis of the Cultural Periodicals of Latin America acquisition and digitization project now underway at the IAI. A further visit in Lima in 2015 to this and other antiquarian bookstores brought a host of new titles to light, some of which did not appear in the *WorldCat* database, like the *Revista cinematográfica* (1914), which have been immensely important in enriching our understanding of intellectual life in Latin America at the beginning of the twentieth century. Similar experiences have also been made in Argentina, Paraguay, Colombia, and, to a certain extent, also in Chile.

All of the above examples underscore what a truly decisive role is played by acquisition trips in building up unique collections in libraries specialized in Latin America and the Caribbean, and in turning an already good, scholarly archive into an archive of outstanding excellence.

NOTES

1. A. G. da Rocha Madahil, "A biblioteca da universidade de Coimbra e as suas marcas bibliográficas," *Boletim da Universidade de Coimbra*, 10 (1932): 186 and 191.

2. Ricarda Musser, "Building up Networks of Knowledge: Printing and Collecting Books in the Age of Humanism in the University City of Coimbra," in: Maria Berbara and Karl A. E. Enenkel, *Portuguese Humanism and the Republic of Letters*, Leiden: Brill (2012), 126.

3. Ligia Cristina Machado, "A Revista Popular (1859–1862) e a nacionalidade de seus colaboradores," in: Tânia Bessone da Cruz Ferreira et al., *O Oitocentos entre livros, livreiros, impressos, missivas e bibliotecas*, São Paulo: Alameda (2013), 122–123.

4. The regional working groups at the Ibero-American Institute were established in 2005 with the aim of consolidating the responsibility of colleagues in acquisition and indexing in the library's integrated workflow with individual countries and raising the level of regional expertise.

5. For instance, the cultural magazine *Carteles*, published between 1922 and 1940.

6. We used recommendations from the German Embassies for logistics agencies in the case of large donations or acquisitions of entire collections for container shipment by sea—a very reasonable way of transport.

7. Past 2016, this program is not any longer financed by the DFG.

Crescent City Connections
to Latin America

A History of the Latin American Library
at Tulane University

HORTENSIA CALVO *and*
GUILLERMO NÁÑEZ FALCÓN

The founding of the Latin American Library (LAL) at Tulane University in 1924 was a reflection of New Orleans' longstanding economic and cultural ties with cities along the Gulf of Mexico and the Caribbean, as well as Tulane's historic orientation towards the region. Perhaps one of its many distinctions vis-à-vis most other repositories of its kind in the country is that the library itself was a natural outgrowth of the French and Spanish colonial past of Louisiana and its continuing commercial and cultural ties with neighbors to the south. With the purchase of the William E. Gates Collection in 1924, Tulane established itself on firm footing as a center for the study of the region. The founding of the present-day LAL marked the beginning of Latin American studies at the university. The acquisition of this stellar collection of Mexicana—rare books and manuscripts from the earliest years of Spanish rule to the Mexican Revolution in the 1910s—came about at the same time that the university endowed a pioneering research institute devoted to the study of Mesoamerica, which was called initially the Department of Middle American Research (DMAR). Funding for both the department and the collection was a gift from an anonymous New Orleans entrepreneur with extensive business interests in Central America. As per the donor's wishes, the purpose of the gift was a gesture of goodwill: "to assist the University in developing more cordial relations between the people of [Middle America] and those of our own [country]."[1]

The early years of the Library of the DMAR, were intimately linked with the fortunes of that department. In true New Orleans fashion, there was rarely a dull moment. The story begins when William E. Gates, an inveterate collector of Mexicana, decided to sell his collection of books and manuscripts at auction through the American Art Association in New York. Before the public sale in 1924, Tulane purchased the entire contents of the catalog—or so it thought. It is not entirely clear how Gates promoted himself as part of the purchase agreement, but he, along with the collection, arrived in New Orleans in short order as the first Director of the DMAR. This was a fateful decision that would have ripple effects for decades to come and almost produced the demise of the entire enterprise.

A self-taught Mayan linguist, with no formal training in anthropology, Gates' limitations became evident from the outset. The idea that Gates himself accompany the collection to New Orleans came from the understanding that he would catalog and sort the material to make it available for research. However, before setting foot in the city, he was already outlining an all-encompassing vision for the new department and asking for more money, a leitmotif of his brief tenure at Tulane. This is evident in a letter to Tulane President Albert Dinwiddie:

> There is something running very strongly in my mind, which I want to put in your mind in advance of my coming. The very moment I get down to New Orleans, about May 1st, I want to begin to make plans to make the Department not merely a scientific research center, in linguistics, archaeology, history and the rest, but a developing center of specific information useful to the Port of New Orleans, and the business that lies behind it. ... I want to begin to gather every kind of information about the Caribbean littoral countries and attach that gathering to all our expeditions and fieldwork, and all our home scientific work. To put it in a word—I want to card-index those countries.... The collection you have bought is already the starting point of all that. I want all kinds of information about plants. About everything that will be of use to international intercourse, travel, and trade. Every single thing of that kind will somehow tack itself onto our special Indian research problems. ... In short, I want to make the dept. not merely outstanding in scientific research, but a storehouse of data that will focalize all this both in and *for* New Orleans.[2]

The DMAR, then, was to be an analog version of the Internet, an indexed storehouse of all knowledge on the countries stretching from Mexico to Panama, and including the Caribbean. The recently purchased collection of Mexicana would be a mere stepping stone to an aggressive acquisitions program:

> To do this work, I plan and have begun to try out having people in the seven to ten great collections in this country, make us cards of everything each has (on different colored cards to show the different collections); put a man on it here to collate them. This man will thus become at once our bibliographer, librarian, and "information man." In time he will cross-index the books and pamphlets into subject matter indices. The whole will thus become, country by country beginning with Honduras which I have already started, a "Bureau of Information and Statistics" of inestimable value, to science, to New Orleans, and to the countries themselves.
>
> For the immediate present.... I want to buy books quite heavily, getting all the advantages that personal presence to select and bargain, and quantity buying will give. Not however of "rarities" and no longer procurable items that made my original collection unique, but the great quantity of general works on these subjects, absolutely necessary for both the Information Bureau, and that type of rounded-out scientific publications, illuminated by these lights from contact-subjects and sciences, which I want to have Tulane's outstanding type—-These purchases in such quantity will soon come to an end, by natural clearing of the bookseller's shelves as they stand. Then a more normal budget will keep it going. But there is every advantage both of economy and for our coming researches, in equipping ourselves here as fast we can, and when chance offers.[3]

There are several things to note. One can see here what made Gates a first-rate collector and a man of vision where collections were concerned. He was clearly passionate about the process of acquisition and showed great experience in the ways of booksellers and advantageous positioning for the buyer. One has to admire Gates' tenacity and savvy in locating hard-to-find research material and the breadth of his ambitions for a first-rate library. That said, it is also striking that Gates' grandiose plans did not include academic research, but rather had a decisive commercial focus, perhaps a reflection of his lack of formal academic training. Unfortunately, the ambitious Gates constantly got ahead

The Library of the Department of Middle American Research, predecessor to the Latin American Library, c. 1930s (courtesy the Middle American Research Institute, Tulane University).

of himself and his budget and that, coupled with an abrasive and suspicious personality, proved to be his downfall. His tenure at Tulane ended barely two years after his initial appointment.

Even before Gates' dismissal, Tulane administrators took immediate action to preserve the integrity of the Library of the DMAR, which was regarded even then as one of the university's treasured assets. On 12 February 1926, Dinwiddie placed the collection under the supervision of the Tulane Library Committee. This would not be the last time that the administrative purview of the library would revert back and forth from the institute to the general library system until it remained permanently under the administration of the latter in the early 1960s.

A few months after Gates' departure, Danish archaeologist and Gates protégé Frans Blom was appointed Director of the DMAR. A sign that the department was being steered on a steadier course, especially given gender roles at the time, was that instead of bringing in Gates' "information man," in October, the library committee impressed upon the university the need to hire "a lady... of general secretarial experience who is at the same time a lady of education and intelligence, able to take charge of the collection and explain it to visitors in the absence of the director," upon which the services of Mrs. E.N. Smith were retained at a salary of $1,500 per year.[4]

In the course of the Gates saga, and especially after his departure, it was discovered that a few of the items listed in the auction catalogue were not originals, but were rather photo static copies of manuscripts in other depositories. Other items in the catalog never made it to Tulane, and it was rumored that Gates had sold some things separately to other institutions, which indeed he had. But missing items, photo static copies, and the tumultuous episode of Gates' tenure in New Orleans aside, the value and importance of the William Gates Collection at Tulane cannot be overstated. The collection, in fact, shaped academic and other priorities for decades to come. For instance, the emphasis on indigenous languages formed the basis for linguistic studies in the Anthropology Department, which prevails today. Gates' collection contained several thousand books, including some of the earliest printed works from Mexican presses, rare first editions of catechisms and confessionals, grammars and vocabularies of Indian languages used to proselytize to native inhabitants, indeed, the instruments of the early Spanish empire. Also included were hundreds of late nineteenth century government publications that he had acquired from other collectors such as Antonio Peñafiel; volumes related to the Emperor Maximilian of Mexico in the mid-nineteenth century, and the administration of Porfirio Díaz, as well as contemporary works and ephemera of the Mexican Revolution. There were also several thousand manuscripts that complemented the collection of rare books. Over time, the DMAR cataloged most of the volumes for the collection that was to reside in the public stacks, but rare items were processed, following the Dewey Decimal classification system, for a caged area, which eventually became the rare books collection. Among the items catalogued in this manner were the *Codex Chalco*, a finely executed nineteenth century copy of a lost sixteenth century pictorial manuscript; Fray Andrés de Olmos' manuscript, *Arte de la lengua mexicana* from 1547; two seventeenth century choral books; and other rare and, in many cases, unique items.

Loose manuscripts from the Gates purchase that did not respond readily to Dewey treatment were simply wrapped in brown paper, tied with a string, and placed on shelves for later processing. The manuscripts fell into several distinct groups. They included Gates' extensive collection of colonial Mexican manuscripts, his file of several hundred letters from the military commandants of the Yucatan dating from the late eighteenth to early nineteenth centuries; the papers of journalist-diplomat Ephraim George Squier; correspondence from the inner circle of the first Mexican Emperor Agustín de Iturbide; the Moctezuma Family Papers, and hundreds of pieces of printed ephemera from the Mexican Revolution, including several dozen original works by legendary Mexican master engraver José Guadalupe Posada.

From the vantage point of today, it is astonishing that documents of this importance remained largely inaccessible and unknown to users for several decades. Two forces may have been at work. On one hand, the study of Latin America at Tulane during this time was largely limited to the archaeologists of the DMAR, and their research focused almost exclusively on native Indian cultures and languages. It was not until later decades that researchers from other disciplines and academic departments, who may have had greater interest in the primary sources of post-contact historical periods, were hired at Tulane. On the other hand, the 1920s predated the professionalization of archival methods, and there was no trained staff to analyze the material or even to house it appropriately. Given these circumstances, perhaps what is surprising is that the collection continued to expand steadily with the addition of key pieces.

Despite a busy schedule of research, teaching and pioneering archaeological expeditions to the Yucatán and Chiapas, there is ample evidence that Frans Blom nevertheless became enthusiastically engaged in the development of the DMAR collections in the early years of his tenure as head of the department. The process, however, sometimes reflected a lack of direction. Two purchases from the 1920s illustrate the point. The Rudolf Schuller Papers consisted of the notebooks, field notes, vocabulary lists, manuscripts, and photographs of an Austrian-born linguist and ethnographer who worked primarily in the Huasteca region of Mexico in the 1920s. This collection fit within the Mesoamerican focus of the DMAR. The papers of ethnologist and archaeologist George Hubbard Pepper, relating to his work with United States Southwest Indians and in the Chaco Canyon, however, did not—despite the intrinsic and extraordinary documentary value of this collection.

By the 1930s, manuscript acquisitions were restricted to the areas of faculty research, that is, Mayan Mexico and Central America. The Tulane expeditions to Mexico and Central America also provided opportunities to purchase ancient documents that today would be prohibited. Among these were several manuscript dossiers of land disputes, the *Crónica de Maní*, the *Crónica de Yaxcukul*, and the *Crónica de Chicxulub*. These dossiers contain documents from the sixteenth to the eighteenth century, and the *Maní*, with its accompanying manuscript map, is reputed to be the oldest example of writing of the Mayan language in alphabetical characters. Among the signature pieces acquired during this time are the Sedley F. Mackie Collection of more than 2,000 volumes of rare printed works relating to Mesoamerica and, particularly, the West Indies. The collection includes many priceless first editions of key works of the colonial period and is especially rich in works relating to European traveler accounts from the seventeenth and eighteenth centuries. In 1933, the library also acquired Fray Pedro de Oroz's priceless 1585 manuscript history of the Franciscan order in New Spain. It was around this time that Blom's connections in Southern Mexico led to the acquisition of the Mixtec *Códice de Huamelulpan* or *Codex Tulane*, a native pictorial manuscript from the mid-sixteenth century painted on a twelve foot strip of deerskin, which has become one of the most iconic pieces of the collection. Today, Tulane houses one of the largest collections of original post-contact Mesoamerican codices in the world.

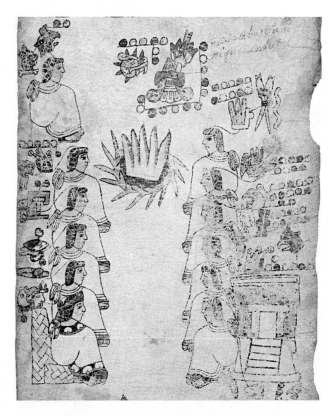

Other unique collections acquired during these early years were two autograph letters by Spanish *conquistador* Hernán Cortés, one of which lays out the first code of laws in the New World.[5] The other letter was written by Cortés on 21 September 1521, three weeks after the fall of Tenochtitlán, and is the earliest known document written by Cortés from the mainland. Also from this time period, the extensive

Códice de Huamelulpan, or *Codex Tulane.* **Paint on deerskin; Mixtec, c. 1550s (courtesy the Latin American Library, Tulane University).**

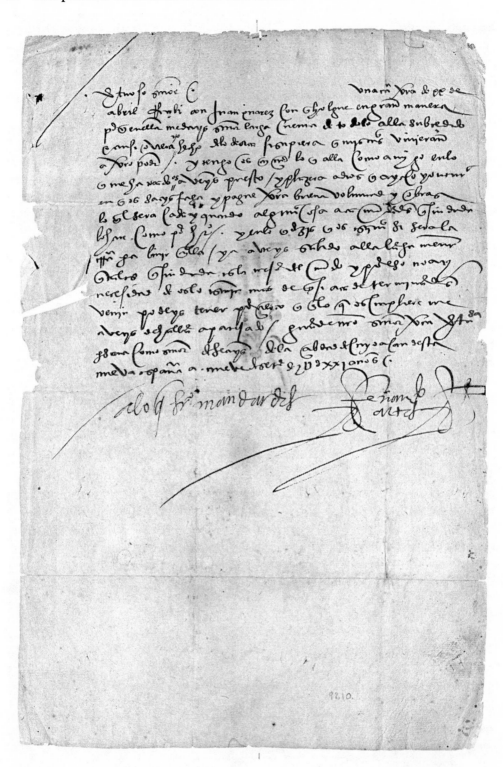

Holograph letter by Spanish conquistador, Hernán Cortés, three weeks after the fall of México-Tenochtitlán, September 1521 (courtesy the Latin American Library, Tulane University).

Viceregal and Ecclesiastical Mexican Collection (VEMC), culled together from various individual groups of documents over time, is especially worthy of note.[6] In 1932, Tulane acquired a collection of about 3,000 miscellaneous, but historically valuable, dossiers dating from the mid-sixteenth century to early Independence, from all parts of Mexico and covering a gamut of subjects. The documents, of great research value in themselves, did not share a cohesive unity of time, place, or subject matter. Rather, there were civil and religious documents relating to Church administration and the Inquisition, relations of members of the various religious orders and the Church, land disputes between Spaniards and Indians, construction of transportation infrastructure and public buildings, and many other matters. Some of the dossiers were several hundred pages. Additionally, there were discrete groups relating to the Benito Juárez period, to the administration of Porfirio Díaz or *porfiriato*, and to the Mexican Revolution of 1910. In 1934, several other items were added, such as a collection of forty-four volumes of administrative papers from New Spain, including a 400-leaf volume of minutes of the Real Audiencia (Royal Audience) from 1575 to 1602, and other bundles of manuscripts acquired separately.

It is from the Viceregal and Ecclesiastical Mexican Collection that two unpublished holograph letters, written in 1682 and 1687, by Mexican writer Sor Juana Inés de la Cruz's mentor, María Luisa Manrique de Lara y Gonzaga, were recently discovered, containing details about the famous friendship of these two extraordinary women.[7] Also in 1933, the DMAR purchased from the daughter-in-law of Captain Callender Fayssoux, aide-de-camp to notorious filibuster William Walker, handwritten records of Walker's armies and invasions of Nicaragua in 1855, 1857, and 1860.

Acquisitions went well beyond unique or rare pieces and manuscripts. The early DMAR staff developed an active library materials exchange program whereby offprints of recent publications on Mesoamerican archaeology, anthropology, linguistics and history were received. These items form the core of an extensive pamphlet collection at the LAL, many of which are not held in other libraries or are not easily obtained. In the meantime, Director Blom adapted easily to the open life of the Vieux Carré in the 1920s and 1930s and became part of a bohemian clique, which included the artist William Spratling, a young William Faulkner, and other literary and artistic figures such as Sherwood Anderson and Natalie Scott.[8] Spratling later settled in Taxco, Mexico where he spawned a veritable renaissance of the Mexican silver industry whose designs were closely aligned with ancient Mexican traditions and contemporary designs in that country and abroad. In fact, there is evidence that Spratling's knowledge of and interest in autochthonous Mexican indigenous design was first sparked by his familiarity with the codices and other rare materials housed at Tulane. Today, the Latin American Library houses the Spratling-Taxco Collection of unique materials relating to the Taxco silver renaissance pioneered by Spratling, and carried out by a number of artists, silversmiths and designers in the mid–20th century.

By the end of the 1930s, Tulane's reputation as a research center for Mesoamerican studies was well established, and the DMAR Library expanded its network of connections. Arthur Gropp was hired as librarian in charge of the collection, and became very active in forging exchanges between Tulane and other libraries in the region.[9] Gropp would later serve as acting co-director of the DMAR in charge of the library after the dismissal of Blom in 1941. In the late 1930s, Duke University, the University of North Carolina–Chapel Hill and Tulane embarked on a cooperative acquisitions and interlibrary loan program for their Latin American collections.[10] Not much is known about the outcome

Holograph letter from María Luisa Manrique de Lara Gonzaga y Luján, Countess of Paredes, to her cousin María de Guadalupe de Lencastre, Duchess of Aveiro, on her friendship with the Hieronymite nun, Sor Juana Inés de la Cruz, 1682 (courtesy the Latin American Library, Tulane University).

of the program or how long Tulane participated, but one can imagine the difficulties of such cooperative arrangements at the time, given the geographical distance of New Orleans from Durham and Chapel Hill in North Carolina. Tulane's collecting responsibilities focused on the Middle American countries (Mexico, Central America and the Caribbean), while Duke and UNC shared responsibility for South America. This cooperative venture is likely one of the first such collaborative programs for Latin American materials in the South. Duke and UNC–Chapel Hill continued their cooperative arrangement after Tulane withdrew its participation.

The decade of the 1940s brought about significant changes. Partly in response to internal turmoil within the Middle American Research Institute (MARI), as the DMAR was now known, in 1942, the library was physically separated from the museum and research facilities of the Institute. The Institute Library was moved to the third floor of the newly built Joseph Merrick Jones Hall in another part of the campus. A 1949 *Tulane Library Handbook for Students* highlighted the library's card catalog "of books and manuscripts pertaining to the life and culture of Mexico, the countries of Central America and the West Indies. Most of the books and journals of this extensive collection are shelved separately in the book stacks."[11] Annual reports from the Tulane library administration confirm that the collection was widely used and saw continued though modest growth during the decade.

In 1950, the study of Latin America was expanded at Tulane with the establishment of the Latin American Area Studies Program, supported by a Carnegie Grant.[12] While the historic emphasis of the library on Middle America continued, the scope of the collections was broadened to include all of Latin America. Nationally, the focus on Latin America diminished during the years of World War II; however, the 1950s brought about several nationwide initiatives to strengthen and support the acquisition and bibliographic control of research materials produced in the region. Initially, the voluntary cooperative agreement known as the Farmington Plan had only included Mexico, but a series of developments led to a concerted effort to strengthen and coordinate the acquisition of research materials produced in a broader array of Latin American countries in United States libraries. The development of statistical surveys of Latin American studies programs around the country resulting from the work of the annual Seminars on the Acquisition of Latin American Library Materials (1956–), field trips to the region by librarians, as well as efforts on the part of the Library of Congress Hispanic Foundation and other actors, effectively expanded coverage to all of Latin America within the Farmington Plan, and the establishment of the Latin American Cooperative Acquisitions Project (LACAP). In 1960, Tulane accepted collecting responsibilities for El Salvador, Honduras, Guatemala and Nicaragua within the Farmington Plan, and in 1962 joined the efforts of LACAP by enlisting its first approval plan with the New York–like book distribution firm of Stechert-Hafner, Inc.[13]

Within Latin American studies, the post–World War II federal support of area studies programs was additionally fueled by the 1959 Cuban Revolution, which refocused international attention, particularly in the neighboring United States, on the region. Reflecting the geo-political climate of the time, the overall broadened scope of the Latin American curriculum within the university, as well as strengthened ties to peer research libraries around the country, the Institute Library was renamed the Latin American Library (LAL) in 1964. Encompassing a decidedly regional scope, the LAL was moved across the street from Jones Hall to the fourth floor of the recently built Howard-Tilton

Memorial Library, where it is still located today, under the administrative umbrella of Tulane's library system, and it remains a discrete collection.

A decade later, LAL continued to expand beyond Mesoamerica and the Caribbean to encompass all geographical areas, relevant disciplines, and also broadened collection policies to include other formats of research material. A key development was the founding of the Tulane University Latin American Photographic Archive (TULAPA) in 1976, a visionary step that represented one of the first such archives in the country devoted to Latin America. The archive was established by co-founders and LAL benefactors Steve and Abbye Gorin.

Two others played a prominent role in the early development of the archive: Thomas Niehaus, Director of the Latin American Library, 1977–1990, and Humberto Rodríguez-Camilloni, Professor of Architectural History in the Tulane School of Architecture. In the late 1970s, Rodríguez opened doors in his native Peru, arranging for the purchase of photographs and drawings by the noted architect-engineer Emilio Harth-Terré (1899–1983) and a collection of photographs by Abraham Guillén Melgar (1901–1985), a documentarian of Andean cultural heritage for fifty years.

Niehaus also purchased important collections such as the photographs of noted Cuzco photographer Martín Chambi (1891–1973), the Nicaraguan images of Judith Hancock de Sandoval, and historic photographs of Guatemala, Panama, Cuba, and Brazil. As the archive became known in academic circles, other collections came into the library in the form of donations, such as the Sidney D. Markman archive of images of architecture in Mexico, Central America, and Spain.

By 1981, a preliminary organization and inventory of the photographic holdings had been developed that numbered some 10,000 images. Also in that year, Ruth Olivera was appointed the first curator of the photographic archive. The collection grew, even as the cost of photographs with research value climbed exponentially. Under director Guillermo Náñez Falcón (1990–2002), the Fernando La Rosa A. Collection of Peruvian and Bolivian images, and the Lorry Salcedo photographs of Afro-Peruvian life and Bahian popular culture were two notable collections acquired that complemented existing 1860s images of Peruvian archaeological sites and colonial monuments in the Ephraim Squier collection.

Under current director Hortensia Calvo (2003-), the archive was renamed the Image Archive to reflect a variety of formats already held as well as recently acquired materials, which include negatives, slides, glass lantern slides, stereoscopic images, postcards, rubbings, original sketches, engravings, and drawings. Major recent acquisitions include hundreds of slides and photographs added to the Merle Greene Robertson Collection of Mayan rubbings; the numerous donations of Jim and Penny Chittim Morrill and the founding of the Spratling-Taxco Collection of photographs and original design drawings by William Spratling, Antonio del Castillo, Margot van Voorhies Carr and other designers associated with the Taxco silver industry; the Alan Boss Collection of Cuban Ephemera with hundreds of photographs and postcards documenting Cuban popular culture since the early 1900s, and the Marcelo Martínez Palma Collection of more than 3,000 stereoscopic glass images of the Yucatán and other cities in Mexico and the Caribbean, among many other acquisitions. In the last thirteen years, the Image Archive has nearly doubled in size, from 60,000 pieces to almost 120,000, and continues to grow. More recently, a comprehensive program is underway to digitize signature collections from the Image Archive to place them as discrete collections within the Tulane Digital Library (TUDL).

By the 1980s, the LAL had expanded considerably in collecting scope and numbers of volumes. The manuscript holdings followed suit, but lacking were descriptions of the collections, finding aids, and archival housing of the documents. This was particularly true of older material. The bound manuscripts in the Gates collection had been cataloged in the 1930s by the Dewey Decimal classification system and incorporated in the library's rare books collection. Countless papers were loose, and the collection now also comprised the VEMC, and others previously noted. Portions of these priceless documents remained, as they had been received, wrapped in brown paper and tied with butcher string, without identification. During the mid-1930s, the library employed persons "who knew Spanish" to begin describing the VEMC documents. Little progress was made. Whatever facility the persons may have had with the language, they lacked knowledge of history, of paleography, of abbreviations, and of colonial Spanish America. Access to materials was severely restricted without proper cataloguing.

In the 1980s, thanks to a sizeable grant from the National Endowment for the Humanities, 85 percent of the collections were cataloged in three years, under the leadership of Guillermo Náñez Falcón, assisted by Ruth Olivera. The resulting card file of collection names, personal and place names, date file, and subjects is among the most detailed and comprehensive for manuscript collections of this kind in the country. The seemingly mundane task of organizing and describing these collections and creating finding aids or, in Gates' lingo of "card-indexing" the collections, laid the groundwork for the subsequent development of the library's outreach efforts. For the first time, the valuable collections acquired during the first years of the founding of the library that had remained in obscurity were accessible not only to Tulane researchers but to a broader number of national and international scholars.

In the 1990s, LAL began to increase its visibility and engagement with wider audiences. Perhaps a turning point in this process was the meeting of the International Congress of Americanists held in New Orleans in 1991. Attracting thousands of scholars from around the world, and held on the eve of the quincentenary of the European arrival to

Immigrants disembarking on the shores of San Martín, Argentina, Samuel Boote, c. 1880s (courtesy the Latin American Library Image Archive, Tulane University).

the New World, the congress was a veritable showcase for the LAL's unique holdings. A splendid exhibit featured the library's stellar collection of original Mesoamerican painted manuscripts, among other collections, and contributed greatly to publicizing its first-rate collections worldwide.[14]

Other initiatives followed that contributed toward greater dissemination and access of the collections. Starting in the late–1990s and continuing for three years, the LAL contributed over 3,000 monograph volumes of Central American imprints to be reformatted on microfilm as part of a SOLINET-led process to preserve "brittle" books. Until the mid–2000s the library also negotiated with commercial microfilm companies to reformat six rare manuscript and pamphlet collections available for sale to other institutions. More recently, digitization projects through the Tulane Digital Library (TUDL) are making rare holdings available freely to researchers worldwide. Perhaps the most visible trend of LAL in more recent years is the efforts to digitize the special collections and to spearhead international collaborative initiatives with partners in several Latin American countries.

Perhaps no other event has transformed the library and opened up possibilities for acquisitions and access as the establishment of the Doris Stone Endowments in 2002, which support the salary of the Director, travel, special public events such as exhibits and invited speakers that promote the collections, and special acquisitions that supplement university appropriated funds. The Doris Stone funds have not only established LAL's finances on a more secure footing, they have also provided a base to seek additional funding in the form of other endowments.

On August 29, 2005, the man-made levies of New Orleans collapsed in the wake of Hurricane Katrina creating a human catastrophe of unprecedented proportions. Located on the fourth floor, LAL's collections were spared from damage, however the basement of the building itself took on almost nine feet of water. Among the collections damaged was the LAL microfilm, of which only a fraction was recovered. These losses were minimal compared to the damage to other parts of the university's buildings and collections, not to mention the loss of life, the human tragedies and devastation of infrastructure throughout the city. LAL was fortunate as the recipient of many gestures of affirmation and hope, like so many that pulled the city together in the months and years after the tragedy. In fact, as occurred in many other parts of New Orleans, the disaster served as a call to action to preserve and protect the patrimony that is housed in the city. One such response came in the form of a generous gift from emeritus historian Richard E. Greenleaf, a long-time champion of libraries and great supporter of the LAL in his many years as a Tulane professor and director of the Latin American Studies Program. Thanks to this endowment, in 2007, the LAL established the Richard E. Greenleaf Fellowships to sponsor short-term visits for scholars residing in Latin America and the Caribbean to come to New Orleans to conduct research at the library. Other gifts support different aspects of the work of the LAL, such as the Jim and Penny Morrill Endowed Fund for Mesoamerican Art History, the Christian-Pradel Endowed Fund, and the Steve and Abbye Gorin Endowed Fund for Photographic Materials.

In 2024, the Latin American Library will celebrate its centennial. It is a fitting time to reflect on its past and future. The LAL is today one of the oldest and most renowned research collections of Latin Americana in the country, with unique materials from thirty countries in the region and the Caribbean. It shares with only two other academic libraries in the United States, the Benson Latin American Collection at the University of Texas–

Austin and the Latin American Collection at the University of Florida–Gainesville, the distinction of being a stand-alone or discrete collection. In the case of Tulane, this is the product of institutional history but, more broadly, a legacy of Louisiana's Spanish and French colonial past and the city of New Orleans' historical cultural and commercial ties to the Gulf of Mexico and circum-Caribbean.

Much has happened to alter the research and library landscape, and academia itself, since the heady days and avid collecting efforts of Gates and Blom. Changes in the information environment in the last two decades have put into question, if not subverted, the traditional paper-based library and related services. So too, the contours of the area studies model, set forth in the wake of Cold War geo-political realities, have been eroded in the present globalized environment.

It is precisely in these times when higher education has grown increasingly mindful of bottom lines, return on investments, and the need to justify the high cost of housing, processing and maintaining growing physical collections that a legacy collection such as the LAL continues to strengthen its role as an asset to the university. Certainly, LAL's acquisitions policies and services continue to evolve in response to changing research trends, user populations and preferences, as well as a rapidly altering technology and information environment. Far from ushering in the demise of paper-based collections, digitization has opened an exciting world of possibilities for libraries such as the LAL. For the first time, scholars in Mexico or Guatemala can view a digitized version of the Codex Tulane from their computer screens at home, comparing it to other codices residing in their own country or around the world, while scholars in any part of the globe can work with any one of the eighteen painted manuscripts in the LAL collection without traveling to New Orleans. While worldwide availability makes on-site travel unnecessary to some users, increased publicity and visibility of collections has also created legions of new users who travel to New Orleans to work with relevant collections on site. Moreover, Tulane's historical emphasis on Latin American studies has only grown, with 60 percent of graduate students in Liberal Arts working on a Latin American topic.[15] Focus on the region is unrivaled across the campus, which is arguably a unique context in the country. LAL continues to be one of the reasons scholars come to visit, teach and work at Tulane. New Orleans is reviving its historical moniker as a "Gateway to the Americas," and Tulane University's Latin American Library will continue to serve as a magnet to scholars from the region, the nation and around the world.

NOTES

1. Deed of gift letter to the Administrators of the Tulane Educational Fund, 2 April 1924. *Albert Bledsoe Dinwiddie Papers*, Tulane University Archives.

2. Letter from William Gates to President Albert Dinwiddie, 21 April 1924. *Albert Bledsoe Dinwiddie Papers,* Tulane University Archives.

3. *Ibid.*

4. Letter from R.S. Cocks to President Albert Dinwiddie, 7 October 1926. *Albert Bledsoe Dinwiddie Papers*, Tulane University Archives.

5. The 1524 Cortés laws are published in Hernán Cortés, *Ordenanzas de buen gobierno dadas por Hernando Cortés para los vezinos y moradores de la Nueva España* (Madrid: J. Porrúa Turanzas, 1960); and Hernán Cortés, *Cartas y documentos [de] Hernan Cortés.* Introduction by Mario Hernández Sánchez-Barba (Mexico: Editorial Porrúa, 1963), 347–353.

6. Michael A. Polushin, *Introduction: The Viceregal and Ecclesiastical Mexican Collection (VEMC)* http://lal.tulane.edu/sites/default/files/lal/docs/VEMCFinalIntroPolushin%20%282%29.pdf.

7. Hortensia Calvo and Beatriz Colombi, *Cartas de Lysi: La mecenas de Sor Juana Inés de la Cruz en correspondencia inédita* (Madrid: Iberoamericana; Frankfurt am Main: Vervuert; México D.F.: Bonilla Artigas Editores, 2015).

8. For an entertaining account of this extraordinary circle of friends, see William Spratling, *Sherwood Anderson and Other Famous Creoles: A Gallery of Contemporary New Orleans. Drawn by William Spratling. Arranged by William Faulkner* (New Orleans: The Pelican Bookshop Press, 1926). A more recent account is provided by John Shelton Reed, *Dixie Bohemia: A French Quarter Circle in the 1920s* (Baton Rouge: Louisiana State University Press, 2012).

9. See *Arthur E. Gropp Library Survey Papers, 1937–1938*, Manuscripts Collection 21, The Latin American Library, Tulane University http://archivolal.tulane.edu/index.php?p=collections/controlcard&id=246&q=gropp.

10. Duke University, "Cooperation in Latin-American Studies Between the University of North Carolina, Tulane University, and Duke University." 1939–1940. Unpublished mimeographed typescript report. Duke University Archives.

11. *Tulane Library Handbook for Students*, 1949 (n.p.).

12. *The Tulane University of Louisiana, Program of Latin American Area Studies* Unnumbered brochure (n.d).

13. Dominick Coppola, "Breakthrough in Latin American Acquisitions," *Stechert-Hafner Book News* 17:1, September 1962.

14. Martha Barton Robertson, *Mexican Indian Manuscript Painting: A Catalog of the Latin American Library Collection*. 47th International Congress of Americanists at Tulane University, New Orleans, Louisiana. July 7–11, 1991.

15. Stone Center for Latin American Studies, Tulane University. Unpublished survey. 2013.

Collections as Collaborators

Documenting and Facilitating Inclusion, Social Justice and Cultural Agency at the Benson Latin American Collection

JULIANNE GILLAND, MELISSA GUY *and* THERESA E. POLK

Twenty-first century research libraries remain at the forefront of the academic mission through collaborations with stakeholders both inside and outside the university. The Benson Latin American Collection at the University of Texas at Austin (UT), which will soon celebrate its one-hundredth anniversary, has a long history of working with partners across our campus and beyond to build collections and make them accessible to faculty, researchers, and students. Collaboration has become central to the Benson's mission in exciting new ways during the last five years, as we launched a formal partnership with UT's Lozano Long Institute of Latin American Studies under unified leadership in 2011, becoming LLILAS Benson Latin American Studies and Collections. This essay examines the LLILAS Benson partnership as an innovative model for integrating special collections and related digital initiatives directly into the scholarly enterprise of a major center for humanities, social sciences, and area studies. Drawing from LLILAS Benson initiatives as well as current collection development and archival practices at the Benson Latin American Collection, we will highlight some of the opportunities we have created for the library and special collection as strategic collaborators. First, opportunities for preservation of and access to material that supports diversity and inclusion, social justice, cultural agency, and human and civil rights for local, national, and international communities. And second, opportunities for advancing document-centered teaching and learning, which promotes the active collaboration of archives and the academy and creates new possibilities for transforming archival theory and practice by engaging researchers and students in the archival enterprise and digital scholarship.

Benson and LLILAS—Forging a Partnership

The Benson Collection was founded in 1921 with the acquisition of a large private collection of Mexican material, and Mexican history and culture continues to be a core strength of the collection to this day. Quickly during the twentieth century, the scope of collection development expanded to include new and rare materials representing every region of Latin America. Today the Benson is one of the premier libraries and archives of Latin American and U.S. Latina/o material in the world, with holdings that include over 1,000,000 books in the circulating collections, over 8,000 linear feet of archival and manuscript material, more than 20,000 maps and 100,000 photographs, and tens of thousands of items in other media including digital resources, sound recordings, video, drawings, and ephemera.[1]

The Institute of Latin American Studies, which became the Teresa Lozano Long Institute of Latin American Studies (LLILAS) in 2000, is the largest Latin American studies program in the United States, offering bachelors, masters, and doctoral degrees and counting over 160 affiliated faculty members in over thirty academic departments. LLILAS is committed to socially engaged scholarship in its degree programs, which emphasize immersion in the language, culture, and history of Latin America, as well as in its numerous scholarly and public programs that engage with campus, local, and international communities throughout the academic year.[2]

In 1971, a new building on the UT campus became the home of these two established anchors of Latin American research and scholarship at the university, Benson and LLILAS. For the next forty years, each institution continued to flourish, and the majority of students, faculty, and researchers engaged in Latin American scholarship assumed that the two were connected, when in fact they were simply good neighbors. That changed in 2011, when the University of Texas Libraries and the College of Liberal Arts established a formal partnership between the two, uniting them under joint administrative leadership as LLILAS Benson Latin American Studies and Collections. The joint mission of the LLILAS Benson partnership is "to raise awareness of past and current issues affecting Latin America and US Latina/o communities through world-class collections, globalized higher education, research, international exchange, and public programming."[3]

Collaboration, Diversity and Inclusion

As an institutional strategy, uniting a library collection such as the Benson and an academic unit such as LLILAS is a new approach for UT. Outside Austin, the partnership has gained recognition among peer institutions as an innovative model, as other research libraries and archives seek to transform from "knowledge service providers" within their universities into "active partners within a rich, diverse learning and research ecosystem."[4] Within this new model for collaboration, librarians and archivists are contributors to digital scholarship and partners in teaching. We will give examples of important initiatives that our institution has launched in both of these areas; but first we will offer a bit more about the Benson's collaboration with other partners beyond LLILAS—at our own university and across Latin America—and how these collaborations have strengthened our institutional support of diversity, inclusion, social justice, and civil and human rights in building our physical and digital collections.

Collaborations with other departments across our own campus have been instrumental in helping us build our collections in ways that actively represent and support the diversity of Latin American history and culture. An important precedent for this kind of inclusive collecting practice was set for the Benson in the early 1970s. The rising importance of Mexican American studies at UT at that time, and the recognition that the Latina/o experience in the United States was a fundamental and important part of the evolving history of Latin America, led us to found the Mexican-American Library Program (MALP) in 1974, a collecting initiative to support research and document the Latina/o experience in the United States. We began systematically acquiring and preserving archival and print materials documenting the U.S. Latina/o experience, emphasizing the acquisition of materials from Texas and the greater Southwest. Forty years later, the Benson's Latina/o collections are perhaps the best in the world. We are the repository for many of the most important collections that document the Mexican American civil rights movement that began in the early twentieth century and continued with the Chicano political movement of the 1960s and 1970s as well as the "Chicano Renaissance" in literature and the arts that began at that time and continues into the present day. The Benson built this collection in close collaboration with the faculty of the university's Center for Mexican American Studies, one of the first of its kind, and still a leader in the academic study of Latina/o history and culture.[5]

Today, in similar fashion, we seek to expand the scope of our collecting practice to more systematically preserve and give access to archival materials, in both physical and digital form, that include and highlight Afro-Latina/o history and culture. In 2014–15 we launched a new initiative to build a Black Diaspora Archive in collaboration with the Department of African and African Diaspora Studies and the John L. Warfield Center for African and African American Studies at UT. Together we have committed to founding and developing an archival initiative centered in large part on the Latin American and Caribbean diaspora experience, which will make the Benson Latin American Collection a major repository for documentary, visual, and artistic materials relevant to research and public education on the black diaspora. We have secured dedicated annual funding to acquire diaspora and Afro-Latina/o archival materials, and we have added to the Benson staff a new professional archivist position specifically dedicated to black diaspora collections, to our knowledge the first such position in the United States.

Digital Initiatives

The Benson Collection has long collected and preserved historical materials that reflect the rich diversity of Latin American histories and document the experience of Latinas/os, of Afro-Latinas/os, and indigenous peoples. Digital collections offer a new challenge and opportunity to provide broad, open access to crucial parts of the historical record, whether in the form of digital surrogates of our physical collections or born digital resources. A number of LLILAS Benson digital initiatives developed over the past several years, many in close collaboration with Latin American partners, have provided new access to fragile or at-risk materials that document political and social histories, particularly of indigenous, underrepresented, and/or politically vulnerable groups. These open digital resources serve not only the scholarly research community, but individuals and communities working to protect and support cultural agency, social justice and equality, and human and territorial rights.

The Archive of the Indigenous Languages of Latin America (AILLA) was founded in 2001 as a collaboration between UT Libraries and the Departments of Anthropology and Linguistics in the College of Liberal Arts with external funding from the National Endowment for the Humanities and the National Science Foundation (ailla.utexas.org). Now part of LLILAS Benson, it is a digital repository of linguistic and anthropological data about the indigenous languages of Latin America and the Caribbean, and its digital holdings include over 280 languages from twenty-two countries. These materials are primarily audio and video recordings, of which there are over 18,000, many accompanied by transcriptions or translations. The archive also includes nearly 10,000 textual and visual resources such as dictionaries, grammars, ethnographic sketches, field notes, and photographs. The archive was created to address the reality that most of the linguistic and anthropological material gathered by researchers has rarely been accessible to the public, to other researchers, and perhaps most importantly, to indigenous communities themselves. With the creation of AILLA, researchers now have access to a free secure repository in which to deposit digitized material—all original material is returned to them—as well as free digitization services. The public has open access to these materials, and the public interface is designed to maximize accessibility for indigenous language communities: the website is designed to work well even with limited Internet capacity. The interface has also been created to accommodate different levels of use, so that contributing depositors or language communities can assign limited access to sensitive materials through passwords or time limits. The archive supports the survival of endangered indigenous languages by giving their speakers access to oral genres of cultural heritage that are disappearing, and the project team has documented cases of verbal performances thought to have become extinct being recovered through AILLA. As an archival project, AILLA has also provided an important example of how data repositories that provide solutions to federally-mandated open-access and retention requirements—which are increasingly the norm for government grant funded research projects—can also become exciting archival initiatives that engage communities and protect cultural heritage.[6]

Primeros Libros de las Américas (primeroslibros.org) is a collaborative effort between universities in the United States, Mexico, South America, and Spain to digitize all existing copies of books printed in the Americas before 1601. This digital repository features some of the first written texts in indigenous American languages (Nahuatl, Mixtec, Huastec, Otomi, Tarascan, and Zapotec), and many multilingual documents. The project, online since 2010, started as a collaboration between the Benson Collection/University of Texas Libraries, Texas A&M University, and the Lafragua and Palafoxiana Libraries in Puebla, Mexico. Today *Primeros Libros* counts thirty partner institutions, including the John Carter Brown Library, Tulane, and Harvard, more than a dozen Mexican institutions, as well as libraries in Spain and South America. Total partner contributions to the project represent nearly than 90 percent of all titles known to exist.

Digital facsimiles of the books have been viewable and fully downloadable on the *Primeros Libros* website since the project launched, but they have not been indexed, and are not yet searchable. A new digital scholarship project at LLILAS Benson seeks to address this problem by using Optical Character Recognition (OCR) software to convert the documents into readable text. Current OCR systems are not capable of providing usable transcriptions of these early books because they cannot read historical documents that are letterpress, multilingual, or do not use modern spelling conventions. New software called Ocular, a historical document recognition system recently developed by computer scientists at the University of California, Berkeley, has created a means for optical character reading of letterpress documents. Now LLILAS Benson researchers, funded by a National Endowment for the Humanities (NEH) grant since 2015, are using natural language processing concepts to expand the Ocular model for use on *Primeros Libros*, incorporating multilingual support into the software and addressing the problems of variable orthography and diacritics. A key feature of this new OCR system is that it automatically identifies the language of each word, enabling new kinds of linguistic research on the text. The LLILAS Benson team is currently in the process of expanding the scope and reach of these tools by allowing the model to "learn" languages like Mixtec or Zapotec from the documents themselves. This exciting digital scholarship project will increase accessibility of the *Primeros Libros* collection for all users, create significant new opportunities for digital analysis of the texts, and produce a new body of historical texts in indigenous American languages. This last aspect is particularly important for research and teaching at LLILAS Benson, where a number of faculty members specialize in indigenous languages and letters. These professors will be able to analyze this new digital corpus of indigenous texts for their own research as well for indigenous language instruction in the classroom.

Post-Custodial Archiving

Moving from examples of digital initiatives that preserve and promote indigenous history and culture to the support of social and political justice and human rights, two major digital archival initiatives that we have launched with partner institutions across Central America have made crucial inroads toward preserving the record of political violence in the region during the past several decades, serving as resources for those who continue to work for justice, reconciliation, and truth in the public record, and also forging a new post-custodial model of archival collection building.

The Benson's foundational project in this area has been the collaboration to create the digital repository of the Archivo Histórico de la Policía Nacional de Guatemala (AHPN). The discovery of the Archive of the National Police in 2005 and subsequent creation of the digital repository provided global access to fundamental resources for the study of the history of Guatemala and human rights in the region. The documents cover a range of topics from the internal armed conflict in Guatemala between 1960 and 1996, to U.S. government-sponsored experiments on sexually transmitted diseases in the 1940s. In collaboration with the Guatemalan archive, the University of Texas built a digital archive that replicates and extends the physical archive. The latter remains intact in the AHPN facilities in Guatemala, and forms part of the historical and cultural heritage of the Guatemalan people. Currently, the digital archive includes more than 10 million documents and, for the first time, offers the opportunity of open access online.[7]

AHPN was groundbreaking for the Benson as a foray into a major post-custodial archival initiative. In line with the definition of the Society of American Archivists, creating a post-custodial digital archive meant that archivists at the Benson did not physically acquire the original records, but instead provided stewardship for digital surrogates of the records that remain in the custody of the AHPN.[8] The project had an immediate impact in supporting the claims against violations of human rights, genocide, and current legal processes in Guatemala, and demonstrated how an archival initiative can not only serve the scholarly research community but can engage activists, students, and general society in the struggle to defend and protect human rights. The success of the AHPN project also inspired Benson librarians and archivists to think in new ways about how to continue and expand this kind of international collaborative work between archivists, scholars, and communities interested in documenting the Central American conflicts and their aftermath.

In 2014 LLILAS Benson organized a symposium called "Archiving the Central American Revolutions" that focused on new critical interpretations of the "revolutionary decades" in Central America and their legacy. The symposium convened not only researchers, but activists involved in the revolutionary processes—solidarity workers, journalists, clergy, and documentary filmmakers. More than just a symposium, the event launched an ongoing project to acquire and archive documentary materials related to the revolutionary and counter-revolutionary era in Central America. The meeting took place in tandem with an exhibition of Benson materials related to the revolutions, featured an archiving workshop led by Benson archivists, and included the opportunity for LLILAS graduate students—trained by our archivists—to conduct oral histories with invited participants about their activist work and experience in Central America. The idea behind each of these activities was to demonstrate the importance of preserving the historical record of these revolutionary movements and the State's responses to them. For infrastructural and political reasons, much of the relevant documentary material in Central America remains at risk, making this archival initiative important in multiple ways: first, in building awareness among the cohort of scholars and activists who participated in the symposium—communicating the need to physically and digitally preserve the materials that they themselves collected over the years, which now lie in file cabinets in their offices, or molding in closets; and second, in making the symposium a catalyst for sustained, collaborative archival preservation efforts between the Central American and U.S. participants in the symposium and their larger networks.

Archive-centered activities related to the symposium were essential to its mission and goals. The exhibition connected to the symposium demonstrated the research value of things like posters and ephemeral materials. It was powerful for symposium participants who lived through the revolution to see that some of these ephemeral things had not only survived but were now safely preserved and permanently accessible to researchers. Likewise, the oral history recording sessions completed with keynote speakers and other participants—all of whom were frontline political leaders in the revolutionary movements of their countries—were an opportunity both to capture key perspectives on the revolutions thirty or forty years out, but also powerful as an act of archive-building embedded within the conference. The archiving workshop led by Benson archivists served to demystify the acquisition and preservation process for these professors and activists, let them know that we want to help them archive what they have, and empower and inspire them to engage their organizations and networks in archiving as well. All of these components—the exhibition, the oral history sessions, and the archiving workshop—served to make not just the work of our archivists and librarians but also the archives themselves into central actors/agents in the symposium and its outcomes.[9]

The Central American archiving initiative has moved forward in the form of a major initiative sponsored by The Andrew W. Mellon Foundation to collaborate with Central American organizations to digitize fragile historical archives and make them available for scholarly access worldwide. Under the auspices of a Mellon planning grant, the Benson partnered with three archival institutions in Central America to digitize selected holdings, with the objectives of both long-term preservation of their unique historical materials as well as online accessibility to a global audience in what would become the Latin American Digital Initiatives (LADI) repository. In developing the project, LLILAS Benson explicitly adopted an approach to archival collaboration informed by post-custodial archival theory. Rather than physically taking custody of partners' collections, we provided the archival training and equipment necessary to adequately preserve, arrange, describe, and digitize the collections locally onsite. Partner institutions prioritized the materials to be included in the project, conducted the digitization work, and created metadata to describe their materials, thus allowing them to retain both physical and intellectual control over their collections throughout the project.[10]

The desire to design a model for post-custodial practice grew out of our experience working with partner organizations through initiatives such as the digital AHPN. We know that more traditional acquisitions models based on taking physical custody of human rights documentation would not serve the needs of our partners, and in fact, that the removal of their records could actually be disruptive to their programming and operations. Furthermore, given historical relations between the United States and Latin America, U.S. intervention in the region, and the appropriation of cultural patrimony, organizations are understandably reluctant to hand over their records to a U.S. institution. This hesitance is even more pronounced for human rights documentation, which can be particularly sensitive. Records such as those contained in the AHPN are the product of a massive state surveillance apparatus turned against its own citizens; and while these kinds of records can support struggles for justice and the full realization of rights, they can also feed the mechanisms of state repression, a reality of which our partners are well aware.

For the initial phase of the pilot project, we identified potential partners that met a few basic criteria: (a) organizations that held collections of high scholarly interest and research value; (b) that those collections documented human rights in the region, and particularly from the perspective of race, ethnicity, or social exclusion; and (c) that potential partners were open to piloting a framework for the collaborative stewardship of archival resources. LLILAS Benson then worked with UT scholars to identify sites that met these initial criteria. The three sites we ultimately chose included the Centro de Investigación y Documentación de la Costa Atlántica (CIDCA) in Bluefields, Nicaragua, the Centro de Investigaciones Regionales de Mesoamérica (CIRMA) in Antigua, Guatemala, and the Museo de la Palabra y la Imagen (MUPI) in El Salvador. At each site, Benson archivists worked with staff to select materials for digitization that were priorities for them given levels of use, local or scholarly interest, uniqueness, or fragility, but also fell within our scope of collections documenting human rights from the perspective of race, ethnicity, or social exclusion. As a point of clarification, our definition of human rights—both for the purposes of this project as well as future work—is a broad one, encompassing not only rights violations by repressive regimes, but also themes of defense of territory, migration, civil society, and cultural identity that are equally central to the realization of and scholarship on human rights in the region. We are interested in records that not only testify to the perpetration of human rights violations and their impacts, but that also document the realization and exercise of rights and agency: that is, the practice of rights, not just their absence.

CIDCA—our partner in Nicaragua—digitized an estimated 900 issues of *La infor-*

mación, a local newspaper that ran from 1917 through 1998 and covered the economic, social, and political life of Bluefields on Nicaragua's Atlantic Coast, and is one of few historical sources documenting indigenous and Afro-descendent communities. CIDCA has the most complete run of *La información* anywhere, but it was in imminent danger of deteriorating and being lost, and many of the issues showed extensive physical damage. MUPI digitized a variety of solidarity and propaganda materials, including posters, pamphlets, and clandestine publications from the Salvadoran conflict, over the period 1979 to 1992. The materials offer a unique perspective from the front lines of the Salvadoran conflict in the voices of some of the principle actors in the resistance. Finally, CIRMA digitized approximately 4,700 news clippings on the theme of violence in Guatemala during the years of 1978–1981 from the Inforpress Centroamericana archive, one of the most highly consulted collections in their holdings. The collection captures how the violence developed and changed shape as Guatemala's internal armed conflict intensified. The Inforpress archive was a primary research source for the team that drafted Guatemala's truth commission report, and has also provided corroborating evidence in several trials relating to the persecution of human rights violations during the conflict.

The Mellon project relied not just on building strong relationships with our Central American partner institutions, but also on the UT campus, and particularly within the UT Libraries. Our colleagues in Cataloging & Metadata Services, Library Information Technology, and Digital Stewardship became close collaborators in providing for the long-term preservation of the digital surrogate files and creating the online digital platform for the resulting digital collections. Together we launched the Latin American Digital Initiatives (LADI) repository in November 2015 (ladi.lib.utexas.edu). Bringing these geographically dispersed collections together in a single digital repository with detailed metadata has allowed them to inform one another, and provide insight into the movement of actors and ideas across borders during the Central American revolutions and counter-revolutions. In addition, we have found compelling connections to other Benson digital collections, for example, linking news clippings from the Inforpress collection to records in the *Digital AHPN*. This has helped build connections between police and newspaper archives, which may aid those who still work on documenting the deaths and disappearances of family and community members.

In terms of connecting collections to research, teaching, and learning, another exciting outcome of the project to archive the Central American revolutions was collaboration with a faculty member to build a graduate history seminar specifically around these materials. The course integrated traditional modes of research along with digital scholarship methodologies in critically interacting with, interpreting, and contextualizing the collections. As the LADI site continues to grow and evolve, and as more researchers and students begin to actively engage it, this dynamic resource will facilitate new insights into human rights scholarship across the region.

As LLILAS Benson moves forward with an ongoing post-custodial enterprise, we are working to build a community of practice among our own archivists and librarians based on the intention and practices evident in the projects described above. In addition, we seek to inform and transform archival theory and practice which will, in turn, alter the work of researchers as well as students, both within Latin American studies and information science.

Collections, Teaching and Learning for a New Generation

The importance of connecting collections to teaching and learning—not only as content but also as practice—cannot be understated. We have given examples of how Benson librarians and archivists increasingly work with faculty to develop and teach graduate and undergraduate courses in the social science and humanities, placing archival materials at their center, and training students in primary documentary analysis and critical thinking. Equally important is the need to train the next generation of archivists and librarians in interdisciplinary approaches.

To this end, in 2011, LLILAS Benson created a dual Master's degree program with the UT School of Information, whose mission is to educate students in "the technologies of information that are changing our behavior, our organizations, and our society … and to help shape a future that reflects social values."[11] To achieve this goal, the School of Information curriculum emphasizes instruction and knowledge "that crosses disciplinary divides, bridges the arts and the sciences, and applies human insights to technological advances."[12] This interdisciplinary approach is reflected in several dual degree programs that allow students to pursue MSIS degrees in information science at the same time that they earn a Master's degree in another academic specialization. As one of these options, the School of Information and LLILAS Benson offer a joint degree program leading to the MSIS and the Master of Arts in Latin American Studies.

Students in the program are able to complete both degrees in three academic years, with course requirements divided equally between the School of Information and Latin American Studies. The program culminates with the completion of a Master's thesis on a topic that combines both information studies and Latin American studies.[13] The Benson Latin American Collection is able to work closely with these dual degree students to facilitate thesis projects as well as paid and volunteer work, providing students with deep experience with our collections and opportunities to work alongside our professional archivists and librarians who are trained as subject specialists for Latin America. This dual degree Master's program gives a new generation of Latin Americanist archivists and librarians the opportunity to advance their own profession in theory and in practice, to continue to advance understanding and intellectual collaboration between archives and departments, and to prepare themselves to be citizens of a global, digital library and archival community.

Conclusion

Reflecting on the LLILAS Benson partnership five years on, general agreement exists among participants that the synergies created by linking a premier academic unit with a world-class library have resulted in remarkable collaborations. We have built on a foundation for preserving and providing access to collections that facilitate inclusion, social justice, and cultural agency, from the creation of the Black Diaspora Archive to our post-custodial approach to safeguarding at-risk materials in Central America. Moving forward, the partnership will help facilitate even deeper ties between LLILAS Benson and stakeholders across the UT campus, and with current and future partners in Latin America.

The LLILAS Benson partnership is no longer an experiment; it is an effective organizational structure that shapes both Latin American studies and information studies education, and is a model for connecting collections to socially-engaged scholarship.

NOTES

1. For more on the history of the Benson Collection, see: Carlos E. Castañeda, "The Human Side of a Great Collection," *Books Abroad* 14, no. 2 (Spring 1940): 116–121; Nettie Lee Benson, "Latin American Collection," *Discovery: Research and Scholarship at the University of Texas at Austin* 7 (1983): 54–61; Adán Benavides, "Benson Latin American Collection," *Discovery: Research and Scholarship at the University of Texas at Austin* 16, no. 1 (2002), 22–23.

2. "LLILAS, ILAS, and the History of Latin American Studies at UT Austin," UT College of Liberal Arts, accessed Aug. 21, 2016, http://liberalarts.utexas.edu/llilas/about/history.php.

3. "LLILAS Benson Latin American Studies and Collections," Teresa Lozano Long Institute of Latin American Studies and Nettie Lee Benson Latin American Collection, accessed Aug. 21, 2016, https://llilas-benson.utexas.edu/. ; "Announcing LLILAS Benson Latin American Studies and Collections," University of Texas Libraries, Aug. 26, 2013, https://www.lib.utexas.edu/benson/announcements/announcing-llilas-benson-latin-american-studies-and-collections.

4. "Mission, Vision, Values," University of Texas Libraries, accessed Aug. 21, 2016, https://www.lib.utexas.edu/vprovost/mission.html.

5. For additional information on the Mexican American Library Program (MALP), see "Mexican American Library Program Celebrates 30th Anniversary Nov. 11," *University of Texas News*, November 4, 2004, http://news.utexas.edu/2004/11/04/nr_library.

6. Susan Smythe Kung and Joel Sherzer, "The Archive of the Indigenous Languages of Latin America: An Overview," *Oral Tradition* 14, no. 2 (2013): 379–388.

7. "AHPN, Digital Archive of the Guatemalan National Police Historical Archive," University of Texas Libraries, accessed Aug. 21, 2016, https://ahpn.lib.utexas.edu/.

8. Richard Pearce-Moses, *A Glossary of Archival & Records Terminology* (Chicago: Society of American Archivists, 2005) Accessed August 22, 2016, http://www2.archivists.org/glossary.

9. "Archiving the Central American Revolutions, Feb. 19–22, 2014," Conference Program, LLILAS Benson, The University of Texas at Austin, accessed Aug. 21, 2016, http://liberalarts.utexas.edu/llilas/_files/conferences/lozanolong2014/LL2014_program.pdf; Brenda Estela Xum, "Archiving the Central American Revolutions: The Value of Documentation in the Reconstruction of History," *Portal* 9 (2013–2014): 9–12.

10. Additional information about the Mellon project and LLILAS Benson's post-custodial archival initiatives can be found in, Theresa E. Polk, "Archiving Human Rights Documentation: The Promise of the Post-Custodial Approach in Latin America," *Portal* 11 (2015–2016): 37–39.

11. "About iSchool," School of Information, University of Texas at Austin, accessed Aug. 22, 2016, https://www.ischool.utexas.edu/content/about-ischool.

12. *Ibid.*

13. "Dual Degree Programs," Teresa Lozano Long Institute of Latin American Studies, accessed Aug. 22, 2016, https://liberalarts.utexas.edu/llilas/student-programs/graduate-program/ma/dual-degrees.php.

Over One Hundred Years
of Collecting Latin Americana
and Caribbeana at the
University of Florida

Lara Lookabaugh, Paul S. Losch *and*
Richard F. Phillips

Introduction

The University of Florida (UF) Latin American and Caribbean Collection (LACC) was founded in 1951 to support emerging scholarly interest in the countries to the south of Florida. As far back as 1939, there had been an Inter-American Reading Room on campus, housing a small assortment of books and journals, but it was not until 1951 that the university library was able to hire a specialized librarian to oversee the development of the collection. Since that time, LACC has grown to become one of the University of Florida's preeminent collections, attracting researchers from around the world to Gainesville. It also has a staff of three librarians, two staff assistants and various student employees. For decades, it was known simply as the Latin American Collection, but the name was modified in 2014 to reflect better its unique strength in the culturally diverse Caribbean region.

LACC has numerous identities. Simultaneously, it is a physical space, an administrative staff, and a circulating collection of books and journals housed in that space and overseen by that staff. There are also the non-circulating rare books, archives and manuscripts, accessible elsewhere in the same building, special collections that bring distinction to UF as a unique repository of cultural materials. Furthermore, there is a broader definition of the "collection" that accounts for those materials related to Latin America and the Caribbean acquired for the university's other libraries, such as those dedicated to the natural sciences, the fine arts and law. LACC is also the foundation of a fast-growing online collection, especially the Digital Library of the Caribbean.

LACC is a place, a human organization, a collection, and a common theme throughout UF's many collections, physical and electronic. It also symbolizes the university's commitment to understanding and appreciating the cultures of Latin America and the Caribbean, cultures that are present in the state's population and its deep international ties. Just as UF has invested substantially in the laboratory infrastructure required for applied fields such as engineering, medicine and agriculture, LACC is an investment in the university's role as a leader in cross-cultural information sharing, built through commitments of resources towards materials, staff, space and technology over the course of decades. While it has enjoyed donations of books, and grant support for specific projects, it is important to note that LACC does not benefit from any kind of major permanent endowment, which is surprising given its history of important work.

The development of UF's Latin American and Caribbean Collection to this day has been shaped and guided by political and economic history, by local needs and by advancing technology. It is a story about how people and personalities, pushed and pulled by their generations, have created and fostered the collection for over a century. In the following essay, we will briefly describe the Latin American and Caribbean Collection and discuss its emergence and development. We will structure the discussion around space, materials, staffing and technology. We will conclude the essay with observations about how its current and future directions of LACC may be understood in light of its past.

LACC as a Space

LACC is physically located in the Smathers Library, the original library building on campus, known from 1967 to 1998 as Library East. It is administratively part of the campus-wide system known as the George A. Smathers Libraries, and it is a unit of the Department of Special and Area Studies Collections. The Latin American and Caribbean Collection effectively functions as a branch library, maintaining its own book stacks, reading room, and reference and circulation desk, putting it in the company of a few peers such as the Benson Collection at the University of Texas at Austin and the Latin American Library at Tulane University.

Facilities for the UF Latin American and Caribbean Collection have evolved over the years. In 1967, LACC was established as a separate reading room in the South Tower of Library East, situated together with the Center for Latin American Studies, and connected to its dedicated stack area through a bridge (now demolished). In 1977, the collection's public service areas and office spaces were relocated to the fourth floor of the North Tower, a space they occupied until 2014. At one point during the 1980s, the library administration briefly considered integrating LACC into the main library for humanities and social sciences, Library West. Faculty, students and alumni rallied to support the concept of a separate collection. LACC's space was renovated in 1996–1997 using funds from the George A. Smathers Endowment. The late U.S. Senator took special interest in Latin American affairs, and was pleased to have his name associated with the building that houses the collection.

In 2014, the newly-renamed Latin American and Caribbean Collection moved into its current public and staff spaces on the third floor, enhanced once more with the further generosity and support of the Smathers family. The new reading room occupies a large spacious room with views out onto the Plaza of the Americas, a central campus quadrangle named at the university's first conference on Latin America in 1931. Visitors are welcomed by staff at a reference/circulation desk between the elevator and the stairwell, and the location offers easy access to the collections of reference materials, current periodicals, microfilm and video formats. The New Book Shelf, where recently cataloged materials are displayed before they go to their permanent locations, reminds users that the collection is constantly evolving through careful selection. There are also exhibit cases and shelving areas set aside to feature topics of special interest, such as Haitian Creole, cookbooks, and Panama Canal history.

LACC's space allows for all kinds of easy interaction. Organized class visits are encouraged, but students and faculty with similar interests may often meet here informally to work together, and many chance meetings occur here. Staff learn about the research interests of students and faculty who become regulars, and about the needs of campus visitors, for many of whom LACC is an obligatory stop. Some undergraduates enter just looking for a quiet place to study business or chemistry and then come to realize that UF places a high value on the cultures of Latin America and the Caribbean. Many of UF's students have family ties to the region, and begin here to explore their own cultural identity as part of their broader education. The space is so prized for its grandeur that occasionally the Center for Latin American Studies or related student/alumni groups ask to use the reading room for events. These requests cannot always be honored, given staffing schedules and the need for study space, but some allowances are made, as this brings in new potential users.

The circulating collection, some 600,000 items, occupies three of the five levels of the climate-controlled stacks wing. Materials classified in the Library of Congress system are on the fourth and fifth levels, which are open for browsing. The third level is mainly occupied by those materials still in the Dewey Decimal System, cataloged prior to 1977, as well as a limited circulation collection. Plans are underway for this area to close to the public, so that it can receive rare materials currently stored elsewhere in the building. LACC aims to serve as a "collection of record" and very little is ever withdrawn. However, the acquisitions of new materials, averaging around 4,000 items per year over the past decade, have created pressures. LACC's 34,000 feet of shelving are over 80 percent full, and so staff are working to identify materials that can be relocated to an off-campus storage facility, and to maintain the stacks. LACC processes approximately 12,000 loans per year (20,000 renewals), accepts 12,000 visitors to the reading room per year, and answers 1300 reference questions.

LACC as a Specialized Body of Information

The stacks, and their contents, are another natural part of what defines LACC. The catalog, at the time of writing, has over 282,000 records for titles housed in the collection, 66 percent in Spanish, 19 percent in English and 10 percent in Portuguese. The geographic and subject scope of the collection is very broad, as it must be to support the research, teaching and public service needs of a campus of nearly 50,000 students, over 20 percent of whom identify as Hispanic. The Center for Latin American Studies has over 200 faculty affiliates in departments all around campus, from art history to zoology, and LACC is involved in meeting these broad information needs. There is no country that is not covered to some degree, and Brazil is of special importance in terms of faculty research. At the same time, the Latin American and Caribbean Collection, as indicated by its name, stands out from other Latin American collections through an emphasis on the Caribbean, and this is determined by geographic proximity and by a national-level commitment to interlibrary cooperation.

LACC mainly houses materials in the humanities and social sciences, but the agricultural and life-science orientation of a land-grant college gives a special history to Latin American studies at UF, and also shapes the collection's holdings. In 1905, various small agriculture schools, teachers' colleges and military academies merged to form the earliest manifestation of the University of Florida campus in Gainesville, Florida. Quickly, education leaders on campus and statewide recognized that agricultural courses and research would take top-level priority at the new institution. Citrus, sugar and cattle production were prominent in Florida, and the study and teaching of techniques relevant to the Latin American environment attracted students from that region. There was also an early emphasis at UF on the social sciences as applied in the rural setting, which continues to this day, in internationally-oriented programs in tropical conservation and development, and Food and Resource Economics. An interest in Florida's Spanish settlements encouraged the study of the colonial history of the wider region.

The expansion of the curriculum accelerated in the 1930s with the establishment of UF's Institute of Inter-American Affairs, and academic programming gained greater momentum after World War II, especially as grants from federal and private agencies helped to fund the development of area studies on campus and nationally. For more than sixty years the libraries have used the services of book vendors to readily support major research and advanced graduate studies in fields as diverse as Southern Cone literatures, the peoples of the Amazon, archaeology of the Inca, food production, religion, wetlands conservation, and climate change. The history and politics of Venezuela and Colombia also have been the topics of numerous seminars and dissertations as have gender studies, women's studies, criminology, and environmental law.

Geographic affinities with Latin America have shaped, and continue to shape the curriculum at UF, and the subjects relevant to the collection. The state has rapidly urbanized and developed global connections, just as Latin America has, and so UF has moved beyond its rural roots. Urban planning, migration studies, public health and international business are emerging fields at UF that involve research connections to Latin America. The College of Arts has prioritized Latin American art and music as areas for future growth. Sustainability, biodiversity and Latin American development are all identified as strategic areas in UF's preeminence strategy. The state's demographics and trade patterns all project heavy connectivity to Latin America as a whole, and our collecting will continue to inform the study of Florida's future.

Apart from local needs, another factor in UF's collection development strategies has been interlibrary coordination. Serving as a national resource for the Caribbean has meant that UF continues to collect heavily from the region, even when there may be an absence of campus activity in a given field. For example, even when state policy discouraged faculty research on Cuba, that country continued to be a major collecting strength, due to long-standing commitments. In the 1950s, UF was tasked with the responsibility of acquiring Caribbean materials by the Farmington Plan. This plan arose from U.S. national policies to hasten post–World War II efforts to train and educate specialists in world affairs and was guided by the Farmington Proposal of 1942 which had an assumption "that American research libraries have the responsibility to acquire foreign publications and build a national library with national interest."[1]

That proposal included specific foreign acquisition programs of the Association of Research Libraries (ARL), which set UF on its mission to collect Caribbeana and to serve as a national resource in this field. Lists of Caribbean acquisitions by UF were published and used as reference sources by other institutions that wanted to be aware of current publications from the region.[2] In 1981, the very distinguished Jamaican bibliographer and scholar Kenneth E. Ingram spent a full year at UF surveying the Caribbean holdings and reporting on strengths and weaknesses.[3] K.E. Ingram was Cambridge-educated, a founder of the Jamaican Librarian Association, and a charming personality. UF librarians were enriched by his visit and work here, and learned much from his intellectual visions and recommendations. Roberto Marte carried out a parallel survey of the Caribbean holdings in languages other than English.[4] Around the same time, Robert Lawless prepared a bibliography on Haiti that drew mainly from the collections.[5] Furthermore, G.K. Hall issued some fourteen volumes of LACC's card catalog.[6] This type of publication was a common way of sharing specialized library holdings with researchers at other institutions in the pre–Internet world.

By sharing its collections in many ways, physically and virtually, LACC contributes to UF's status as a "National Resource Center" in Latin American Studies under the U.S. Department of Education's Title VI program. A 1998 study funded by ARL looked at UF as a purveyor of Caribbean-themed interlibrary loans and found heavy lending by UF.[7] Much of this lending is to other state universities in Florida where course offerings in Latin American studies are steadily increasing, but UF also serves as a resource to its ARL colleagues who depend on its collections to support advanced research. Since 2010, LACC has supplied via interlibrary loan an average of around 1400 items per year to researchers at other institutions, and this represents about 18 percent of LACC's total annual lending. For decades, UF has welcomed many visiting researchers to our campus each semester and the UF Center for Latin American Studies awards each year travel money for research visits.

The circulating collections are complemented by the rare book, manuscript and archival collections of the university, and these include one-of-a-kind materials not available elsewhere. These special collections holdings truly enrich UF's regular and steady receipts of contemporary publications from mainstream book and journals sources in Latin American and Caribbean Basin cultural markets. Dr. Margarita Vargas Betancourt is the current curator of LACC's special collections, and has been working diligently to provide greater access to them, through description and digitization.

A few of the notable and special acquisitions over the years include the purchase of the Rochambeau Haitian Revolution Papers at auction in London in the 1950s, the receipt by gift of the Braga Brothers Cuban sugar company business files archive in the 1980s, and purchases of rare Cuban books and manuscripts from vendors Maury Bromsen and Howard Karno in the 1990s. While documenting the colonial plantation society has been a traditional strength of the collection, recent acquisitions have tended to emphasize the twentieth century, and to document reactions to that colonial model, notably the Cuban Revolution.

One major recent donation was the extensive holdings of the Panama Canal Museum (PCM)–coupled with the award of a large grant for the preservation of these rare materials, all of which nicely coincided with the centennial of the opening of the Canal in 1914, affording the Libraries an opportunity to host workshops, panels and exhibits. Topics of interest have ranged from race and the Canal work force, the commercial impacts of the Canal, and the ecological and environmental nature of the isthmus. That donation was just one example of how UF's existing collections sometimes attract new ones, since donors are aware that their materials will "fit" and be appreciated as part of an overall strategy of the library to emphasize Latin America and the Caribbean as areas of distinctive collecting. Another recent endowment in UF's Price Library of Judaica will allow the Libraries to bridge two areas of strength, by developing collections on Jewish communities in the Americas.

LACC as a Human Organization

While LACC is a space, and a collection of printed matter, it would not be what it is without the human element. In fact, this may be the most important part of the collection, which reflects the dedication of its staff and its supporters throughout the decades. Credit must be given as far back as John J. Tigert, University President from 1928 to 1947. Tigert had been U.S. Commissioner of Education, and was very aware of the growing interest in Washington in increased cultural relations with Latin America. He had a vision that Florida's future would be connected to Latin America, and he made ties with the region a priority when he arrived in Gainesville.

In 1930, soon after it was announced that the University of Florida was creating an Institute of Inter-American Affairs (today's Center for Latin American Studies), an article appeared in *Library Journal* describing the aims of the institute, and how the library would support this ambitious work.

> [I]t is easy to realize how vitally the University of Florida Library is concerned with the development of the Institute in its various phases. [...] As yet the collection of these allied subjects is not large, but a bibliography of all material now in the library has been compiled. Books are being purchased and periodical subscriptions are being placed as rapidly as funds are available. Letters have been written to the Ministers of Education and to the Presidents of the Institutions of Higher Learning in the various countries in hopes of establishing an exchange list and in this way securing much valuable material. The field is very fertile and it is hoped that much will be accomplished to the mutual benefit and pleasure of all concerned.[8]

Although no author is credited, the article may very well have been written by UF librarian Henrie Mae Eddy, who had once been a Spanish teacher and who had compiled bibliographies of Spanish-language sources in Florida history. Unfortunately, the economic difficulties of the 1930s delayed much of the work that was being contemplated in the article. Conditions eventually improved, and, in 1939, Miss Eddy oversaw the creation of an Inter-American Reading Room as part of the Institute of Inter-American Affairs. An article in the campus paper described the reading room. "Although relatively young in the program of the institute, the reading room is slowly gaining attention and it is the hope of the officials of the Institute that the material sent to this department will provide of value to the students in acquiring knowledge of Latin America."[9] There are still a few books in the stacks today with markings indicating that they were once cataloged for this reading room that was an early forerunner of today's LACC.

Miss Eddy might have been part of that pioneering generation of Latin American studies librarians, but tragedy struck in a fatal plane crash in Rio de Janeiro in August 1939. The famous radio announcer Red Barber had worked in the library as a student at UF and was in New York when he read of her death. Many years later, he recalled the strong impression that this news had made on him:

> My mind remembered Robert Browning's line, "A man should die at his pinnacle moment." Miss Eddy had so wanted to see this place, this beautiful harbor. We read the story carefully. It was a mys-

tery crash. It had been a completely beautiful, bright day, with no limit on visibility. So, my wife and I conjectured, Miss Eddy had seen the harbor of Rio de Janeiro. She had lived to see it. Then she died. She didn't live to be disappointed by it, this thing she had wanted so passionately to see.[10]

Miss Eddy's passing, and the advent of World War II further delayed the development of the library's collections and services related to Latin America. In Ronald Hilton's first edition of the *Handbook of Hispanic Source Materials and Research Organizations in the United States* (1942), the University of Florida did not merit any mention.[11] However, it did receive some praise for its efforts by the time the second edition of the *Handbook* was published (1956):

> The reasonably adequate resources for studies in Hispanic fields to be found in the University of Florida Library are primarily a matter of growth during the past decade. Such progress as has been achieved has been without outside funds, and with no large donations of books. The first sizeable gift, and a very helpful one, was that of a thousand or so volumes from the Latin American library of the late Joseph B. Lockey. [...] Another thousand or more volumes were later acquired by inheritance from the university's Institute of Inter-American Affairs and from the personal library of A. Curtis Wilgus, when the institute was superseded by the School of Inter-American Studies and Dr. Wilgus became its director in 1951.[12]

The arrival of historian Curtis Wilgus indeed helped to spur the library's work, as he brought with him significant experience related to the field. Wilgus had been active in the Inter-American Bibliographical and Library Association, a Washington-based group that included librarians from the Library of Congress and the Pan American Union and functioned as something of a predecessor to Seminar on the Acquisition of Latin American Library Materials (SALALM), a national group that Wilgus helped to establish in 1956. The old Institute of Inter-American Affairs at UF had been housed in the student union, and its work had focused, due to scant resources, mainly on exchange programs and cultural activities. Under Wilgus, however, the new school's offices were established in a new addition to the library building, a location that made clear the increasing emphasis on faculty research and on graduate training. The school, in 1964, became today's Center for Latin American Studies, and the center continued to be housed in the library until its current building was erected in 1970.

The postwar period was one of great growth in U.S. higher education, and UF took advantage of the opportunities to achieve its longstanding aim to become a leader in Latin American studies in the library field and elsewhere on campus. For example, the University of Florida Press began to develop a specialty in Latin American topics that continues to this day. From 1949 to 1978, the press published the *Handbook of Latin American Studies*, the preeminent guide to current publications in the field, and UF faculty members have been important contributors for decades to this ongoing work.

The UF Libraries soon began to hire specialized staff and to become more involved in national-level work in Latin American Studies. While Curtis Wilgus was vital in getting university support for the library, it was Dr. Irene Zimmerman who led the library's efforts for over two decades in the field. She was the first bibliographer formally charged with a Latin American and Caribbean assignment and specialization. Dr. I.Z. (as she was known) arrived at UF in 1951 from Kansas. She is remembered as a hard working individual, true especially on Friday afternoons as longtime staff pleasantly recall even today. It was under her vision and leadership that great growth of UF's exchange programming occurred, as Dr. I.Z. was an avid correspondent with numerous libraries and archives in the Caribbean and beyond. These exchange agreements were vital for procuring hard-to-acquire items from around the region.

In a working paper for SALALM 1977 entitled "Latin American Studies and Library Development," William E. Carter wrote, "Above all else, the Latin American Collection of the University of Florida is the creation of a single person, Dr. Irene Zimmerman."[13] He continues:

> Dr. Zimmerman's situation exemplifies the truth behind probably most Latin American Collections. They would never have existed and would not continue to exist without the selfless dedication of key individuals. These are the collections' patrons, in the best sense of the word. They are the persons who know the collection best, and who look upon it as their composite child. Without their constant concern, those of us in the academic departments of universities would find ourselves bereft of resources.[14]

In 1956, the UF Libraries hosted the first Seminar on the Acquisition of Latin American Library Materials at Chinsegut Hill, a country estate near Brooksville that belonged to the university at the time. Since that time, SALALM has been held at UF on two other occasions, 1977, and again in 2005 to celebrate the organization's golden anniversary during its fiftieth annual meeting. Curtis Wilgus and Irene Zimmerman were elected to honorary membership in the organization for their contributions, as were two of their successors at UF, Rosa Mesa (Collection Head, 1977–1991) and Richard Phillips (Collection Head, 1993–2014).

Rosa Quintero Mesa was a Cuban exile who came directly from Havana in 1961 as a government documents expert. She was part of a contingent of noted Cuban bibliographers that settled in Gainesville and included Fermín and Elena Peraza, and she produced *Latin American Serials Documents,* a massive country-by-country list of Latin American serials held at U.S. institutions.[15] Mesa worked concurrently in the libraries with Dr. Irene Zimmerman, and became Collection Head in 1977 with the retirement of Dr. I.Z. that same year. Doña Rosa (as she was called) worked tirelessly building UF holdings of Caribbean imprints. She was remembered in an obituary published in the 1997 *SALALM Newsletter* as a committed and focused Latin Americanist librarian who made great contributions to the field.[16] The obituary reads, "According to her peers, there was almost nothing related to Latin America, especially in history and politics, that she was not aware of."[17] The *Miami Herald* described her as an "unofficial expert on Latin American affairs" due to the fact that patrons very rarely left the library empty-handed. "If her staff can't find it, Mesa will."[18]

Praise of Zimmerman and Mesa's dedication can lead us into a discussion of the numerous faculty and staff who have worked ensuring the Latin American and Caribbean Collection's success and survival at the University of Florida. There has always been more staff working on the university's Latin American and Caribbean collections (outside of LACC proper) than just those individuals assigned full-time to the topic. Without the skilled assistance of the Acquisitions and Cataloging departments, the collection development and reference work carried out in LACC would not be possible. For example, Jean Hixson was the section chief of cataloging for Latin American and Caribbean imprints from 1949 until her retirement in 1979. She served as the rapporteur at that first SALALM conference in 1956 and made a brief appearance at the fiftieth annual meeting, encouraging the membership to continue the work she had helped to start.

UF Director of Libraries Stanley West was very supportive. During his tenure (1946–1967) the first LACC specialized staff were hired, the microfilming program was launched, the first SALALM meeting was hosted, and funds were first appropriated for travel and ongoing acquisitions. His successor, Gus Harrer, was another UF library director that provided leadership (1968–1984) to the UF Latin American and Caribbean Collection. For example, Dr. Harrer engaged UF as a major partner in the Association of Caribbean University, Research and Institutional Libraries (ACURIL), often flying his small private plane with other UF librarians as passengers to Trinidad and other islands to attend conferences that furthered collegiality and coordination. UF's Map Librarian Helen Jane Armstrong joined in those ACURIL sessions, and developed excellent Caribbean map collections at UF.

Dale Canelas was director of UF Libraries from 1985 through 2006, and took an active role in national and international projects supporting Latin American and Caribbean bibliography, serving on advisory boards and numerous task forces. Current UF Dean of Libraries Judith Russell has enthusiastically ramped up LACC programming, giving maximum priority to user services, digital efforts, grant work, exhibits, alumni and donor relations, and overall improvement of collection quarters. She has also been effective in marshaling statewide coordination from other members of the State of Florida academic library community, especially with the goal of creating centralized storage facilities in the near future.

The LACC has been favored by UF collection development officers over the years, including Sam Gowan, Sal Miranda, John Ingram, and (more recently) Patrick Reakes. Others have made contributions in various ways to technical services, including Jorge Gonzalez, Peter Bushnell, Justino Llanque-Chana, and Cecilia Botero. Digital leadership at UF Libraries was under Erich Kesse for many years, and today draws from the talents and inspiration of Laurie Taylor, Digital Scholarship Librarian. Digital exhibits, and all exhibiting, come under the responsibility of Lourdes Santamaria-Wheeler. There are many others whose service is also worthy of mention, but space does not allow us to go further

Technology and the Future of LACC

LACC, as a place, an organization and a collection of printed material would not be where it is today if it were not for the technological advances that have expanded its reach over time. UF's leadership in areas such as microfilming, shared cataloging and digital libraries, have all been connected to the LACC's work and give some directions for its future.

Following the Farmington Plan designation, the UF Libraries received a series of grants from the Rockefeller Foundation and embarked on several years of microfilming in Caribbean archives, generating unique holdings of newspapers and manuscripts from diverse places such as Haiti, Suriname, the Dominican Republic, and Trinidad and Tobago. Service copies were placed at all host facilities as UF's work went forward. Beyond the UF microfilming done in the Caribbean Basin in the 1950s, UF set up cameras in Gainesville and did in-house filming for many years of a number of Caribbean newspapers and scarce monographs.

UF cameras at one point in the mid–1990s were generating over one million pages of microfilm text annually (figure includes some Florida, Africana and Judaica filming as well as Caribbean exposures). Many UF projects over the years have been the result of creative cooperation with outside entities, coordinated by LACC. For example, in the late 1980s the Smathers Libraries supplied large amounts of raw negative film stock to the Biblioteca Nacional do Brasil (National Library of Brazil) for use by their camera crews. The end result of such innovative coordination was that Brazilian newspapers were microfilmed by these international partners, while UF gained service copies of hundreds of unique titles. Decades later, UF cooperated with the Center for Research Libraries to convert many of those reels (*Diário de Pernambuco,* and *Jornal do Commercio*) into online resources.

LACC has gradually expanded its collections to include audiovisual and digital materials. During the early 1970s, the UF Libraries housed a "Latin American Data Bank," a very early attempt at collecting data in card punch and tape form. However, the main advances from computerization have come in the areas of online cataloging and in digital collections, and this work at UF took on special significance because of LACC's rich holdings. UF has long been a national leader in terms of the cataloging of Latin American and Caribbean materials, and this role has been enhanced through shared cataloging.

In the 1970s the UF Libraries were one of the first institutions beyond the original Ohio group to activate OCLC cataloging, and e-service platforms. As far back as the 1940s, UF had been designated a "card contributor" for Caribbean bibliographic records within the old *National Union Catalog* (*NUC*) efforts. Always a powerhouse in technical services operations, pioneering librarians such as Jean Hixson and Nancy Lynn Williams took UF into automated national serials and authorities projects (CONSER, ENHANCE, and NACO), which did much to promote Caribbean and Latin American processing and workflows. This yielded efficient results both locally in UF Libraries, but also globally as connectivity mushroomed in the 1980s–1990s, and into today's virtual e-reality. UF was also an early online public user catalog institution, with NOTIS coming up in the early 1980s.

UF has also been a leader in digitization. Grants received from The Andrew Mellon Foundation in the 1990s allowed for conversion of some of the microfilm collections that had been created decades earlier, and led to the earliest digital access to such holdings. Today's Digital Library of the Caribbean (dLOC) can trace its roots to this Mellon grant and to the United States Department of Education Technological Innovation and Cooperation for Foreign Information Access (TICFIA) funding received by Florida International University (FIU), dLOC's administrative headquarters in Miami. dLOC now has millions of pages of Caribbeana in free and open electronic access, with partner libraries and archives across Florida, the Caribbean Basin region, and beyond. Page views since 2006 are some 40 million and climbing. FIU and UF dLOC staff provide systems support and development, and have provided dozens of training workshops with partners in the Bahamas, Belize, Aruba, Haiti, and many other locales. UF is currently working with the National Library of Cuba to carry out joint projects related to cataloging and digitization.

Conclusion

Given the rapidly diversifying demography of the state of Florida's population, coupled with tightening funding for book and journal acquisition, the concept of resource sharing will continue to shape the manner in which LACC operates. Statewide coordinated purchasing agreements are being achieved, and digital access is a growing reality, with UF playing a leading role in the field. The history shows that there has long been a balance between the local and the international, in-person service and the construction of technological systems that reach a broader audience. LACC is still an important space, but its impact goes well beyond its physical location. Its contents, through technology and through the work of its staff, continue to grow and evolve in order to meet the needs of users near and far.

We can conclude with an anecdote that gives an idea of how UF's current work is connected to its past. Not long ago, a member of the LACC staff came upon the name of a relatively unknown woman who had taught Spanish in the 1890s at the Florida Agricultural College, a small institution which would later form part of the University of Florida. The librarian researching her name discovered that this teacher, Aurora de Mena, had been forced into exile during the Cuban struggles for independence in the 1890s. Digging deeper, the UF librarian then discovered for sale on eBay an 1896 monograph authored by de Mena, *The Pearl Key or Midnight and Dawn in Cuba*.[19] The price was modest, but the purchase turned out to be remarkable treasure for a number of different reasons. According to *Worldcat*, UF's copy, plucked from an online auction site, was only the second reported by any library anywhere—startling given the active collecting of academic libraries, archives, and scholars with focus on Cuba, women's narratives, and Caribbean history.

Aurora de Mena was very likely the first "Latin Americanist" faculty member (male or female) at UF, at a time when the school was a local "cow college," and it took over 100 years for the library to acquire a copy of her work. Since then, it has been displayed prominently in some recent exhibits, including one on Cuban revolutionary women. Efforts are now underway to digitize the item and make it available online—linking the history and the future of LACC in one book, a story that has involved many people dedicated to improving the flows of information between Florida and the wider world.

NOTES

1. Ralph D. Wagner, *The History of the Farmington Plan* (Lanham, MD: Scarecrow Press, 2002), 1–2.

2. University of Florida Libraries, *Caribbean Acquisitions* (Gainesville: University of Florida, 1958).

3. Kenneth Ingram, *Report on the Holdings of the University of Florida Libraries Related to the English-Speaking Countries of the Caribbean* (Gainesville: University of Florida, 1982).

4. Roberto Marte, *The Non-English Speaking Caribbean Holdings of the University of Florida Libraries* (Gainesville: University of Florida, 1983).

5. Robert Lawless, *Bibliography on Haiti: English and Creole Items* (Gainesville: Center for Latin American Studies, University of Florida, 1985).

6. University of Florida Libraries, *Catalog of the Latin American Collection* (Boston: G. K. Hall, 1973).

7. Jennifer Cobb Adams and Richard F. (Richard Frederick) Phillips, *The University of Florida's Latin American Collection: A Case Study of Unilateral Specialization in Caribbean Materials* (Gainesville: University of Florida, 1998).

8. "An Institute of Inter-American Affairs," *Library Journal*, November 1, 1930, 887.

9. "Inter America Institute Has Long and Interesting Periodical List," *Alligator*, August 11, 1939.

10. Red Barber and Robert W. Creamer, *Rhubarb in the Catbird Seat* (Lincoln: University of Nebraska Press, 1997), 131–132.

11. Ronald Hilton, *Handbook of Hispanic Source Materials and Research Organizations in the United States* (Toronto: University of Toronto Press, 1942).

12. Ronald Hilton, *Handbook of Hispanic Source Materials and Research Organizations in the United States* (Stanford, CA: Stanford University Press, 1956), 158.

13. William E. Carter and Irene Zimmerman, "Latin American Studies and Library Development: The Florida Experience," *Final Report and Working Papers of the Annual Meeting of the Seminar on the Acquisition of Latin American Library Materials* 22 (1979): 129–133.

14. Carter and Zimmerman, "Latin American Studies," 130.

15. Rosa Quintero Mesa, *Latin American Serial Documents: A Holdings List* (Ann Arbor, MI: University Microfilms, 1968).

16. Stacey Carr, "Rosa Quintero Mesa, 1923–1997," *SALALM Newsletter* 25, no. 2 (1997): 42.

17. Carr, "Rosa Quintero Mesa," 42.

18. Fabiola Santiago, "UF Boasts Largest Collection of Caribbean Publications," *Miami Herald*, January 31, 1982.

19. Aurora de Mena, *The Pearl Key or Midnight and Dawn in Cuba* (Jacksonville, FL: Vance Printing Co., 1896).

Promoting and Maintaining Collaborative Collecting

A Case Study

HOLLY ACKERMAN *and* TERESA CHAPA

Introduction

In place for more than seventy years, the University of North Carolina at Chapel Hill (UNC) and Duke University Cooperative Acquisitions Program for the Collecting of Latin American Library materials is one of the oldest in the country. The agreement, based on a geographic division by country, commits both Duke and UNC to acquire core materials from throughout Latin America and the Caribbean to support undergraduate curricular needs. Additionally, each institution acquires research-level materials and expensive items including data, films, and microform based on its area responsibilities. The division by countries has worked well for our joint agreement despite the shifts in academic interests and movement of faculty through the years.

Key to the success of this cooperative collecting program has been the confidence and trust we share that both partners are solidly committed to the process. The on-going dialogue between the Latin American librarians, our user community and, oftentimes our vendors, keeps the agreement current and relevant. This sort of engagement and continual reassessment gives the librarians the confidence to promote the two collections as one specialized library, albeit housed on two campuses. When faculty support of the concept of one shared collection has met resistance, the local librarian has been able to find viable solutions based on individual needs. For the most part, the shared collections concept has been well-received mostly due to the spirit of cooperation that has been in place between Duke and UNC campus-wide. Many other cross-campus library partnerships that have been in place for decades also contribute to the continued vitality of the program.

History

Asked about the roots of our Latin American collaborative collection development (LACCD), Duke University Librarian and Vice Provost for Library Affairs, Deborah

Jakubs, who in 1986 was the first full-time Duke Librarian for Latin America and Iberia, remarked, "In the beginning, collecting on Latin America was really fueled by the faculty—at Duke it was John Tate Lanning, J. Fred Rippy and Alan Manchester.[1]" The historical record confirms and amplifies Dr. Jakubs' evaluation.

Leadership for Latin American studies could be seen as early as 1915 and 1916 at the respective annual meetings of the American Historical Association (1915 in San Francisco in tandem with the Panama Pacific Exposition) and the American Congress of Bibliography and History (1916 in Buenos Aires), where pioneering scholars met to acknowledge the need for and establish the governing structure for a history journal focused exclusively on Hispanic America.[2] One of their prime objectives for starting the journal was to have a reliable source for collecting and publishing multiple bibliographies in the field, something they found missing in other journals. Indeed, bibliography was recognized as the foundation of scholarship and of equal importance to published research.

The resulting journal, *The Hispanic American Historical Review* (*HAHR*), was initially supported largely by individual contributions but after 1922 lacked sufficient funds to continue until its editor, James A. Robertson, a former Duke faculty member, suggested to William K. Boyd, the Chair of the Duke History Department that Duke should take it on.[3] In 1926, *HAHR* came to Duke under Robertson' direction with financial subsidy from the University. UNC Professor William Pierson served as Associate Editor. The journal became and remains the leading history journal in the field, making the Triangle area an early focal point for scholarship on Latin America and strengthening the informal collaboration at the faculty level between UNC and Duke. It should be remembered that Duke was only founded in 1924 (though it incorporated Trinity College which was founded in 1859), unlike UNC which was chartered 135 years earlier in 1789. Hence, Latin American studies grew in tandem with the new university as a fundamental part of an emerging institutional identity.

Starting in 1914, a similar process unfolded at UNC where Prof. William Pierson published a *Syllabus of Latin American History*. It circulated nationally, serving as an aid and stimulus to teaching in the field.[4] In 1935, UNC Professor Sturgis Leavitt successfully advocated within the American Council of Learned Societies (ACLS), for creation of the *Handbook of Latin American Studies*, which remains one of the primary bibliographical tools of scholarship in this area. By 1940, UNC had officially established an Inter-American Institute, one of the first in the nation. The two universities were proceeding on parallel paths but had not yet signed binding collaborative documents on Latin America either between academic departments or libraries.

Essentially, when Latin American studies began to flourish at Duke and UNC it was a fledgling discipline in the United States, with faculty located primarily in departments of history, politics and Romance studies. As Duke History Professor J. Fred Rippy succinctly argued in a memorandum to Duke President, William Preston Few in 1928 asking for funds to purchase library materials from Latin America, "Our greatest handicap is lack of books. This is a new field. We have been buying books in other fields for from ten to twenty-five years. We have just begun to buy them in this field."[5] Clearly, attention to the libraries was high on the agenda from the start.

The purchase that Rippy successfully requested was the library of Francisco Pérez de Velasco, a Peruvian bibliophile whose collection consisted of over 3,000 items on Peru, Chile, Spain, Ecuador, Colombia and Bolivia.[6] The sale was arranged on behalf of the owner at that time by Víctor Andrés Belaúnde Diez Canseco, a Peruvian diplomat in exile in the

United States. A decade later Belaúnde and UNC Professor Sturgis Leavitt would organize an exchange with support from UNC President Frank Porter Graham, the Pan American Union and the Institute for International Education to bring hundreds of Latin American students to UNC to study English during summer school in 1941.[7] In 1942 another group of one hundred studied at Duke. The interaction with Belaúnde is but one example of the parallel development of the two programs. Additional purchases of rare books would continue at Duke as would a tradition of north-south exchange at both institutions.

During these early years, preparing bibliographies, sharing syllabi and buying books during field research trips were primarily faculty functions. Housing, processing and circulating the books were the primary library functions. However, as faculty succeeded in establishing the field of Latin American studies and library collections grew in size and complexity, librarians gradually took on bibliographic and acquisitions aspects of collecting. At Duke, cooperation between faculty and librarians was heightened during the 1930s as the Depression reduced faculty positions nationwide and two recent Ph.D.s in Hispanic fields took up careers as library staff.[8]

The collaborative relationships that had characterized faculty publishing could now be seen in formal library agreements reached in the 1930s. Though these were not specific to Latin America, they set the stage for the next decade when Latin American collaborative collecting would begin in earnest. The early stages of collaboration resulted in system wide achievements such as a shared catalog, experiments in joint collecting and conceptualization of the rationale and principles for shared collections. After a series of attempts to collect collaboratively in the basic humanities, social sciences and physical sciences, the two libraries evaluated what had worked and what hadn't. They agreed that the best candidates for collaboration were instances where professors were already working closely with the library and with each other; their scholarship was interdisciplinary and there was formal administrative approval for both ad hoc and systematic cooperation.[9] Latin American studies seemed to be a perfect test case.

In 1940 libraries at UNC, Duke and Tulane Universities received a six year grant from the Rockefeller Foundation for collaborative collection development on Hispanic America.[10] Tulane would eventually leave the partnership giving testament to the crucial role played by proximity in pre-digital collaboration. However, the meta-frame guiding collecting would remain in the UNC/Duke collaboration from 1940 to the present.

Responsibility for collecting would be based on geography with each institution collecting from all countries in support of basic undergraduate education but leaving deep collecting to one or the other institution based on a geographical split. Originally the division called for UNC to be responsible for the Southern Cone and Venezuela while Duke focused on the Andean nations and Brazil, making the two local universities responsible for all of South America while Tulane expanded its prestigious collection on Middle America and the insular Caribbean. Once Tulane left the collaboration, Duke took on Mexico, Central America and the English Speaking Caribbean while UNC added the French and Spanish Speaking Caribbean.

Each library formed a "conference committee" which met monthly. Minutes of each conference were circulated among the three partners. Members of the conference included pertinent librarians and several faculty members representing diverse disciplines. At Duke, conferences were attended by B. Harvie Branscomb, the University Librarian (1939–1941) who saw the alliance as an opportunity to practice his concept of "the professor assisting the librarian in the library and the librarian assisting the professor in the classroom."[11] Branscomb was an early advocate of bibliographic instruction, open stacks and faculty participation in requiring "student shelf browsing"—new best practices for librarians that were just being debated and incorporated in professional repertoires. He saw Latin American studies as a testing ground for these concepts thus further strengthening the faculty/library connection on Latin America and providing support for collaboration at the highest level of the Libraries.

During the 1940s the war years intervened in committee structures as faculty joined the war effort and purchasing patterns were disrupted when shipping was delayed or ended. Oddly, the collections expanded as a result. For example, in 1940 John Tate Lanning wrote to Nelson Rockefeller who was then in Washington serving as the Coordinator of the National Defense Commission of Cultural and Commercial Relations with Latin America.[12] Lanning suggested sending copies of the *HAHR* to every known Latin American intellectual, newspaper and institution of learning "to provide a means of keeping in professional touch with their peers in the United States." Subsequently, 1250 free copies of the journal were sent to Latin American counterparts for many years. Though no exchange was required, many organizations reciprocated thus creating a substantial expansion of the joint collection. Faculty who had been sent to serve in U.S. embassies in Latin American countries during the War spent their off hours perusing book shops coordinated closely with the librarians at home. Ingenuity was maintaining collaboration under difficult conditions.

When the Rockefeller Foundation's support ended in 1946 both universities maintained library budgets and part-time Latin Americanist staff thus allowing collaborative collection development to continue. A systematic review of materials continued into the 1970s when a major project to make newspaper subscriptions available for research use was undertaken. The 1950s to the 1990s were times of incremental building and maintenance. As collections expanded, each institution hired a full time Librarian for Latin America with Berta Becerra, a former Professor of Library Science at the University of Havana coming to UNC in 1960 and Deborah Jakubs named Librarian for Latin America and Iberia at Duke in 1986.[13]

The next big step in increasing solidarity between the two collections came about following the failure of a joint UNC/Duke application for designation as a Title VI, National Resource Center Program of the U.S. Department of Education in 1987. Each university had written its own grant text and the two were loosely edited and jointly submitted. Professor Lars Schoultz, Director of what was then the Institute of Latin American Studies at UNC met with reviewers in Washington to seek feedback on where the application went wrong. It turned out that bigger is not always better and that the application had greatly exceeded the size limit. The staff reviewer did comment that one great strength of the application was the collaborative library work.[14]

Schoultz then threw himself into the pursuit of both a stronger, better-stated alliance and alternative sources of funds. Natalie Hartman, current Associate Director of the Duke program, says that the receipt of $550,000 in1990 from the Mellon Foundation was largely the result of Schoultz's persistence and innovative programming.[15] He had found that the Mellon Foundation was interested in consortial structures as a means to improving higher education and forged a more sincere and substantive partnership with Duke. Among the innovative projects presented in the grant were two related to the libraries: a plan to subsidize international buying trips by the subject librarians and a second project to prepare cross-campus subject guides.[16]

Collaborative collecting received a second boost when the Consortium in Latin American and Caribbean Studies at the University of North Carolina at Chapel Hill and Duke University was created in 1990 and in 1991 was designated as a Title VI Center, a distinction it has maintained since then. Thoughtful planning with the Mellon Foundation and the presidents of each university produced endowments for the two programs which included a small materials budget and travel budgets for the respective librarians.[17] These resources allow for pre-planning for participation in international book fairs and systematic search for ephemeral materials that match the scholarly and programmatic needs of each library and of the consortium.

The five key factors discussed below which have promoted and maintained a successful collaboration include:

- Administrative support
- Multiple reinforcing collaborations
- Proximity
- Parallel cooperation among faculties
- Shared vendors

Administrative Support

Library-level administrative support has been fundamental to the success of the Latin American acquisitions partnership. Fiscal support is core for this agreement and each library has always provided a separate funding stream specifically allocated for Latin American material. There have been occasions that UNC, a public university, has faced budget cuts that have resulted in a reduction of state funding for library acquisitions. In spite of these funding decreases, the commitment to our cooperative agreement has been given high priority and other funding sources have been provided to supplement the reduction. In addition to the necessary fiscal support for materials, the administration at both libraries has given the Latin American librarians the independence to oversee the particulars of the agreement including the autonomy to make all decisions related to the management of the cooperative acquisitions plans. Library administrators have also been generous in providing funding for acquisitions trips and granting professional work release time to engage in international travel and to accept leadership roles in national and regional library groups including the Seminar on the Acquisition of Latin American Library Materials (SALALM), the Center for Research Libraries' consortium, Latin Americanist Research Resources Project (LAARP) and Latin American Studies Southeast Regional Libraries (LASER) consortium, a SALALM affinity group.

Multiple Reinforcing Collaborations

Two inter-campus institutional structures, the Triangle Research Library Network (TRLN) and the Consortium in Latin American and Caribbean Studies at the University of North Carolina and Duke University, have been essential to the longevity and success of our cooperative collecting agreement. These collaborative organizations, the former established in the 1930s and the latter, in the early 1990s, have provided additional institutional support, visibility and, in the case of the Consortium, additional funding. TRLN provides us with structural support including a shared online catalog that, in addition to Duke and UNC, includes North Carolina State University and North Carolina Central University. The unified search capability the TRLN catalog offers is another reinforcement of the unified library concept.

This longstanding cooperative buying agreement for Latin America has served as a model for similar acquisitions agreements between Duke and UNC for other world areas. In most cases, the acquisition responsibility follows the geographic division model while in other cases, a subject-level approach has been established for collection building. An interesting combination of both subject and geographic divisions is the agreement for East Asia. Duke is responsible for Japanese imprints and specialized Western language materials on Japanese studies while UNC takes primary responsibility for titles printed in China, with a special emphasis on history, literature, and religion as well as specialized titles on Chinese studies in Western languages. In addition, Duke takes responsibility for Chinese imprints on contemporary popular culture, the social sciences and art history. With the development of each agreement the librarians involved have had the flexibility to determine the specific division of responsibilities based on the strengths of the library collections and the needs of each institution.

Proximity

Central to the success of the Duke-UNC Latin American cooperative agreement is the advantage of our physical proximity. With a distance of approximately 8 miles between the two universities, the ability to move between campuses has been simplified in recent years with an express bus that runs continually, including weekends, during the academic year. The ease of quickly traveling to our neighboring institution allows students to take advantage of a cross-campus course enrollment program. In an effort to promote inter-action between the universities, all campus community members are encouraged to use this mode of transportation to attend the various programs and events continually being offered including working group meetings and the Consortium's annual film festival. For LACS Consortium members the bus is yet another way that we encourage the concept that we are one unified academic program with the ability to move easily between campuses to browse the library collections and to consult with either librarian for specialized reference assistance.

Intercampus delivery of library materials and correspondence is simplified by the Triangle Research Library Network (TRLN) truck that makes a daily run to the four area libraries. This service facilitates the informal sharing of materials between librarians and also provides library users the guarantee of promptly receiving interlibrary lending and borrowing requests from any of our partner libraries. This is an additional layer of support that brings home the notion of one shared collection.

Parallel Cooperation Between Faculties

The Duke and UNC Latin American and Caribbean Studies programs share a long history of informal cooperation dating back to the early 1900s. Formal academic collab-oration, as previously discussed, was initiated by an unsuccessful grant application in

1987. A successful grant from The Andrew W. Mellon Foundation came soon after to solidify our programs. In 1991 the relationship was again strengthened with a Title VI National Resource Center and Foreign Language and Area Studies award. The formalized partnership and deep collaboration has resulted in a broad range of activities from scholarly lectures to community outreach events. Throughout the years of the collaborative program the libraries and the LACS librarians have been integral partners. An example of the support we receive is annual funding from the Mellon Foundation and the joint Title VI National Resource Center (NRC) grants allocated for library materials and acquisition trips.

The NRC funding supports many intercampus events including an annual conference that brings together faculty and graduate students from both campuses. The LACS librarians have been conference participants in various capacities as presenters, panel organizers and moderators. This meeting and other Consortium programs provide excellent engagement opportunities with faculty, students and community members and oftentimes result in informal library consultations. Attendance at these events is crucial in order to remain current with research trends and interests on both campuses.

The Consortium's annual North Carolina Latin American Film Festival, is held on both campuses and at other venues throughout the Triangle, including local universities, community colleges and community centers. The Consortium's lending library, held at UNC, offers films to the local university community and to the general public as a way of providing outreach. In order to facilitate access and promote broad use of this formidable collection, the UNC Libraries have entered records for these films in the online catalog.

The Consortium's commitment to the instruction of less commonly taught languages began in 1992 with the establishment of the Yucatec Maya Institute. This highly-specialized and unique summer program supports curricular interests at UNC in the departments of Romance Studies, Linguistics and Anthropology and has also served to recruit Maya specialists to join these academic units. This interest has resulted in much library-related activity including a very generous donation of over 13,000 volumes on Maya studies by George E, and Melinda Y. Stuart. The area studies librarian acquires Yucatec Maya language and other supporting hard-to-acquire materials by traveling to the region.

With the establishment in 2010 of the Duke Haiti Lab, an innovative research center focused on Haitian studies, interest in offering language courses in Haitian Creole grew. Elementary and intermediate level courses are now offered through the Romance Studies Department. As in the case of Maya studies at UNC, the Duke Library has supported both the Haiti Lab and the Haitian Creole language program by acquiring retrospective newspapers and other research materials to strengthen the Haitian collection at Duke. In many cases, the digitized content has been uploaded to the Digital Library of the Caribbean (dLOC) and other open access digital collections. In addition, Duke, in partnership with Vanderbilt University and the University of Virginia, provides access to Vanderbilt's elementary and intermediate K'iche' Maya via high quality video conferencing. Duke, in turn, offers its Haitian Creole courses while UVA offers elementary Tibetan.

Portuguese language and history have also been a focus of joint attention. UNC has a long-standing program of Portuguese language and literature which has recently been supplemented at Duke by the hiring of two tenure track faculty who have designed a major in Brazilian and Global Portuguese Studies as well as a Brazil Initiative to develop deeper connections with Brazil through faculty and student research exchanges, university and industry conferences, and by bringing leading Brazilian scholars, public officials and artists to the Triangle. A lab devoted to Global Brazil has also been funded at Duke and provides programming of interest on both campuses.

Duke and UNC faculty take advantage of our LACS-related programming and have developed strong cross-campus relationships that fortify our consortium. The K'iche' Maya course offerings have encouraged UNC faculty to travel to Duke to attend classes. Faculty and students from various disciplines with interests in focused research topics join interdisciplinary Consortium working groups. These working groups conduct discussion sessions, hold seminars and invite distinguished intellectuals in their field. In many instances the group's work concludes with the publication of a scholarly publication. Recently the Latin American Political Imaginaries working group, coordinated by Professor Arturo Escobar (Department of Anthropology, UNC) Professor Walter Mignolo (Literature Program, Duke), Professor Michal Osterweil (Global Studies, UNC) and UNC anthropology graduate students, produced *Tejiendo de otro modo: feminismo, epistemología y apuestas descoloniales en Abya Yala*. The Abya Yala working group culminated in the publication of *Teorizando las literaturas indígenas contemporáneas* (A Contracorriente Press, 2015), edited by UNC Associate Professor of Romance Studies, Emilio del Valle Escalante. Shared scholarly interests across the campuses also result in shared research projects. A recent collaboration has been awarded an American Council of Learned Societies Collaborative Research Fellowship. Professors Orin Starn, (Department of Cultural Anthropology, Duke) and Miguel La Serna, (Department of History, UNC) received this award for a study that will result in a co-authored book on an aspect of twentieth-century Peruvian history.

Shared Vendors

Even though the cooperative agreement's geographic division continues to serve as our underlying framework, we approach these country assignments with flexibility. Haiti and Peru are two current examples of how our local curricular and research interests require us to continually revisit and reassess the state of the current arrangement and require us to work closely to modify our approval plans, when appropriate. Duke's Haiti Lab, inaugurated in 2010, has generated the need for deep collecting at Duke despite the responsibility for Haiti being historically at UNC. In the case of Peru, Duke's primary responsibility, both Duke and UNC have faculty whose primary research and coursework focuses on this Andean country. These are examples where the cooperative agreement has been modified to support the current needs on each campus. In the case of research-level materials from Guatemala, Duke has primary collecting responsibility but UNC has curricular interest in Maya studies. In this case, UNC acquires materials to meet the needs of its scholars while depending on Duke's collection for other subjects.

In an effort to coordinate the selection and acquisition of materials from Mexico, Spain (including Latin American content) and Argentina, we have made the decision to use the services of the same vendors in an effort to avoid duplication while broadening the breadth and depth of our collections. In each case we have worked closely with our *libreros* to understand the mission of our joint effort to maximize our budget allocations while strengthening our holdings. The result of the sharing of vendors has been very positive and has given us excellent coverage for these countries with little duplication.

When asked how this shared collaboration has worked from the vendors' perspectives, we have been told that there are no real issues as long we are available for consultation. Our Mexican vendor's method is particularly inventive. He approaches our two approval plans as one and from this starting point he can adjust the materials using the particular preferences of each campus. The resulting reduction in duplication of Mexican materials reinforces our decision to coordinate our acquisitions at the vendor level.

Continuing Strengths and a Major Challenge

Important traditions continue even as new challenges and opportunities arise. For example, at UNC noted Caribbean historian Louis A. Pérez, Jr., and at Duke Brazilian expert John D. French have continued traditions of bibliography and journal editing with publications such as *Archives of Cuba = Los archives de Cuba* and *Oxford Bibliographies Online; The Cuban Revolution*[18]and *Oxford Bibliographies Online; Neoliberalism.*[19] Faculty and librarians have also continued editorial leadership within leading academic journals. *HAHR* continues under the direction of Duke historians Jocelyn Olcott, Pete Sigal and John D. French while the leading journal in its field, *Cuban Studies (Estudios cubanos)* was published at UNC from 2004 to 2009 with Louis A. Pérez, Jr., as Editor in Chief and Teresa Chapa serving as Bibliography Editor, a collaboration that assured comprehensive collection on Cuba.

The greatest challenge to collaboration presently resides both with the library as a whole and Latin American collections specifically. The general problem is the need for publishers to value collaborative licensing. Here, TRLN has made some progress with English language books through a shared e-book program but much remains to be negotiated in relation to shared electronic journals. In Latin American and Caribbean studies digital publishing is still in a formative stage and the problem is finding reliable products as well as shared terms of use.

At the core of successful collaboration lie flexible commitment and measurable reward. For example, a review of Spanish language books on Mexican subjects demonstrates how collaboration has expanded the titles held. For 2015, of 120 books held at the two institutions only ten are duplicate titles and these are on subjects of curricular interest to both universities. The collaborating librarians are encouraged by these results to maintain and expand joint efforts. In 2015, as UNC celebrated one hundred years of Latin American Studies and the Consortium observed a twenty-fifth anniversary, it was agreed that joint collaboration continues to be worth the effort.

Notes

1. Deborah L. Jakubs, February 9, 2016. Interviewed by Holly Ackerman.

2. Roscoe R. Hill, "Dr. James Alexander Robertson 1873–1939," *The Hispanic American Historical Review* 19 (2). Duke University Press (1939): 127–129. http://www.jstor.org/stable/2507436.

3. Charles E. Chapman, "The Founding of the Review," *The Hispanic American Historical Review*, 1 (1), Duke University Press (1918): 8–23. And, John Tate Lanning, "The Hispanic Collection," Chap in *Gnomon, Essays for the Dedication of the William R. Perkins Library* (Durham, NC: Duke UniversityLibraries, 1970), 80–95.

4. Louis A., Pérez, Jr., and Beatriz Riefkohl Muñiz, *One Hundred Years of Latin American Studies at the University of North Carolina at Chapel Hill, 1915–2015* (Chapel Hill, NC: Institute for the Study of the Americas, 2015).

5. J. Fred. Rippy, "Memorandum to William Preston Few on the Latin-American Collection." James

Fred Rippy Papers, Duke University Archives, David M. Rubenstein Rare Book & Manuscript Library, Duke University, 1928.

6. R.O. Rivera, "The Peruvian Collection of Duke University," *The Hispanic American Historical Review*, 10 (1) Duke University Press (1930): http://www.jstor.org/stable/2506180.

7. Pérez and Riefkohl Muñiz, *One Hundred Years of Latin American Studies.*

8. Lanning, "The Hispanic Collection."

9. Patricia B. Dominguez and Luke Swindler, "Cooperative Collection Development at the Research Triangle University Libraries: A Model for the Nation," *College and Research Libraries* 54 (1993): 470–496.

10. Cooperation in Latin-American Studies Between the University of North Carolina, Tulane University and Duke University. John Tate Lanning Papers, Duke University Archives, David M. Rubenstein Rare Book & Manuscript Library, Duke University, 1939.

11. Cooperation in Latin American Purchases, Duke-UNC-Tulane. Cooperative Programs Files, Collection Development Department, UNC-CH Libraries, 1941. And, B. Harvie Branscomb (1894–1998) in Donald G. Davis, *Dictionary of American Library Biography*, Second supplement, Vol. 3 (1941 [2003]): 37.

12. John Tate Lanning, Carbon copy of letter to Nelson Rockefeller. John Tate Lanning Papers, Duke University Archives, David M. Rubenstein Rare Book & Manuscript Library, Duke University, 1940.

13. Pérez and Riefkohl Muñiz, *One Hundred Years of Latin American Studies.*

14. Lars Schoultz, February 22, 2016. Interviewed by Teresa Chapa.

15. Natalie Hartman, February 23, 2016. Interviewed by Holly Ackerman.

16. Alice Joyce, "It's Full Speed Ahead." *Carolina Alumni Review.* Fall: 50–54.

17. Hartman, interview.

18. Louis A. Pérez, Jr., and Rebecca Scott, *The Archives of Cuba = Los archivos de Cuba* (Pittsburgh: University of Pittsburgh Press, 2003). And, Louis A. Pérez, Jr., "The Cuban Revolution," in *Oxford Bibliographies* in Latin American Studies, http://www.oxfordbibliographies.com.proxy.lib.duke.edu/view/document/obo-9780199766581/obo-9780199766581-0027.xml (accessed 6 March 2016).

19. John D. French and Matthew Lymburner, "Neoliberalism," in *Oxford Bibliographies* in Latin American Studies, http://www.oxfordbibliographies.com.proxy.lib.duke.edu/view/document/obo-9780199766581/obo-9780199766581-0078.xml (accessed 6 March 2016).

Building Shared Latin American and Iberian Research Collections

2CUL as Case Study of an Enduring Collaborative Model

SEAN PATRICK KNOWLTON *and* SÓCRATES SILVA

Introduction

In May of 2012, Cornell University Library (CUL) and Columbia University Libraries (CUL) embarked on an enduring partnership to collaboratively build Latin American and Iberian Studies research collections under the direction of a shared Latin American and Iberian Studies Librarian position based at Columbia University. This transformative collection development model is one of a series of resource-sharing agreements of the 2CUL partnership (pronounced "too cool") that aims to pool "resources to provide content, expertise, and services that are impossible to accomplish acting alone."[1] With the explicit aim of expanding both the depth and breadth of global scholarly resources, initial efforts purposely targeted eliminating unnecessary duplicate acquisition of low-use print materials published in the region, primarily in Spanish and Portuguese, and redirecting resources toward acquiring additional materials, often in new collecting areas. This essay provides the background, rationale, means of collaboration, and an assessment of collection building to date. Furthermore, this essay reports on lessons learned, to include the challenges of liaison work at two institutions and the implications of collecting deeply while addressing local faculty interests.

Background

Research collections share a common mission to enable meaningful scholarship, such as the writing of scholarly monographs, articles, and dissertations, in addition to supporting instruction at the graduate and undergraduate levels. To this end, in most aspects, academic libraries no longer directly compete with each other; to the contrary, they are interconnected and interdependent, it is in their DNA.[2] 2CUL is indicative of the general direction of networked academic libraries in the twenty-first century, whether motivated by efficiencies, budgetary or storage concerns, enhancing quality of research collections, or meeting emerging research needs. These interconnected networks explode traditional concepts of ownership and access and instigate heretofore-untapped areas of collaboration that will benefit all scholars, local and beyond, for generations.

Consider the case of BorrowDirect, the foundation upon which this collaborative model functions. Today, students, staff, and faculty at Columbia and Cornell have on-site borrowing privileges and can initiate interlibrary borrowing requests for monographic materials from some of the most comprehensive research collections in the United States: Brown, Columbia, Cornell, Dartmouth, Duke, Harvard, Johns Hopkins, the Massachusetts Institute of Technology, Princeton, University of Chicago, University of Pennsylvania, and Yale. Materials requested via a common online interface largely arrive within four days and within two days via expedited delivery between Cornell and Columbia. Often, multiple copies in all published editions of monographs, including Latin American and Iberian imprints, are, for all practical purposes, as accessible via BorrowDirect as they are locally. In short, BorrowDirect is efficient, cost-effective, and popular.[3] Additional collaborative efforts beyond BorrowDirect further impact collection building, especially at Columbia University Libraries, and their import will only increase. These notably include the Manhattan Research Library Initiative (Columbia University, New York Public Library, and New York University) and the Research Collections and Preservation Consortium (ReCAP), a multi-institutional, joint-ownership preservation repository (Columbia University, New York Public Library, and Princeton University).

The year 2009 was pivotal in shaping 2CUL in general and, ultimately, this specific 2CUL collaboration. In order to reduce overall spending at the university as a response to the global financial crisis, Cornell University announced a Staff Retirement Incentive[4] that shepherded 432 staff members to early retirement from the institution,[5] including David Block, the Ibero-American Bibliographer, whose position was not replaced. The financial crisis kick started the initial phase of 2CUL, in which "the two libraries joined forces to address budgetary challenges posed by the economic recession and to improve library efficiencies, enhance quality, promote innovation, and meet new and emerging academic needs.[6]

The first 2CUL collaborative collection development effort in global studies led by a shared librarian position began in 2010 and swiftly demonstrated the impact of this approach. Robert H. Davis, Librarian for Russian, Eurasian & East European Studies for 2CUL, reduced duplication rates for newly acquired Russian imprints from 14 percent to 1.6 percent in the first two years of shared collection building while reallocating funds to acquire additional materials, which resulted in a more diverse collection than previously acquired when selected in isolation.[7] To assess this effort, Cornell conducted a survey of Slavic and Eastern European studies faculty, which revealed a high degree of satisfaction with Davis's approach.[8]

Overview of 2CUL Model for Latin America and Iberia

The 2CUL Latin American and Iberian Studies collection development agreement aims to unite the individual strengths of two historically important, yet distinctive research collections under the coordination of one librarian based at Columbia University. The principal focus is to reduce unnecessary acquisition of duplicate print materials and redirect funds toward the acquisition of additional titles, thus building shared collective capacity. 2CUL is conceived as a long-term partnership; Cornell and Columbia are dedicated to building shared global collections for the foreseeable future. Although collection building is conceived collaboratively, all material budgets remain separate and material continues to be acquired distinctly at each institution. Any and all savings identified through 2CUL efforts are reinvested into the collections; 2CUL is about getting more, not less. In the end, 2CUL seeks to make both libraries more resilient and adept in serving immediate instruction and specialized research needs in these vital global areas.[9]

Since the immediate local research and instructional needs of scholars must be met in a convenient and timely manner, both libraries continue to duplicate core materials. Core materials essentially include major print and digital reference works in any language, U.S. and British university press publications, and other major publishers publishing works in English, and established authors and their related criticism.

Overview of Latin American Studies at Cornell and Columbia

Cornell and Columbia entered this collaboration with distinct and historically comprehensive Latin American and Iberian research collections built in support of robust programs at both institutions.

Cornell's Latin American Studies Program (LASP) offers a minor in Latin American Studies for undergraduate and graduate students, a "Foreign Language Across the Curriculum" initiative, and other programming, including hosting visiting scholars. LASP consists of approximately eighty faculty members. Key departments for collection development include: Anthropology, City and Regional Planning, Development Sociology, History, History of Art, International and Comparative Labor Relations, Government, and Romance Studies. Agricultural sciences and nutrition are areas of distinct interest at Cornell.

The Institute of Latin American Studies (ILAS) at Columbia University is the center for research, teaching, and discussion on the region and supports a Center for Brazilian Studies, has a special focus on Mexican studies, and is a National Resource Center, together with New York University. It hosts visiting scholars and organizes programming related to the region. ILAS offers an interdisciplinary MA program in Regional Studies—Latin America and the Caribbean (MARSLAC), an undergraduate major in Latin American and Caribbean Studies, and a graduate Certificate in Latin American Studies. Approximately ninety faculty members are affiliated with Latin American studies at Columbia. Key departments for collection development in the region include: the Department of Art History and Archaeology, the Graduate School of Architecture, Department of History, the Department of Latin American and Iberian Cultures, the Department of Political Science, the School of International and Public Affairs, and Spanish and Latin American Cultures (at Barnard College).

Based on a review of faculty interests as expressed via profiles on the Cornell and Columbia websites, the following countries represent the highest level of interest across campuses, in order of rank: Mexico, Brazil, the Caribbean in general, Argentina, Peru, Venezuela, the Dominican Republic, Chile, and Spain.

Overview of Research Collections

The historically comprehensive research collections held at Cornell and Columbia complement each other in several areas. Columbia has invested deeply in the Spanish-speaking Caribbean, Central America, the Southern Cone, and Spain. At the same time, Cornell has historical and current strengths in the Andes, principally Peru and Bolivia, two nationally recognized research collections. Both research collections are heavily invested in Brazil and Mexico in the humanities but especially so in the social sciences. Subject contrasts emerge from Columbia's intensive investments in architecture and fine arts while Cornell has a notable dedication to labor issues. Complementary subject strengths include economic development, history, languages and literature, political science, sociology, and anthropology.

Materials are acquired in English, Spanish, and Portuguese, and in other European and indigenous Latin American languages. Spanish-language monographs dominate the titles published in the region, followed by Portuguese. Catalan is a very distant third that begins the long tail distribution that includes Galician, Mayan languages, Basque, and Quechua, with additional languages held only in the single digits.

Collection Analysis Methodology

To prepare for shared collection building, monographic holdings at both institutions were analyzed to afford a clear understanding of recent collecting patterns. Rich Entlich, Collection Analyst at Cornell University Library, conducted a test-case analysis of all relevant call number ranges for Colombian imprints. This in-depth analysis yielded data with a significant specificity of detail. However, to scale this method for all twenty-three countries would have required dedication of time and labor beyond that available for the analyst. Learning from this initial approach, the 2CUL librarian then utilized the expert search features of the *WorldCat* database via the *FirstSearch* interface to mine data that identified and compared country-specific imprints held at Cornell and Columbia with an eye for overlap/duplication versus uniqueness within the collections. This librarian-initiated method provides big-picture numbers useful for high-level decision-making specifically geared toward reviewing approval plans with library vendors. Using *World-Cat*-cataloged records presents some obvious methodological challenges: newly acquired titles often are present only in local pre-cataloging queues and imprints published in many Latin American countries for a given year may not arrive in library collections until many months into the following year.

The statistics and charts that follow reveal library holdings at each institution of monographic imprints published in the region itself, not those about the region published elsewhere, including in the United States. This is an important distinction as 2CUL collaborative efforts, above all, aim to refocus shared collecting patterns of materials acquired from the region via library vendors based in Latin America, Spain, and Portugal. Titles held by Columbia (*but not by Cornell*) are in Columbia blue, titles held by Cornell (*but not by Columbia*) are in carnelian, and the sections in green are titles held in common (each institution holds a copy of the same edition of a publication).

Graph 1 reveals that, in the case of 2000–2011 Mexican imprints, Columbia holds approximately 7,600 titles not held at Cornell while Cornell holds 2,300 titles not held

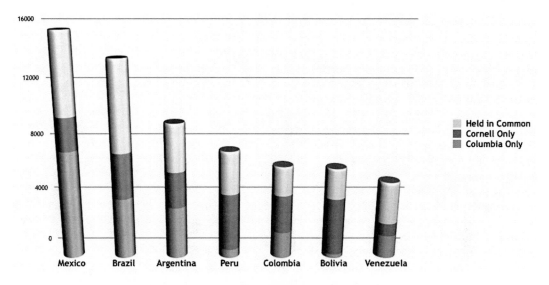

Graph 1: Most-Collected Countries (2000–2011)

at Columbia. Together, Columbia and Cornell hold in common (or duplicate) an additional 5,600 titles. These duplicated titles encompass 36 percent of the grand total of the 15,500 titles acquired from Mexico in just over one decade. The graph also clearly illustrates intensive collecting efforts of Mexican, Brazilian, and Argentine imprints at both institutions during the period of study. On average, 39 percent of imprints from the seven most-collected countries are duplicated at both institutions.

As evidenced by Graph 2, Cornell's historical and ongoing dedication to collecting Peruvian and Bolivian imprints stands in sharp contrast to Columbia's efforts, which are considerably more limited. As previously mentioned, Cornell's holdings in Peru and Bolivia are recognized as nationally significant collections. Despite two very distinct

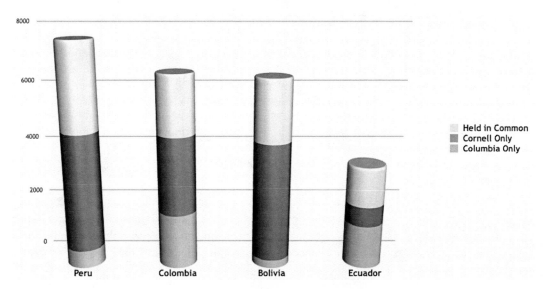

Graph 2: The Andes (2000–2011)

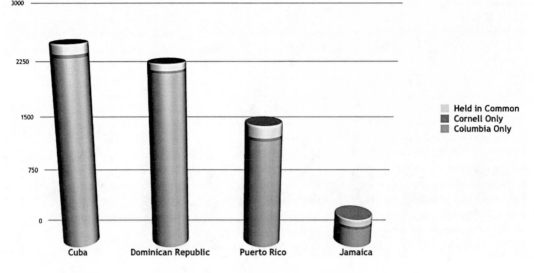

Graph 3: The Caribbean (2000–2011)

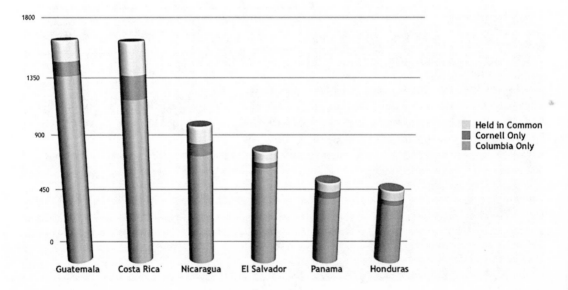

Graph 4: Central America (2000–2011)

collecting patterns, the analysis reveals a shared collection overlap of 36 percent on average for these countries.

Columbia's dedicated efforts to build both Caribbean and Central American research collections is unmistakable, as evidenced above (Graphs 3 and 4), more so in contrast to Cornell's collection, which does not share this collection goal. Accordingly, the collection overlap is similarly minute and likely consists of materials that fit the category of core materials.

The collection analysis further revealed a balanced approach to collecting materials from the three most collected Southern Cone countries. In the case of each country, the

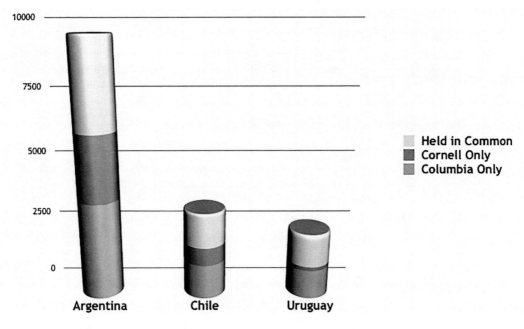

Graph 5: Southern Cone (2000–2011)

percentage of titles held in common (duplicates) is significant: Argentina (35 percent), Chile (40 percent) and Uruguay (50 percent).

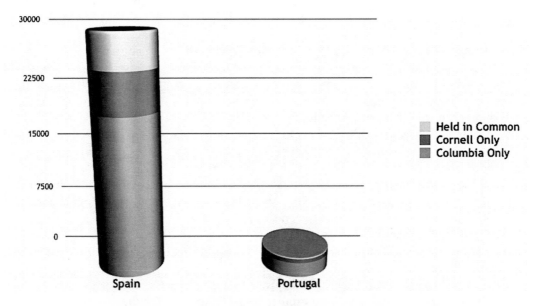

Graph 6: The Iberian Peninsula (2000–2011)

Of particular note, Graph 6 illustrates the combined holdings of Spanish imprints at Cornell and Columbia totals nearly 30,000 publications. These materials vastly outstrip those from Portugal and nearly double those from the next most collected country within

2CUL, Mexico. In fact, Spanish imprints more than double the research holdings of Brazilian imprints for this decade. It is noteworthy to point out that many of these Iberian imprints are, in fact, on Latin American and Caribbean topics and that many Latin American and Caribbean authors publish in Spain and Portugal. To date, addressing the collecting patterns and harmonizing vendors for Spain remain a pending task and a future goal.

Titles Held in Common/Duplicate Holdings

The collection analysis of 2000–2011 titles reveals that, on average, the combined Latin American and Iberian research collections of Cornell and Columbia include a 25 percent duplication rate. The seven countries with the highest level of duplication average a 43 percent duplication rate. For the second-most-collected Latin American country within 2CUL, Brazil, a full 46 percent of imprints are held in common, representing over $20,000 in annual expenditures dedicated to acquiring duplicate titles for a single country. The countries with the highest percentage of duplication within 2CUL for the period of study are Venezuela (54 percent), Uruguay (50 percent), Brazil (46 percent), Chile (40 percent), and Mexico (36 percent).

Library Vendors

Columbia and Cornell actively collect library materials published in twenty-one Latin American and Caribbean countries, including Puerto Rico, as well as Spain and Portugal. While the librarian selects many titles annually via firm orders, the vast majority of titles are acquired via profiled approval plans with established library vendors. Columbia and Cornell work closely with approximately fifteen vendors based in the regions of collecting with which we had active approvals for monographic materials. The working relationships with many of these vendors can be counted in decades; accordingly, some vendors can rightly claim a paramount role in building these research collections.

The exigencies of building collaborative collections, however, necessitated a complete analysis and reevaluation of existing approval plans with the goal of refocusing and harmonizing vendors within a shared vision. In keeping with 2CUL's goal of improving efficiencies, vendor relationships were assessed by their track record in budgeting, shipping, facility in communicating and selecting materials, and their ability to provide MARC records moving forward. The 2CUL Librarian communicated his intentions to all vendors of Latin American and Caribbean materials, meeting with them where possible, as well as consulting with acquisitions staff at both institutions to solicit their input. New approval plan profiles were created at both institutions with the input of our vendors, who suggested better approaches and adjusted their workflows to meet the new requirements. Overall, the new collection profiles respect and continue the historical patterns of collecting by carefully delineating areas of common interest and areas of local specialization. A consistent goal of reducing duplication within each country to a target of 10 percent was established. In practice, however, this target goal has proven to be the opening salvo for an ongoing conversation as vendor workflows, material availability, and in-country conditions all result in unique, country-by-country, approaches to meeting 2CUL goals. Common interests of collecting at both institutions are difficult for some vendors to parse out; further direction might be needed.

Collection Analysis (2012–2015)

A collection analysis of the first three years (2012–2015) of 2CUL collaborative collection development activity reveals a meaningful shift in collection overlap that illustrates the profound and positive impact of a collaborative approach to building research collections.

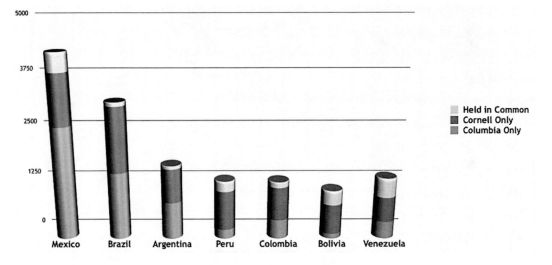

Graph 7: Most-Collected Countries (2012–2015)

Of the seven most-collected countries of publication (Graph 7), Brazilian imprints saw the most dramatic decline in duplicate titles, from 46 percent to 3 percent. True to the goal of 2CUL, all savings realized were, instead, reinvested into building a deeper and more diverse Brazilian research collection. Overlapping Mexican imprints saw a 25 percent reduction, from 36 percent to 11 percent of titles acquired. The 2CUL collaborative approach, in short, reduced overall duplication of materials from the seven most-collected countries by an average of 24 percent. From these countries, only 1775 titles (12 percent) published in 2012–2015 and cataloged to date, appear in the local holdings of both Columbia and Cornell. Again, true to the intentions of 2CUL, the entirety of the budget allocations for these countries remained in place since 2CUL is about getting more, not less.

Holdings of Andean publications saw a fifty percent reduction in overlapping titles (from 36 percent prior to 2CUL to 18 percent).

The balanced collecting approach to the three most-collected Southern Cone countries carried forward into the 2CUL collaboration. However, the collection became more diverse overall with a significant reduction in overlap (from 52 percent to 14 percent, a reduction of 38 percent).

A review of the first three years of dedicated effort within the 2CUL collaborative collection development agreement reveals a distinct overlap landscape. True, the seven

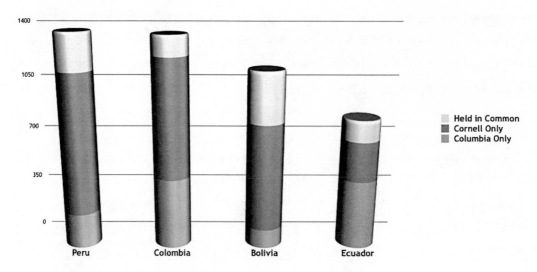

Graph 8: The Andes (2012–2015)

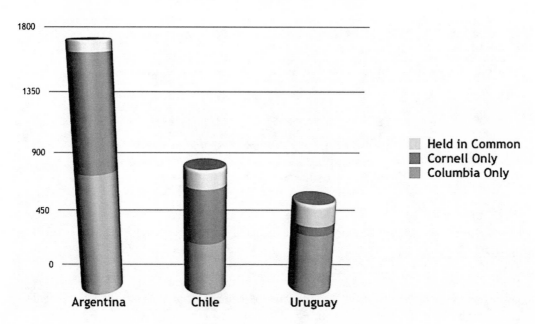

Graph 9: The Southern Cone (2012–2015)

countries with the highest percentage of overlap (Graph 10) remain essentially intact except for Bolivia replacing Brazil. However, the percentage of overlap reduction from the 2000–2011 analysis speaks volumes about the effects of 2CUL and the hard work of our library vendors: Uruguay (27 percent reduction), Chile and Mexico (25 percent reduction), Ecuador and Venezuela (23 percent reduction), and Peru (22 percent reduction), as well as Bolivia trailing at a 4 percent reduction.

The reallocation of resources at the heart of 2CUL has led the way to more diverse collections. New approval plans include Catalan monographs (Spain), graphic novels (Latin America, Spain and Portugal), Portuguese monographs (Portugal), and the non–

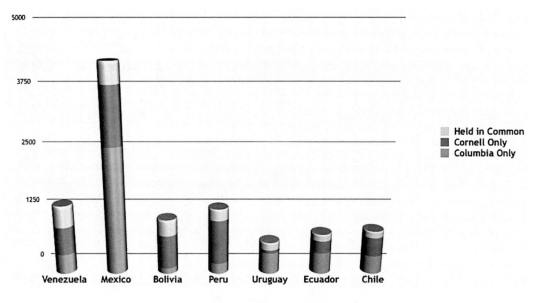

Graph 10: Countries with the Most Overlap (2012–2015)

Hispanic Caribbean. The latter approval plan has significantly expanded the collection of Haitian imprints, up from 88 titles published between 2000 and 2011 to over a hundred additional titles published between 2012 and 2015. In addition, Cornell and Columbia participate in the Collaborative Collection Development Agreement for Brazil within BorrowDirect institutions with these realized savings, further increasing the bibliodiversity of research collections.

Outreach and Research Services

While the focus of this essay is on collection development, we are aware that this particular and unique position raises questions about other responsibilities typical of subject librarians in academic research libraries. In addition, collection development does not exist in a vacuum. Librarians make decisions about collection development through information gleaned from liaison work, reference consultations and instruction, and other proxies that account for scholarly interest. We would like to address efforts and limitations encountered in the 2CUL model as they relate to work outside of ingesting collections and think through what these efforts and limitations in the model could imply.

As mentioned previously, the 2CUL Librarian is located at Columbia and visits Cornell a couple of times a year. These visits are funded for one to two days per semester. Liaison efforts to the Cornell community during the period under discussion consisted of a newsletter to faculty called *Apuntes,* which outlined collection development efforts, a presentation to the faculty of the Latin American Studies Program (LASP), and individual visits with faculty and graduate students. These visits can be challenging to schedule as they necessarily fall within a short period of time. Approaches to scheduling these meetings have ranged from invitations via the LASP listserv to individual emails sent out to targeted faculty. As with any building of faculty liaison programs, these relationships take time to establish and the approaches have had various degrees of success. In addition to the outreach efforts to faculty and students, it has been equally as important to spend time during visits establishing contacts with colleagues at Cornell, librarians and staff, who are working with interrelated scholarly communities. These are colleagues who work with patrons on an everyday basis. While these collegial relationships might be taken as a matter of course when working side-by-side, they become absolutely essential in this long-distance model as these colleagues are a source of referrals and a bridge to the local community.

Local Cornell librarians address library instruction and the majority of the reference interactions adeptly with an understanding that they can refer more complex Latin American and Iberian-related questions (typically those relating to primary sources, statistics, and data) to the 2CUL Librarian. In turn, the 2CUL Librarian addresses these via email, telephone, Skype, or during the campus visit. In addition, the 2CUL Librarian maintains research guides, a Cornell email account, and a directory presence on the Cornell Library website.

We do not have measurable benchmarks accounting for the absence of a physically present librarian at Cornell's Olin and Uris Libraries' Research and Learning Services department during these years. While we know that local expertise is valuable, we assume that the distributed reference model mitigates this need. We can speculate that "pounding the pavement" and "being embedded" can have an impact on the uptick of reference and instruction requests, that in-person presence in a department can be helpful in assisting with student success and making connections between faculty and the suite of services offered at libraries, and that conversely email marketing is a less effective way to reach people, but we cannot measure this the same way we can measure collection duplication reduction—not least because outlining realistic liaison expectations and measuring impact has been a vague process at research libraries to begin with.[10] Community conversations about these roles are taking place at both institutions and the implications of these conversations for the 2CUL model will hopefully be clearer in the near future.

It is useful to point out that in some areas the 2CUL collection development approach redistributes priorities to inter-institutional commitments, national strengths and subject representation away from an individualized local approach to collecting for current faculty and graduate student needs. This was not principally the scale upon which these collections were built in the first place. That being said, faculty and graduate student requests for materials that duplicate 2CUL content are small and do not significantly skew duplication percentages upward. Requested items are ordered as a matter of good relations and in acknowledgment that these requests fulfill a local need. Duplication of core materials and the BorrowDirect network serves as a safety net for local research needs.

Concerns

It might be helpful to outline some concerns about the 2CUL model with regard to support that would help fulfill institutional missions of discovery and preservation. Curatorial projects such as exhibits and digitization of archival sources that require long-term project management and careful institutional navigation become a bigger challenge when one is not on-site. While these projects have been traditionally marshalled by special collections librarians and archivists, global area studies expertise can be instrumental in surfacing and interpreting unique materials to a broader audience. These curatorial efforts would also fall in line with the increasingly horizontal distribution of this work in research libraries. Cornell's historical and current strength in the Andes merits continuous cross-institutional commitment that implies time investment to carry out these kinds of projects.

In general, the Latin American and Iberian publishing markets have yet not embraced e-books to the same degree as U.S. and European publishers. Nonetheless, current significant investment in this collaborative collection development project is premised on the dominance of print materials and patrons' ability to borrow print materials across institutions. The advent of an e-book dominant marketplace will require 2CUL to reevaluate collecting assumptions, where the status quo of leasing electronic content presents a different set of questions about stewardship and the contractual limitations of borrowing. This model opens opportunities for shared licensing negotiations—an aspect of 2CUL that this essay has not touched upon is the joint purchase of electronic resources—but it also raises larger unresolved questions about long term preservation of the historical record in e-book leasing models that favor access for the current user at the potential detriment of future scholars. The Manhattan Research Library Initiative (MARLI), a partnership between Columbia University, New York University and New York Public Library is partly addressing this question with initiatives that complement licensing of e-book packages with one of the partners collecting the corresponding print and being the repository of record.

Space planning is an ongoing issue for most research libraries. Finite space at the Research Collections and Preservation Consortium (ReCAP), a multi-institutional, joint-ownership preservation repository (Columbia University, New York Public Library, and Princeton University) brings forth questions about further collaborative collection development efforts that might reduce duplication of low use material. These questions have not been cemented into specific efforts, as of yet. It is also not clear how these potential efforts might affect the 2CUL arrangements. Global studies collections are in part bordering levels of uniqueness in the network that mirror special collections holdings, and these specific partners might be part of the handful of libraries that could be collecting some content.

Conclusion

It is still quite early in this collaboration to truly assess the long-term impact of the 2CUL collection development model for Latin American and Iberian studies (LAIS). In short, Cornell and Columbia Libraries both continue to collect deeply true to their historical patterns; however, the shared approach has dramatically increased the diversity of materials acquired for the collections. This collaborative approach collects global studies content at a scale that is increasingly rare at research libraries. The collection serves not only the institutional audience at both universities, but an external network with material with subject and country content that is frequently held only held at a few libraries. 2CUL has sought to increase the diversity of LAIS content for its users and maintain its position of leadership in collecting global studies material.

NOTES

1. "About 2CUL | 2CUL." 2016. https://www.2cul.org/node/17.

2. J.G. Neal, "Advancing from Kumbaya to Radical Collaboration: Redefining the Future Research Library," *Journal of Library Administration* Vol. 51, No. 1 (2010): 66.

3. D.A. Nitecki and P. Renfro, "Borrow Direct: A Case Study of Patron-Initiated Interlibrary Borrowing Service," *The Journal of Academic Librarianship* Vol. 30, No. 2 (2004).; D.A. Nitecki, C. Jones and J. Barnett, "Borrow Direct: A Decade of a Sustained Quality Book-Lending Service," *Interlending & Document Supply* Vol. 37, No 4 (2009): 192–198.

4. M. Opperman, "Cornell Announces Retirement Incentives for Long-Service Staff," February 27, 2009, https://statements.cornell.edu/2009/20090227-retirement-incentives.cfm (accessed 16 July 2018).

5. S. Kelley, "Opperman Salutes 432 New Retirees," *Cornell Chronicle*, April 16, 2009.

6. "About 2CUL | 2CUL." 2016. https://www.2cul.org/node/17.

7. R.H. Davis, "The Theory into Practice: 2CUL and the Implementation of Meaningful Collaborative Collection Development," 9th Columbia University Libraries Symposium, New York, March 16, 2012.

8. G. Glazer, "Survey: Resource-Sharing 'Opens up the Doors' for Cornell and Columbia Library Users," *Cornell Chronicle*, December 2, 2011.

9. Columbia University Libraries, 2012. "Columbia and Cornell University Libraries Announce Latin American and Iberian Studies Collection Development Agreement," May 2, 2012, https://www.library.cornell.edu/about/news/press-releases/2cul-announces-latin-american-and-iberian-studies-agreement (accessed 16 July 2018).

10. B. Rockenbach, J. Ruttenberg, K. Tancheva and R. Vine, "Association of Research Libraries/Columbia University/Cornell University/University of Toronto Pilot Library Liaison Institute," June 2015, http://www.arl.org/storage/documents/publications/library-liaison-institute-final-report-dec2015.pdf (accessed 16 July 2018).

Collaborative Collection Development the Brazilian Way

The Brazil BorrowDirect Program

JANA LEE KRENTZ

Latin American library collections have had a long and successful history of cooperation for over fifty years. Cooperative programs focusing on Latin America, many of which are described in this book, have prospered and thrived, and encompass the fields of preservation, cataloging and collection development. Their influence and effectiveness can be demonstrated by the fact that they have become models for other area studies collaborative programs. Collaborative or distributed resources projects emerged as a solution to expanding publishing and rising costs of Latin American materials, and the desire to offer our researchers access to as many resources from Latin America as possible.

Collaborative collection development programs among Latin American collections have emerged on the international, national, regional and local levels. The Latin American Research Resources Project (LARRP) is a consortium of Latin American library collections founded in 1995, who among other things, have agreed to collect "noncore" materials for specifically chosen countries, regions or subjects. LARRP is the gold standard among Latin American collaborative collection development programs. It emerged as a national program but quickly expanded to include partners in Latin America and the Caribbean. The Seminar on the Acquisition of Latin American Library Materials (SALALM), an organization of librarians and booksellers with a focus on Latin America, has been fertile ground for nascent collaborative efforts. Regional consortia sprung up within SALALM that also promote cooperative projects and distributed resource programs. For example, the California Cooperative Latin American Collection Development Group (CALAFIA) and the Midwest Organization of Libraries for Latin American Studies (MOLLAS) both undertook initiatives to cooperatively collect Mexican imprints. Locally, institutions with strong Latin American collections who had close proximity to one another, have embarked on collaborative collection development strategies, such as those at Duke and the University of North Carolina, Yale and Harvard, Columbia and Cornell, and the University of California, Berkeley and Stanford. The success of such programs has emboldened Latin Americanist librarians to establish similar programs, and imbued individuals with the confidence needed to uncover possibilities, experiment and create.

Process

Building on the success of these initiatives, a discussion was held at the Latin American North East Libraries Consortium (LANE) meeting that took place at SALALM in 2012, proposing the development of a collaborative collection development agreement for the coverage of Brazil. Initiated by Fernando Acosta-Rodríguez, Librarian for Latin American Studies at Princeton, the conversation centered on the need to provide a deeper coverage of Brazilian materials for our constituents. It was decided that LANE was too large and diverse a group for such an agreement. BorrowDirect, a library resource sharing partnership of twelve academic institutions within the Ivy Plus consortium, already had an infrastructure in place, and seemed the ideal platform for such an agreement. It was also felt that BorrowDirect participants represented those institutions within LANE who possessed strong Brazilian components within their curriculum. In addition, the members of LANE who were interested in crafting an agreement were all from institutions who counted themselves as a member of BorrowDirect and the Ivy Plus Library Group.

There was a considerable delay between the initial discussion at LANE and the creation of the agreement. This was due, in part, to the fact that several key Latin American librarian positions within BorrowDirect institutions were vacant. Immediately after those positions were filled, e-mails were exchanged discussing various facets of the agreement, and possible meeting dates. It was determined that a meeting to draft an agreement should be placed outside of the national SALALM meeting to allow for the time needed for careful deliberations.

To prepare for the meeting, Brazilian publishing data by region was collected from booksellers specializing in Brazil. Sean Knowlton, who was then the Latin American and Iberian Studies Librarian at Columbia University, and Fernando Acosta-Rodríguez and his staff at Princeton gathered together statistics and data on the book trade in Brazil, and prepared detailed spreadsheets that summarized the Brazilian monographic holdings among BorrowDirect institutions and other key institutions from 2008 to 2012. The data was broken down by year and by region in Brazil. The *WorldCat* database, a global catalog of library collections, was used to compile the data, and the "Valladares search-strings" were employed as a model.[1] (The "Valladares search-strings" are search criteria developed by Miguel Valladares in his 2009 WorldCat analysis and comparison of LANE Latin American library collections.) *WorldCat* duplication rates among BorrowDirect libraries were analyzed to create a baseline. Although *WorldCat* data is imperfect, the analysis performed by Acosta-Rodríguez and Knowlton gave participants a reasonably good understanding of the strengths and weaknesses of the BorrowDirect collections, and allowed for comparisons to broader publishing output figures. Another factor that figured into preparations were the meetings, agendas and discussions of the BorrowDirect library directors and university librarians. These were important in order to judge the timing of the submission of the agreement, and negotiate the climate in which it would be received.

A gathering took place on April 15, 2014, at Columbia University attended by eight librarians: Fernando Acosta-Rodríguez (Princeton), Sean Knowlton (Columbia/Cornell), Patricia Figueroa (Brown), Lynn Shirey (Harvard), Jana Krentz (Yale), Nancy Spiegel (University of Chicago), Joe Holub (University of Pennsylvania), and Jill Baron (Dartmouth). Several salient points were examined during the day: the division of Brazil between institutions, duplication of monographs from the large Brazilian publishing centers, cataloging, the role of vendors, budget constraints, project evaluation and assessment, and collecting scope and exclusions. Libraries proceeded to designate and divide Brazil by states, claiming one or more states or regions according to their budget. An agreement was drafted and subsequently modified via e-mail and in Google Docs. It was based on the model of a Memorandum of Understanding (MoU) crafted by the Ivy Art and Architecture Group (IVAAG) in 2013 that focuses on collecting global contemporary art. By the end of 2014, the MoU for collecting Brazilian monographs was completed. Since the 2014 meeting, Duke University has joined BorrowDirect and has entered into the Brazil agreement. Behind the scenes, individual librarians consulted with their cataloging and technical services directors as well as collection development officers. Some were required to submit proposals for the MoU committees within their institutions for approval. The MoU was discussed extensively at a series of separate meetings of collection development officers and library directors at the Ivy Plus meetings and BorrowDirect meetings. The final step was to obtain the signatures of respective university librarians or library directors in order for the MoU to take effect. This was completed in December of 2014, and the agreement went into effect with 2015 imprints. The initial agreement is for a time period of three to five years.

It should be noted that in 2015 the Ivy Plus Libraries Group created a new position for Director of Collections Initiatives. The Director coordinates program planning and project management for precisely this type of program. In the future, at least within the BorrowDirect and Ivy Plus communities, the process of developing a similar agreement should be much facilitated. The current Director has taken an interest in the Brazil agreement, and is currently considering making the program part of an Ivy Plus beta initiative on assessment of collaborative collection development programs.

Why Brazil?

Latin American librarians began to see a growing interest in Brazilian studies nationwide, and a need on campuses for Brazilian materials from all regions, not just from the large publishing centers of Rio de Janeiro and São Paulo. Increased publishing in Brazil, the high price of Brazilian books, high shipping fees, and flat materials budgets have reduced libraries' ability to supply faculty and students adequately with research materials.

Brazil is the world's fifth largest country in terms of population, and is the largest country in Latin America in terms of population and geographic areas.[2] It is officially divided into five macro-regions consisting of three or more states: North, Northeast, Center-West, Southeast and South. The macro-regions have been created according to physical, political, social, ethnic, and economic similarities which vary widely from each other. The Brazilian publishing market is ranked ninth in the most recent International Publishers Association Global Publishing Statistics.[3] This increased output of publishing, together with the factors listed above, make it impossible for any one institution to comprehensively collect relevant scholarly monographs from Brazil. From the MoU:

> A recent assessment by a major vendor of Brazilian materials to U.S. academic libraries reveals that they annually process approximately 3,600 academic titles (equivalent to a $133,000 annual materials budget). The vendor further estimates that a truly comprehensive collecting focus for Brazil could arrive at 5,000 titles at a cost of $150,000 annually. Barring a fundamental shift in materials budget

allocations at the local level, academic libraries will have to collaborate to provide researchers deeper and more diverse access to Brazilian monographs. By comparison, Harvard, the Borrow Direct member with the largest Brazilian collection by a wide margin, acquires only about half of that amount, according to figures obtained from Worldcat. Barring an unlikely fundamental increase in materials budget allocations at the local level, academic libraries will have to collaborate to provide present and future researchers deeper and more diverse access to Brazilian monographs.[4]

Most libraries buy core materials which originate in and around Rio de Janeiro and São Paulo. Yet, faculty and students focus their research on other parts of Brazil and require monographs published in those regions. Anecdotally, faculty and students tell librarians that they often purchase their own materials from these regions while undertaking field research. The goals of the Brazil BorrowDirect agreement are to respond to this need, to increased bibliographic diversity and comprehensiveness for Brazil, and to provide access to a Library of Congress-level collection. There is also the likelihood that the Library of Congress may someday cease collecting foreign imprints, in which case, we risk having no copies of Brazilian scholarly monographs available to researchers in the U.S. As an additional goal, the institutions involved in the BorrowDirect agreement wish to reduce duplication within the northeastern collections.

The Agreement and Scope of the Collaboration

In order to realize these goals, the BorrowDirect participants resolved to redistribute the coverage of Brazilian monographs along regional lines. Participants were encouraged to identify a specific region or state collecting focus that would complement existing local collection and research strengths much as the LARRP Distributed Resources Program model, and was grounded in their individual budget capacities. Some institutions claimed a whole region, others took responsibility for one or more states (see Appendix 1). This would allow for significantly better coverage outside of the megacities of São Paulo and Rio de Janeiro as well as increase the coverage of small presses and publishers originating in these regions. It would effectively create one mega-collection of Brazilian materials within the northeastern region of the U.S. Member institutions would continue to collect materials from São Paulo and Rio de Janeiro as driven by local research needs. Participants agreed to "collect all relevant newly published monographs in selected subject areas from dedicated regions of Brazil," replace lost or stolen titles, and to attempt to acquire retrospective materials if available and if funds allow.[5] Participating libraries affirmed a long-term commitment to collect and maintain an in-depth research-level collection. This includes the obligation for preservation, sufficient acquisitions funds, and personnel such as selectors with language and subject expertise, and ordering and cataloging support.

The librarians who met in April 2014 spent much time deliberating spreadsheets and tables to determine the subject range of materials to be collected. Law, medicine and some areas of the fine arts were excluded. This was due to the fact that most of the participating libraries have separate libraries and separate selectors for these disciplines. In addition, some Latin Americanist librarians may have to collaborate with librarians at their institutions who are responsible for music and other areas of art in order to make materials selections. Materials that do not circulate such as *literatura de cordel* are excluded from the agreement as are textbooks and devotional texts. Coverage includes a wide range of subjects: history, politics and government, social sciences, humanities, economics, literature and language, music and performing arts, popular culture, religion, philosophy, psychology, education, communication and media, and general reference works (see Appendix 2). The MoU covers published monographic imprints in print format. However, participating libraries may collect non-print materials such as physical media, and web-based and other born-digital resources when possible and reasonable. A limit of $100 was placed on each item, although occasionally an item may exceed that limit in which case the vendor will send a slip notifying the librarian. The idea of limiting by dollar amount guarantees that the collaborative collection development agreement focuses on current, non-special collections materials.

Latin Americanist librarians have a very special relationship with their vendors in Latin America. The Latin American business model, unlike the U.S. or European models, is very much based on personal respect and social relationships, which evolve into a close-knit relationship or sense of extended family. Most of the principal bookdealers situated within Latin America are also members of SALALM, a fact that brings both librarians and vendors into even closer social proximity. With personal relationships in the balance, many librarians endeavor to work with all vendors, even those competing for the same country. In the case of Brazil, there are three Latin American vendors who provide materials to U.S. libraries. Although one of these vendors provided the statistics and data upon which the initial project assessment was made, it was essential that the agreement not favor one vendor over another. All participants concurred that this is fundamental in maintaining a climate of healthy competition among vendors in order to meet the goal of having a broader/deeper collection on Brazil. The vendors' role in the agreement is pivotal in ferreting out materials outside of the big publishing centers. The bookdealers had many questions, and there were some concerns especially that a Brazilian collaborative collection development program might cause a reduction in orders for monographs and approval plans. In fact, the opposite is true with many participating libraries increasing the number of Brazilian books that they purchase for the collections. After clarification and reassurances, the vendors have done much to contribute to the success of the collaborative program by supplying hard-to-find Brazilian books to participating libraries. Partnership with bookdealers is vital. The Brazilian cooperative collection development agreement could not have launched without the initial data provided to us by vendors. Success of the program cannot be achieved without their support.

Shared Responsibility

The BorrowDirect institutions who signed the MoU, agree that the materials that each library collaboratively collects are for the benefit of the full group. The benefits include those stated above: to reduce lacunae and redundancy, and to create "a shared collection of great diversity, depth, and comprehensiveness that could not be created singly by any of the member institutions.[6] Therefore, the agreement was grounded in a number of fundamentals. Participants agree to inform each other of any changes or amendments to the scope of their commitment. Reasonable efforts must be made to "ensure timely acquisition, bibliographic access, and other processing."[7] They also agree to make reasonable efforts to retain works which fall within their area of responsibility, and ensure long-term preservation of these materials. (The Ivy Plus Collection Development

Group is currently working on a revision of the MoU template that will include language about retention). Materials collected under this agreement must be available to BorrowDirect patrons on a priority basis through interlibrary loan, document delivery or on-site consultation, depending on the participating libraries' circulation and lending policies.

Terms

Finally, the MoU is subject to review by collection officers of the participating institutions every three years, and lasts indefinitely unless ended by the majority of institutions. The Latin Americanist librarians involved will review performance of the agreement and report back to the heads of collections on an annual basis. They meet regularly at both SALALM and LANE meetings, and communicate via e-mail to review the agreement, and to identify and act on any issues that arise. Lengthy meetings can be called outside of SALALM and LANE, if required. Any modifications must be communicated to the collection development officers of the BorrowDirect group, and the MoU may be modified by them. A thirty-day notice is required for member libraries who wish to terminate the agreement, and the agreement will be terminated if the number of active participants falls to fewer than five.

Assessment and Tracking

The matter of assessment was discussed but a methodology was not formally decided upon, although the librarians who crafted the MoU felt that project evaluation was essential for the success of the agreement. The matter is still pending. Recently, as stated above, the Director of Collection Initiatives has taken an active interest in assessing the program and is considering using it as a beta program for evaluating collaborative collection development agreements within the Ivy Plus Libraries Group.

The question of how the data necessary for a reasonably good evaluation will be gathered remains unanswered. Discussion has revolved around the use of the "Valladares search strings" to assess the uniqueness or redundancy of items that are acquired through the agreement despite the flawed data. It was decided that, at least initially, each librarian would submit a report that would include the amount spent on each of their assigned areas, and number of titles collected. In addition, each librarian should review the materials coming in to ensure that they meet the required collection profile.

Recommendations for tracking titles purchased through the agreement were submitted by the cataloging team at the University of Pennsylvania, and were discussed via e-mail. The team suggested that a note for internal view be added to the record at the point of processing for every item received through the BorrowDirect agreement. It would inform any future Latin Americanist librarian contemplating deaccessioning the item that it was acquired for the agreement and, therefore, every effort should be made to preserve or replace the item. The second suggestion was for a 583 note stating that the item was purchased for the BorrowDirect agreement. 583 notes are local notes that indicate who donated an item, if the item is signed, etc. These notes would only be searchable through a keyword search in the local library's online catalog. They would not be searchable in a national-level database like *WorldCat*. The note would be added at the point of acquisition. At this time, it is not known if any of the participating libraries have adopted either one of these suggestions. Since many of the participating institutions do not plan any deaccessioning programs in the near future, it is not an urgent question. It should be noted, however, that, for most libraries, there is a challenge over how to note retention decisions within purchase and/or bibliographic records in ways that are both actionable and scalable.

Potential Hurdles

Besides the question of how to evaluate the success of the agreement, there are a few matters that pose potential complications for the Brazilian BorrowDirect program. Many of the titles purchased through the agreement will require original cataloging. Correct original cataloging is a complicated and time-consuming process. Books needing original cataloging often end up in the cataloging backlog, a perennial area of concern for libraries, and its elimination is the goal of all cataloging departments. There is no doubt that at some institutions participation in the Brazil BorrowDirect program would contribute to local cataloging backlogs. A shortage of cataloging staff nationally, the number of catalogers is predicted to drop significantly due to the aging and subsequent retirement with new cataloging hires that have not kept pace with those leaving the profession.[8] In addition, some institutions are unwilling or unable logistically to give the Brazilian BorrowDirect books priority in their cataloging queues. Staff shortages and local practices hindered the creation of a 583 field. It, therefore, becomes difficult to even identify books purchased through the MoU. To compound this predicament, many local library management systems and online catalogs make it difficult, if not impossible, to search by state, rather than country. This also informs future assessment of the program as a whole.

Continued reductions in collections budgets may also endanger the nascent program. Ironically the program was conceived precisely because cuts to Latin American collection budgets combined with increased publishing in Brazil hinder librarians from collecting comprehensively. At the April 2014 meeting at Columbia University, much thoughtful consideration was given to the problem of dwindling budgets. Most librarians had to divert some of their existing funds to provide for the agreement. Several were lucky enough to receive extra funds from their collection managers to accommodate all the costs of the new acquisitions for the program. University librarians and library directors were required to approve the MoU to ensure their long-term commitment to the program. However, the shadow of future budget cuts is ever present. Librarians may find themselves in a situation in which they will have to reallocate their already meager collections budget to cover the program, in effect, robbing Peter to pay Paul. Even so, collaborative collection development programs like the Brazil BorrowDirect project are our best solution to stretch our collection dollars and provide comprehensive research materials for our clientele. The BorrowDirect Brazil agreement follows in the footsteps of many successful and long-term collaborative collection development programs on Latin America. There is no reason to think that the newest of them all will not do the same.

Appendix 1. Institutional commitments
by region and state[9]

REGIONS	Brown	Chicago	Columbia	Cornell	Dartmouth	Duke	Harvard	Penn	Princeton	Yale
Norte										
Acre (AC)								X		
Amapá (AP)								X		
Amazonas (AM)								X		
Pará (PA)								X		
Tocantins (TO)								X		
Rondônia (RO)								X		
Roraima (RR)								X		
Nordeste										
Alagoas (AL)			X	X						
Bahia (BA)	X									
Ceará (CE)			X	X						
Maranhão (MA)			X	X						
Paraíba (PB)										X
Pernambuco (PE)										X
Piauí (PI)			X	X						
Rio Grande do Norte (RN)			X	X						
Sergipe (SE)			X	X						
Centro Oeste										
Distrito Federal (DF)									X	
Goiás (GO)									X	
Mato Grosso (MT)									X	
Mato Grosso do Sul (MS)									X	
Sudeste										
Espírito Santo (ES)							X			
Minas Gerais (MG)		X								
Rio de Janeiro (RJ)* excluding city								X		
São Paulo (SP)* excluding city							X			
Sur										
Paraná (PR)							X			
Santa Catarina (SC)					X	X				
Rio Grande do Sul (RS)					X	X				

Appendix 2. Subject Profile[10]

Cinema: Comprehensive coverage of works pertaining to national, regional and international cinema in all areas including social and political aspects and history.

Communication and media: Comprehensive coverage of works dealing with journalism, the press, radio, television, digital media, advertising, publishing, and the book trade.

Economics: Comprehensive coverage of works on economics at the local, national, regional and international levels. Include all major topics of interest such as economic development, globalization, finance, banking, trade, foreign investment, industry, agriculture, mining, tourism, employment, labor, and sustainability. Include also works on economic theory,. Include official documents and NGO imprints.

Education: Comprehensive coverage of works dealing with historical, social, and policy aspects. Exclude textbooks.

General reference works: Comprehensive coverage of works of bibliographies, dictionaries, and guide to major repositories of books and archives.

History: Comprehensive coverage of works dealing with national, regional, and local history during all periods. Include works dealing with the history of other parts of Latin America and history of relationship with other parts of the world. Also includes history of science, historiography, biography, genealogy, archaeology, and prehistory, numismatics, and philately.

Literature and language: Excessive, in-depth coverage of novels, short stories, poetry, drama, literary essays, literary criticism, and cultural studies in all languages including those of indigenous and other minority populations. Include graphic novels. Include also works on translation studies, linguistics, philology, indigenous languages, and grammars.

Music and performing arts: Comprehensive coverage of works pertaining to musical and theatrical performances in all genres. Exclude sheet music.

Philosophy: Comprehensive coverage of works dealing with philosophy.

Politics and government: Comprehensive coverage of works dealing with politics and government (national, state and local), international relations, comparative politics, public policy, social movements, and civil society. Include official documents and NGO imprints.

Popular culture: Comprehensive coverage of works dealing with historical and social aspects of music, dance, festivals, folklore, customs, myths, recreation, sports, and other areas. Include manifestations of traditional as well as alternative and counter-cultures.

Psychology: Comprehensive coverage of works dealing with psychology. Includes psychoanalysis. Exclude clinical psychology except when dealing with historical or social aspects.

Religion: Comprehensive coverage of works dealing with historical and social aspects of all religions.

Social sciences: Comprehensive coverage of works in sociology, cultural and social anthropology, emigration and immigration, race and ethnicity, gender, environment, urban planning, demography, criminology, public health, social change, conditions, and participation.

NOTES

1. Miguel Valladares, "Latin American & Iberian Library Collections at LANE Institutions: 1999–2009, 10 Years of Comparative Data with Historical Information Since 1996." (A LANE report, ca. 2009), accessed June 23, 2016, http://salalm.org/wp-content/uploads/2012/04/Lane_1966–2009_Data.pdf.

2. "Brazil," *Europa World Online*, accessed June 23, 2016.

3. Rüdiger Wischenbart, "IPA Global Publishing Statistics," *World* 114, no. 12, 189 (2013): 7–46.

4. "Draft Memorandum of Understanding: Collaborative Collection Development Agreement for Brazil Within BorrowDirect Institutions" (unpublished document, April 2014), 1.

5. *Ibid.*, 1.

6. *Ibid.*, 3.

7. *Ibid.*, 3.

8. Magda A. El-Sherbini, "Cataloging and Classification: Review of the Literature 2005–2006." *Library Resources & Technical Services* 52, No. 3 (2008): 150.

9. "Memorandum of Understanding: Collaborative Collection Development Agreement for Brazil within BorrowDirect Institutions" (unpublished document, April 2014) 5.

10. *Ibid.*, 6–7.

A Case Study of Small-Scale Collaborative Approval Plans for Latin America Collecting

PHILIP S. MACLEOD *and* LAURA D. SHEDENHELM

Introduction

Academic libraries in the United States are familiar with publishing in the context of North America and Western Europe, where often a single or a handful of vendors can provide most of the resources needed. Collecting research materials from Latin American countries poses some distinctive challenges that might not be known to or not considered by these institutions. The region has a vast number of countries and languages to consider. From the southern border of the United States with Mexico down to Tierra del Fuego, there are twenty independent nations and one overseas department found on the two American continents. Additionally, there are at least another twenty-six independent countries, territories, colonies and overseas departments among the islands of the Caribbean. For the sake of comparison, remember that Brazil alone is geographically larger than the lower forty-eight contiguous United States. Compounding the difficulties of adequately covering this immense geographic expanse there is the multiplicity of languages to be considered: Spanish, Portuguese, French, Dutch, English, and an estimated 550 to 700 indigenous languages spoken throughout the region as described in chapters four through six of Lyle Campbell's *American Indian Languages*.[1] Librarians dedicated to building Latin American collections rely on multiple small firms who specialize in a particular country or a combination of countries or regions within this territory to acquire the items our scholars need.

Beyond the number of languages to consider and the amount of territory to traverse in Latin America in order to obtain materials, there is also the question of availability for any given title. Take the example of a best seller such as J.K. Rowling's *Harry Potter and the Chamber of Secrets*, the second book in this popular series. According to Shmuel Ross, this book was released in 1999 in the United States with a print run of 500,000 copies.[2] In contrast, consider the 1967 first edition of Nobel laureate Gabriel García Márquez's *Cien años de soledad*. This work, which is often on required reading lists for high schools and colleges, was released in Buenos Aires with a print run of only 8,000 copies. This was supplemented later that year by three later releases of 20,000 copies each.[3] These examples demonstrate that the variance in the size of print runs between North American and South American publication is enormous. This deviation is significantly greater in the case of works from Central America where the printings are very small—normally less than 1,000 copies. As a result, acquiring titles as soon as they appear is imperative. This is why it is vital to work with vendors who are intimately acquainted with the specific region, who know the publishing industry players, and who understand the idiosyncrasies of local publishing patterns. Having a specialized vendor with these skills and contacts makes the difference between getting or not getting works that our library patrons want.

Background

James Burgett, John Haar, and Linda L. Phillips begin their 2004 guide to collaborative collection development with the statement, "For decades, librarians have been tantalized by the potential for combining the strengths of their libraries to build collections, union catalogs, delivery services, automation systems, and, most recently, digital libraries."[4] Exemplifying such cooperation, the libraries of Emory University and the University of Georgia (UGA) are members of the GETS consortium (University of Georgia, Emory University, Georgia Technical University and Georgia State University), among other cooperative programs in the state. GETS allows patrons to borrow materials directly from the member libraries or seek expedited interlibrary loan requests.

Burgett, Harr, and Phillips also succinctly identify a major impetus behind our statewide cooperative programs when they write, "Formal programs of collaboration have become a matter of broader and more urgent interest among libraries of all types and sizes as means of controlling erosion in the quality of collections and services."[5] Budgetary issues are among the "compelling incentives" they identify for libraries to consider when deciding on further cooperation. Peggy Johnson reiterates this view when she indicates, "Library cooperation has become even more essential in today's environment of constrained budgets...."[6] At the end of the first decade of the twenty-first century, all of the library budgets for institutions of higher education in Georgia were under financial pressure. In light of the active cooperation already in place, the Latin American bibliographers for UGA and Emory began exploring opportunities for more collaborative projects.

The idea of collaborative collection development has been deliberated for many years. See, for example, the section "Landmarks in CCD [cooperative collection development] evolution" in Burgett, Harr, and Phillips[7] where they describe national-level projects by the Association of Research Libraries, the Center for Research Libraries, the Farmington Plan, and the Global Resources Program,[8] among others. The Farmington Plan was particularly important for cooperative collection development related to Latin American titles.[9] Ralph Wagner[10] describes the significant contribution to building our collections provided through one of the outgrowths of the Farmington Plan: the Latin American Cooperative Acquisitions Program (LACAP). It was a coordinated attempt to obtain multiple copies of Latin American imprints for academic libraries in the United States from the late 1950s to the early 1970s. He highlights both a strength and a weakness (especially for our purposes) of LACAP when he writes " the broad duplication of the blanket orders [through LACAP] tended to make Farmington Plan country assignments less significant. It also showed what could be accomplished by direct, on-scene negotiations between sellers and representatives versed in American libraries' [needs]."[11] In other words, the strength comes from the in-country, timely acquisition of the titles, while the weakness lies in the duplication of the titles acquired.

Many of the discussions about cooperative collection development occur at both national-level and regional-level meetings. Indeed, this is illustrated by the title of the 1984 meeting of the Seminar on the Acquisition of Latin American Library Materials (SALALM): *Collection Development: Cooperation at the Local and National Levels*.[12] Various approaches to cooperative collecting of Latin Americana were presented at that meeting. In general, debates center on creating broad coverage with unique titles among the cooperating institutions as seen in the Duke–University of North Carolina, Chapel Hill Consortium[13]; the Research Library Cooperative Program among Stanford University, the University of California at Berkeley, and the University of Texas at Austin[14]; the Latin American and Iberian Studies cooperation in the 2CUL partnership between Cornell University and Colombia University[15]; the Harvard-Yale Mexican Collaborative Collection Development Agreement, the new BorrowDirect Brazilian Collaboration[16]; and the memoranda of agreement of the CALAFIA regional group of Latin American libraries in California for collecting materials from the northern and southern Mexican states.[17] There are also programs that combine funds to acquire expensive titles such as the Shared Purchase Program of the Center for Research Libraries.

The CALAFIA agreements are especially interesting to us because of the minimal funding each institution agreed to commit to these purchases: $1,500 for each of the northern states and $1,000 for each of the southern states. However, these examples also demonstrate that most existing Latin American collaborative programs are usually found at institutions with long-standing and extensive Latin American holdings, even when the expenditures are quite small. There is no comparable level of cooperative collecting in Georgia for materials from Latin America. Regardless that there was not a lengthy history of collecting Latin American works, the circumstances in the state were suitable to begin thinking about closer cooperation.

At the 2010 meeting of SALALM in Providence, Rhode Island, we met to consider possibilities for collaborative collecting. A number of options were discussed, but we decided to test a small-scale plan to broaden our collecting within the state of Georgia for the Spanish-speaking countries of Central America. A presentation by Jesús Alonso-Regalado at the 2009 SALALM conference in Berlin had provided an example of a modest plan for sharing materials between the campuses of the State University of New York at Binghamton and Albany.[18] Caryl Ward briefly describes the 2009 expansion of this collaboration for Puerto Rican and Chicano Studies resources.[19] Part of the reason to focus on Central America is that the materials can be difficult to obtain and acquiring the titles soon after publication is optimal. Both institutions have limited collection budgets for Central America, yet there is student and faculty interest at both institutions in the study of the region. While neither institution had a faculty member whose research focused exclusively on Central America, the growing Latino population in the state and the concomitant immigration issues that tracked back to Central America were of particular concern for several departments at both schools, including linguistics, history, and sociology. We compared our interactions with our respective faculty and students and a natural division between the two institutions appeared. Topically, investigations centered on literature and linguistics at the University of Georgia while, at Emory, other areas of the humanities and social sciences were the cores of research. Accordingly, we decided to divide our acquisitions along those lines. The aim was to maximize the purchasing power of each university and increase the number of unique titles each school received from their Central American approval plans.

The University of Georgia had an established approval plan with a vendor for Central American imprints. Given that Emory did not have an approval plan that focused exclusively on Central American imprints, the bibliographer deemed it appropriate to start an approval plan with the same firm. We agreed that we both would continue to utilize multiple vendors and other forms of acquiring materials as necessary on a firm-order basis. The timing of the SALALM meeting was such that the newly established cooperation could begin with the new fiscal year. One of the difficulties was to coordinate the differing fiscal cycles of each institution: UGA runs July through June, while Emory has a cycle of September through August. However, we decided that we would only include the titles received during our individual budget year regardless of the dates. We wanted to get the program in place rapidly. Since the UGA fiscal cycle had already started and Emory needed to set up an approval plan, we determined the best approach was to craft an informal arrangement between the bibliographers with assistance of the vendor, rather than pursue a formal memorandum of agreement between the libraries.

As noted above, both institutions acquire materials outside of the approval plans. Emory's bibliographer regularly attends international books fairs, especially the Guadalajara Book Fair. This book fair frequently has strong representation from the Spanish-speaking Central American countries in our study, thus allowing for broader collecting opportunities. For the purposes of this article, these acquisitions are not counted as books received through the approval plans, but do factor into the analysis of uniqueness. The Emory bibliographer provides a list of the titles he buys at the fair to the vendor in order to minimize the possibility of internal duplication or overlap with the UGA plan.

There are a few more specifics about our cooperative plan. We agreed that there were certain types of works that both institutions would need. For instance, reference titles (such as historical dictionaries) and the works of certain well-known writers (for example, Sergio Ramírez or Horacio Castellanos Moya) would be critical for both collections. We also agreed that, if a particular title were requested, we would buy it for our respective collections, regardless of its being held by the other institution.

The First Year

We began the program during FY 2010–2011. The target budgets for the approval plans were $1,800 for Emory and $3,000 for UGA. The UGA plan had been created several years earlier and the bibliographer did not want to reduce the amount just to attain parity. This did not prove to be an obstacle, however, as Emory's budget varied over time, reaching a high of almost $2,500 in FY 2013–2014 and again in 2016–2017. One of the issues we considered was the cost difference between literary works versus social sciences titles—literature and literary criticism tend to be less expensive. While doing the analysis, we noted that Emory averaged between fifty to seventy books each fiscal year, while UGA's receipts fluctuated over time, with a low of sixty-four to a high of 166. This may reflect the differences in our budgetary cycles, or it may be related to the buying and shipping of the materials from Central America. In either case, the total amount of funding for UGA averaged the $3,000 target amount.

Methodology

As each approval shipment arrives, each bibliographer reviews the invoices and enters the titles received by their institution into spreadsheets. The bibliographers periodically exchange the spreadsheets and search the titles received by the other institution against their own catalog, noting any duplication. (We counted as a duplicate a previous edition or printing of a given work. Some of these were acquired through means outside of the approval plans, especially if specifically requested by faculty or students.) At the end of the spring semester, the two spreadsheets are combined into one document and a preliminary analysis for uniqueness is done. Even though the fiscal years are not yet complete at that time, this analysis provides information for discussions the bibliographers have with each other and with the book vendor during the annual SALALM conference. The final analysis is completed and shared at the end of Emory's fiscal year.

Results of Central American Cooperation

Below are sample tables representing the results of the first fiscal year (2010–2011) and the latest fiscal year (2016–2017). Table 1 reveals the maximum amount of duplication between our institutions during our experiment. Of the titles we received, 25 percent were the same (i.e., each school received copies of the same twenty titles). In the statistical analysis, this results in forty books. Only 3 percent of the titles were variant editions held by either school. We determined that 9 percent of the titles purchased outside of the approval plans proved to be duplicated at the other school. The total amount of duplication is 37 percent. However, this is still a total uniqueness factor of 63 percent.

Table 1. UGA/Emory 2010/2011

UGA	Total UGA Titles Received 2010/2011	Overlap EMU Titles Received 2010/2011	EMU titles firm ordered or Prior Approval Plan	EMU earlier edition of title	Unique UGA Titles FY 2010/2011
Costa Rica					
Guatemala	43	9	8		26
Honduras					
Nicaragua	36	5	3	1	27
Panama					
El Salvador	19	6			13
UGA Totals	**98**	**20**	**11**	**1**	**66**

EMU	Total EMU Titles Received 2010/2011	Overlap UGA Titles Received 2010/2011	UGA Titles received on Approval in prior years	UGA earlier edition of title	Unique EMU Titles FY2010/2011
Costa Rica	7		2		5
Guatemala	27	9		2	16
Honduras	9		1	1	7
Nicaragua	8	5			3

(continued on page 138)

EMU	Total EMU Titles Received 2010/2011	Overlap UGA Titles Received 2010/2011	UGA Titles received on Approval in prior years	UGA earlier edition of title	Unique EMU Titles FY2010/2011
Panama	2				2
El Salvador	7	6			1
EMU Totals	**60**	**20**	**3**	**3**	**34**
Grand totals	**158**	**40**	**14**	**4**	**100**
Percentages		**25%**	**9%**	**3%**	**63%**

Based on the relative success of the first year, we realized we could further minimize the duplication in the Central American approval plans. At the SALALM conference in 2011, both bibliographers met with our vendor to discuss our initial findings. Our conversation reinforced the division of subject collecting responsibilities between the two institutions. This meeting clarified the understanding of all parties regarding the details of the informal agreement for the collaboration, and helped the vendor concentrate on elimination of duplication between the two approval plans.

As can be seen in Table 2, which corresponds to the most recent fiscal year of this study (2016–2017), we have significantly reduced our duplication rate within the approval plan to 1.46 percent and enhanced the number of titles that are unique (92.7 percent) between our institutions. If we had not considered purchases outside of the approval plans, our uniqueness rate raises to 98.54 percent.

Table 2. UGA/Emory 2016/2017

UGA	Total UGA Titles Received 2016/2017	Overlap EMU Titles Received 2016/2017	EMU titles firm ordered or Prior Approval Plan	EMU earlier edition of title	Unique UGA Titles FY 2016/2017
Costa Rica	37	1	1	1	34
Guatemala	2				2
Honduras	17				17
Nicaragua					
Panama					
El Salvador	8		1		7
UGA Totals	**64**	**1**	**2**	**1**	**60**

EMU	Total EMU Titles Received 2016/2017	Overlap UGA Titles Received 2016/2017	UGA Titles received on Approval in prior years	UGA earlier edition of title	Unique EMU Titles 2016/2017
Costa Rica	14		1		13
Guatemala	2		2		0
Honduras	13				13
Nicaragua	35				35
Panama					
El Salvador	9		3		6
EMU Totals	**73**		**6**		**67**
Grand totals	**137**	**1**	**8**	**1**	**127**
Percentages		**0.73%**	**5.84%**	**0.73%**	**92.7%**

While we received no duplicated titles through the approval plan from 2011–2015, there were ten in 2015–2016 (4.98 percent), and one (0.73 percent) in 2016–2017. Duplication from a variant edition only occurred in 2011–2012 and 2016–2017 (1 percent or less), while duplication from outside orders ranged from a low of seven to a high of sixteen (5 percent-7.96 percent) during the same period. Our total numbers for this collaboration can be seen in Table 3, which shows an overall uniqueness rate of 88 percent. Again, if we only consider as duplication the twenty titles (forty books) both universities received through the approval plan in 2010–2011 plus the eleven duplicate titles during 2016–2017, the uniqueness rate raises to 93 percent for the duration of our agreement to date.

Table 3. UGA/Emory 2010–2017

UGA	Total UGA Titles Received 2010–2017	Overlap EMU Titles Received 2010–2017	EMU titles firm ordered or Prior Approval Plan	EMU earlier edition of title	Unique UGA Titles FY 2010–2017
Costa Rica	159	0	14	1	144
Guatemala	198	9	24	0	165
Honduras	54	0	1	0	53
Nicaragua	147	5	12	1	129
Panama	50	0	10	0	40
El Salvador	59	6	6	0	47
UGA Totals	**667**	**20**	**67**	**2**	**578**

EMU	Total EMU Titles Received 2010–2017	Overlap UGA Titles Received 2010–2017	UGA Titles received on Approval in prior years	UGA earlier edition of title	Unique EMU Titles 2010–2017
Costa Rica	106	1	3	1	101
Guatemala	110	10	3	2	95
Honduras	54	0	1	1	52
Nicaragua	52	7	0	0	45
Panama	44	6	0	0	38
El Salvador	90	7	1	1	81
EMU Totals	**456**	**31**	**8**	**5**	**413**
Grand totals	**1,123**	**51**	**75**	**7**	**990**
Percentages		**5%**	**7%**	**1%**	**88%**

Expansion of Cooperative Program

We were so encouraged by the first-year results of our Central American project we decided to see if we could expand this process to other areas. We discovered that we use the same book dealers for other Latin American countries. Because our collecting patterns varied widely with some of the countries, we decided that another small-scale collaborative effort best suited our needs. During fiscal year 2011–2012 we looked at Puerto Rico and Dominican Republic as a possibility, especially given the growing research interests in the Caribbean among both Emory and UGA faculty. The topical divisions for collection responsibilities are the same as those for Central America, but the funding levels are very different. Emory already had a plan in place for $2,000 annually, while UGA could only set aside $500 annually for a new plan that began in 2012–2013. For this project, we simplified the data that we collected for duplication. We just counted any time a title was already held by the other institution. Our experience with the Central American plan had showed us that attempting to track duplication due to outside buying and considering earlier editions/printings was challenging.

Results of Dominican Republic/Puerto Rico Cooperation

In anticipation of the new plan, UGA did some retrospective buying with the vendor during the first year, which may have contributed to the higher duplication rate during 2011–2012, as seen in Table 4. Another contributing element, and one which will probably always be in play, is that the duplication is primarily among the core literary titles that the faculty members at both institutions require for teaching and research. There was a 36 percent duplication rate from the 168 titles acquired during the first year, but that still provided for a 64 percent uniqueness factor.

Table 4. UGA/Emory 2011/2012

UGA (firm orders first year only)	Total UGA Titles Received 2011/2012	Overlap EMU Titles Received 2011/2012	Unique UGA Titles FY 2011/2012
Dominican Republic	31	14	17
Puerto Rico	68	38	30
UGA Totals	**99**	**52**	**47**

EMU (Approval Plan)	Total EMU Titles Received 2011/2012	Overlap UGA Titles Received 2011/2012	Unique EMU Titles FY 2011/2012
Dominican Republic	47	7	40
Puerto Rico	22	2	20
EMU Totals	**69**	**9**	**60**
Grand totals	**168**	**61**	**107**
Percentages		**36%**	**64%**

Emory and UGA received a combined total of eighty-four books annually in both fiscal years 2012–2013 and 2013–2014. The result was a 17 percent duplication rate and an 83 percent uniqueness factor for each of those years. The eighty-two titles received during fiscal year 2014–2015, however, showed a 29 percent duplication rate with a uniqueness factor of only 71 percent. In FY 2015–2016 a total of ninety-two titles arrived, but the duplication rate rose to 34 percent and the uniqueness factor decreased to 66 percent. Table 5, covering 2016–2017, provides a comparative view to the initial year that was seen in Table 4. As can been seen, the uniqueness of the titles we receive ranges between 66 percent-88 percent for the time we have been tracking our cooperative acquisitions for the Dominican Republic and Puerto Rico.

Table 5. UGA/Emory 2016/2017

UGA	Total UGA Titles Received 2016/2017	Overlap EMU Titles Received 2016/2017	Unique UGA Titles FY 2016/2017
Dominican Republic	9	4	5
Puerto Rico	5	2	3
UGA Totals	**14**	**6**	**8**

EMU	Total EMU Titles Received 2016/2017	Overlap UGA Titles Received 2016/2017	Unique EMU Titles FY 2016/2017
Dominican Republic	48	4	44
Puerto Rico	27	1	26
EMU Totals	**75**	**5**	**70**
Grand totals	**89**	**11**	**78**
Percentages		**12%**	**88%**

The aggregate results for this cooperative plan are in Table 6. While we have not reached the same level of uniqueness that we saw in the Central American project, we anticipate that it will remain closer to the 70 percent to 80 percent range. We forecast that variations in the uniqueness rate of this collaboration will continue. In any given year, both universities will need to receive certain key literary titles—the number of these critical works published varies from year to year.

Table 6. UGA/Emory 2011–2017

UGA	Total UGA Titles Received 2011–2017	Overlap EMU Titles Received 2011–2017	Unique UGA Titles FY 2011–2017
Dominican Republic	72	31	41
Puerto Rico	110	55	55
UGA Totals	**182**	**86**	**96**

EMU Received 2011–2015	Total EMU Titles Received 2011–2015 Unique EMU Titles FY 2011–2015		Overlap UGA Titles
Dominican Republic	220	24	196
Puerto Rico	186	30	156
EMU Totals	**406**	**54**	**352**
Grand totals	**588**	**140**	**448**
Percentages		**24%**	**76%**

Conclusion

When we began pondering the intention of collaborative collection development for Latin Americana in Georgia, we noted that there is a somewhat traditional impression that it could only be undertaken by large institutions with historically strong collections in particular regions or subject areas. This was born out in much of the literature on collection development—only large-scale programs were discussed. We believed, however, that collaboration on a lesser scale was possible. There was a strong economic impetus for this project at both of our institutions. We also have confidence that there are other localities where similar projects can be implemented. There are multiple universities across the nation that have faculty interested in Latin American studies, for example, but without any specialist in their university library. Even where such specialists exist, many now have responsibilities for multiple subjects within the library. Given today's economic reality and budgetary situations, academic libraries must explore creative options to fulfill our patrons' expectations and research needs. We believe we have shown in this project that institutions with smaller budgets and collections are equally adept at finding these creative solutions. Collaborative collection development need not only be the purview of the oldest and largest universities, nor need to be on a grand scale.

There are a number of concerns that go along with this type of collaborative project.

Bibliographers must trust one another to uphold their commitments to the agreement. Regular communication is essential to the continued success of the undertaking. The informal agreement between Emory's and UGA's bibliographers was easy to implement, yet it may only last as long as the current subject specialists remain in their particular positions. Our respective institution's research and collecting priorities might change over time or the budgets we have for these collecting areas could be altered radically. Increased or new job responsibilities may lessen the time we have to devote to this collaborative effort.

In spite of all this, we have shown through this project that complementary collections can be built cooperatively on a small scale. Our methodology and approach are simple and can be reproduced in other locations and with other topics or regions. It can be set up among two or more institutions. The time commitment is minimal, but it is imperative that bibliographers have a thorough knowledge of their individual collections and are closely acquainted with the research and teaching needs of their faculties.

NOTES

1. Lyle Campbell, *American Indian Languages: The Historical Linguistics of Native America* (Oxford: Oxford University Press, 1997).

2. Shmuel Ross, "Harry Potter Timeline: The Life and Times of Harry Potter and His Creator," *Infoplease*, 2016, accessed 27 May 2016, http://www.infoplease.com/spot/harrypottertimeline.html.

3. *Captain Ahab's Rare Books*, 2016, accessed 27 May 2016, http://www.captainahabsrarebooks.com/shop/ahab/574.

4. James Burgett, John Harr and Linda J. Phillips, *Collaborative Collection Development: A Practical Guide for Your Library* (Chicago: American Library Association, 2004), 1.

5. Burgett, *Collaborative Collection Development*, 2.

6. Peggy Johnson. *Fundamental of Collection Development and Management*, 3rd ed. (Chicago: American Library Association, 2014), 345.

7. Burgett, *Collaborative Collection Development*, 8–13.

8. Center for Research Libraries Global Resources Network, "Shared Purchase Program," 2016, accessed 27 May 2016, https://www.crl.edu/collections/cooperative-collection-building/shared-purchase-program.

9. Ralph D. Wager, *A History of the Farmington Plan* (Lanham, MD: Scarecrow Press, 2002), 210–211.

10. Wager, *A History*, 359–362.

11. Wager, *A History*, 362.

12. Barbara G. Valk, ed., *Collection Development: Cooperation at the Local and National Levels: Papers of the Twenty-Ninth Annual Meeting of the Seminar on the Acquisition of Latin American Library Materials, University of North Carolina, Chapel Hill, North Carolina, June 3–7, 1984* (Madison, WI: SALALM Secretariat, 1987).

13. The Consortium in Latin American and Caribbean Studies at the University of North Carolina at Chapel Hill and Duke University, *Library Collections*, 2016, accessed 27 May 2016, http://jhfc.duke.edu/latinamericauncduke/resources-2/library-collections/.

14. Stanford University Libraries, *Research Library Cooperative Program*, 2016, accessed 27 May 2016, https://library.stanford.edu/using/research-library-cooperative-program.

15. Gwen Glazer, "Cornell, Columbia Libraries to Share Latin American, Iberian Studies Collections," *Cornell Chronicle*, May 9, 2012, accessed 27 May 2016, http://www.news.cornell.edu/stories/2012/05/librarys-2cul-partnership-columbia-expands.

16. Yale University Library, *Latin American Collection*, 2016, accessed 27 May 2016, http://web.library.yale.edu/collection-development/latin-american-collection.

17. CALAFIA (California Cooperative Latin American Collection Development Group), *Memorandum of Agreement: North Mexican State Materials*, last modified May 17, 1997, accessed May 27, 2016, http://web.stanford.edu/~c0y0t8/calafia/northmex.pdf. CALAFIA (California Cooperative Latin American Collection Development Group). *Memorandum of Agreement: South Mexican State Materials*, last modified May 17, 1997, accessed May 27, 2016, http://web.stanford.edu/~c0y0t8/calafia/southmex.pdf.

18. Jesús Alonso-Regalado, "Enriching Collections with Limited Funds: Getting the Most Out of Book Fair Acquisitions and Cooperative Projects," Paper Seminar on the Acquisition of Latin American Library Materials, Berlin, Germany, July 3–8, 2009. *Downloads SALALM 54*, 11, accessed May 27, 2016, http://www.iai.spk-berlin.de/uploads/tx_wftag/salalmdownloads.pdf.

19. Caryl Ward, "Expanding Access to Latino Studies Research," *LibraryLinks* (Fall 2009/Spring 2010): 9, accessed 27 May 2016, https://www.binghamton.edu/libraries/about/documents/LibraryLinks_Spring2010_FinalVersion.pdf.

Collecting Collaborations

Lynn M. Shirey

Since the founding of SALALM (Seminar on the Acquisition of Latin American Library Materials) in 1956, successful initiatives in the areas of preservation, access and collection development have proliferated and flourished. Early collecting agreements for Latin American materials included the Farmington Plan and the RLG Conspectus (both for foreign language materials in general). Partnerships were forged between the University of North Carolina Chapel Hill and Duke University libraries, and the Stanford University and UC Berkeley libraries. Further efforts by Latin Americanist librarians to diversify and deepen academic collections began in 1995, with the Distributed Resources Project (DRP). One of several projects carried out under the auspices of the Latin American Research Resources Project (LARRP), it is a coordinated attempt to focus collecting activities at different institutions on particular countries, regions or topics. Under the agreement, 7 percent of each librarian's budget for Latin American monographs is redirected to each library's committed area or topic. In 2011 the libraries of New York University, Colombia University and New York Public formed the Manhattan Academic Research Library Initiative (MaRLI), in order to "coordinate their research collecting, eliminating overlap of specialized materials and identifying opportunities for shared collecting. They will be able to do so by making their collections mutually available to researchers."[1] Columbia and Cornell University libraries are sharing collections as well as professional staff for Latin America and Slavic areas under their 2CUL rubric. Most of the large research libraries participate in related projects such as LAMP (preservation) and LARRP (open access), which are consortia funded programs managed by the Center for Research Libraries (CRL).

Other collaborative agreements for borrowing, lending, preservation and storage, often led by regional consortia, have also proliferated. Some of these efforts have a direct effect on collections collaborations. BorrowDirect, a patron initiated interlibrary loan tool, was established by a small group of Ivy League libraries in 1999, and has grown to twelve current members. This initiative has generated increased potential for coordinated collecting among peer institutions.

Publishing and Acquisitions Trends

Statistics for global publishing have risen steadily in recent years. The numbers of titles published in Latin America has followed suit: according to the Centro Regional para el Fomento del Libro en América Latina, El Caribe, España y Portugal (CERLALC), new titles and reprints published in the region increased from 59,568 in the year 2000, to 194,009 titles in 2013.[2]

Scholarly information is becoming available in a growing array of physical formats: film, television, photography and games; datasets and tools. Libraries now need to collect, host and preserve digital formats of various kinds, in addition to print. Researchers require an expanding variety of genres as well: comics, graphic novels, posters, ephemera, pamphlets, artists' books, zines; maps and statistics. However, library acquisitions budgets, and libraries' capacity for storage and processing, are not keeping a pace with all this activity.

As the universe of research materials expands, library collections are amassing increasingly similar collections (so called vanilla). When budgets are stretched, librarians narrow their collecting scopes and acquire what seems to be most needed: usually the output of university presses and established publishers from major cities. Foreign language collections funding in the U.S. is particularly vulnerable to budget cuts.

Harvard and Yale

Harvard and Yale universities are in many ways peer institutions: located in the northeast, prestigious, private and Ivy League, they are 135 miles and a short two-hour train ride apart. They compete energetically with one another in both academics and sports. They offer similar academic programs and each rely upon a network of general as well as specific subject libraries, which in turn have comparable collecting interests, strengths and materials budgets. The main libraries at each campus (Widener and Sterling Memorial) are large collections of research materials in the humanities and social sciences, published worldwide in many languages. Bibliographers and curators at each institution build, maintain and promote research collections based on geographical areas[3]: Africa, the Middle East, Slavic countries, South Asia, Latin America, Western Europe and others.

Experiment

Could Harvard and Yale collaborate to form deeper, shared Latin American collections? At stake in this very traditional environment were academic reputation as well as size, quality and ease of access of their library collections. In the fall of 2003, Dan C. Hazen (Associate University Librarian for Collections, Harvard) and Lynn M. Shirey (Acting Librarian for Latin America, Spain and Portugal, Harvard) discussed the idea of a collecting collaboration with colleagues at Yale University. We drafted a proposal that we then shared with our colleague César Rodríguez, who was then Yale's Curator of the Latin American Collection.

Following the lead of earlier institutional agreements for shared collection development, the goal of our project was to expand Harvard and Yale's combined collecting capacity for Latin American research materials. Each library was already attempting to acquire a broad range of publications from Latin America, including core titles for research and teaching, secondary titles, collections of ephemera, government documents, and other special materials in the fields of humanities and social sciences. Evidence in the WorldCat database, vendors' lists that indicated the destinations of their approval selections, and informal assessments all showed that we were building largely duplicative collections. Each institution was faced with slowly increasing or stagnant acquisitions budgets, and librarians were working hard to keep up with an expanding universe of materials.

We imagined a duplicate core collection for teaching and research that would be available on site at each institution for our most active academic programs. By means of careful efforts to reduce non-core duplication, however, we hoped to achieve a broader collective coverage of selected areas between the two libraries. The saving achieved through non-duplication could be employed to collect regional newspapers, film and television, ephemera and visual materials, and elusive government publications. These materials could be shared. In all cases of non-duplication, perceived demand and usage by local faculty and students would be respected.

Methodology

Following a series of preliminary draft proposals and initial meetings among librarians in early 2004, we agreed to proceed with a series of steps. Faculty support was essential for a collaborative effort to work. Librarians at each institution met with respective faculty members who worked primarily on Latin American topics. We assured them that core collections would continue to be at hand and that we would duplicate one another's holdings of other materials whenever there was a perceived interest or a direct need. General faculty support for the proposal was obtained at both Yale and Harvard.

Vendor selection was an essential component of the proposed plans. It was imperative that we identify vendors who would be willing and able to work with us. Given that both Harvard and Yale have strong academic interests in Mexico and Chile, and that we had solid and experienced shared vendors in place, we decided to focus our efforts on the publishing output of these countries. We approached the following vendors: Books from Mexico, Libros de Todo México, and Herta Berenguer Publicaciones Chilenas with our idea, and their representatives indicated willingness to collaborate with us. We decided to experiment with different collecting scopes for each country. The use of divergent collecting parameters would provide us with two sets of experiences for evaluation.

Mexico

Mexico has a highly decentralized publishing industry, distributed across its thirty-one states and the Federal District (Mexico DF). It seemed logical to divide collecting responsibilities by region of publication. Each bibliographer analyzed the respective strengths of their library's holdings from this perspective, and together attempted to divide the Mexican states in an equitable fashion. After some deliberation, it was decided that Yale would collect second-tier monographs and more ephemeral and special materials from the northern Mexican states and Mexico DF, the capital; Harvard would focus on the southern states for similar materials. Libros de Todo México was chosen as the provider for the northern states (they had begun business as México Norte); and Books from Mexico/Mexico Sur was selected to provide materials from the Mexico DF, and the southern Mexican states. Each vendor would supply both Harvard and Yale with essential core titles published in their regions, creating duplicate collections. A designated vendor would supply none-core materials for one or the other institution.

Chile

The Chilean publishing industry is more centralized than Mexico's, and based largely in Santiago and Valparaíso. Chilean materials were provided at that time by one principal (and shared) vendor: Herta Berenguer Publicaciones Chilenas. In this instance we defined our collecting topically: Harvard would collect deeply in biography, communications, philology and linguistics, philosophy, religion and social sciences. Yale would focus on non-core materials in history, literature, anthropology and archaeology, as well as government documents.

Mechanics and Ongoing Evaluation

In the initial stages of the project we asked our three vendors to separate their shipments into core and non-core materials. Packages and invoices were to be clearly marked to designate them as one or the other. In addition, we requested that non-core materials for Harvard be shipped to Yale; and that non-core shipments for Yale be sent to Harvard. Librarians at each institution would evaluate the other's materials and thus have the opportunity to evaluate the vendor's selection with the materials in hand, and to decide to order additional copies of non-core titles if warranted by local interest.

After prompt examination, the materials were sent on to the library of destination. In order to ensure complete understanding of the project by the technical services staff involved, a visit was organized at Yale for Harvard staff (technical services and bibliographers) in late 2004. We spent the better part of a day reviewing the purpose and mechanics of the project and established personal connections with all involved. We completed the final versions of our approval plan documents in late 2004, and initiated the project with 2005 imprints.

Amendments to Project

Over time it became apparent that the effort involved in bibliographer review of the partner library's non-core shipments was time consuming, sometimes messy, and not essential to the project. Our vendors had demonstrated their understanding of the scope of materials. In addition, their annotated lists clearly indicated which materials were duplicated by Harvard and Yale, and which were unique to each library. We decided to eliminate this procedure by mid–2006.

The Chilean shared approval was problematic from the beginning. It was difficult for our vendor to obtain the non-core materials we had hoped to uncover, and Chilean publishing output was smaller and less diverse than we had expected. For these reasons, combined with budget shortfalls, we agreed to cancel this part of the project by 2007.

Project Assessment

From the start, we realized that project evaluation would be a challenge. Advanced searching in the *WorldCat* database is problematic due to the number of cities of publication in Mexico; in addition, significant numbers of library holdings are not loaded into the system for long periods of time. The *WorldCat Collection Analysis* tool is not subscribed to by all libraries, and we were unable to experiment with it. Institutional catalog reporting tools could not provide the kind of data we needed. Once Harvard became a BorrowDirect member in 2011 (Yale had joined in 1999), we became hopeful that statistics obtained there would help to measure the flow of materials between the two institutions. Although we can measure the amount of lending by numbers for Mexican publications, we cannot parse that information by city or state.

In the absence of hard data we continue to rely upon alternate methods of evaluation. We receive regular budget reports from our vendors that indicate our expenditures on core and non-core items. We continue to inspect and review any non-core shipments that arrive, and study our vendors' lists of titles, each of which includes a series of receiving libraries for each entry. We look for a stable pattern of duplication and non-duplication for our areas between the two libraries, and order additional items as necessary.

Lessons Learned

Communication with vendors is of upmost importance to the success and efficiency of a shared collecting project. This is sometimes a challenge when relying upon foreign vendors who are sometimes unavailable—often travelling to acquire our materials! Library staff and administrators should also be reminded of the project and kept up to date on any changes or developments. Documentation should be clear and available for new administrators and technical services staff. Ongoing institutional support is essential for any long term collaborative collection project. Budget fluctuations lead to confusion for vendors and staff alike.

Evaluation of collaborative collecting projects has so far proved to be very difficult, and continues to be problematic for early collaborative efforts like LARRP's Distributed Resources Project, and recent ones like the BorrowDirect Brazil program. Members of the DRP staff at BorrowDirect are actively exploring tools and methods for future use in this area.

NOTES

1. *The New York Public Library, Columbia University and New York University Forge Historic Collaboration* (Columbia University Libraries News and Events, 2011), accessed June 13, 2106, http://library.columbia.edu/news/libraries/2011/20110318_marli.html.

2. *El espacio iberoamericano del libro 2014* (Bogotá: CERLALC-UNESCO, 2014), 84.

3. In 2015, the curator of the Latin American Collection became responsible for publications about Latin America published worldwide.

Beyond Print

Developing Music Collections

DAISY DOMÍNGUEZ

Latin Americanist collection development focuses mostly on writing, whether in print or digital formats. To the extent that audiovisual collection development is discussed, it tends to center around film. Music, which is so integral to Latin American and Caribbean[1] identity, is often ignored even though it represents a form of media that literally calls out to us. All collections supporting programs that seek to better understand Latin America, regardless of whether or not the institution has a music department and/or program, will benefit from sound recording collection development. Just as musicological circles have come to acknowledge the way that music permeates our society,[2] and can be seen as "a way of knowing the world,"[3] so too should librarians of all stripes advocate for and promote music collection development as a way to supplement the breadth of our print and film collections. Through a cross comparison of various Latin American music collections in the United States and a discussion of music collection development resources, this essay serves as a call for a heightened emphasis on music collection development.

Latin American Music Library Collections in the United States[4]

There are several unique and/or notable Latin American and Caribbean music collections in the United States. Librarians seeking to develop sound recording collections may find it helpful to understand how these collections have been built and to search their available online metadata.

Latin American Music Center, Indiana University Libraries, Bloomington

Founded in 1961 by Chilean composer and musicologist Juan Orrego-Salas, the Latin American Music Center (LAMC) at the Jacobs School of Music at the University of Indiana, Bloomington (IU)[5] currently acts as a center dedicated to the promotion of music through concerts, courses, competitions, performances, research, and other activities. Its music collection, noted as among the best of its kind in the world,[6] is housed at the William & Gayle Cook Music Library at IU. Built almost solely by donation, the music collection is managed by Emma Dederick, Associate Librarian, and a singer, violinist, and pianist. Donations are supplemented by occasional purchases made by students and others affiliated with the Center who are able to acquire material from Brazil, Colombia, and Venezuela, as well as ongoing purchases made with the Cook Music Library's acquisitions budget. The Cook Music Library's budget supports the LAMC as well as the entire music program.

Although the music collection's holdings are cataloged, there is no absolute way to find all their holdings in the library catalog. This is due to the difficulty of flagging all approval plan items and the large backlog, which include three recently donated special collections: the Guillermo Espinosa Collection, which contains the renowned Colombian composer's papers, scores, recordings, and mementos[7]; the Juan Orrego-Salas Legacy Collection, which includes the scores, photographs, and correspondence of Chilean composer, musicologist and LAMC founder[8]; and the Alfonso Montecino Collection, which includes scores and correspondence donated by the Chilean pianist and Indiana University Jacobs School of Music Professor Emeritus.[9]

Currently, searching the local subject heading designation "Latin American Music Collection" in IUCAT[10] (Indiana University's online library catalog) retrieves 9,269 items. Sound recordings do not circulate but most books and scores in stacks may be borrowed via Interlibrary loan. For most sound recordings, faculty and students request lists ahead of time and they, as well as many other items, are digitized for in-house access only. CDs and DVDs are circulated in-house only. A campus-wide music and video digitization project called the Media Digitization and Preservation Initiative (MDPI)[11] is being developed for archival purposes.

The Díaz-Ayala Collection, Florida International University Libraries, Miami

The Díaz-Ayala Cuban and Latin American Popular Music Collection[12] at the Florida International University (FIU) Special Collections & University Archives began as a donation by Cuban music collector Cristóbal Díaz-Ayala. It is composed of approximately 150,000 items housed in the Sound and Image Department, headed by Tom Moore, a librarian and musician, with reference support by librarian Verónica González. Gayle Williams, Latin American & Caribbean Information Services Librarian, also supports this collection through the acquisition of books and sound recordings as well as instruction services and referrals.[13] Mr. Díaz-Ayala continues to acquire material for the collection and has extensive connections with other collectors who also donate. The collection database is accessible online.[14] A useful online collection development resource is the downloadable full-text of the *Encyclopedic Discography of Cuban Music 1898–1960*.[15]

Because the Díaz-Ayala Collection is considered to be a special collection, materials do not circulate. To facilitate the collection's use, the facility is equipped with turntables which play various sound recording formats, a cassette player, a computer station, etc. A digitization project is underway for the 78 rpm recordings, sound clips of which are accessible on the FIU dPanther digital repository online.[16] The collection offers three annual scholarships allowing national and international graduate, undergraduate, and independent scholars to visit and work with the collection on campus for a period of one week.

Belfer Audio Archive, Syracuse University Libraries

The Belfer Audio Archive at the Syracuse University (SU) Libraries' Special Collections Research Center maintains a collection of Caribbean and Latin American popular music dating from 1950 to 1962. Two Cuban brothers, Joseph and Max Bell who owned a music store called Music Box in New York City, donated the collection in 1963.[17] The collection, which is not separate from the Audio Archive or known by a particular collection name, is composed of about 20,000 45 rpm recordings which are not yet cataloged and an unknown number of 78 rpm recordings. This collection is also donation-based. It consists of historical recordings made by Hispanic musicians but issued by U.S.—particularly New York City—companies, as well as others from the Caribbean and Central and South America. Dr. Jenny Doctor, Director of the Belfer Audio Archive, and a historical musicologist, manages this collection. Doctor works with librarian and sound archivist Patrick Midtlyng, responsible for the preservation of the physical collections and accessibility through metadata collection, and two audio engineers, Robert Hodge and Jim Meade, who clean or otherwise conserve the physical recordings before transferring them to digital formats.

A relatively small number of recordings have been digitized. Doctor notes that since music is one of the most restrictive forms of media (due to copyright issues), it would be difficult to make this material accessible to the public. When someone requests access to a 78 rpm recording, it is digitized for access as well as preservation, and made available for listening in the Special Collections Reading Room only. Because most of this collection's metadata is not online, it is currently relatively unknown and unused.

Digitization is particularly important for historical collections where patrons will only be able to access recordings if they have been digitized, for preservation and/or access. Since it is not common for libraries to have audio preservation specialists, several interviewees suggested that librarians interested in building sound recording collections consult the freely available *ARSC Guide to Audio Preservation.*[18]

The Catholic University of America
Latin American Music Center

Located in Washington, D.C., the Latin American Center for Graduate Studies in Music, also known as the Latin American Music Center, was founded in 1984 by the Benjamin T. Rome School of Music. The School of Music offers graduate degrees in music with Latin American music concentrations in cooperation with the Organization of American States (OAS) and the Inter-American Music Council.[19] The OAS donated a music collection to the center which was augmented in 2008 by the music collection of the Brazilian American Cultural Institute (BACI).[20] Scores, composers' manuscripts, and other publications in the Latin American Music Center's collection are included in the Latin American Music Catalog.[21] Additional Latin American music books and scores held in the Catholic University of America Music Library are accessible though the Washington Research Library Consortium (WRLC) catalog.[22]

The Frontera Collection, UCLA

The Strachwitz Frontera Collection of Mexican and Mexican American Recordings[23] is a joint project of the Digital Library of the University of California, Los Angeles (UCLA); the Arhoolie Foundation; and the UCLA Chicano Studies Research Center (CSRC). It is known as "the largest repository of Mexican and Mexican American popular and vernacular recordings in existence."[24] The Arhoolie Foundation owns the collection; the CSRC digitizes the music; and UCLA Library and Digital Library host the website. The Frontera Collection features 90-second clips of over 115,000 recordings owned by the Arhoolie Foundation, and which grew out of Arhoolie Records but is separate from it. It does not have the right to license this material, which includes Arhoolie Records' material as well as others.[25] This collection was received through donation and has been expanded through further donations by Chris Strachwitz, president of the Arhoolie Foundation and founder and president of Arhoolie Records, as well as others.

Other Collections

Other library collections are not primarily devoted to Latin American music, but contain unique materials. The Rubén Blades Archives at Harvard University maintains both commercial and privately produced sound and audiovisual recordings as well as print material and ephemera. The Rubén Blades finding aid, which describes the collection in detail, is available online.[26] Princeton's Mendel Music Library maintains the Puerto Rican Music Collection, with over 350 recordings of a variety of genres released in the 1960s and 1970s. The collection is accessible through the Princeton catalog[27] using the phrase "Puerto Rican Music Collection."[28] Fernando Acosta-Rodríguez, Librarian for Latin American Studies, Latino Studies, and Iberian Peninsular Studies at Princeton University Library, also notes that Princeton maintains a "Cuban post-revolutionary music imprints collection of over four hundred titles, consisting mostly of scores and sheet music, as well as some monographs and pamphlets, all published in Cuba after 1959. A list of all the titles in the collection can be generated by searching for 'Cuban post-revolutionary music imprints' in our library catalog."[29] The University of California at Santa Barbara Library maintains the Edouard Pecourt Tango and Latin American Music Collection which includes 20,000 sound recordings and thousands of pieces of sheet music, discographies, and books, and ephemera. A finding aid is available.[30]

Librarians interested in specific genres or regions of music should also seek out specialized libraries. For example, the City University of New York's Dominican Studies Institute Archives and Library has small but unique CD, LP, and DVD Dominican music collections. The collections are listed online[31] as well as in in-house finding aids for the historical music collections of composer, conductor, and musician Rafael Petitón Guzmán. Likewise, the National Jukebox at the Library of Congress[32] is an online resource containing several dozen Spanish language recordings.

The Unique Nature of Music Libraries

Music libraries bear distinctive characteristics that make it difficult for non-specialists to use them as an exact model for building music collections. Understanding these differences at the outset will help librarians who are not music specialists to use the resources in these collections more wisely.

Several of the librarians working in music library collections have strong music backgrounds, and their collections are intended to support users from music departments or schools, making their collections performance and/or research based. Because many music library interactions relate to music as a discipline, questions from users in other humanities disciplines may be rare. Librarians who are building music collections for non-music users will most likely be in the opposite position because they will be trying to encourage faculty to incorporate music into their teaching and consequently need to make recommendations and focus more on outreach. Some of the collections listed above are indeed primarily maintained by librarians without music degrees who serve a broader constituency. Verónica González of the Díaz Ayala Collection does not have a music background and notes, "The Diaz-Ayala collection at FIU serves a multidisciplinary community of researchers in areas such as history, sociology, linguistic, musicology and ethnomusicology, Latin American and Caribbean studies, among many other disciplines."[33]

Latin American music collection development depends more on strong personal and professional networks than on standard collection development publications or tools like websites and databases. Because most of the collections discussed above are donation-based, and only supplemented by acquisitions, interviewees were unable to point me to standard collection development resources. Dederick notes that staffers and students with strong working relationships in other countries have been particularly helpful in building the collection's holdings from Argentina, Mexico, and Spain. Though she, as the librarian, is not the principle liaison in this capacity, the concept is similar to Latin Americanist librarians who maintain close working relationships with book vendors based in Latin America. These librarians depend on trips to book fairs and on book buying trips to expand their collections. Latin Americanist librarians who have regional contacts with musicians or music distribution networks could work to increase awareness about collections such as the LAMC at IU in order for them to make acquisitions from these regions more common. That music from certain countries, regions, or genres is not represented in U.S. library collections does not necessarily indicate that they do not exist, but that they are difficult to obtain without establishing these professional connections. Dederick notes that lack of contacts makes obtaining material from countries like Guatemala, Honduras, Nicaragua, Panama, and Paraguay particularly difficult.

Librarians might also incorporate music into established book buying trips in order to add unique music recordings to their own collections. Those who are not able to do so may inquire whether vendors based in Latin America are able to add music to their approval plans or firm order plans. Some of these vendors offer music or are willing to acquire music based on a profile submitted by a librarian. Sarah J. Adams, Director of the Eda Kuhn Loeb Music Library at Harvard University, relies on book vendors like Susan Bach, who provides recordings lists for Brazilian music.[34] I confirmed that other book vendors, such as Atlantis Livros Ltda., E. Iturriaga & Cia, Libros de Barlovento, and Puvill Libros S.A. offer music for the regions they cover as well. As Gayle Williams noted, some Latin Americanist librarians are already involved in music collection development efforts.[35] For example, at Harvard, Adams also has a shared approval plan for Spanish and Portuguese with Lynn M. Shirey, Librarian for Latin America, Spain, and Portugal in the Widener Library at Harvard University, who also selects many titles and sends notices to Adams.

Collection Development

Besides working with Latin-based vendors, taking book buying trips, and visiting books fairs, there are a myriad of tools that can aid librarians in building and expanding a Latin American music collection. Strategies for seeking out sound recordings such as networking with other librarians, perusing specialty journals, online sources and even radio stations can sometimes be time-consuming, but are very effective. A highly recommended source and perhaps one of the most impressive for those collecting historical recordings is the Audio Preservation Fund.[36] Because many private historical recording collections are being offered to institutions that may not be in a position to accept, Jenny Doctor of the Belfer Audio Archive says that the Audio Preservation Fund functions as a clearinghouse for libraries that can accept materials for free or for the cost of shipping.[37] This is an important resource for librarians like CUNY Dominican Studies Institute Assistant Librarian Jhensen Ortiz who wants to ensure that historical musical records are not only held by private collectors, but are made accessible to all.[38]

Word of mouth also seems to be an effective way for librarians to learn about resources. Interviewees learn about music at the Latin American Studies Association and World History Association conferences. Others find and purchase recordings at local stores or flea markets such as Casa Amadeo in the Bronx. González of FIU's Díaz-Ayala Collection learns about new music recordings from musicologists and researchers in general. By doing extensive reading online and getting in touch with library collections and musicologists who are often also performers, Ortiz has become familiar with historical Dominican and U.S.-based record labels like Ansonia Records, Seeco Records, Tico Records, and Verne Records.[39] David Seubert, Curator of the Performing Arts Collection at the UCSB Library, recommends that non-music librarians find a mentor who has already built a collection of sound recordings.[40]

There are a number of online distributors and vendors of Latin American music recordings that can aid librarians in building Latin American music collections. Several online sources noted may be used to find and/or purchase Latin American music, including YouTube, Amazon.com, F.Y.E., iTunes, Pandora, and Yahoo Music. Other websites geared specifically toward Latin music are Batanga Radio,[41] which works like Pandora, wherein users are able to enter the name of an artist or song, thereby creating a personal radio station that plays songs by that artist or similar ones; Descarga,[42] which offers a large selection of Afro-Latin CDs as well as instructional material, books, films, and a newsletter and reviews; and Museo del Disco,[43] an online music supplier.

The UNESCO Collection of Traditional Music website[44] makes the collection development process easier by including short sound files and a searchable database that allows filtering by genre and country. This collection spans the 1960s through the first decade of the twenty-first century, and includes some previously unreleased work. It is especially interesting for academic libraries since the recordings often come with substantial notes.

The website features a "Tools for Teaching" section with lesson plans on a select number of genres. The Latin American categories are a bit eclectic, including only "American Indian," "Caribbean," and "Latin."

Other distributors cover more specialized materials. For Brazilian music, Tom Moore at FIU recommends online music distributors Saraiva[45] and Tratore.[46] Dederick of IU's LAMC recommends subscriptions to digital streaming music databases with substantial Latin American holdings as one way to jump start a music collection. Though not an online service, Adams of the Music Library at Harvard takes part in the Library of Congress's PL 480 Cooperative Acquisitions program, which includes Brazilian sound recordings.[47] Libraries subscribing to this service will receive a selection of non-returnable classical, folk, and popular Brazilian music CDs from the Library of Congress Overseas Offices in Rio de Janeiro, Brazil.[48]

Journals

Browsing through journals, both academic and popular, give the librarian a good sense of new artists and trends. *Ethnomusicology*, which is available via the full-text database *JSTOR*, does not exclusively cover Latin American material, but when it does, it includes scholarly articles and reviews of monographs, audiovisual, and sound recordings. *Latin Beat Magazine*[49] provides news, reviews, radio hits lists, a calendar of events and regional music columns primarily on salsa and Caribbean music. It ceased publication in 2012 but the website remains active. Other journals mentioned include *Early Music, Jazz Times, Jazzis*, and *Pitchfork*. Remezcla,[50] a website dedicated to news about Latin American and Latino culture, offers opportunities to discover new Latino and Latin American music. Some scholars also use historical Spanish language newspapers to learn what music was played at the time.

Radio

Radio and television are also essential sources for learning about music. Besides satellite radio, some specific stations and programs noted include KPFK's Global Village shows, especially those hosted by Betto Arcos. Others include the Zeta radio station in California, the "Tiene Sabor" radio show on WWOZ, and the NPR programs "Soundcheck" and Alt Latino, hosted by Jasmine Garsd and Felix Contreras, and which focuses on Latin Alternative music and Latino culture.[51] Afropop Worldwide,[52] a radio program and online magazine about the music of the African Diaspora, includes interviews, discographies, reviews and more. Also of note is the 1992 PBS series *Americas*, whose DVDs contain supplementary reading material.

Databases and Indices

Music databases are another way to learn about and explore musical genres. Browsing through the databases can be very valuable in identifying musicians and sound recordings. For more basic background information these include the encyclopedia-style entries found in *Oxford Music Online* and Wikipedia, both of which include discographies. Some artists not easily found in scholarly databases are included on free websites. Thus the latter are important in order to avoid overlooking promising or substantial musicians and music. Important indices are *Music Index Online*, which indexes over 475 journals and includes full text for articles going back to 1970, and *RILM Abstracts of Music Literature,* which targets international music and indexes less common material like ethnographic recordings, electronic resources, conference proceedings, dissertations, and festschriften. In addition, scholars should also consult area studies resources, like one of the staples of Latin American Studies, *HAPI Online* (*Hispanic American Periodicals Index*). A quick search for the subject term "music" pulled over 4,000 records. Currently, only two music journals and one fine arts journal which includes music are being indexed: *Cuadernos de música, Artes visuales* and *Artes escénicas, Latin American Music Review,* and *Revista musical chilena.*[53] The large number of articles found may have been published in non-music journals, and include some titles which have been confirmed to have ceased, including *Anuario interamericano de investigación musical, Boletín inter-americano de música, Revista brasileira de música,* and *Revista musical de Venezuela.* The *International Index to Music Periodicals Full Text* (IIMP) covers over 440 international journals, in some cases dating back to 1874. *International Index to Performing Arts* (IIPA) includes over 97 musical theatre and film music journals. RISM, the *Répertoire International des Sources Musicales* or *International Inventory of Musical Sources,* catalogs print music resources. RIPM, or the *Retrospective Index to Music Periodicals,* indexes 18th through 20th century music-related periodicals. One interesting and highly specialized resource is *Latin American Choral Music,*[54] a free index containing about 13,000 entries dating from 1500 to the present.[55]

Obstacles to Building a Collection: Cataloging

One of the challenges to collecting Latin American music materials is the lack of cataloging records. At least one library noted having a sizeable backlog of music materials including Latin Americana. The large backlog is due, in part, to the fact that many items have no authority records in the Online Computer Library Center (OCLC). Therefore, no bibliographic records can be made, and the materials are set aside for future cataloging. The lack of authority and bibliographic records could indicate several things. First, that U.S. and possibly even Latin American institutions are not collecting music in a comprehensive manner. In the case of music from the colonial period, for example, Orrego-Salas notes that the majority of it is not available in published form.[56] The dearth of materials in collections leads to the absence of bibliographic records available nationally.

Catalogers may also not be trained in creating music authority records and in submitting them to the Library of Congress Name Authority Cooperative Program (NACO). John Wright, Authority Control Librarian at Brigham Young University's Harold B. Lee Library, explains that catalogers who create authority records for music titles in the NACO program must be trained and then given an independent status by a NACO Music Funnel coordinator. The funnel project consists of a group of libraries that have joined together to contribute name authority records to the national authority file, and consolidate their efforts to make a more significant contribution in terms of quantity. Wright notes that even when librarians in Latin America are trained and are working independently, "[t]here are some practical and logistical realities that may make it difficult for all to participate in NACO."[57] Wright notes, "[P]articipants are required to create English language authority records and code them as such ... [by] ... making their notes in English, and they have to have access to the LC-NACO authority file via a national utility like OCLC or SkyRiver."[58]

Non-music librarians interested in building music collections should also note that music cataloging is more specialized than the cataloging of print materials. Ellen Jaramillo, Catalog Librarian at Yale University, explains, "Cataloging music materials requires the use of descriptive cataloging rules written and standardized specifically for music materials, (as opposed to descriptive rules for print materials), and in most cases music catalogers have a vast knowledge of music and/or performance prior to their library school and cataloger training."[59] Catalogers cannot catalog these materials if they have not been trained in descriptive cataloging of music materials or to read music. To compound the problem, few academic libraries have been filling vacant catalog librarian positions. Jaramillo explains that annually libraries lose staff who have the skills and certification to create authority records in special materials like music, and to contribute them to NACO or OCLC, because they are not being replaced. Non-music librarians would be wise to keep these cataloging and access issues in mind and plan out who will be taking responsibility for music cataloging for any items you acquire. A special training effort geared towards catalogers based in the U.S. and abroad who deal with Latin American music may go a long way toward making these recordings accessible more quickly.

Conclusion

The original intention in writing this essay was to advocate for sound recording collection development. It is an accessible form of media that anyone, regardless of academic background, can relate to, and, therefore, can be easily introduced into classroom instruction. Jhensen Ortiz, who is building a historical collection of 45, 78 and 33 rpm records for the CUNY Dominican Studies Institute Archives and Library, notes that having the accompanying physical artifact is also important because it contextualizes artists' music and lives. The text on record sleeves contains information on musicians' early careers that can lead to the discovery of other musicians and music scenes. Examining the sleeve of a merengue album with a somewhat controversial depiction of national identity, Ortiz notes that the artifact's imagery says a lot about the blending of musical and national identity, how these are understood, and how the music was promoted. Having a score collection also enhances our understanding. A score contains lyrics that can be used when the library makes an homage or tribute to the artist. Chilean composer and musicologist Juan Orrego-Salas, founder of the LAMC at IU, regards the increased representation of Latin American composers in music performance programs in the U.S. as one of the LAMC's contributions to the dissemination of Latin American music.[60]

Whether a Latin Americanist librarian chooses to focus on scores, historical music recordings, specific genres, particular countries or regions, or a combination of these, music collection development work will undoubtedly enrich their broader collection, and possibly unearth unique material that will be made known to future generations. Depending on how heavily involved a librarian becomes in collection development, certain things should be taken into consideration. Properly maintaining historical music collections in particular will require continuing education or the addition of staff trained in digitization and preservation, and is something to seriously consider as collections are developed. Building a collection will also be a time intensive undertaking, particularly at first. However, this should not detain librarians from this meaningful endeavor.

Decide on the collection focus, read all the literature available, use the resources listed above, and reach out to the librarians at the music collections listed, and other musicologists and researchers with specific questions in order to build a network. Educate librarians and faculty on how to incorporate music into their collections and instruction. Advocate for databases and indices to include more Latin American music material. There are many ways to ensure that the Latin American musical legacy endures not just in living rooms and on dance floors but within academia, thereby enriching scholarly discussions and projects across multiple disciplines.

NOTES

1. All future references to Latin America include the Caribbean as well.

2. Daniel Zager, "Collection Development and Management," *Notes* 56, No. 3 (March 2000): 569.

3. Nicholas Cook, *Music a Very Short Introduction* (New York: Oxford University Press 1998): vii, quoted in Daniel Zager, "Collection Development and Management," *Notes* 56, No. 3 (March 2000), 569.

4. I would like to acknowledge and thank all of the people who answered my questions and/or allowed me to interview them about their music collections, cataloging, and collection development practices: Sarah Aponte, Fernando Acosta-Rodríguez, Sarah J. Adams, Emma Dederick, Tom Diamant, Verónica González, Sal Güereña, Ellen Jaramillo, Julianna Jenkins, Tom Moore, Jhensen Ortiz, David Seubert, Gayle Williams, and John Wright.

5. http://music.indiana.edu/lamc.

6. Latin American Music Center, "Overview," http://music.indiana.edu/lamc/about/overview.shtml.

7. http://music.indiana.edu/lamc/research-resources/special-collections/espinosa-collection/index.shtml.

8. Latin American Music Center, "Juan Orrego-Salas," http://blogs.music.indiana.edu/lamcconference/exhibits/juan-orrego-salas/ Accessed August 29, 2016.

9. Jacobs School of Music, "IU Latin American Music Center Receives Alfonso Montecino Legacy Collection," http://info.music.indiana.edu/web/page/normal/23980.html Accessed August 20, 2016.

10. www.iucat.iu.edu.

11. https://mdpi.iu.edu/.

12. http://latinpop.fiu.edu.

13. Gayle Williams, telephone interview by author, February 25, 2016.

14. http://latinpop.fiu.edu/advsearch.cfm.

15. http://latinpop.fiu.edu/discography.html.

16. Verónica González, e-mail message to author, February 15, 2016; http://dpanther.fiu.edu/dPanther/collections/DZA.

17. Council on Library and Information Resources, "Popular Music of Latin America and the Caribbean, 1950–1962: Belfer Archive's 45 RPM Collection," http://www.clir.org/hiddencollections/registry/hc.0351. Accessed February 15, 2016; Jenny Doctor, telephone interview by author, January 5, 2016.

18. http://www.clir.org/pubs/reports/pub164.

19. "Latin American Music Center," http://lamc.cua.edu/. Accessed February 15, 2016.

20. "Latin American Music Catalog," libraries.cua.edu/music/lamcatin.cfm. Accessed February 15, 2016.

21. *Ibid.*

22. http://catalog.wrlc.org/search/index.php.

23. frontera.library.ucla.edu.

24. Chicano Studies Research Center, "CSRC Archival Projects," http://www.chicano.ucla.edu/library/csrc-archival-projects.

25. Tom Diamant, telephone interview by author, December 31, 2015.

26. Sarah J. Adams, e-mail message to author, January 4, 2016. http://nrs.harvard.edu/urn-3:FHCL.Loeb.Faids:mus00027.

27. http://library.princeton.edu/.

28. Fernando Acosta-Rodríguez, e-mail message to LALA-L, April 3, 2014.

29. Fernando Acosta-Rodriguez, e-mail message to author, March 1, 2016.

30. http://www.oac.cdlib.org/findaid/ark:/13030/c8x06971/.

31. https://www.ccny.cuny.edu/dsi/library-music-collection-cd.

32. http://www.loc.gov/jukebox/.
33. Verónica González, e-mail message to author, December 15, 2015.
34. Sarah J. Adams, interview by author, January 8, 2016.
35. Gayle Williams, telephone interview by author, February 25, 2016.
36. http://audiopreservationfund.org/.
37. Jenny Doctor, telephone interview by author, January 5, 2016.
38. Jhensen Ortiz, interview by author, January 13, 2016.
39. *Ibid.*
40. David Seubert, e-mail message to author, February 13, 2016.
41. http://www.bradio.com/.
42. www.descarga.com.
43. www.museodeldisco.com.
44. www.folkways.si.edu/unesco.
45. http://www.saraiva.com.br/cds.
46. http://tratore.com.br/.
47. Sarah J. Adams, interview by author, January 8, 2016.
48. Library of Congress Overseas Offices, Rio de Janeiro, Brazil, "Cooperative Acquisitions," https://www.loc.gov/acq/ovop/rio/rio-coop.html. There are currently five CD assortment categories with different pricing levels; more information is available at https://www.loc.gov/acq/ovop/rio/rio-compactdiscs.html.
49. http://www.latinbeatmagazine.com/.
50. http://remezcla.com/music/.
51. Jhensen Ortiz, e-mail message to author, January 20, 2016.
52. www.afropop.org.
53. Orchid Mazurkiewicz, e-mail message to author, January 1, 2016.
54. www.latinamericanchoralmusic.org.
55. Paula Covington, e-mail message to LALA-L, September 13, 2010.
56. Juan Orrego-Salas, "Introduction," in *Scores and Recordings at the Indiana University Latin American Music Center*, ed. Ricardo Lorenz, Luis R. Hernández, and Gerardo Dirié (Bloomington: Indiana University Press, 1995), ix–x.
57. John Wright, e-mail message to author, February 10, 2016.
58. *Ibid.*
59. Ellen Jaramillo, e-mail message to author, February 15, 2016.
60. Juan Orrego-Salas, "Introduction," xiii. *Scores and Recordings at the Indiana University Latin American Music Center* includes a short list of publishers of scores on pages xix–xxxii and encourages interested readers to contact the LAMC for more information.

Collecting the Law
of Latin America

History, Challenges and Trends
in U.S. Law Libraries

Julienne E. Grant *and*
Teresa M. Miguel-Stearns

Law libraries are specialized information centers dedicated to the collection, dissemination, and preservation of legal materials. The American Association of Law Libraries categorizes law libraries by type: academic, government, and private.[1] Patron groups for these libraries vary, but include students, faculty, attorneys, judges, and members of the public. As with any kind of library, law libraries strive to tailor their collections to serve their primary user groups; thus, U.S. law libraries focus on acquiring and providing access to U.S. federal and state materials. A browse through the shelves of many U.S. law libraries, however, will reveal that foreign materials of varying levels of quantity and quality are also available for consultation. The main purpose of this essay is to explore, in historical and modern terms, how U.S. law libraries have approached collecting materials associated with one particular area of the globe—Latin America.[2] After an historical overview of Latin American collections in selected U.S. law libraries, the essay will focus more specifically on collection development approaches and trends. The multiple challenges presented in acquiring legal materials from and about this region will also be discussed, along with various methods that have been utilized to successfully meet those challenges.

What Are Latin American Legal Materials?

Before diving straight into the topic at hand, a short introduction to the kinds of materials under discussion is warranted. The term "Latin American legal materials" is admittedly general in the sense that there are twenty countries in the defined region, each with a unique judicial system and legal publishing tradition. It would be too large an endeavor, though, to report on how U.S. law libraries approach collecting materials from and about each of the twenty nations. Thus, the term "Latin American legal materials" will be used here as a broad rubric to encompass primary and secondary materials pertaining to the laws of Latin American countries—published in all formats within the region, as well as outside of it. Significant variations involving specific countries, however, will be indicated where applicable.

It is essential to briefly examine the law of Latin America itself in order to understand the types of Latin American legal materials available directly from the region, as well as the importance of the various legal texts. To begin with, it is erroneous to suggest that there is a universal set of rules that applies to all twenty nations—a so-called Latin American legal regime. Each country has its own constitution, set of national and local laws, and domestic courts structure. Despite variations in legal systems, however, all twenty Latin American nations follow the civil law tradition to some extent. The civil law tradition, which was introduced by the various European colonizing powers, has its roots in the Roman Republic and generally rejects the notion of judge-made law.[3] These countries' most important legal materials are thus the laws themselves, which are first published in official government gazettes.[4] Individual laws may subsequently be published chronologically as sets of session laws, and further organized by topic in codes that provide comprehensive frameworks for private, commercial, penal, and other areas of law. Digitized versions of gazettes, legislation, codes, and executive branch directives are now routinely posted on government websites, although archival coverage and accessibility vary from country to country.[5]

In addition, constitutions, treaties, and court opinions contribute to the corpus of Latin American legal materials. The first constitutions of newly-independent Latin American nations were drafted in the nineteenth century and have been superseded multiple times in most instances.[6] William S. Hein & Co.'s *World Constitutions Illustrated* database offers digitized versions of historical and current Latin American constitutions in the vernacular, as well as modern versions in English translation. The texts of treaties involving Latin American nations also add to the body of Latin American law. Treaties may be compiled and indexed in print, and many are now available on the World Wide Web. Latin American court opinions are likewise primary legal documents, although these decisions are not often precedential (unlike in common law jurisdictions where the doctrine of *stare decisis* applies).[7] Opinions of the upper-level Latin American courts are published in court reporters in varying levels of thoroughness and regularity, and a number of Latin American tribunals are now posting their decisions online.

Included in the body of Latin American legal resources is secondary literature published in a variety of formats. Although legal scholarship or doctrine (*doctrina*) is not considered to be a source of law per se in Latin America, it is highly valued and utilized heavily as persuasive authority.[8] *Doctrina* may be found in a number of sources, including treatises and law reviews. Other secondary legal literature includes textbooks, encyclopedias, and dictionaries, although their contents may not necessarily rise to the level of *doctrina*. There are a number of publishers in Latin America that specialize in legal materials, including Librería Porrúa in Mexico, Rubinzal-Culzoni in Argentina, Editorial Jurídica in Chile, and Saraiva in Brazil. Although numerous Latin American law reviews are now available electronically, electronic book publishing has not yet had a huge impact in the region.[9]

Latin American legal materials published in English are not plentiful. Although Latin American constitutions are routinely translated into English, there are relatively few translations of Latin American codes on the market.[10] Decisions of Latin American courts are likewise not regularly translated into English. In terms of secondary literature, there is a casebook in English on Latin American law, several monographs about the legal systems of individual countries, and books about specialized areas of law in some jurisdictions. A small number of U.S. law schools publish law reviews that focus on Latin America (*Law and Business Review of the Americas* and *University of Miami Inter-American Law Review*). *Latin Lawyer* is an online magazine that concentrates on business law developments. The Law Library of Congress (LLC) and the Organization of American States (OAS) have both published series on the legal literature and laws of Latin American countries, although much of this material is now outdated. In sum, there is a clear deficit of contemporary Latin American legal literature available in English in the forms of direct translations and analysis.

The types of Latin American legal materials that have historically been available for U.S. law librarians to acquire for their institutions' collections include primary sources, such as government gazettes and codes, and secondary doctrinal literature in the form of treatises. Prior to the advent of the World Wide Web in the 1990s, these sources were available almost exclusively in print, but some are now available in both print and electronic formats, and some only electronically. Although most U.S. law libraries hold only a small percentage of the available print resources, there are a number of repositories that have rich acquisition histories. In order to understand the current challenges and trends in collecting Latin American legal materials, it is useful to explore how several of these noteworthy print collections began and have evolved over time.

Latin American Collections in U.S. Law Libraries

The history of U.S. law libraries begins in the pre-colonial era with the private collections of practicing attorneys. These early collections, which were largely composed of tomes focusing on English law, became the foundations for institutional law libraries. Bar libraries, more specifically, began emerging in the nineteenth century and were supported largely by membership subscriptions. One such library was that of the Association of the Bar of the City of New York which was founded in 1870. Between 1881 and 1889, an extensive catalog of the library's holdings (about 36,000 books) was compiled showing the collection already included Latin American materials.[11] The library's efforts to acquire resources from the region continued into the twentieth century, with developing relationships between the library and booksellers in Brazil, Argentina, Uruguay, Peru, Bolivia, Ecuador, and Colombia.[12] By the 1940s, the library was attempting to collect "the reports, session laws and codes" for every Latin American country.[13]

As the Association's membership increased, so did visits to the library, and the facility responded by adding more books. By 1962, its holdings surpassed 320,000 volumes.[14] Although demand for Latin American materials specifically was not chronicled, the library produced a bibliography on "Doing Business in Latin America" that same year, which suggests that members were increasingly utilizing materials from the region. Indeed, the Association's library was one of a small handful of U.S. law libraries that housed major Latin American collections during that time period.[15] In the early 1990s, however, the library essentially stopped acquiring foreign law resources due to space and budget concerns, along with changes in its patron base. The New York City Bar Association subsequently donated some of its Latin American materials to the Law Library

Microform Consortium (LLMC) for digitizing, and the remaining items were gifted to the Jacob Burns Law Library at the George Washington University Law School.[16] Although the New York City Bar's library no longer houses a Latin American collection, the fruits of its earlier efforts to develop one have certainly not been wasted.

The Los Angeles County Law Library (now LA Law Library) also began as a bar association library in the late nineteenth century. The library received inadequate funding, however, and its stewardship was turned over to the County in 1891, along with its collection of more than 4,000 volumes. The library's first foreign books were purchased in 1894: twenty-eight volumes of Mexican and Spanish law.[17] In 1941, the library began to focus earnestly on its Latin American acquisitions and hired a consultant, Helen L. Clagett, to develop the fledgling collection. Dr. William B. Stern, who served as foreign law librarian from 1939 to 1970, provided some insight into why the library focused so heavily on Latin America at that time. Writing in 1945, he asserted, "Changed political conditions and viewpoints focus attention on our Latin-American neighbors. Information on their legal life becomes of paramount importance."[18] In 1959, Dr. Stern indicated that over half of his library's foreign law queries involved Mexico, primarily due to its geographic proximity.[19]

The LA Law Library continued to devote financial and personnel resources to its foreign law collection generally, and its Latin American collection specifically. The library was included in the lists of major Latin American collections in U.S. libraries in 1957, 1960, and 1970.[20] In a 1972 survey of foreign and international collections in selected U.S. law libraries, Los Angeles County ranked fifth by collection size (213,000), and listed Mexican state gazettes as its area of specialization.[21] In a similar 1988 survey, the library identified itself as collecting the government gazettes of Brazil, Chile, Bolivia, Mexico, Guatemala, and numerous other Latin American nations.[22] A 1992 article suggested that the library's foreign law collection often matched or exceeded those available in the home countries' libraries, with the Latin American and Mexican collections highlighted as examples.[23] The LA Law Library continues to focus on its extensive foreign law collection, with Latin America being an important part; the library currently collects most of the Latin American government gazettes in print, along with codes, selected case reporters, and practitioner-oriented materials.[24]

The collections of the great U.S. law school libraries also evolved during the nineteenth and twentieth centuries, with the twentieth century bringing increased demands for foreign materials. Both world wars contributed to this heightened demand, and academic law libraries acquiesced in order for their law schools to remain competitive.[25] At the University of Michigan in Ann Arbor, the law library purchased a private collection of Mexican and Spanish law books in 1922.[26] Professor Hessel E. Yntema explained that the library's Latin American collection continued to expand in the 1940s as a result of aviation, which increased foreign trade, which in turn created legal problems. He concluded that the "comparative study of the laws of the Americas, especially those affecting international commerce, is of special and immediate interest."[27] In 1950, the director of the Michigan law library, Hobart R. Coffey, travelled to Central and South America (to every country except Bolivia and Paraguay) to purchase additional materials.[28] Michigan's law library continues to collect Latin American materials fairly heavily and currently has an approval plan with RettaLibros in Montevideo for items from Uruguay, Paraguay, Brazil, Cuba, and Venezuela.[29] A number of other U.S. law school libraries have historically emphasized Latin America in their collections and remain dedicated to highlighting that area.[30]

The U.S. law library with perhaps the most extensive history of collecting from this region is the Law Library of Congress. First established as a separate department of the Library of Congress in 1832, the LLC has evolved into the world's largest with about 2.9 million volumes.[31] It is renowned for its collection of foreign law, which covers almost all of the world's nations, including those of Latin America. According to its website, the LLC attempts to acquire government gazettes, constitutions, codes, session laws, case reporters, and a variety of other primary and secondary literature for all major national, state, and equivalent jurisdictions.[32]

The complete history of the Law Library of Congress' Latin American collection would be voluminous, but an attempt will be made here to capture its highlights. In August of 1848, just three months after the termination of the U.S.-Mexican War (1846–1848), the U.S. Congress directed the Law Library to procure all available Mexican constitutions and laws.[33] Four years later, Congress appropriated $1,700 for more Mexican materials, as well as Spanish law books.[34] In 1911, Law Librarian Dr. Edwin Borchard reported that the Law Library was "making a systematic effort to bring its collection of foreign law to a state of high efficiency," including that of Latin America.[35] In 1915, Dr. Borchard added to the Latin American collection after an acquisitions trip to eleven Latin American countries.[36] In 1923, the library hired Dr. John Thomas Vance to travel to Mexico to obtain legal materials for the Library. Vance, who was fluent in Spanish and had worked in the Dominican Republic, was appointed Law Librarian in 1924.

Vance created a strong foundation for the current collection during his nineteen-year tenure as Law Librarian of Congress. In 1940, Vance described the Law Library's most recent efforts to "gather as complete collections as possible of the legislation and jurisprudence" of the twenty Latin American nations.[37] In keeping with the Library's emphasis on Latin American materials, the Latin American Section was formed in January 1943. The section offered reference services focusing on the region, as well as translations of Latin American legislation as requested by members of Congress.[38] Before his death in April 1943, Vance acquired 5,500 volumes of legal materials for the library during a six-month trip to Latin America.[39] In 1943, the American Bar Association's Special Committee on the Facilities of the Law Library of Congress reported:

> Latin America has been, ever since the coming of Dr. Vance, a very important field for the activities of the Law Library of Congress. Both through blanket orders placed to secure complete coverage of current legal publications, and through continuous checking of dealers' offers, library lists, etc., every effort is being made to keep complete and up-to-date collections of laws, codes, court decisions, legal treatises, and other pertinent legal material for each of the Latin American republics. Efforts are constantly being made to fill in the gaps in the collections, both through correspondence and through the utilization of the Library of Congress representatives in Latin America.[40]

One year later, the same committee stated that the library's Latin American collection was "probably more nearly complete than those which exist in any other library," due to Vance's attention.[41]

After Vance's death, the LLC continued its dedication to the Latin American collection by inviting the head of the Biblioteca del Poder Legislativo del Uruguay (Congressional Library of Uruguay) to serve as a consultant in 1946.[42] In 1948, the library initiated a project to microfilm the gazettes of every Mexican state and territory up until 1920.[43] By 1956, the Law Library's Latin American collection was perhaps quantitatively the largest in the world.[44] In 1957, the Latin American Section was renamed the Hispanic Law Division to reflect the inclusion of Spain, Portugal, their possessions, the Philippines, and Puerto Rico in its scope of coverage. The Hispanic Law Division was one of five of the Library's geographic-linguistic divisions that covered the world at that time. Helen L. Clagett served as the division's chief until her retirement in 1971.[45]

In the mid–1960s, Ms. Clagett provided a fascinating glimpse of the division's activities during that time period. She indicated that growing Congressional interest in the region had actually created minor "'research explosions'" within the division.[46] The U.S. Supreme Court also sought research assistance for several cases, including *Banco Nacional de Cuba v. Sabbatino,* which is still the Court's leading case on the Act of State Doctrine.[47] Ms. Clagett attributed part of the proliferating demand for Latin American legal materials to events such as the "Sovietization" of Cuba, the revolution in the Dominican Republic, the presidential succession problem in Argentina, and attacks on the legal status of Guantánamo.[48] According to her, other contributions to the increasing interest in Latin America included the implementation of long-term programs such as the Alliance for Progress.[49]

Ms. Clagett also reported on general reference service the division provided in the early 1960s. In 1965, she indicated that 147 topics had been covered during the prior two years.[50] Examples of reference questions that the division fielded included additional topics related to Cuba, such as the constitutionality of Cuba's revolutionary courts' "'war crimes'" trials, the legal issues surrounding Fidel Castro's ransoming of prisoners in 1962, and the impounding of Cuban planes in the United States by creditors of the Cuban government in the early 1960s.[51] Other queries involved the extradition from Florida of a former president of Venezuela (Marcos Pérez Jiménez) in 1963, and the 1956 disappearance of a Columbia University professor who had been highly critical of the Dominican Republic's Rafael Trujillo.[52] One patron asked whether a foreigner could sit on the bench of any of the Latin American supreme courts.[53]

Although much of it is now outdated, the Law Library of Congress has contributed substantially to the bibliographic literature for Latin American legal materials. Dr. Edwin Borchard published a guide on the law and legal literature of Argentina, Brazil, and Chile (1917), and similar guides were published in the 1940s as part of a project with the Center of Inter-American Legal Studies.[54] Guides published during that period covered Colombia (1943), Cuba, Haiti, and the Dominican Republic (1944), Mexico (1945), Bolivia (1947), Chile (1947), Ecuador (1947), the Mexican States (1947), Paraguay (1947), Peru (1947), Uruguay (1947), Venezuela (1947), and Argentina (1948). The Mexican and Peruvian guides were updated in 1973 and 1976, respectively. The Hispanic Law Division (and its chief, Ms. Clagett, in particular) was instrumental in the publication of most of the aforementioned guides. In addition, the division produced an *Index to Latin American Legislation* that was published as a two-volume set covering 1950–1960, with later supplements covering 1961–1975. The *Index* was automated in 1976 and evolved into the web-based *Global Legal Information Network* (GLIN).[55] GLIN lost financial support from the U.S. government in 2012.[56]

The Law Library of Congress has continued its role as the largest law library in the world, with substantial emphasis on its foreign law collection and related services. Foreign legal specialists who are currently on staff include several whose primary jurisdictional emphasis is a Latin American nation—specifically, Argentina, Brazil, Mexico, and Nicaragua.[57] The Law Library now has a Global Research Directorate with two divisions—Foreign, Comparative, and International Law Divisions I and II. The services and responsibilities related to Latin America are part of Division II.[58] The Law Library supports online initiatives, including the *Global Legal Monitor*, the *In Custodia Legis* blog, and the comprehensive *Guide to Law Online: Nations of the World*. The Law Library also provides online access to its recent reports on various legal topics related to foreign jurisdictions, including the 2009 constitutional crisis in Honduras and the legal implications of Fidel Castro's resignation in 2008.

In sum, the early institutional law libraries in the United States included Latin American materials in their collections, and those collections generally increased in size over time to reflect demand. Factors such as the development of aviation, the proliferation of international trade, geographic proximity, and events in Cuba have all been cited as contributing to this surge in demand. Although there is not a current published list of major Latin American collections in U.S. law libraries, the government law libraries on such a list would certainly include the LA Law Library and the Law Library of Congress. Academic law libraries listed would undoubtedly include those at the University of Michigan, Yale (Lillian Goldman Law Library), Harvard, the University of Texas at Austin (Tarlton Law Library), and the University of Miami. A few private law libraries, such as those of the New York City Bar and global law firm Baker & McKenzie, once had large print collections of Latin American materials.[59] Law firm print collections in general, however, have dwindled or even disappeared in recent years, due to space and budget concerns.[60] As U.S. law libraries continue to add and withdraw Latin American materials, it is useful to take a closer look at the factors and selection tools influencing collection decisions.

Approaches to Collection Development

Law libraries approach collection development much like other types of libraries; that is, their primary goal is to meet users' needs. As aforementioned, different types of law libraries focus on different patron groups. Law school libraries concentrate on their own faculty and students, private law firm libraries acquire materials with their own attorneys in mind, and public court libraries primarily serve the judges and clerks of the court's jurisdiction, as well as members of the public and local attorneys. Law school libraries will likely collect at the instructional or research levels, perhaps emphasizing areas where its programs are strongest, as well as areas where its faculty are conducting research.[61] Law firm libraries will collect in practice areas in which their firms specialize, and public law libraries will likely emphasize primary and secondary materials covering the laws of their own jurisdictions. Law libraries must also decide whether to actually develop a collection in a particular area, or buy on demand.

Law libraries, like most libraries, fashion collection development policies that may address such issues as cost, currency, language, format, and institutional priorities.[62] Space may also come into play. Legal materials in particular make special demands in terms of currency, official status, and authenticity. Legislation may not be applicable if it has recently been amended, and attorneys cannot properly utilize and cite to digitized law if it is not official and authenticated.[63] In terms of foreign law, some law library collection development policies are broad, while others focus on legal system types, regions, or even specific countries. The University of Michigan Law Library's collection development policy, for example, provides parameters for the general category of civil law jurisdictions, noting that it will continue to collect extensively for Bolivia, Guatemala, and Panama as part of a Primary Collecting Responsibilities Agreement.[64] Michigan's policy also includes a supplemental memo for Mexico.[65] The collection development policy of Yale's Lillian Goldman Law Library divides foreign law by region, and includes a section on Latin America.[66] Duke's Goodson Law Library describes its general approach to collecting foreign law, but attaches an Appendix that designates collecting levels by jurisdiction (materials from Mexico, for example, are collected at the research level).[67]

In approaching their collection decisions, law school libraries must also be cognizant of binding standards for American Bar Association (ABA) accreditation, as well as the requirements for membership in the American Association of Law Schools (AALS). Although the *ABA Standards* do not explicitly require that foreign law be part of a law school library's core collection, they do prescribe that the library should support "special teaching, scholarship, research, and service objectives."[68] Thus, the *Standards* essentially require that law school libraries appropriately support a curriculum that includes courses with global content. The *AALS Bylaws*, although not binding in terms of ABA accreditation, require that member law schools adhere to certain rules to maintain their memberships in good standing. Although the bylaws do not specify that an AALS member library should collect foreign law, they do demand that the collection "serve any special research and educational objectives."[69] Just as with the *ABA Standards*, the *AALS Bylaws* suggest that a member library should adequately support a curriculum with international content.[70]

As the demand for international and foreign legal materials has proliferated, so has the need for library personnel who specialize in foreign, comparative, and international law (FCIL). Although there is currently no set of core competencies for FCIL librarians, the law library literature has addressed this with recommendations for various skills that should be required for these types of positions.[71] These recommendations run the gamut from geographic competencies, to foreign language facility, to curiosity and patience. Although not recent, a 1976 article denoted what one author viewed as necessary qualifications for a librarian in charge of Latin American legal collections—at least bilingual, preferably multilingual, familiarity with publishing firms, authors, and pertinent subject matter, and "knowledge of the workings of the various Latin American nations."[72] A number of U.S. FCIL librarians who currently select Latin American legal materials do meet these requisites and are certainly Latin Americanists in their own right.

There are a number of current sources that provide guidance for developing FCIL collections.[73] There is also historical literature providing direction for collecting Latin American legal materials, including a detailed article authored by Dr. William B. Stern in 1945.[74] In 1965, the International Association of Law Libraries (IALL) hosted a panel that Stern himself chaired on the topic of Latin American law. There, panelist Professor Michael A. Schwind of New York University advised librarians not to attempt to cover the entire Latin American region. It is possible, he said, to "have an excellent Latin American law library without trying to get all the books published in all the Latin American countries."[75] In 1970, Professor Fernando J. Figueredo had this piece of advice:

> It is very important that the acquisitions librarian realize that the establishment of a collection of Latin American legal materials also depends on the kind of institution that is going to use it and for what purpose. It must be remembered that all of the Latin American republics operate legally in civil law systems, and thus the language of the statutes tend to be more significant than the corresponding court opinions.[76]

In reviewing the Spanish legal encyclopedia *Nueva Enciclopedia Jurídica* in 1978, Jorge L. Carro essentially proclaimed that the purchase of this encyclopedia could substitute for an entire Latin American collection for law libraries on a tight budget."[77]

The American Association of Law Libraries (AALL) has historically provided guidance for collecting materials from this region. During its early years as an organization, AALL had an active Committee on Securing Latin-American Laws. In its 1910 report, the Committee recommended:

> ... that considerable information concerning the laws of the Latin-American countries could be obtained from the official gazettes of the different countries, as the laws and decrees of the various Latin-American countries are promulgated in these official gazettes before the same take effect. It might be well for the Association or the libraries interested to subscribe for these official gazettes. If the Association should take up this matter it is suggested that the correspondence be conducted in Spanish, as it is understood but little attention is paid to letters in English, and while the correspondence should be carried on in a business-like way, it would also be well to keep in mind that the Latin-American countries are accustomed to forms of diplomacy even in business matters unknown in this country, and communications should be in diplomatic form to receive attention.[78]

During the 1940s, the Association had an active Committee on Cooperation with Latin American Law Libraries. In 1971, the Association published a *Union List of Basic Latin American Legal Materials*, edited by Kate Wallach. The Association subsequently published *Basic Latin American Legal Materials, 1970–1975*, authored by Juan F. Águilar and Armando E. González.

In the 1980s, the Association had an informal but active Latin American Law Librarians (LALL) group.[79] A workshop on Latin American law and reference services was offered at the 1988 AALL Annual Meeting in Atlanta, which featured a number of papers and compiled bibliographies. At that workshop, Yale's Daniel L. Wade presented the results of a survey he had conducted that was "intended to provide an impressionistic snapshot of the collecting of Latin American legal materials in this country."[80] Part of the survey results listed the collection development practices pertaining to Latin American materials for thirty-six U.S. law libraries. Harvard, for example, was emphasizing Brazil and Uruguay, while Georgetown was heavily collecting Mexican materials.[81] The University of Detroit noted "recent intense faculty interest in Central American law" and the University of Miami was adding books purchased from Northwestern's Latin American collection.[82] Continuing with its tradition of fostering Latin American legal collections, the Association currently has a vibrant Latin American Law Interest Group that is part of its Foreign, Comparative, and International Law Special Interest Section.[83]

The advent and ubiquity of the World Wide Web has greatly impacted the development of online Latin American law collections. Most Latin American governments now have transparency laws in place requiring that government information, such as government gazettes, be posted on the Web.[84] Links to Chile's 2008 *Ley de Transparencia* (Law of Transparency)[85] are actually prominently displayed on Chilean government websites. The country's Biblioteca del Congreso Nacional de Chile (Library of the National Congress of Chile) has a highly sophisticated web portal that provides access to Congressional bills, laws, legislative history, and Chilean codes, with explanations of some legislation available in sign language and audio files. Online access to upper-level Latin American court opinions is now relatively common. Many Latin American law reviews are also now available online; two of Mexico's most prestigious law schools, for example, host open access journal repositories.[86]

The posting of Latin American government gazettes, codes, court opinions, and law reviews online has diminished the need for collecting these items in print, although some U.S. law libraries continue to do so. Secondary material in the form of treatises, as well as English translations of primary material, continue to be available almost exclusively in print. Reflecting the need to still collect Latin American legal materials in print, Lillian Goldman Law Library's *Collection Development Policy* clearly even states that it still relies heavily on print materials from and about Latin America.[87] Interestingly, the acquisition of Latin American legal materials in print remains perhaps as challenging as it was over one hundred years ago.

Challenges in Acquiring Latin American Legal Materials

Historical Challenges

U.S. law libraries have always faced challenges in acquiring Latin American legal materials. Franklin O. Poole of the Association of the Bar of the City of New York described frustrations he encountered in purchasing foreign law books in the early twentieth century:

> The Latin American field has presented the most difficulties. The law book trade is not organized. The dealers know little or nothing about publications outside of their own city or it would seem in many cases, outside of those they themselves issue; and most unfortunately they do not in most instances appear to desire business relations with North American buyers.[88]
> … Difficulty has been experienced in arranging for continuations. It has been our experience that these can only be obtained by periodical prodding. Except for Colombia, Brazil, Uruguay, and the Argentine we have so far been unable to secure catalogues showing current legal publications, and these catalogues are somewhat irregular and do not give satisfactory information as to all the publications in those countries.[89]

Some twenty-five years later, in 1942, Miles O. Price, Law Librarian of Columbia University, nostalgically described his adventures collecting legal materials from "South of the Border." Mr. Price noted that prior to World War II, he had relied on Dutch dealers to supply the library with their law books and periodicals from South America. However, dissatisfaction with price and service from the Dutch dealers, combined with the closing of European markets due to the war, precipitated his nearly six-month trip to South America, including to Brazil, Uruguay, Argentina, Chile, and Peru. Mr. Price noted several advantages to traveling to the area and buying directly from booksellers in these countries:

> First, it permitted actual inspection of the available material, infinitely better in book selection than the best dealer's catalog. Furthermore, it turned up material not listed anywhere, as far as I had discovered. Second, prices were much lower than dealers' quotations. Fairly typical comparisons were $39 instead of $200; $150 for $480; $165 for $500; 90 cents for $9, etc. I saved nearly twice the cost of my entire trip, less my salary, in Santiago alone, based upon actual quotations in hand. Third, and vastly important, I was able to secure complete sets and other material which otherwise would have been unobtainable…. Fourth, advantageous contacts were established for future purchases.[90]

Mr. Price explained the need for legs, luck, and lingering to obtain the best legal material in the region: legs for traipsing around a city, luck in stumbling upon obscure bookstores and even more obscure books, and lingering around a bookstore long enough to work one's way into the basement, for example, where Mr. Price found many valuable hidden treasures.[91] Of course, knowledge of Spanish was essential too, since the second language at the time was French, not English.[92] Mr. Price observed that some bookshops were found in unexpected places while others were logically located next to law schools and the courts.[93] He noted that prices in Argentina and Uruguay were much higher than in other countries in South America.[94] He described many fine libraries in the region "though the service and organization expected in the United States are not yet common."[95]

Dr. William B. Stern of the LA Law Library described his library's acquisitions process at the Fourth Seminar on the Acquisition of Latin American Library Materials (SALALM) in 1959.[96] Dr. Stern explained that the library attempted to use established general bookdealers and importers for acquisitions. However, he noted that general dealers often "fail in the field of law" even though they might excel in other academic areas.[97] Dr. Stern explained:

> Our Library deals therefore with bookdealers, book agents (who may work from their home or governmental office), stationery stores, department stores, etc. to the extent necessary... [M]ost of our correspondence with Spanish speaking countries is conducted in Spanish ... [P]urchases are in the long run less expensive than gift requests and exchanges. Gifts and exchanges are likely to be received sporadically; claiming of overdue or missing parts is difficult and on the whole useless ... exchanges are frequently a one way street.[98]

Dr. Stern continued with a discussion of the difficulty in acquiring government gazettes, illustrated with specific examples from various countries.[99]

Professor Fernando J. Figueredo reported on the "burdensome task" of acquiring Latin American legal materials to SALALM in 1970.[100] He shared what he believed were some of the difficulties in collecting legal materials from the region, including possessing legal knowledge of all the different countries, language barriers, general lack of good indices, delays in publication and distribution, and acquiring official publications due to bureaucratic obstacles.[101] Professor Figueredo advised against using the commercial Latin American Cooperative Acquisitions Program (LACAP) for legal materials but was, surprisingly, a proponent of exchanges with Latin American law schools.[102] Professor Figueredo opined that the best way to acquire legal publications was through bookstores or bookstore-publishing companies, rather than from the publishing houses directly, so that one can obtain publications from a variety of publishing houses. The author also suggested reviewing the few general catalogs of Latin American materials that are received by university libraries. Professor Figueredo concluded with an ambitious proposal to establish five centers of acquisitions in Latin America—Argentina, Chile, Brazil, Venezuela, and Mexico—in cities with established booksellers. In each of these centers, local lawyers and law school professors would recommend and select books for U.S. law libraries. Professor Figueredo maintained that such a program was already underway in Argentina and Venezuela.[103]

In 1984, Ellen Schaffer, referring to Professor Figueredo's 1970 work, provided an update on the difficulties in obtaining Latin American legal materials.[104] Ms. Schaffer summarized the necessary skills needed to establish and maintain a Latin American legal collection in a U.S. law library: "good fortune combined with language knowledge, a familiarity with the legal systems involved, a tenacity of spirit, and a sense of humor."[105] Rather than focusing on these problems, however, Ms. Schaffer provided creative solutions and methods for successfully acquiring needed legal publications. Ms. Schaffer first pointed to some of the classic bibliographic and reference works in the area, and then shared success stories with various publishers and bookdealers in Latin America.[106] She then suggested ways of contacting government offices, businesses, universities, and people in the region who could all conceivably assist a U.S. library acquire legal materials.[107] Ms. Schaffer provided appendices of central banks, statistical agencies, and approval plan bookdealers.[108]

21st Century Challenges

Many of the observations, concerns, and methods expressed by Latin American acquisitions experts in the twentieth century remain true and accurate today. For example, prices in Argentina are generally the highest in the region; legal bookstores are often near law schools and courts, but also in obscure corners of the city; the book trade in some Latin American countries is still highly unorganized; catalogs are incomplete; visiting the region is essential in order to establish connections with booksellers and find material that cannot be found elsewhere; and Spanish language skills are essential (as is Portuguese if collecting Brazilian legal materials).

Additionally, there are still very specific challenges to collecting Latin American legal materials and these challenges continue to vary by country. The Latin American countries with the most impact in legal publishing today are Argentina, Brazil, Chile, Colombia, and Mexico. Peru, Uruguay, and Venezuela (especially before the country's economic collapse and paper shortage) also contribute significantly to the development of law in the region. Publishers in countries such as Bolivia, Ecuador, and Guatemala produce important material pertaining to indigenous law, while human rights materials flow from almost every corner of the region, Ciudad Juárez to Patagonia, Rapa Nui to Rio de Janeiro.

Although there has been a proliferation of laws (including legislation, decrees, and regulations), court decisions, and doctrine from the primary countries in particular, collecting relevant and useful materials can be difficult. Developing sustainable collection plans for the region is a constantly evolving process.

Overcoming the Challenges and Creating a Great Collection of Latin American Legal Materials

Latin American Legal Systems

The countries most important to a law library will depend on the emphasis of the collection, both historical and current. If current business law is important, for example, the acquisition of legal materials from Panama might be emphasized, as the country has seen a significant increase in foreign investment and commercial activity in recent years. If a focus of the collection is human rights, many of the Latin American countries, including Argentina, Chile, Paraguay, Guatemala, and Nicaragua, will have important texts to contribute. If the collection has a focus on legal history, Chile and Argentina will provide a plethora of material. If constitutional law is an emphasis of the collection, treatises about the decisions of Colombia's Constitutional Court, one of the first in the world and upon which many are modeled, will be of high importance.

When collecting primary law of Latin American countries, one cannot rely solely on one's knowledge of U.S. law and collection techniques to guide acquisitions. Additionally, one must keep in mind that, as aforementioned, each country's legal regime is unique despite having deceptively familiar legal systems, such as democratically elected leaders and legislators, and an independent judiciary. Each country is also unique in how the various sources of law are weighted.

The design and development of Argentina's government, for example, was heavily influenced by the United States. The Argentine legislature has two chambers, and there are multiple levels of judiciary culminating in a single high court. This is where the similarities end when translating collection practices for U.S. legal materials to those of Latin America. As discussed previously, the Argentine legal system, like those of all former Spanish colonies in Central and South America, is rooted in the civil law tradition. As a result, legislation is organized differently and assigned a particular hierarchy. Also, writings of prominent scholars, especially in the form of annotations to legal codes (such as the civil code) are given higher weight than in the United States. Finally, court decisions (*jurisprudencia*) are generally, but not always, accorded lesser weight, if any, than court decisions in the United States.[109] Teresa Miguel-Stearns explains some of the specific anomalies of Argentine jurisprudence:

> The *Corte Suprema de Justicia de la Nación* (CSJN), Argentina's highest tribunal, was created in 1853 by the Argentine Constitution and modeled after the Supreme Court of the United States of America. It has seven justices (as opposed to nine in the United States). The decisions of the U.S. Supreme Court and scholarly treatises of North American jurists continued to influence Argentine jurisprudence throughout the 19th century. As a result of this U.S. influence, the CSJN follows notions of judicial review similar to the U.S. Supreme Court. The CSJN will only hear *a posteriori* controversies where the parties have standing, the case is ripe, and the controversy is not moot. Thus, the CSJN does not hear *a priori* (abstract) cases as do many other high courts in the region following civil law tradition.
>
> One significant difference between the CSJN and the Supreme Court of the United States is that the decisions of the CSJN bind only the parties to the ruling of the Court; there is no express doctrine of *stare decisis*. Over time, however, the CSJN has successfully persuaded the lower courts to follow the rulings of the CSJN by stating, for example, that it is the "moral duty" of the lower courts to follow the nation's supreme tribunal. The CSJN subsequently scolded lower courts for not following CSJN decisions and declared that such behavior undermines the judiciary as an institution. Lower courts have generally been complicit such that although not expressly stated in the Constitution or elsewhere, the decisions of the CSJN have evolved into binding precedent in many regards, though to what extent remains unclear. From the founding of the CSJN, its decisions have been published in the *Fallos de la Corte Suprema de Justicia de la Nación,* the official print court reporter (which is available in full-text pdf on the Court's website).[110]

This is just one example of the basic structure and influence of a high court. Each of the Latin American countries' judiciary is organized differently and its decisions are granted varying degrees of weight. Each country's court decisions are also published, if at all, in its own manner. A quick way to gain an understanding of each country's legal system is by reviewing any of several guides to understanding the legal system of a foreign country.[111]

The Distribution of Latin American Legal Publications

Understanding the varied nature of the legal systems for each country will help a collector determine what is important to the collection. The next challenge is learning what is generally being published in each country. There are several ways to gain an understanding of what is available in print in any given country. First, legal research guides often contain bibliographical information that will be helpful. Second, local students and scholars from the area are a valuable source of information. Third, traveling to foreign book fairs is beneficial for a variety of reasons. Fourth, there are now neutral (not attached to any publishing house) vendors based in many Latin American countries that sell legal materials to libraries.

Research Guides

Research guides, such as those on the GlobaLex and LLRX websites, as well as topical and country-specific research guides created by law librarians around the world, can be fruitful starting points for gaining an understanding of the legal literature of a particular country. For example, the Argentine GlobaLex guide, written by Argentine lawyer and law librarian, Gloria Orrego-Hoyos, has a section on the current legal codes along with information about the country's legal publishers.

Local Scholars

Another source of information about current legal publications from Latin America is graduate students at the law school who are from the region. Every few years, it is a worthwhile effort to speak with students from Latin America to get their opinions on which publishers are the strongest. Graduate students are often thrilled to be able to suggest titles in their area of expertise, share who the most prolific legal scholars are in their respective countries, and explain the current state of legal publishing. Visiting professors and scholars from Latin America can also be very helpful for the same reasons.

Book Fairs and Bookstores

Attending national book fairs in Latin American countries is an excellent way to meet vendors, to understand the quantity and quality of legal texts published in a country, and to explore university presses, small publishers, subject-specific publishers, government presses, and non-profit and NGO publishers. Book fairs allow the collector to gain a deep understanding of the legal publishing scene in that country and how it is changing over time. For example, just in the last two decades, LexisNexis bought many significant local legal publishers in various countries, including Abeledo Perrot (Argentina), Ediciones Técnicas (Chile), and Dofiscal (Mexico); and then sold them in 2008 to a Dutch company, Legal Publishing Group.[112] Thomson Reuters purchased Legal Publishing Group in 2011, acquiring Abeledo Perrot and the others.[113] Thomson Reuters also purchased La Ley (Argentina), Revista Dos Tribunais (Brazil), and more. Thus, the legal publishing industry continues to evolve at a rapid pace.

Book fairs also provide an opportunity to acquire unique items for the collection from smaller publishers or government presses that are not yet on the radar of local vendors or distributors. Attendance at book fairs provides an excellent opportunity to meet with a local vendor, walk around together, and educate the vendor on the subject matter, publishers, and types of materials that are important to the law library. Shopping together is generally a great way to educate a vendor on the priorities of the law library.

Lastly, while at book fairs it is easy to explore the city in order to find bookstores that sell legal materials. Many of these bookstores will be adjacent to courthouses and law schools. Some will be the storefront of the publisher; others will have books from many publishers. Still other bookstores will be in obscure locations throughout the city.[114]

Neutral Booksellers

Most of the vendors who distribute and sell Latin American legal materials to libraries in the United States today[115] understand the general business model employed by U.S. libraries. That is, libraries will pay for books or other materials after the items have arrived at that library; most libraries do not pay in advance for anticipated acquisitions. However, smaller vendors from smaller countries often struggle to provide all the information required for U.S. libraries to establish the vendor in university financial systems. Knowledge of Spanish (and Portuguese for Brazil) is essential for fluid and accurate communications.

Generally, vendors prepare and send lists of books, pamphlets, and other material they acquire and are offering for sale to U.S. libraries, although these lists are often incomplete since many of the vendors do not deal exclusively in the sale and distribution of legal materials.[116] Librarians then review the lists and send purchase orders back to the vendor for certain titles. If firm orders are not done in a timely fashion, the library risks missing the opportunity to acquire material due to short print runs. Many established vendors with whom a law library has a good, ongoing relationship, will respond quickly to rush requests, and often notify the librarian of special purchase opportunities.

Some of the larger countries have multiple vendors. For example, Brazil is home to at least two significant distributors of legal books, Susanne Bach Books and Atlantis Livros. Additionally, Librería García Cambeiro, based in Buenos Aires, has an office in Brazil (LatBooks Brasil) and distributes law books from Brazil to U.S. libraries as well. Each vendor has its own process for acquiring, offering, and pricing legal material. In countries where there are multiple vendors, it is always worth comparing the titles, publishers, and prices in order to ensure the library is acquiring the best legal texts the country produces and the best price.

Other countries have less established legal vendors. Mexico, for example, is surprisingly weak and unstable in the distribution of legal materials. In recent decades, several distributors have combined, separated, ceased operations, and reappeared. None is particularly strong in the distribution of legal materials, but several irregularly offer a small and varied quantity of legal materials from a country that produces a massive amount of legal texts. In this situation, it is worth utilizing every vendor possible, reviewing and comparing their lists, and establishing close ties with the vendors so they remember to acquire legal materials as they travel about purchasing other non-legal texts. It is also well-worth going to the annual Feria Internacional del Libro de Guadalajara (International Book Fair of Guadalajara) in order to understand the magnitude of the legal publishing industry and to try to forge connections with publishers directly. Some publishers, such as Porrúa, will sell directly to U.S. libraries, but only after much persistence and effort by the librarian.

The currency or recency of legal materials received in U.S. libraries also varies by country. In Brazil, where most publications are released once or twice annually, the materials are received in U.S. libraries rather quickly and efficiently. In Central America, where publications are sporadic and printed in short runs, it is often hard for vendors to acquire material at all. Sometimes, however, they are able to find items on second or third sale.

One way to combat the problem of delinquent distribution is to establish an approval plan with a vendor. For example, if a library generally purchases the most important human rights material from Central American countries, that library can enter into an approval plan with a Central American vendor for a certain annual dollar amount and leave the selection to the vendor. In this way, the vendor, when traveling throughout the region, will not hesitate to purchase a relevant item knowing that the vendor has a budget and can make the independent judgment as to whether a certain item is relevant to the collection.

Approval plans generally take several years of refinement before they run seamlessly. The librarian must review each shipment of materials and communicate both good and poor acquisitions to the vendor so that the vendor can better understand the library's profile. The librarian also needs to monitor the vendor's spending. However, once a vendor knows the library's profile and budget, a library can greatly benefit from the acquisition of timely, relevant materials, and the librarian's time can be spent performing other activities.

Exchanges

Historically, exchanges were thought to be an effective way of obtaining legal serials from foreign law schools at a low or no cost. However, over time, these exchanges have proven unsustainable because they are difficult and time-consuming to track, and because so many serial publications in Latin America, such as law reviews, are short-lived. Such efforts inevitably either become one-sided with U.S. law libraries sending long-standing and regularly published law reviews without equal reciprocation; or break down altogether due to change in personnel and other disruptions to the original agreement. Rather, standing orders with a reliable vendor have proven much more effective. With a standing order, a vendor knows to send the next volume or issue of a serial as soon as it is published. This is similar to an approval plan arrangement in that there is an agreement in place that does not require the vendor to obtain permission from the library before sending material.

Collaborative Acquisition and Collection Development Initiatives

Collaborative efforts in acquisitions and collection development have historically been a means of addressing the specific challenges related to crafting collections of Latin American legal materials. In the second half of the twentieth century, acquiring law books from Latin America was becoming more systematic but still inconsistent. In September 1958, with the support of Congress and several libraries participating in the Farmington Plan, William H. Kurth of the Library of Congress embarked on a three-month trip to Mexico and South America to acquire Latin American research materials (including some law) for the Library of Congress and the supporting libraries.[117] Prior to departure, Mr. Kurth circulated an extensive questionnaire in which libraries indicated areas of interest and specific titles for acquisition.[118] Upon his return, he issued over 100 field reports. Some general observations of the publishing industry in Latin America included that many titles and government publications are printed in short runs of one-to-two thousand copies, which make them difficult to locate; and periodicals are a struggle for the local book trade as well as the international one.[119] Commenting on Kurth's trip, as well as cooperation initiatives in more general terms, Dr. Stern wrote:

> First of all, we suggest a greater degree of cooperation among American libraries. All investigating and purchasing missions should be cooperative enterprises. We are very grateful to the Library of Congress in sharing the results of Mr. Kurth's recent trip with other libraries.... The Los Angeles County Law Library has recently engaged in a series of cooperative acquisition projects for unusual foreign materials free of charge.[120]

In 1970, Mario Goderich, Law Librarian at the University of Miami, stressed the need for cooperative acquisitions.[121] He provided many excellent reasons for such an undertaking, including the ability to increase holdings nationwide, eliminate duplication, meet increasing demands for specialized material, and address space issues. He acknowledged the difficulties, such as meeting local needs, owning appropriate material rather than having to borrow it, and sustainability. Mr. Goderich shamed the library profession for allowing the commercialization of acquisitions in the Latin American Cooperative Acquisitions Program (LACAP); and praised the Farmington Plan, though far from perfect, as the first national attempt at cooperative acquisitions.[122]

Mr. Goderich also highlighted the "Chicago Plan" of the 1930s and 40s. The Chicago Plan involved a group of law librarians from four law libraries in Chicago who formed an association to, among other activities, collaborate on collection efforts. After creating a union list and noting significant duplication and serious gaps in their collections, they agreed to each take responsibility to collect in certain areas and share freely with the other members.[123]

After noting these noble collection development programs, Goderich challenged law librarians to renew cooperative efforts. He gave several possible reasons for their reluctance including the independent nature of many law libraries, institutional rivalry, local patron needs, and inherent difficulties in dividing collection development responsibilities.[124] Nonetheless, Goderich was certain that "time will take its toll; and these attitudes will give way to necessity." He called on the American Association of Law Libraries to formulate a national plan, but reminded readers that "the responsibility for change and adaptation lies within each one of us."[125]

Collaborative collection development is obviously not a new idea but it is enjoying a renaissance and gaining momentum in this twenty-first century era of tightened budgets. Although cooperative book-buying trips like those of William Kurth in 1958 are infrequent today due to greater access to legal material with established book vendors in the region, there are many other opportunities for cooperation.

In the northeast United States, the Northeast Foreign Law Librarians Cooperative Group (NEFLLCG) endeavors to spread collection responsibilities among its member libraries, informally, to cover much of the world. NEFLLCG, formerly known as the New York Law Library Group (NYLLG), overlapped for several years with an earlier effort at collaborative collection development initiated by members of the Research Libraries Group Law Program Committee wherein certain libraries were asked to take primary collection responsibilities (PCRs) for various countries.[126] The same idea permeated NYLLG and today's NEFLLCG. Original NYLLG members were the law libraries of Columbia, Fordham, New York University, and Yale. Original NEFLLCG members were the NYLLG law libraries plus the University of Pennsylvania. NEFFLCG met bimonthly and the Law Library of Congress and Harvard attended the meetings as observers.

Today, NEFLLCG has expanded to include Georgetown and Harvard. The group meets twice annually and maintains an evolving list of countries to which members have self-assigned vigorous collecting responsibilities (VCRs). VCR is loosely defined and also organic. A few years ago, as budgets continued to shrink, members agreed that a VCR should include acquiring codes and judicial decisions, usually in the vernacular, and some legal monographs. VCR assignments have changed over time depending on faculty needs and financial constraints. NEFLLCG also maintains a spreadsheet of foreign and international legal databases to which members subscribe. This is purely informative, and there is no agreement regarding who is responsible for maintaining a subscription to a particular database, and no obligation to license a database at any time. Members agree that database subscriptions are subject purely to the needs of the institution at a moment in time.

Conclusion

U.S. law libraries have a long and rich history of collecting Latin America legal materials, and they continue that tradition today. Politics, migration, and trade are but a few reasons why access to legal information from Latin America is crucial to the community of scholars, politicians, and lawyers in the United States. Advancements in travel and technology make collecting easier in many respects, such as access to vendors and publishers, and speed in acquiring material; and more difficult in other respects, such as navigating the overwhelming volume of materials flowing from the region while simultaneously seeking the hard-to-find but important texts. There is no single source for magically creating and maintaining a comprehensive collection. Rather, just as it did 100 years ago, collecting the law of Latin America takes time, patience, diligence, and hard work.

Notes

1. American Association of Law Libraries, "Types of Law Libraries," accessed April 23, 2016, http://www.aallnet.org/mm/Careers/lawlibrarycareers/Types-of-Law-Libraries.html.

2. For purposes of this discussion, the term "Latin America" refers to the twenty nations that signed (with the United States) the 1948 charter establishing the Organization of American States (OAS). Charter of the Organization of American States, April 30, 1948, 2 U.S.T. 2394, 119 U.N.T.S. 3 (entered into force December 13, 1951), http://www.oas.org/dil/treaties_A-41_Charter_of_the_Organization_of_American_States.htm.

3. John Henry Merryman and Rogelio Pérez-Perdomo, *The Civil Law Tradition: An Introduction to the Legal Systems of Europe and Latin America*, 3rd ed. (Stanford: Stanford University Press, 2007), 23.

4. For an explanation of the hierarchies of the legal instruments of individual Latin American countries, see Rubens Medina and Cecilia Medina-Quiroga, *Nomenclature & Hierarchy: Basic Latin American Legal Sources* (Washington, D.C.: Library of Congress, 1979).

5. For detailed information on electronic legal resources of individual Latin American countries, see Marci Hoffman, ed., *Foreign Law Guide* (BrillOnline *Reference Works*: Koninklijke Brill NV, 2015), http://referenceworks.brillonline.com/browse/foreign-law-guide.

6. Ángel R. Oquendo, *Latin American Law*, 2nd ed. (New York: Foundation Press, 2011), 126.

7. Some Latin American courts, however, do issue binding precedent in certain instances. See Teresa M. Miguel-Stearns, "Judicial Power in Latin America: A Short Survey," *Legal Information Management* 15 (June 2015): 100–107.

8. M.C. Mirow, *Latin American Law: A History of Private Law and Institutions in Spanish America* (Austin: University of Texas Press, 2004), 197.

9. Julieta Lionetti, "E-Books in Spanish Latin America: The New El Dorado or a Mirage?" *Publishing*

Perspectives, August 29, 2012, http://publishingperspectives.com/2012/08/e-books-in-spanish-latin-america-the-new-el-dorado-or-a-mirage/#.VrjvyGdIg5s.

10. For example, Lawrence Publishing in Baton Rouge, Louisiana, offers English translations of several Latin American codes in print, but these are not updated with the frequency required to keep them current.

11. George Martin, *Causes and Conflicts: The Centennial History of the Association of the Bar of the City of New York 1870–1970* (Boston: Houghton Mifflin, 1970), 326; William J.C. Berry, comp., *Catalogue of the Library of the Association of the Bar of the City of New York* (New York: J.J. Little, 1892).

12. Franklin O. Poole, "Foreign Law Books—How to Secure Them," *Law Library Journal* 8 (January 1916): 71.

13. Alfred B. Lindsay and Fred B. Rothman, "Resources of Law Libraries in New York City," *Law Library Journal* 36 (1943): 11.

14. Martin, *Causes and Conflicts*, 348.

15. Columbus Memorial Library, "Major Latin American Collections in Libraries of the United States," Appendix C in *Final Report of the Second Seminar on the Acquisition of Latin American Library Materials June 19–20, 1957* (Austin: Institute of Latin American Studies, University of Texas, 1958); Marietta Daniels Shepard, *Major Latin American Collections in Libraries of the United States*. Cuadernos Bibliotecologicos no. 1 (Washington, D.C.: Unión Panamericana, Secretaría General de la Organización de los Estados Americanos, 1960).

16. Richard Tuske, Director of the Library, New York City Bar Association, e-mail message to Julienne E. Grant, April 27, 2016.

17. Gail H. Fruchtman, "The History of the Los Angeles County Law Library," *Law Library Journal* 84 (1992): 697, 699 (quoting *L.A. Daily J.*, November 22, 1949: 1,2).

18. William B. Stern, "Latin-American Law Books in Anglo-American Law Libraries," *Law Library Journal* 38 (1945): 4.

19. William B. Stern, "The Acquisition of Latin American Materials at the Los Angeles County Law Library," in *Final Report and Papers of the Fourth Seminar on the Acquisition of Latin American Library Materials June 18–19, 1959* (Washington, D.C.: Library of Congress, 1960), 104.

20. Columbus Memorial Library, "Major Latin American Collections"; Shepard, *Major Latin American Collections*; Kent E. Miller and Gilberto V. Fort, *Major Latin American Collections in Libraries of the United States*. Cuadernos Bibliotecologicos 1 (rev.) (Washington, D.C.: Secretaría General, Estados Unidos Americanos, 1970).

21. Igor I. Kavass, "Foreign and International Law Collections in Selected Law Libraries of the United States: Survey, 1972–1973," *International Journal of Law Libraries* 1 (1973): 126, 131.

22. Ellen G. Schaffer and Thomas R. Bruce, eds. *Directory of Foreign Law Collections in Selected Law Libraries* (Littleton, CO: Fred B. Rothman, 1991).

23. Fruchtman, "Los Angeles County Law Library," 699.

24. Neel Agrawal, Global Law Librarian, LA Law Library, telephone conversation with Julienne E. Grant, April 19, 2016.

25. Christine A. Brock, "Law Libraries and Librarians: A Revisionist History; or More Than You Ever Wanted to Know," *Law Library Journal* 67 (1974): 345.

26. Margaret A. Leary, "Building a Foreign Law Collection at the University of Michigan Law Library, 1910–1960," *Law Library Journal* 94 (Summer 2002): 408 n55.

27. Hessel E. Yntema, "Research in Inter-American Law at the University of Michigan," *Michigan Law Review* 43 (December 1944): 553.

28. Leary, "Building a Foreign Law Collection," 410.

29. Alex X. Zhang, Reference Librarian, University of Michigan Law Library, e-mail message to Julienne E. Grant, April 27, 2016.

30. The Harvard Law School Library, for example, has approval plans for Colombia and Uruguay. The law library also shares a plan with Harvard's main research library (Widener) that provides extensive coverage of human rights in Argentina and Brazil. The law library is also setting up approval plans for Venezuela, Argentina, Brazil, and Cuba. J. Bridget Reischer, Collection Development Librarian for Foreign and International Law, Harvard Law School Library, e-mail message to Julienne E. Grant, April 29, 2016.

31. Law Library of Congress, "About the Law Collections," last updated September 22, 2015, https://www.loc.gov/law/about/collections.php.

32. *Ibid.*

33. Library of Congress, *Law Library of Congress: A Brief History of the First Hundred and Fifty Years 1832–1982* (Washington, D.C.: Library of Congress, 1982), 7.

34. *Ibid.*

35. Dr. Edwin Borchard, "Guides to Foreign Law Literature, Extract from Report of the Librarian of Congress for 1910–11," *Law Library Journal* 4 (January 1912): 35.

36. Library of Congress, *Law Library of Congress*, 14.

37. John Thomas Vance, "Need for a Center of Latin-American Legal Study," *ABA Journal* 26 (September 1940): 707.

38. Harold M. Stephens, chair. "Report of the Special Committee on the Facilities of the Law Library of

Congress," *Annual Report of the American Bar Association* 69 (1944): 293. The American Bar Association authorized the creation of this committee in 1932 to address what it deemed to be the overall neglect of the Law Library and the need for its development. John F. Dockweiler, "The Nation's Principal Repository of Legal Literature," *American Bar Association Journal* 24 (May 1938): 404.

39. Dr. Eldon R. James, "Report of the Special Committee on the Facilities of the Law Library of Congress," *Law Library Journal* 37 (November 1944): 101.

40. Stephens, "Report of the Special Committee," 293.

41. Dr. Eldon R. James, "Report of the Special Committee," 99.

42. "Uruguayan Librarian to Consult on Latin-American Collection," *American Law and Lawyers* 8 (April 9, 1946): 4.

43. Ronald Hilton, ed., *Handbook of Hispanic Source Materials and Research Organizations in the United States.* 2nd ed. (Stanford: Stanford University Press 1956), 100.

44. *Ibid.*, 101.

45. Obituary, "Helen Lord Clagett, Library of Congress Official," *Washington Post*, January 14, 1989; "Mrs. Clagett played a major role in building the largest collection of Hispanic legal materials ever assembled and received numerous commendations for her work in preparing guides to the law and legal literature of Latin American republics." Library of Congress, *Annual Report of the Librarian of Congress for the Fiscal Year Ending June 30, 1971* (Washington, D.C.: G.P.O., 1972), 67.

46. "Summary of Annual Report 1964–1965 Law Library of Congress," *International Association of Law Libraries Bulletin* 16 (1966): 22 (reproduced from the *L.C. Information Bulletin* 24 (September 7, 1965): 482–84).

47. *Banco Nacional de Cuba v. Sabbatino*, 376 U.S. 398 (1964); The Act of State Doctrine bars U.S. courts from questioning the validity of a foreign country's sovereign acts that occur within its own territory.

48. Helen L. Clagett, "Reference Work and Bibliographical Studies at the Law Library of the Library of Congress in the Field of Latin American Law," *International Association of Law Libraries Bulletin* 15 (November 1965): 7.

49. *Ibid.*, 8.

50. *Ibid.*, 10.

51. *Ibid.*

52. *Ibid.*

53. *Ibid.*, 11.

54. Dr. John Thomas Vance initially proposed the idea for the Center of Inter-American Legal Studies in 1940. The Center was funded by the U.S. State Department, and before the funds were exhausted, the Law Library produced legal guides for most Latin American countries—with the notable exception of Brazil. Such a guide would have supplemented Dr. Borchard's 1917 work. See Clagett, "Reference Work," 13.

55. Claire M. Germain, "Digitizing the World's Laws," in *The IALL International Handbook of Legal Information*, ed. Richard A. Danner and Jules Winterton (Surrey, England: Ashgate, 2011), 192.

56. There are now plans for a GLIN 2. See the GLIN Foundation website, http://www.glinf.org/rfi-rfp/vision-glin2.

57. Law Library of Congress, "About the Organization," last updated February 28, 2014, https://www.loc.gov/law/about/organization.php.

58. Luis Acosta, Chief, Foreign, Comparative, and International Law Division II, Global Legal Research Directorate, Law Library of Congress, e-mail message to Julienne E. Grant, January 12, 2016.

59. See Daniel L. Wade, "Survey of Latin American Law in U.S. Law Libraries," in *Workshop on Latin American Law and Law Related Reference Sources* (unpublished 1988): C1; Jon R. Bauman, *Pioneering a Global Vision: The Story of Baker & McKenzie*, Chicago: Harcourt Education Group, 1999, 70–71.

60. See, e.g., Jean P. O'Grady, "12 Building Blocks of a Digital Law Library," *Law360* (January 5, 2015).

61. Frederick W. Dingledy, Benjamin J. Keele, and Jennifer E. Sekula, "Collection Development, Acquisitions, and Licensing," in *Law Librarianship in the Twenty-First Century*, 2nd ed., ed. Roy Balleste, Sonia Luna-Lamas, and Lisa Smith-Butler (Lanham, MD: Scarecrow Press, 2014), 139.

62. *Ibid.*, 140.

63. For a discussion of official and authentic digital law, see Germain, "Digitizing the World's Laws," 193–97.

64. University of Michigan Law Library, *Collection Development Policy* (Last reviewed and updated August 27, 2014): 16–22, https://www.law.umich.edu/library/info/about/Documents/Collection%20Development%20Policy.pdf; See also, Wade, "Survey of Latin American Law," C2.

65. Barbara H. Garavaglia, "UPDATE: Collection Development Policies and Other Basic Tools for Building a Foreign and International Law Collection," GlobaLex, August 2013, http://www.nyulawglobal.org/globalex/International_Foreign_Collection_Development1.html.

66. Lillian Goldman Law Library, *Collection Development Policy: Latin America*, accessed April 28, 2016, http://library.law.yale.edu/latin-america.

67. Goodson Law Library, *Collection Development Policy* (Revised May 2014), Appendix B, https://law.duke.edu/sites/default/files/lib/collectiondevelopment.pdf.

68. American Bar Association, Section of Legal Education and Admissions to the Bar, *ABA Standards and Rules of Procedure of Law Schools 2015–2016*, Standard 606(c)(3).

69. Association of American Law Schools, Bylaws of the Association of American Law Schools, Inc., Section 6–8(a)(iii) (Adopted December 29, 1971; Amended through January 2016).

70. AALS did draft a list of recommended titles in Latin American law for its member libraries. See Association of American Law Schools, *Latin American Law: Draft List of Suggested Titles for Member School Libraries* (Chicago: Association of American Law Schools, 1966).

71. See, e.g., Neel Agrawal, "Training in FCIL Librarianship for Tomorrow's World," *Law Library Journal* 105 (Spring 2013): 199–229; Daniel L. Wade, "Wisdom from Mount Nebo (Hiei): Advice to a Young Person Aspiring to Become a Foreign and International Law Librarian," *Legal Reference Services Quarterly* 25 (2006): 51–71.

72. Oscar M. Trelles, II, "Latin American Legal Literature: Problems in their Acquisition and Comparative Reflections," *International Journal of Law Libraries* 4 (1976): 105.

73. See, e.g., Garavaglia, "UPDATE: Collection Development Policies."

74. Stern, "Latin-American Law Books."

75. William B. Stern, "Latin American Law: A Coming Task for Law Librarians," *Law Library Journal* 59 (1966): 48.

76. Fernando J. Figueredo, "Acquisition of Latin American Legal Materials: A Burdensome Task," *Law Library Journal* 64 (1971): 48.

77. Jorge L. Carro, "The Use of Legal Encyclopedias as an Alternative Approach in Building Up Collections of Spanish and Latin American Legal Materials," review of NUEVA ENCICLOPEDIA JURÍDICA, Francisco Seix, Ed., 1950-, *International Journal of Law Libraries* 6 (1978): 289.

78. O.J. Field, Frederic B. Crossley, and Robert B. Anderson, "Report of the Committee on Securing Latin-American Laws," *Law Library Journal* 3 (October 1910): 24.

79. Nancy Paul, "Special Interest Section News," *American Association of Law Libraries Newsletter* 18 (December 1986): 128.

80. Wade, "Survey of Latin American Law," C1.

81. *Ibid.*, C8–11.

82. *Ibid.*

83. American Association of Law Libraries, Foreign, Comparative & International Law Special Interest Section, Latin American Law Interest Group, http://www.aallnet.org/sections/fcil/cmtesgroups/Latin-American-Law.

84. See Teresa Miguel, "The Digital Legal Landscape in South America: Government Transparency and Access to Information," *International Journal of Legal Information* 40 (2012): 39–133; Marisol Florén-Romero, "Open Access to Legal Information: Mapping the Digital Legal Information of Mexico, Central America, the Spanish Speaking Caribbean, and Haiti," *International Journal of Legal Information* 40 (2012): 417–515.

85. Law on the Transparency of Public Functions and Access to Information on Public Administration (*Ley de Transparencia de la Función Pública y de Acceso a la Información de la Administración del Estado*), Law 20.285, *Diario Oficial* (August 20, 2008).

86. Sergio D. Stone, "Law Reviews," in Bianca Anderson et al., "Research Guide to Mexican Law," *Legal Reference Services Quarterly* 1 (2016): 58.

87. Lillian Goldman Law Library, *Collection Development Policy: Latin America*.

88. Poole, "Foreign Law Books," 69. Poole goes on to list several booksellers with whom he has established business, noting that he must often pay in advance. He also notes that friends of the library as well as the U.S. diplomatic corps have assisted in securing books for the library of the Association of the Bar of the City of New York.

89. *Ibid.*, 71.

90. Miles O. Price, "South of the Border Book Buying," *The Legist* 2, no.4 (1942): 35.

91. Miles O. Price, "Notes of a Law Book Scout in South America," *Law Library Journal* 35 (1942): 95. Unrelated to book buying but interesting nonetheless, Mr. Price observed, "Law students and law school appearances generally, are strikingly similar to ours, except that the percentage of women seems higher." *Ibid.*, 99.

92. *Ibid.*, 99.

93. *Ibid.*, 95.

94. *Ibid.*, 97.

95. *Ibid.*, 98.

96. Stern, "Acquisition of Latin American Materials," 104. In a separate but related article, Dr. Stern emphasized the importance of foreign law collections generally (as trade opened up at the beginning of the twentieth century and the world was at war at that time), and the necessity of Latin American legal systems specifically (given the changing political conditions of many Latin American countries). Dr. Stern explained the unique aspects of civil law jurisdictions, including a discussion of the importance of codes, precedent and *stare decisis, amparo,* and judicial decisions. He also provided the titles to some relevant bibliographical works and other essential legal materials—constitutions, statutes, regulations, treaties, court reports, periodicals,

and treatises—that form the basis of a comprehensive Latin American legal collection. Stern, "Latin-American Law Books," 4.

97. *Ibid.*, 110.

98. *Ibid.*

99. *Ibid.*, 111–116. Acquiring gazettes continues to be problematic in the 21st century. Beatrice Tice, "Foreign Official Gazettes: Solving a Collection Conundrum," *Law Library Journal* 97 (2005): 299.

100. Figueredo, "Acquisition of Latin American Legal Materials," 46. A similar article focusing on the difficulty in obtaining legal materials from "Third World Countries" is, Arno Liivak, "Third World Materials as Catalyst for Access Dominated Solutions to the Problem of Western Libraries," *International Journal of Law Libraries* 78 (1976): 4. See also, a discussion of ongoing problems of "delinquent distribution and publication and … the absence of adequate indices." Trelles, "Latin American Legal Literature," 106.

101. Figueredo, "Acquisition of Latin American Legal Materials," 46–48.

102. *Ibid.*, 49–50. The Latin American Cooperative Acquisitions Program (LACAP) was a cooperative effort for acquisitions of library materials from Latin America, not specific to legal materials, from 1959 to 1973. A commercial international bookseller, Stechert-Hafner, Inc., oversaw the program. For more information, see M.J. Savary, *Latin American Cooperative Acquisitions Program: Imaginative Venture* (New York: Hafner Pub. Co., 1968).

103. *Ibid.*, 50–51.

104. Ellen Schaffer, "Legal Materials from Latin America and the Caribbean: Some Ideas for Acquisition," *International Journal of Legal Information* 12 (1984): 103.

105. *Ibid.*

106. *Ibid.*, 103–107.

107. *Ibid.*, 110–111.

108. *Ibid.*, 112–116.

109. See Miguel-Stearns, "Judicial Power," 100.

110. For an expanded treatment of courts in Latin America, see Miguel-Stearns, "Judicial Power," 100.

111. See, e.g., "GlobaLex: Foreign Law Research," New York University, accessed April 20, 2016, http://www.nyulawglobal.org/globalex/index.html. See also, Claire Germain, *Germain's Transnational Law Research: A Guide for Attorneys* (Ardsley-on-Hudson, NY: Transnational Juris Publications, 2006); Richard A. Danner and Marie-Louise Bernal, eds. *Introduction to Foreign Legal Systems* (New York: Oceana, 1994).

112. "LexisNexis to Sell Local Publishing Operations in Argentina, Chile, and Mexico to Legal Publishing Group," *Business Wire*, March 28, 2008, accessed April 23, 2016, http://www.businesswire.com/news/home/20080328005443/en/ LexisNexis-Sell-Local-Publishing-Operations-Argentina-Chile.

113. "Thomson Reuters Acquires Legal Publishing Group," *Reuters*, January 19, 2011, accessed April 23, 2016, http://www.reuters.com/article/idUS225830+19-Jan-2011+HUG20110119.

114. Obscure bookstores are a long-standing phenomenon. See Price, "A Law Book Scout," 71.

115. For a list of current Latin American vendors, see Teresa Miguel-Stearns, "List of Latin American and Iberian Distributors," last updated by Cate Kellett in 2015, last accessed on April 23, 2016, http://www.aallnet.org/ sections/fcil/cmtesgroups/Latin-American-Law.

116. This problem was first noted more than fifty years ago. See Stern, "Acquisition of Latin American Materials," 110.

117. Robert Vosper and Robert Talmadge, eds., *Farmington Plan Survey: Final Report* (Washington, D.C.: Association of Research Libraries, 1959), 33. The supporting libraries included the National Library of Medicine, University of California Los Angeles, University of Kansas, University of North Carolina, Cornell University, New York Public Library, University of Florida, University of Miami, University of Indiana, University of Pennsylvania, and Los Angeles County Law Library. The Farmington Plan expanded to cover major Latin American countries in 1958. *Ibid.*, 75. See also, William H. Kurth, "Cooperative Maintenance of Acquisition Agent in Latin America," in *Final Report and Papers of the Fourth Seminar on the Acquisition of Latin American Library Materials, June 18–19, 1959* (Washington, D.C.: Library of Congress, 1960), 4. See also, Howard F. Cline, *Latin America and the Farmington Plan: A Working Draft with Recommendations* (Washington, D.C.: Library of Congress, 1958).

The Farmington Plan was the response to a 1942 proposal made at the meeting of the Library of Congress Librarian's Council in Farmington, Connecticut, to divide the responsibility of acquiring library materials among U.S. libraries for the benefit of the world. The Association of Research Libraries became a sponsor and the plan became operative in 1948 covering three European countries. Robert B. Downs, "The Significance of Foreign Collection for U.S. Materials: Problems of Acquisitions," *Foreign Acquisitions Newsletter* 34 (1971): 2. The Farmington Plan required that libraries accept all materials acquired within the scope of their commitment, without taking into account local needs and financial constraints, which ultimately lead to its demise in 1972. Peggy Johnson, *Fundamentals of Collection Development and Management* (Chicago: American Library Assn., 2004), 242. See also, Ralph Wagner, *A History of the Farmington Plan* (Lanham, MD: Scarecrow Press, 2002).

118. Vosper and Talmadge, *Farmington Plan Survey*, 34.

119. Kurth, "Cooperative Maintenance," 5.

120. *Ibid.*, 116–117.

121. Mario Goderich, "Cooperative Acquisitions: The Experience of General Libraries and Prospects for Law Libraries," *Law Library Journal* 63 (1970): 57.

122. *Ibid.*, 58.

123. Goderich, "Cooperative Acquisitions," 63.

124. *Ibid.*, 60.

125. *Ibid.*, 61.

126. Daniel L. Wade, "Building a Medium-to-Large Foreign Law Collection," in *Introduction to Foreign Legal Systems*, eds. Richard A. Danner and Marie-Louise Bernal (New York: Oceana, 1994). See also Wade, "Survey of Latin American Law," C2.

The CUNY Dominican Studies Institute Library

Bringing the Community to the Academic Library

SARAH APONTE *and* NELSON SANTANA

Documenting Latino/Hispanic Immigrants Through U.S. Repositories

Formal repositories have been established throughout New York City to document the experience of the Latino/Hispanic population. Since the 1970s, some librarians and archivists have made it a priority to identify, preserve and make available bibliographical and archival materials of underrepresented groups to "represent better the American experience."[1] In the 1980s, the New York State Archives changed what had been a traditional practice of exclusion and began to incorporate communities that were not adequately represented in New York's historical records.[2]

It is important for individuals to have access to repositories that contain the histories of their people. A study conducted by Dabbour and Ballard of the Oviatt Library, housed at California State University, found that Latino students used the physical library more than their white counterparts.[3] The study also found that, when compared to white students, Latino students consulted archival or rare book materials with lesser frequency than white students.[4] It is important for users to know about the resources that are available to them, but most important is the ability to have access to the material.

The legacy of Latino/Hispanic population in New York City is housed in multiple research units within the City University of New York (CUNY), which is the largest urban public institution of higher learning in the United States, and in terms of ethnicity, one of the most diverse in the world. CUNY is comprised of twenty-four institutions including eleven senior colleges and seven community colleges. Each institution is located in one of New York City's five boroughs.

Among the major Latino groups in New York City, Puerto Ricans and Dominicans created the Centro de Estudios Puertorriqueños (Center for Puerto Rican Studies) (Hunter College, CUNY) in 1973 and the CUNY Dominican Studies Institute (City College) (CUNY DSI) in 1992, respectively—two institutions housed in the City University of New York that started as research units, afterward spawning a library and eventually an archive. The Mexican community in the New York metropolitan area established the CUNY Mexican Studies Institute in 2012, housed at Lehman College.

The work done by the Centro de Estudios Puertorriqueños, the CUNY Mexican Studies Institute, and the CUNY Dominican Studies Institute is a fundamental contribution to the understanding of the past and present of the Puerto Rican, Mexican, and Dominican populations in the New York metropolitan area and in the United States at large. They are an essential and vibrant part of the life of Latino communities in New York society and within the American nation today. These institutions contribute to the development of knowledge about the respective ethnic populations that they focus on, as well as to the challenges that such initiative faces as to its dissemination and further development within New York academia. This knowledge is important for policymaking purposes, for the self-awareness and preservation of identity of these communities, and for the healthy integration and acceptance of those communities within the U.S. cultural mosaic of the early 21st century.

A crucial component in the success of these Latino/Hispanic library/archives is the manner in which staff engage the Latino-Hispanic community. Librarians, archivists and staff of repositories must at all times be attentive to community needs, the concerns of individuals, and the relationships between institutions and the community.[5] There should always be cooperation between archives and the community and the mere transfer of records should not mark the end of the relationship between donor and archives, but rather the beginning.[6]

Another component in documenting Latino/Hispanic groups is the perceived issue of multiple identities. Mario Ramirez calls upon Latino/Hispanic archivists to "question how notions as 'Latino' and/or 'Hispanic' are conceptualized" so that Latino/Hispanic archivists "can proceed to reconsider the types of materials, events, organizations, and/or individuals" that are brought into repositories and "designate as 'representative'" of themselves, "thereby questioning the very notion of constructing a representative body of historical material."[7]

In addition to the work done by individual repositories to preserve a culture, there have also been collaborative efforts among these institutions. For instance, the Centro de Estudios Puertorriqueños (Centro) has earned the respect of the U.S. Puerto Rican community and created links with community groups including genealogical associations and visual artists, writers and musicians.[8] The Centro has had a role in the creation of other repositories including the New Jersey Hispanic Research and Information Center, and served as the model for the creation of the CUNY Dominican Studies Institute.[9] In similar fashion, the CUNY Dominican Studies Institute has served as a model for the creation and establishment of other units housed within academic walls. A notable example is that the CUNY DSI has been regularly approached by administrators, academic personnel and community members interested in modeling the CUNY DSI not only in its intellectual capacity but also in its physical structure. We can mention the recently approved Haitian Studies Institute at Brooklyn College, CUNY.

Founded in 1992, the CUNY Dominican Studies Institute is the only university-based research entity outside the Dominican Republic fully devoted to the study, dissemination and production of knowledge about Dominicans. CUNY DSI houses the first and only Dominican Library and Dominican Archives in the United States that collect primary and secondary source material pertinent to Dominican studies. Through its

Dominican Library and Dominican Archives as well as its Research Unit, CUNY DSI is engaged in a number of projects that contribute to deepen and enhance the historical and cultural consciousness of and about Dominicans in the United States as well as in the country of origin.

The CUNY Dominican Studies Institute has built and continues to build relationships with community and civic leaders known as pillars of the New York Dominican community and grassroots organizations. It highlights programs and research activities that were designed keeping in mind its stakeholders, prioritizing the organization of activities that are free-of-charge, programmed in the evenings, and bilingual. The Dominican Archives and Dominican Library continue to serve as a gathering place of the best scholarly minds interested in Latino/Dominican studies. The multipurpose facility has become an educative center for community residents, undergraduate students, and school children, as well as an institution that promotes top notch and competitive academic scholarship and research about the Dominican experience within the United States, especially within New York City.

City College Libraries System

The City College Library System is the largest within the City University of New York. This library system includes six libraries and an archive. The original library has served as a federal depository since 1884, and to this day the library houses 230,000 government records. To date, the libraries hold more than 1.6 million print volumes, and makes accessible 200,000 electronic books and 77,000 electronic journals. The mission of the City College Library System is simple: the libraries are "committed to acquiring, preserving and providing access to records of enduring value that document the history of City College—the nation's first public institution of higher education and one of the most ethnically diverse institutions in the world—and its alumni, faculty and students throughout its history."[10] Access is granted to members of the City College community (students, faculty, staff, special researchers etc.)

The library attempts to complement every division within City College. According to CCNY Chief Librarian Charles Stewart, one librarian is assigned to each discipline and the library makes every effort to provide invaluable resources to both the students and faculty. Among the college's mission is to produce and disseminate scholarly research, an area in which librarians play a key role in ensuring that faculty and their students have the necessary books, journals, and other resources to carry their research.[11]

The model of reference service has changed drastically over the years and will continue to change. There once was a point in which reference was mostly delivered in person with someone sitting at the reference desk. Currently, a growing number of users have their questions answered through the convenience of email or chat like. The "Ask a Librarian" service available at the City College Cohen Library's web site. In the past, there were moments when three to four librarians would sit at the reference desk of large libraries. Today, one will usually find one librarian. Sometimes during the hectic periods of the spring and fall semesters, a second librarian may assist users.

Librarians at City College have different ways in which they connect with faculty and students. One way in which City College librarians connect with faculty is by networking at gatherings such as conferences, meetings, or other events. Some of the information literacy courses that take place begin with a simple conversation that librarians strike up with faculty in a myriad of events. The CUNY DSI Chief Librarian is part of the City College Library's liaison system in which librarians assigned to different disciplines reach out to faculty and other types of instructors at City College. In addition to providing library instruction to students, a way in which librarians at City College drive traffic and also promote the library is by participating in Freshman Inquiry Writing Seminar (FIQWS) courses, a six-credit special topic course in which freshmen enroll. Each FIQWS class must attend two mandatory information literacy workshops in the library during the semester that the course is held. The Dominican Library, however, falls into a very unique space. The Dominican Studies Librarian provides instruction to college students who enrolled in courses in the humanities such as history and Spanish. The Dominican Library also hosts a diverse group of users ranging from kindergarten to high school as well as graduate students, educators, and community residents interested in learning about the resources found in the library.

The CUNY Dominican Studies Institute has a long-standing relationship with the public school City College Academy of the Arts (CCAA). Each year, approximately eighty students from the CCAA's sixth grade make a necessary stop at the CUNY DSI Archives and DSI Library when visiting City College in order to learn about the resources available to them. In addition, every year, for six consecutive Fridays, CUNY DSI faculty and staff teach a seminar to eighth grade students. Through lectures and discussions, they study Dominican history, folklore, race, and immigration, in the same manner as college students and professionals within academic walls. By the end of the seminar, the students have a stronger understanding of Dominican culture and experience how college professors ask questions, conduct research, and solve problems. The seminar incorporates primary and secondary resources from the Dominican Archives and Dominican Library. Guest lecturers such as members of the Dominican artistic and academic community in New York City have been invited to participate in the seminar.

When Dominican migration became a popular research topic among U.S. scholars in the 1970s and 1980s, it became the general notion that the first major wave of Dominican emigration occurred in the 1960s, due to the death of dictator Rafael Leónidas Trujillo in 1961. Needless to say, the first known major wave of Dominican migration occurred between 1882 and 1924, when an estimated 5,000 Dominicans entered the United States through Ellis Island.[12] Perhaps even more astounding is the fact that in 1613, according to archival records in the Netherlands, a man named Juan Rodríguez—born in Santo Domingo—became the first official immigrant resident of what today is known as New York.[13]

The Creation of the Dominican Research Library

Prior to the creation of the CUNY DSI Library, students, educators, scholars, and others in and outside the university were unable to access free and accessible information on Dominican issues even in the Latino reference sections of existing libraries. Dominican reference sources in CUNY libraries and other university libraries of the tri-state area were scarce or non-existent. In spite of the growing visibility of Dominicans in New York, the special needs of this population were inadequately served by public library collections. The New York Public Library had some sources relating to the history of the Dominican

Republic, yet these materials were dispersed throughout several branches. Notable holdings also existed in private institutions such as Columbia University and New York University, but these were practically inaccessible due to restrictive policies. These materials were only available to people affiliated to these institutions such as faculty, students and staff as well as "Friends of the Library" who could afford to pay high annual registration fees. The creation of the CUNY Dominican Studies Institute in 1992 began to address this dearth of information by producing and publishing research on Dominicans. Subsequently, CUNY DSI gave birth to the Dominican Library in 1994 and the Dominican Archives in 2002.

There were several events that took place prior to 1992 that culminated in the founding of the CUNY DSI. In the late 1980s, the Council of Dominican Educators (an independent, grass-roots volunteer group of teachers and instructor-activists from throughout the different Dominican communities of New York City) began a dialogue about the need of an academic institution committed to fostering Dominican studies. At the time of the Institute's founding in 1992, peoples of color found themselves embroiled in a struggle with law enforcement and the Dominican community was no exception. As a result of Ronald Reagan's war on drugs in the 1980s, communities of color in urban cities were vilified in the media. U.S. media outlets such as *The New York Times* and *The New York Post* depicted Dominicans as thugs, thieves, and drug lords.[14] Dominican activists, predominantly those who worked in educational settings, understood that Dominicans needed an academic space to produce, preserve and disseminate information pertinent their population and culture in the same manner as African Americans, Mexicans and Puerto Ricans had previously done.

In January 1932, the George Cleveland Hall Branch Library opened its doors, marking the first time a Chicago Public Library opened in a predominantly African American neighborhood. Vivian Gordon Harsh, who had been a branch librarian since 1924, became both the first African American branch head and the first director of the George Cleveland Hall Branch.[15] Not to be outdone, New York City's vibrant African American population brought about the creation of the Division of Negro Literature, History and Prints that opened in 1925. Currently, this important repository is known as the New York Public Library's Schomburg Center for Research in Black Culture and houses more than ten million items in its five divisions that include an archive, arts and artifacts division, and a division devoted to moving images and recorded sound, among others.

In similar fashion, Latin American communities in the United States have followed in the footsteps of their African American brothers and sisters and have established their own repositories. The legacy of Latino/Hispanic immigrants is not housed in one, but in multiple repositories. Since Mexicans comprise the largest Latino/Hispanic group in the United States, there are multiple libraries and repositories that document the experience of Mexicans, Mexican Americans and Chicanos in the United States including the Chicano Studies Research Center at the University of California, Los Angeles (UCLA) and Mexican American Collection at Stanford University, among others. The Cuban Heritage Collection at the University of Miami is the most extensive repository dedicated to documenting the experience of Cubans and Cuban Americans, containing both primary and secondary sources.

The CUNY Dominican Studies Institute began as a pilot project in 1992 with a planning grant made available by the City University of New York. By 1994, CUNY DSI had met the conditions required by the CUNY Board of Trustees to approve it unanimously as an integral component of the City University of New York., Dr. Silvio Torres-Saillant was appointed as its first director. This milestone marks the official "birth" of the CUNY Dominican Studies Institute as we know it today. At the time, there were some information resources available related to Dominicans located in the two small offices assigned to the Institute. The materials were scattered inside file cabinets or in shelves with no organization. In the process of organizing these materials, a Word Perfect "catalog" listing the available sources was prepared. At the same time, after much lobbying, the City College administration assigned a larger space for the Dominican Studies Institute and as of today this constitutes the main offices of the Institute but within a much more expanded space.

The library opened "officially" in April 1994 sharing the same office space as the Institute, featuring a seminal collection of books that belonged to CUNY DSI's founding director. Nearly a year later in March 1995, letters were mailed requesting donations to the Council of Dominican Educators, the academic community, community organizations, and individuals whose research dealt with Dominicans in the United States.

Since the collection did not exist before, there was no work plan initially and no written policy defining its scope, content, and purpose. A core collection was assembled representing the basic works of Dominican studies with donated materials. The materials were donated by Dr. Silvio Torres-Saillant, Dr. Ramona Hernández, Dr. Daisy Cocco De Filippis, Dr. Franklin Gutiérrez, Ana García-Reyes, and Anthony Stevens-Acevedo, to mention a few. Sister institutions were visited for advice and mentorship. Nélida Pérez, former Director of the Library and Archives from Centro de Estudios Puertorriqueños, was of tremendous help and a mentor as well as Judith Selakoff from the Library for Caribbean Research at the Research Institute for the Study of Man in New York City.

By this time, there were very limited personnel working at the Dominican Studies Institute and the work had to be divided between administrative and library duties. The Institute was able to hire students to assist in the day-to-day operations. Gradually, while supported all along by book donations from the Dominican community and from scholars, the library started to attract the attention of visitors from throughout CUNY, the community at large, local and out-of-state colleges and universities, and researchers from several parts of the world. Soon, the library became a central component of the Dominican Studies Institute and required special attention.

A Time for Transition

After securing a permanent director line for the Institute, Dr. Torres-Saillant left to head the Latino-Latin American Studies Program at Syracuse University. In 2002, Dr. Ramona Hernández assumed the position of director. The first major step was to physically separate the library from the main office. With all the donations that the library had received as well as the increase in visitors, the library had already outgrown the space shared with the office. Through her lobbying of the college's administration, Dr. Hernández was able to secure more space across the main Institute's office and the library moved there temporarily. After negotiations with the main library of the College, the Dominican Library relocated to a space on Cohen Library's first floor. The Institute was able to secure for a dedicated staff for its library for the first time.

The Library as an "Independent" Entity

In the new temporary space, the Library began its outreach to New York City public schools, establishing successful relationships and conducting workshops with students as well as with teachers. But again, the Library continued to outgrow its own temporary space and visitors complained that it was located in a very difficult to find area (it was literally in the basement of the Cohen Library, one flight below the main entrance). Meanwhile, the Institute had hired a highly specialized and recognized archivist, Idilio Gracia Peña and with his leadership, the Archives was established. By the end of 2004, after much lobbying, the Institute was able to secure a grant from the New York City Council to build a space for the Archives and the Library adjacent to the Cohen Library. In May 2006, the Library moved from the first floor or "basement" to the main floor of the Cohen Library and continued to function there until the construction of the new facility began. Due to a lack of any alternate space available, all the collections and equipment of the Dominican Library had to be stored while the construction was completed, and for the first time since its inception, it remained closed until the inauguration of the new facilities.

From an In-House Catalog System to WorldCat

Before sharing information about the new state of the art space of the Dominican Library inaugurated in December 2008, it may be useful to discuss changes in the library's catalog since the creation of the Word Perfect "catalog" in 1994. Dr. Frank Moya Pons, a well-known Dominican historian, worked as Director of Research at CUNY DSI since its inception to the late 1990s. He recommended a more user-friendly method that allowed sharing the in-house database with our users. The Word Perfect document was transferred to ProCite, a software tool that organized the materials in separate bibliographic entries. The holdings were in a more organized format but were not available via a web-based library system. Researchers who were unable to visit did not know the richness of the collection. In order to discover specifics of the collection, they had to contact library staff to obtain customized lists of Dominican Library resources. Library staff spent countless hours preparing and organizing bibliographies dealing with specific topics for researchers.

The date the collection listing was transferred from ProCite to a web-based SQL server database was celebrated as a milestone in the history of the Dominican Library. Still, this catalog could only be searched by entering the Dominican Studies Institute website directly. Dominican Library holdings were not findable in the WorldCat database. It was therefore critical to integrate our holdings into WorldCat.

In 2009, the City College Library (under the guidance of former Chief Librarian, Pamela Gillespie) recognized the need for parity and for the Dominican Library collection to be more visible. The Library agreed to facilitate the creation of a location code so that the name of the Dominican Studies Institute appeared next to our holdings in CUNY Plus, the CUNY Libraries system catalog. The old catalog was transferred so the holdings became visible in the WorldCat/ CUNY Plus system. Participating in these shared systems made our holdings more broadly accessible and made our library operations more efficient. Library holdings have developed over the years from a core collection to a comprehensive research collection of Dominican-related books, manuscripts, doctoral dissertations, newspaper clippings, audiovisual resources and other materials. The library has been transformed from a local resource to a recognized international resource.

Dominican Library Users

Since the Dominican Library is based inside a university, the majority of users are people affiliated with academia: undergraduate and graduate students, professors, and researchers who conduct research in anything that encompasses Dominican studies. Dissimilar from other libraries within the CUNY system and most academic libraries, the Dominican Library distinguishes itself in that it is accessible to people not affiliated with the university; making it conveniently available to those who live in the community where the college is situated. The library is strategically located in the storied neighborhood of Harlem, which includes a sizable Dominican population; it is also adjacent to Washington Heights, the neighborhood with the most vibrant Dominican presence in the United States; and lastly, this unique reference library is less than 10 minutes away from the Bronx, the New York City borough with the largest population tracing their ancestry to the Dominican Republic.

In the year of 2010, the Dominican population in the U.S. approximated 1.5 million and New York is home to 604,844 people of Dominican ancestry.[16] Similar to public libraries, this specialized Dominican library is accessible to the public, so long as users present valid state identification to security upon entering the building. The library continues to attract local community members and seasoned researchers from around the world. In addition, it welcomes researchers who visit from the Dominican Republic, often frustrated by the lack of information on U.S. Dominicans in the country's libraries. The library is open to the general public, not just academics. We do not have to worry like Virginia Woolf did in her book *A Room of One's Own* when she complained about being denied entrance to the Library: "I had no wish to enter had I the right, and this time the verger might have stopped me, demanding perhaps my baptismal certificate, or a letter of introduction from the Dean."[17]

The Dominican Library has a long-lasting interaction with the Dominican community. It has contributed towards enriching the nation's historical heritage through its bibliographical documentation of a very pronounced segment of society. The CUNY DSI Library's commitment to community service is carried out mostly through its collaboration with public schools and community-based, non-for-profit service and cultural organizations. Through its partnership with school teachers, school groups regularly visit the exhibits and workshops organized by the Library on various Dominican topics. The exhibits themselves, besides the in-house produced ones, are often co-sponsored with artists, scholars, and institutions both from the U.S. as well as from the Dominican Republic.

As a haven for rare books and other materials, the Dominican Library houses bibliographical sources that are nearly impossible to acquire because so few original copies exist. The library houses several books that were published prior to the 1960s; including rare books that date back to the nineteenth century. It contains an increasingly bilingual collection of books, manuscripts, doctoral dissertations, academic publications, newspaper clippings, audiovisual resources and other publications on matters relating to the Dominican community.

Since the CUNY DSI Library came formally into existence, it has distinguished itself for its highly specialized collection. Its national visibility continues to grow and the library has become the mecca of Dominican studies in the United States. As the only collection of its kind in the United States, it is filling a significant gap in information services to Dominicans and others studying the Dominican experience. Throughout the years, the Library has received acknowledgments in multiple publications, including books and journal articles.

The CUNY DSI Library's main tool to evaluate the effectiveness of its work and its impact in meeting the needs of its audiences has been, so far, the direct response from its patrons, written and oral, or follow-ups to our regular service as well as to our workshops, exhibits, and co-sponsoring and co-hosting of events. Through this direct feedback the library learns about what the special needs of its patrons are. Overall, the main finding from this user-input throughout the years has been the need for expanded library hours and for on-site research technology and tools. The best ways the library has been able to effectively respond to these needs has been the approval of additional staff, as well as the much improved premises constructed in 2008 with New York City Council capital funds.

Digital Library Initiatives

The Dominican Library has teamed up with numerous digital resources, such as the CUNY Academic Works, the ARTstor/Shared Shelf Digital Library and the Digital Public Library of America to digitize and make the Library's materials even more accessible.

CUNY Academic Works is CUNY's open access institutional repository. The Dominican Library's involvement with CUNY Academic Works has resulted in a massive broadening of the scope through which the Institute's publications and exhibits can be accessed online. From August to December of 2015, CUNY DSI publications have been downloaded by over fifty-nine institutions including various U.S. government agencies (Department of Veterans Affairs, The City of New York and the NYC Housing Authority), not to mention commercial entities like Al Jazeera America LLC, Shock Hardy & Bacon, and the Aga Khan Foundation. The highest number of downloads resulted from educational institutions. While most of the downloads are from the United States (348), DSI publications have been also downloaded from twenty-nine different countries from around the world.

Most of this information may be hosted on external websites, yet they link back to the DSI's main page, giving researchers easy access to information about the Institute itself. Compared to other services, CUNY Academic Works brings a massive benefit in that any uploaded publication is easily discoverable, whether it be through a Google search, via the CUNY OneSearch catalog, or even by means of the *WorldCat* database. CUNY DSI is the first, and so far, the only CUNY research institute with a prominent presence in CUNY Academic Works.[18]

The ARTstor Digital Library enhances scholarship and teaching through the use of digital images and media. Similar to the JSTOR database, ARTstor provides digital collections online. Shared Shelf is an open source component that allows access to those that do not have a subscription to the database. So far, the Dominican Library has used both Shared Shelf and ARTstor to showcase photos belonging to the First Blacks in the

Americas Project, a CUNY DSI online platform focusing on the history of the early inhabitants of African ancestry of today's Dominican Republic. The library is steadily expanding on the First Blacks ARTstor/Shared Shelf project, constantly adding new content. In the near future we plan on introducing a second digital project based on the history of Dominican artists in the United States. CUNY DSI is the first and only CUNY research institute to have its collection on this prestigious database.[19]

The Dominican Library has also managed to make the content of the First Blacks in the Americas available through the Digital Public Library of America (DPLA). The DPLA helps unify materials of libraries, archives, and museums and makes them freely available to anyone in the world. As of now, the DPLA contains the same content found on ARTstor.[20]

Key Challenges for the Dominican Library

The Dominican Library has several key challenges, the most crucial being funding and space. Like any library housed in a public institution of higher education, the Dominican Library is dependent on government funding. Funding for most departments, research centers, and institutes has been cut drastically. Over the years university departments have disappeared or have been reduced to programs. Space is another challenge that CUNY DSI Library faces since donations of books and other materials have drastically increased over the years. In addition, the demands from the student body as well as the community are increasing at an unparalelled pace. Regularly, CUNY DSI faculty and staff are approached by members of the community to host events such as book presentations, lectures and meetings at our premises. Due to the limited space and dedicated personnel, CUNY DSI is unable to host these events.

Conclusion

Since its beginnings in 1994 as a spontaneously assembled collection of books created to respond to an immediate demand for bibliographic resources on the part of researchers, students and members of the public following the events of the recently established CUNY Dominican Studies Institute, the Dominican Library, with the support of the City University of New York and the community that buttressed the founding of CUNY DSI, has made strides in becoming a full-fledged, firmly established research entity that uniquely combines the service to the scholarly constituency and the public at large interested in the latest scholarship about Dominicans, their society, history, and culture.

Appendix

The CUNY DSI has received credit in various publications attesting to the success of our effort to serve the academic community. Below a list of publications that acknowledge CUNY DSI since its inception:

Alvarez López, Luis. *Dieciséis conclusiones fundamentales sobre la anexión y la guerra de la restauración (1861–1865)*. Santo Domingo: Editorial Argos, 2005.

Alvarez López, Luis. *Estado y sociedad durante la dictadura de Trujillo.* Santo Domingo: Editora Cole, 2001.

Azzari, Margherita, and Leonardo Rombai, eds. *Amerigo Vespucci e i mercanti viaggiatori fiorentini del Cinquecento.* Firenze, Italy: Firenze University Press, 2013.

Brennan, Denise. *What's Love Got to Do with It?: Transnational Desires and Sex Tourism in the Dominican Republic.* Durham: Duke University Press, 2004.

Candelario, Ginetta. "Dominican Studies Institute." *Oxford Encyclopedia of Latinos and Latinas in the United States.* Editors Suzanne Oboler and Deena J. González. New York: Oxford University Press, 2005.

Canino, María J., and Silvio Torres-Saillant. Eds. *The Challenge of Public Higher Education in the Hispanic Caribbean.* Princeton: Markus Wiener Publishers, 2004.

Cocco De Filippis, Daisy. *Desde la diáspora/A Diaspora Position: Selección bilingüe de ensayos/A Bilingual Selection of Essays.* New York: Alcance, 2003.

Cocco De Filippis, Daisy. *Para que no se olviden: the lives of women in Dominican history, a selection.* 1st edition. New York: Ediciones Alcance, 2000.

Davis, Mike. "Magical Urbanism: Latinos Reinvent the U.S. Big City." *New Left Review.* No. 234 (March/April 1999): 3–43.

Diaz, Junot. *Drown.* First Edition. New York: Rverhead Books, 1997.

Gallin, Anne, Ruth Glasser, and Jocelyn Santana, eds. *Caribbean Connections: The Dominican Republic.* Washington, D.C.: Teaching for Change, 2004.

Gray, Dulce María. *High Literacy and Ethnic Identity: Dominican American Schooling in Transition.* Lanham, MD: Rowman & Littlefield, 2001.

Helmreich, Williams. *The New York Nobody Knows: Walking 6,000 Miles in the City.* Princeton: Princeton University Press, 2013.

Hernández Vázquez, Francisco, and Rodolfo D. Torres. *Latina Thought: Culture, Politics, and Society.* New York: Rowman & Littlefield, 2003.

Hoffnung-Garskof, Jesse E. *A Tale of Two Cities: Santo Domingo and New York After 1950.* Princeton: Princeton University Press, 2010.

Howard, David. *Coloring the Nation: Race and Ethnicity in the Dominican Republic.* Oxford: Signal, 2001.

Itzigsohn, José, and Carlos Dore-Cabral. "Competing Identites? Race, Ethnicity and Panethnicity Among Dominicans in the United States." *Sociological Forum.* Vol. 15, no. 2 (2000): 225–247.

Kaplan, Marion A. *Dominican Haven: The Jewish Refugee Settlement in Sosúa, 1940–1945.* 1st edition. New York: Museum of Jewish Heritage, 2008.

Kugel, Seth, and Carolina González. Nueva York: The Complete Guide to Latino Life in the Five Boroughs. 1st edition. Nueva York: St. Martin's Griffin, 2006.

López, Nancy. *Hopeful Girls, Troubled Boy: Race and Gender Disparity in Urban Education.* New York: Routledge, 2003.

Louie, Vivian. *Keeping the Immigrant Bargain: The Costs and Rewards of Success in America.* New York: Russell Sage Foundation, 2012.

Martínez-San Miguel, Yolanda. *Caribe Two Ways: Cultura de la migración en el Caribe insular hispánico.* San Juan, P.R.: Ediciones Callejón, 2003.

Méndez, Danny. *Narratives of Migration and Displacement in Dominican Literature.* 1st ed. *Routledge Interdisciplinary Perspectives on Literature.* New York: Routledge, 2012.

Moya Pons, Frank. *La otra historia dominicana.* Santo Domingo: Libreia La Tinitaria, 2008.

Paulino, Edward. "Birth of an Archives." *New York Archives*. Vol. 3, no. 3 (Winter 2004): 6–7.

Paulino, Edward. *Dividing Hispaniola: The Dominican Republic's Border Campaign Against Haiti, 1930–1961*. Pittsburgh: University of Pittsburg Press, 2016.

Pessar, Patricia. *A Visa for a Dream: Dominicans in the United States*. Boston: Allyn and Bacon, 1995.

Pita, Marianne D., and Sharon Utakis. "Educational Policy for the Transnational Dominican Community." *Journal of Language, Identity, and Education*. Vol. 1, no. 4 (2002): 317–328.

Pon, Michael. *The Strongbox*. CreateSpace Independent Publishing Platform: 2015.

Reyes-Santos, Alaí. *Our Caribbean Kin: Race and Nation in the Neoliberal Antilles*. New Jersey: Rutgers University Press, 2015.

Rivera, Carmen. *To Catch the Lightning and the Downfall of Rafael Trujillo*. South Gate, CA: NoPassport Press, 2015.

Rodríguez de León, Francisco. *El furioso merengue del norte: Una historia de la comunidad dominicana en los Estados Unidos*. New York: Editorial Sitel, 1998.

Rodríguez Guglielmoni, Linda M., and Miriam M. González Hernández, eds. *Enlaces: Transnacionalidad—el Caribe y su diáspora—lengua, literatura y cultura en los albores del siglo XXI: 7ma Conferencia Internacional de Escritoras y Críticos Literarios del Caribe*. New York: Latino Press, 2000.

Rosario-Andújar, Julio. "Felisberto Hernández y el pensamiento filosófico. Series: Wor(l)ds of Change: Latin American and Iberian Literature." Vol. 43. New York: Peter Lang, 1999.

Roth, Wendy. *Race Migration: Latinos and the Cultural Transformation of Race*. Stanford, CA: Stanford University Press, 2012.

Santana, Jocelyn. *Dominican Dream, American Reality*. New York: Jocelyn Santana, 2006.

Sellers, Julie A. *Merengue and Dominican Identity: Music as National Unifier*. Jefferson, NC: McFarland, 2004.

Snyder, Robert W. *Crossing Broadway: Washington Heights and the Promise of New York City*. Ithaca, NY: Cornell University Press, 2014.

Suárez, Lucía M. *The Tears of Hispaniola: Haitian and Dominican Diaspora Memory*. Gainesville: University Press of Florida, 2006.

Sunshine, Catherine, and Deborah Menkart, ed. *Caribbean Connections: Moving North*. Washington, D.C.: Network of Educators on the Americas, 1998.

Torres-Saillant, Silvio. *An Intellectual History of the Caribbean. Series: New Directions in Latino American Cultures*. New York: Palgrave Macmillan, 2006.

United Way of New York City. *Neighborhood Profile*. No. 5 Washington Heights/Inwood Manhattan Community Disctrict 12. New York: United Way of New York City, 1994.

Vega García, Susan A. "Latino Reference Resources." *Choice* Vol. 40, no. 3 (November 2002): 399–408.

Wucker, Michele. *Why the Cocks Fight: Dominicans, Haitians, and the Struggle for Hispaniola*. New York: Hill and Wang, 1999.

Ybarra, Raul L., and Nancy López. *Creating Alternative Discourses in the Education of Latinos and Latinas: A Reader*. Counterpoints: Studies in the Postmodern Theory of Education (Book 253). New York: Peter Lang International Academic Publisher, 2004.

NOTES

1. Tracy B. Grimm and Chon A. Noriega. "Documenting Regional Latino Arts and Culture: Case Studies for a Collaborative, Community-Oriented Approach." *The American Archivist* 76, no. 1 (2013): 95–112.

2. Nélida Pérez. "Two Reading Rooms and the Librarian's Office: The Evolution of the Centro Library and Archives." *Centro Journal* 21, no. 2 (2009): 199–219.

3. Katherine S. Dabbour and James D. Ballard. "Information Literacy and U.S. Latino College Students: A Cross-Cultural Analysis." *New Library World* 112, nos. 7–8 (2011): 347–364.

4. *Ibid.*, 355.

5. Tracy B. Grimm and Chon A. Noriega. "Documenting Regional Latino Arts and Culture: Case Studies for a Collaborative, Community-Oriented Approach." *The American Archivist* 76, no. 1 (2013): 95–112.

6. Dominique Daniel. "Documenting the Immigrant and Ethnic Experience in American Archives." *The American Archivist* 73, no. 1 (2010): 82–104.

7. Mario H. Ramirez. "The Task of the Latino/a Archivist: On Archiving Identity and Community." *InterActions: UCLA Journal of Education and Information Studies* 5 no. 1 (2009): 1–12.

8. Nélida Pérez. "Two Reading Rooms and the Librarian's Office: The Evolution of the Centro Library and Archives." *Centro Journal* 21, no. 2 (2009): 199–219.

9. *Ibid.*, 216.

10. The City College website: https://www.ccny.cuny.edu/.

11. C. Stewart, personal communication, July 30, 2014.

12. Ramona Hernández. "The Dominican American Family." In *Ethnic Families in Americas: Patterns and Variations*, edited by R.H. Wright and C.H. Mindel. Translated by R.W. Habenstein, 148–173. Boston: Pearson, 2012.

13. Anthony Stevens-Acevedo, Tom Weterings, and Leonora A. Francés. *Juan Rodríguez and the Beginnings of New York City*. New York: CUNY Dominican Studies Institute, 2013.

14. Silvio Torres-Saillant and Ramona Hernández. *The Dominican Americans*. Westport, CT: Greenwood, 1998.

15. Laura Burt. "Vivian Harsh, Adult Education, and the Library's Role as a Community Center." *Libraries & the Cultural Record* 44 (2009): 234–255.

16. Ramona Hernández, and Anthony Stevens-Acevedo. "Dominican Immigrants." In *Multicultural America: An Encyclopedia of the Newest Americans*, edited by Ron Bayor, 471–532. Santa Barbara, CA: Greenwood, 2011.

17. Virginia Woolf. *A Room of One's Own*. New York and Burlingame: Harcourt, Brace & World, 1957.

18. http://academicworks.cuny.edu/dsi_pubs/.

19. http://www.sscommons.org/openlibrary/welcome.html#2|7730395|City20College20Dominican20 Library20First20Blacks20in20the20Americas.

20. http://dp.la/search?utf8=%E2%9C%93&q=City+College+Dominican+Library+First+Blacks+in+ the+Americas.

Latin American and Caribbean Documentary Memory in the Digital Age

FERNANDO ACOSTA-RODRÍGUEZ *and* LUIS A. GONZÁLEZ

Introduction

Digitization occupies a salient place in the evolving information landscape of Latin American and Caribbean studies, primarily supporting academic research and teaching in the field, but equally important for providing broad-based engagement with information resources by non-academic communities throughout the hemisphere and around the world. Foregrounded in open-access models and principles of national and international collaboration, Latin American and Caribbean studies research collections based in North American memory institutions have adopted digitization with the objective of meeting the information needs of both academic and non-academic users in the digital age.

This essay examines the main contributions of five open-access primary resources digitization projects that have been created to support the study of Latin America and the Caribbean within the last decade as part of a collaboration between institutions in the United States, Latin America, and the Caribbean: the *AHPN: Archivo Digital del Archivo Histórico de la Policía Nacional de Guatemala*; *Brasil: Nunca Mais digit@l*; *Archivo Mesoamericano*; *Digital Archive of Latin American and Caribbean Ephemera*, and the *Digital Library of the Caribbean (dLOC)*. The essay provides an overview of each project, describing not only the unique contents that have been preserved and made freely accessible via the Internet, but also the innovations and novel contributions introduced by these projects in various realms—from project governance to description methodologies, from innovative search functionality to availability of previously inaccessible cultural, historical and ephemeral materials as well as human rights documentation. We also try to situate these projects within the broader context of digitization initiatives in memory institutions, addressing key issues in the literature: inter-institutional collaboration; funding and sustainability; preservation and curation of endangered content; access and ethical issues surrounding privacy and the involvement of originating communities or stakeholders; copyrights and permissions; and the debate on the interaction between archives, memory, and power. We close with a discussion of lessons learned in how to undertake and manage digitization projects, address ongoing challenges, and consider future directions for these kinds of initiatives.[1]

Digitization: Background and Foreground

Systematic digitization initiatives among academic and research libraries in North America can be traced back to the mid–1990s. This was certainly the case among members of the Association of Research Libraries (ARL), the prominent non-profit organization of research institutions based in the United States and Canada. A membership survey taken in 2006 shows that digitization activities among ARL institutions steadily increased throughout the second half of the 1990s, accelerated during the turn of the century, and continued to grow, though at a slower pace, afterward. In 2006, the majority of survey respondents (66 out of 68, or 97 percent) stated that they were involved in digitization activities at some level.[2] These findings are consistent with other surveys conducted during the same period on the adoption of digitization by U.S.-based academic libraries.[3] While the original motivations for implementing digitization in most institutions included both the preservation of library materials and improving access to collections, over time digitization for access has become the predominant motivation. Digital creation has come to be seen as an adequate strategy to bring greater visibility to and, more explicitly, greater use of library collections.[4]

Similar patterns are broadly present in the development of digitization activities coordinated by North American academic libraries in the field of Latin American and Caribbean studies. The *Brazilian Government Documents* project and the *Presidential Messages* database project were two of the pioneer digital projects in the field. These two successful initiatives were established in the mid–1990s as a result of larger collaborative endeavors between national and international institutions with funding principally derived from private grants. Funded by the Andrew W. Mellon Foundation in 1994 and coordinated by the Latin American Materials Project (LAMP), a cooperative initiative administratively based at the Center for Research Libraries (CRL),[5] the *Brazilian Government Documents* project is a digital collection of official serial documents issued by the national government as well as by provincial governments in Brazil.[6] Composed of page images of publications that go back to the nineteenth century, the freely accessible database was an early experiment with digitization from microfilm.[7] Likewise, the *Presidential Messages* database consists of official publications, in this case documentation from the office of the presidents of Argentina and Mexico, covering the period from the early nineteenth century to the present.[8] This initiative was supported by the Latin Americanist Research Resources Project (LAARP).[9] As with the Brazilian collection, *Presidential Messages* involved remediation from microfilm to digital format. Due largely to high costs of rekeying text, the quality of microfilm images, and the state of development of Optical Character Recognition (OCR) software available at the time, project managers opted for simple interfaces that delivered very basic search functionality. Essentially collections of page images, none of these early databases are full-text searchable. Individual pages or sections of text in a volume are linked to the table of contents or an index where available. Both initiatives, however, share an overriding objective: to provide online access to materials of significant research value that were scarce, in some cases fragile or deteriorating, and often scattered in various locations.

As forerunners, *Brazilian Government Documents* and *Presidential Messages* reveal core features present in the subsequent, more advanced digitization endeavors that are the focus of this article. Inter-institutional collaboration, access and preservation as project objectives, support for open and free access to online content as well as substantial reliance on external sources of funding are all elements that continue to characterize more recent digital activities among academic libraries. Nevertheless, the five projects to be reviewed below belong to what we might conceivably call a second generation of digitization initiatives. The digitally reformatted materials accessible through these portals represent a wide range of media from conventional text-based sources such as official publications, historical newspapers, and archival manuscripts to non-text content such as photographs, maps, artifacts, and audio and video materials. In contrast to first generation initiatives, these online portals provide users with sophisticated tools that transform the portal's search functionality, a result of the combination of new technologies with rich descriptive metadata and flexible processing workflows to manage and curate digital content. In their respective ways, these projects represent remarkable models for preserving and providing open access to the documentary memory of the hemisphere.

AHPN: Archivo Digital del Archivo Histórico de la Policía Nacional de Guatemala

Even though its existence had for decades been denied by Guatemalan authorities, personnel from that country's Procurador de los Derechos Humanos (Office of the Human Rights Ombudsman) accidentally discovered in 2005 a vast archive of abandoned files that documented in extraordinary detail the activities of that country's Policía Nacional (National Police) from 1881 to 1997, the institution having been disbanded as required by the peace accords ending Guatemala's thirty-six-year civil war that were signed the year before. Throughout the second half of the twentieth century, the Policía Nacional had been a collaborator and enforcer in the government's brutally repressive counterinsurgency campaign that, led by the army, ended the lives of more than 200,000 people.[10] Officially named the Archivo Histórico de la Policía Nacional de Guatemala (AHPN), or National Police Historical Archive of Guatemala, and since 2009 under the custody of the Archivo General de Centroamérica (General Archive of Central America) (Guatemala's national archive), the AHPN revealed the inner workings of the Policía Nacional and the government's engine of repression. Hundreds of thousands of internal communications, identification records, personnel lists, complaints, reports, orders, operational plans, surveillance photographs, logs to investigation files, and many other types of documentation started to shed light on decades of government surveillance, control, persecution, and elimination of political opposition.[11] The archive gave Guatemalan society the opportunity to discover what had occurred to many of those killed and disappeared during the conflict, to prosecute perpetrators of human rights abuses, and to start a process of recovery of the historical memory of their country.[12]

To help turn that opportunity into a reality, soon after discovery the AHPN launched a massive and risky effort to preserve, catalog and digitize the approximately 80 million pages of records that constitute the archive and make it one of the largest unexpurgated repositories of police files ever made available to human rights investigators anywhere in the world. Many foreign governments, international cooperation agencies and organizations from around the world have collaborated with the AHPN in this endeavor by providing substantial financial and political support as well as equipment, technical assistance and specialized training.[13] As a result, more than 19 million pages have been cataloged, digitized and made available as of 2016, with more being added as progress continues.[14] To safeguard the integrity of the information as well as the security of the individuals who work at the archive, all of the data is permanently protected in four separate digital repositories that serve as backup centers. They are located at the AHPN's facilities, at the headquarters of the Archivo General de Centroamérica, at the Schweizerisches Bundesarchiv (Swiss Federal Archives), and at the University of Texas at Austin.

In addition to serving as one of the backup centers, the University of Texas at Austin (UT) has closely collaborated with the AHPN by hosting and maintaining since 2011, the *AHPN: Archivo Digital del Archivo Histórico de la Policía Nacional de Guatemala*, an open-access website that makes all of the documents digitized to date and transferred by the AHPN available for consultation.[15] The collaboration has permitted the AHPN to fulfill one of its most fundamental functions: to offer public access to the information contained in the documents that it holds.[16] Thanks to this collaboration the documentation is available without restrictions to representatives from public entities and human rights organizations in Guatemala and elsewhere prosecuting cases of human rights abuses, to families and friends of the killed or disappeared who seek the truth of what happened to their loved ones, and to journalists, scholars, historians, students and independent researchers everywhere.[17]

The AHPN digital archive hosted by UT mirrors the physical archive that remains at and are preserved in the facilities of the physical AHPN in Guatemala. In conformance with professional archival principles, it respects the original order of the physical archive and reflects the administrative structure of the Policía Nacional. To find documents within the millions of pages already available through the site, the bulk of which were produced between 1960 and 1997, users must browse through the hierarchical structure of the archive in a manner analogous to working with the physical archive. Keyword searching capabilities are limited as most of the images in the database have little accompanying metadata and the available name index is small. The website does offer various resources to assist researchers, including brief introductory instructions and sample search strategies, an in depth user guide with examples of how to locate specific types of documents, finding aids integrated into the structure of the archive which describe each category of records, and a link to the electronic publication of *From Silence to Memory*, an essential source for understanding the organizational structure and functions of the Policía Nacional.[18]

The deployment of the *AHPN: Archivo Digital del Archivo Histórico de la Policía Nacional de Guatemala* and the international collaboration that made it possible represent a remarkable example of the post-custodial archival model that has been adopted by the UT Libraries and in particular by its Human Rights Documentation Initiative.[19] In contrast to the traditional acquisition model where a resource rich institution, often a U.S.-based university research library, takes physical custody of an archive in order to preserve it and facilitate access to its content, the post-custodial archival model seeks instead to establish a collaborative relationship where the original custodian retains physical and intellectual custody and provides digital copies to partners with the resources and technical expertise necessary to provide long-term preservation and access. In practical terms, the post-custodial model implemented at the UT Libraries means that digitization and description of the documentation is conducted onsite by the original custodian and the partner library provides the technical resources required for long-term digital preservation and access. The original custodian does not only contribute content and labor, but also subject expertise and knowledge of their own material that will be positively reflected in the quality of the descriptive work and that will greatly aid future users of the archive. The partner library in return helps to build preservation capacity, provides technical assistance and training in archival best practices, and may even provide digitization equipment. It also provides the infrastructure required for long term preservation and access.[20]

As has been noted by Theresa E. Polk, the Benson Latin American Collection's Post-custodial Archivist, the post-custodial approach can be particularly suitable to human rights archival documentation. The traditional acquisition model can often be less palatable to holders of human rights records who are understandably reluctant to relinquish custody of their materials as that option may not only disrupt their programmatic and operational needs, but could also represent a loss of cultural and historic patrimony.[21] The success of the *AHPN: Archivo Digital del Archivo Histórico de la Policía Nacional de Guatemala* helps to make a strong case in favor of the post-custodial archival model as a preferred approach in such cases and represents an extraordinary example of the benefits that it can bring to the partners involved.[22]

Brasil: Nunca Mais digit@l

Brasil: Nunca Mais digit@l is an open-access initiative that provides access to official human rights documentation related to the Brazilian military dictatorship era (1964–1985).[23] In this partnership between Brazilian and international institutions, the Latin American Materials Project (LAMP) has played a long-standing role in the preservation and dissemination of this remarkable collection. *Brasil: Nunca Mais* is the name given to a singular collection of the official records of political trials from the military regime that ruled Brazil for two decades. These official records expose flagrant human rights violations perpetrated by Brazilian authorities since the start of military rule in 1964 up to 1979, when an amnesty law was introduced, paving the way for a carefully controlled transition to democratic rule. Public disclosure of these records provided undeniable evidence of the widespread and systematic use of torture by the Brazilian regime against political opponents.

The content and existence of this documentation is unique. In his comparative study of military regime justice systems, *Political (In)Justice*, political scientist Anthony Pereira asserts that there is no comparable archive to *Brasil: Nunca Mais* in Argentina or Chile, countries that also endured repressive military regimes during the same years.[24] The collection consists of 707 political trials from the Supremo Tribunal Militar (Superior Military Court). With the connivance of the civilian judiciary, the Brazilian military regime established a parallel court system to try political opponents. The Supremo Tribunal Militar served as the court of appeal for civilians accused of breaking the national security law. According to Pereira, the existence of this military court system gave the dictatorship the appearance of legality, fairness, and due process.

The riveting story behind the origins of the *Brasil: Nunca Mais* project is worth retelling here, if only briefly.[25] These documents were secretly copied from the original files stored in the archives of the Supremo Tribunal Militar in Brasília. This top-secret operation lasted nearly six years and was coordinated by Cardinal Paulo Evaristo Arns,

Archbishop of São Paulo, and the Reverend Jaime Wright of the Presbyterian Church/USA in Brazil. Active in the human rights movement under the dictatorship, these religious leaders had direct knowledge of the political violence routinely practiced by the authorities. Through their work with human-rights lawyers, they learned that the court files included detailed accounts by defendants in the form of sworn testimony on acts of torture practiced against them while in custody. They realized that accessing and disclosing this kind of evidence would bolster human rights advocacy. Cardinal Arns and the Reverend Wright enlisted a small team of trusted lawyers to access records of the Supremo Tribunal Militar. Most of these lawyers were involved in the defense of political prisoners seeking protection under the amnesty law passed in 1979. Under the law, defense lawyers were permitted to retrieve the court files from the tribunal for a period of twenty-four hours to prepare their cases. The project coordinators used this opportunity to reproduce, first via photocopying, then reformatting, more than one million paper copies into 543 rolls of microfilm, the complete set of 707 political trials archived in Brasília. The World Council of Churches based in Geneva financially supported the project from beginning to end.

Analysis and dissemination of the stunning findings from the *Brasil: Nunca Mais* project unfolded along two tracks. The most important track, known as Project A, is the authoritative report published in twelve bound volumes analyzing state-sponsored political torture from various perspectives.[26] Three of the twelve volumes consist of excerpts drawn from actual sworn testimonies in the court files of victims describing instances of torture. Other volumes identify the victims of torture by name as well as the names of individual torturers, including information on military judges, medical examiners, informants, officials and collaborators of the repressive apparatus. Documented cases of deaths resulting from torture as well as cases of forced disappearances are the subject of another volume. A massive compilation of statistical data about the 283 different types of torture that emerged from the court documents forms another volume.

While Project A serves as a meticulously organized index to the collection of 707 complete court cases from the Superior Military Court archive, Project B was conceived as a book publication that summarized the main findings for a wider readership. Written by professional journalists under the supervision of Reverend Wright and originally released in Brazil by Editora Vozes in 1985 under the title *Brasil: Nunca Mais*, this book is today considered a foundational moment in the construction of the social memory of the crimes of the Brazilian dictatorship.[27] The book instantly became a best seller and retains its status as one of the most important non-fiction works published in Brazil.[28] The English-language edition, *Torture in Brazil: A Report*, appeared in 1986.[29]

Concerned with the uncertainties of the transitional period that began in 1979, the project organizers decided to send the complete microfilm set and other Project A materials abroad for safekeeping. Initially, microfilm, computer files, and other important documentation generated by the project were sent to the headquarters of the World Council of Churches in Geneva. The complete paper copies of the 707 cases plus a set of the physical, twelve-volume report *Brasil: Nunca Mais* were donated to Arquivo Edgard Leuenroth at the Universidade Estadual de Campinas (Unicamp), the State University of Campinas. Twenty-five bound copies of Project A were distributed to human rights organizations, libraries, and universities within Brazil and abroad. Cardinal Arns, however, wanted to find a permanent home for the materials that had been sent to Switzerland. He was interested in finding an academic institution that would make this material widely available for research. This prompted Reverend Wright to contact academic institutions in the United States. In 1987, Wright agreed to donate the collection of 543 rolls of microfilm to the Latin American Materials Project (LAMP) at the Center for Research Libraries (CRL) in Chicago.[30]

In 2011, the São Paulo regional office of the Ministério Público Federal, or Federal Prosecutor's Service, contacted CRL to explore a cross-institutional collaboration to digitize the complete set of microfilm rolls of *Brasil: Nunca Mais*.[31] An autonomous institution within the Brazilian government, the Federal Prosecutor's Service has constitutional powers to protect the public interest and other fundamental rights in Brazil.[32] For years, the São Paulo office has been active in human rights litigation involving claims from citizens persecuted by the military regime. Specifically, Brazilian officials asked LAMP to fund the cost of duplication of the complete collection of 543 rolls. LAMP enthusiastically agreed to collaborate, paying for the creation of duplicate negatives of the complete collection, the ideal medium for digital reformatting. The main Brazilian institutional partners—the Ministério Público Federal (Federal Public Ministry), the Arquivo Público do Estado de São Paulo (Public Archive of the State of São Paulo), and Armazém Memória—coordinated the complete digitization operation, allocating additional resources and funding for the project, using the copy of the microfilm set that LAMP provided. The full-text searchable database uses indexing and text recognition software developed by DOCPRO, the Brazilian information technology firm that has created software used in digital initiatives of the Biblioteca Nacional (National Library of Brazil) and other prominent academic institutions in Brazil. The site is hosted on servers managed by the Ministério Público Federal in São Paulo.[33]

In the open-access digital portal, the original *Brasil: Nunca Mais* core collection of court cases and Project A report has been enhanced with additional sources. This new content includes both text and non-text materials. Among the text-based materials, the collection of records from the World Council of Churches consists of correspondence related to planning and funding the *Brasil:Nunca Mais* project, review articles and press clippings from the Brazilian and international press addressing the impact of the publication of the book *Brasil: Nunca Mais*, and reports from national and international human rights organizations on political violence in Brazil during the period of military dictatorship. Unpublished documents and reports regarding denunciations of arrests, torture, killings and forced disappearances collected by the Comissão Justiça e Paz de São Paulo (Commission for Justice and Peace) from the Archdiocese of São Paulo have also been digitized and made available via the online portal. Previously inaccessible, the information offers glimpses into Cardinal Arns' early work in human rights advocacy prior to his involvement with *Brazil: Nunca Mais*. Non-text materials include videos of filmed statements by key figures in the planning and development of the project, including lawyers Eny Raimundo Moreira and Luiz Carlos Sigmaringa Seixas, as well as Luiz Eduardo Greenhalgh and Paulo Vannuchi who contributed chapters to the book publication.

Other enhancements to *Brasil: Nunca Mais digit@l* include a new finding aid that provides abstracts (*sumários*) of relevant information for each of the 707 legal cases in the collection.[34] Organized into six sections, each abstract provides the names of the defendants, the nature of the charges levelled against them, court rulings, and other key information that helps explain the stages of a case as it went through the military court bureaucracy. Crosslinks to the digitized court cases facilitates easy access to the original source from which the information was retrieved. Significantly, the data and findings originally collected for Project A were subjected to a comprehensive review by a team of researchers at the Pontifícia Universidade Católica in São Paulo.[35] This review has determined that data from forteen legal cases was not entered into the database created by the original team of investigators who produced the Project A report. Several factors may account for this gap in the original data. As noted, the project unfolded under very precarious conditions. Copies of some court records became available at a moment when data processing and analysis was already too advanced to add additional information. Other factors could have been the poor quality of the photocopies as well as inconsistent and incomplete data in the military court records themselves.

Over the years, the *Brasil: Nunca Mais* documentation deposited at Unicamp's Arquivo Edgard Leuenroth has been the most heavily used collection at the prominent repository specializing in Brazilian contemporary history.[36] This collection has supported usage by both academic and non-academic constituencies. Numerous documentaries, books, and graduate theses have been written using these records. Researchers have explored a broad range of topics related to student and labor mobilization and leftist movements during the dictatorship era.[37] In recent years, non-academic use has increased due to the passing of financial reparations laws. Victims of political persecution by the military dictatorship and their relatives have been referencing these documents to back up legal claims for reparations from the Brazilian government.[38] Reportedly, as many as 325 consultations by researchers and individuals were recorded from 1987 to 2003.[39] Since the launching of the *Brasil: Nunca Mais digit@l* portal in 2013, boosting visibility and wider access to the collection, the use of these records has increased exponentially as shown by a recently released report from the São Paulo regional office of the Ministério Público Federal especially furnished to the authors of this article.[40] In the period from September 2013 to August 2016, website traffic metrics show a total of 125,953 visits to the site by as many as 83,772 unique visitors. Pageviews, the total number of pages accessed or viewed on a site (and another key metric), totaled 285,154 in this three-year period. This important metric is helpful to understand both the quality of the content accessible via the site as well as the usability or ease of navigation on the site. That pageviews more than doubled the number of visits to the portal in a three-year period is a respectable indicator of the productive interaction that users have had with the content on the portal. Furthermore, 2.7 million documents were downloaded in the same period. Additionally, data about the geographic location (countries and cities) from which a session originates reveals the impact that digitization has had on facilitating greater access and visibility to these remarkable records. While the overwhelming majority of the sessions originate within Brazil, the open-access portal has been accessed by users from all corners of the world. Significantly, *Brasil: Nunca Mais digit@l* served to anchor the work of the Comissão Nacional da Verdade (CNV), the National Truth Commission, established by the Brazilian government in 2012 to investigate the human rights abuses committed in the country between 1946 and 1988, with particular attention to post–1964 events.[41]

Unveiling the crimes of the military dictatorship was the core mission of the original *Brasil: Nunca Mais* project. From the beginning, however, this mission had broader pedagogical motivations. The right to truth and the right to memory were deemed critically important principles in the construction of a democratic society. The digitization project stems from the same motivation. As stated on its site, *Brasil: Nunca Mais digit@l* seeks "to provide education for historical memory, for the development of social relations foregrounded in human rights."[42] Reproduction of the material available through the online portal is authorized, provided that the original source is quoted and *Brasil: Nunca Mais digit@l* is acknowledged. No formal permissions requests are necessary to use any of the materials on the portal.[43]

Archivo Mesoamericano

A collaboration between Indiana University (IU) and three leading research and memory institutions in Central America and Mexico, *Archivo Mesoamericano* is a searchable digital archive of rare contemporary historical and ethnographic video materials based on the collections of the Latin American partners: the Instituto de Historia de Nicaragua y Centroamérica (IHNCA) (Institute of History of Nicaragua and Central America), based in Nicaragua; the Museo de la Palabra y la Imagen (MUPI) (Museum of Word and Image) in El Salvador, and the Centro de Investigaciones y Estudios Superiores en Antropología Social (CIESAS) (Center of Higher Research and Studies in Social Anthropology) from Mexico.[44] *Archivo Mesoamericano* combines two interrelated but originally distinct projects, the Central American and Mexican Video Archive (CAMVA) and the Cultural and Linguistic Archive of Mesoamerica (CLAMA) into a single online portal. While CAMVA focused on digitization of historical and ethnographic video materials, CLAMA sought to digitize audio and photographic sources relating to minority languages and cultures held by partner institutions in Mexico and Central America.[45] Funding for this multi-year digitization initiative stemmed from the short-lived Technological Innovation and Cooperation for Foreign Information Access (TICFIA) program managed by the U.S. Department of Education.[46] Created in 1999, TICFIA promoted the use of new electronic technologies as a means to improve the quality of education in the United States through better access to a wide-range of international instructional and research resources. During its existence, TICFIA funded nearly forty projects dealing with different world regions, including nine projects specifically focused on Latin America and the Caribbean.[47] The abrupt and premature ending of the TICFIA program in 2011 thwarted the completion of the CLAMA project as originally envisioned.

While a few video recordings go back to the 1970s, the bulk of the individual video titles represented in *Archivo Mesoamericano* were filmed during the 1980s. This period in Central American history was marked by profound political struggles as well as by social and economic transformations. The triumph and travails of the Sandinista Revolution in Nicaragua and the emergence of a guerrilla movement in El Salvador stand out as perhaps the most salient phenomena in the region. Though spared from the political turmoil that caused rifts in the isthmus, Mexico was nonetheless shaken by social and economic instability. The impact of these transformations on Mexican rural populations of predominantly indigenous background often resulted in land loss, social dislocation, and accelerated migration, particularly external migration to the United States.

Traces of the impact of these transformations on people's lives were captured on film, providing unique first-hand perspectives on the rise of social movements led by women, students, peasants, and workers. Similarly, the videos provide unparalleled access to social and cultural aspects of the everyday lives of communities in the Mexican and Central American countryside. Reflected in these filmed materials are religious and folk ceremonies and rituals, civic celebrations and official commemorations, as well as *saberes tradicionales*, or traditional knowledge and practices now recognized as intangible cultural heritage, such as traditional medicine, that are amenable for linguistic and ethnographic analyses.

Although cultural, political, and social themes predominate in the digital video collection, the scope and provenance of the content in *Archivo Mesoamericano* is very diverse. Only the Mexican video materials were originally conceived with a clear scholarly or educational objective. These were collected in the course of research conducted by CIESAS-affiliated anthropologists mainly working in rural regions of Chiapas, Oaxaca, and Veracruz. In contrast, the materials contributed by both IHNCA and MUPI come from a variety of sources, including raw footage and documentaries produced and/or collected by media organizations (television and radio networks) in both Nicaragua and El Salvador.[48]

A full review of the remarkable video content digitally available in *Archivo Mesoamericano* is beyond the scope of this article, but a few highlights deserve attention. Two good examples of depictions of intangible cultural heritage in Mexico are the documentaries *Saberes de las parteras indígenas en los Altos de Chiapas* and *K'in Santo ta Sotz'leb* (or *Día de Muertos en la Tierra de los Murciélagos*). Filmed in 2004, the first documentary explores the work of indigenous midwives in the highlands of Chiapas in southern Mexico and efforts to keep the practice alive through formal training programs led by the Organización de Médicos Indígenas del Estado de Chiapas (OMIECH) (Organization of Indigenous Physicians of the State of Chiapas). The documentary is narrated in Spanish with segments in Tzotzil, a Mayan language spoken in southern Mexico. The other, *K'in Santo ta Sotz'leb* shows how Tzotzil families from Zinacantán in Chiapas prepare for the Day of the Dead, one of the most important religious celebrations in their community.

Several landmark documentaries produced by Radio Venceremos, the media arm of the insurgency during the Salvadoran civil war (1980–1992), have been digitized and made accessible through *Archivo Mesoamericano*. Filmed in guerrilla-controlled zones, works such as *La decisión de vencer* (1981), *Carta de Morazán* (1982), and *Tiempo de audacia* (1983), explore the process of revolution in El Salvador, providing powerful visual testimonies of the struggle.[49] Another important set of video materials covers the Esquipulas process, the series of negotiations that led up to the peace accords that brought an end to the armed conflicts in Central America.

During the Sandinista period, prominent Nicaraguan authors and intellectuals were politically active. Celebrated poet Ernesto Cardenal and novelist Sergio Ramírez occupied key government positions, the latter as Vice President, the former as Minister of Culture. The digital archive contains speeches and interviews by both writers on the occasion of cultural and political events during the 1980s. Also available is a rare filmed speech by Julio Cortázar upon accepting the Orden de la Independencia Cultural "Rubén Darío" (Rubén Darío Order of Cultural Independence) award in 1983. Established by the Sandinista government, the honor recognized Cortázar "for his intellectual position in agreement with the yearnings for freedom of Latin American peoples and his profound identification with the Sandinista popular revolution."[50] A key figure in the Latin American literary boom, Cortázar was a staunch and eloquent advocate of leftist and progressive political movements.

Beyond the creation of a freely available regionally-focused digital video archive of previously inaccessible materials, *Archivo Mesoamericano* introduced innovative technological approaches for the digital preservation, annotation, and discovery of video collections. The Digital Library Program at IU Libraries developed the open-source software that made this innovation possible, combining video segmentation with annotation capabilities. The software was originally developed for the *Ethnographic Video for Instruction & Analysis Digital Archive (EVIADA)*, a collaborative digital preservation initiative supported by Indiana University.[51] Two TICFIA grants permitted enhancements to the segmentation and annotation capabilities of the software to support teaching and learning in an online environment, a key component of the program's guidelines. Two back-end software tools that are particularly innovative are the Annotator's Workbench and the Controlled Vocabulary Manager. The Annotator's Workbench enables curators to divide video files into segments, representing scenes, specific actions or events in a timeline structure that are then annotated and described using metadata. Stored in the Controlled Vocabulary Manager, the metadata, or the terms used to describe the content of the video collection, are seamlessly imported into the Annotator's Workbench. This controlled list of search terms draws from various sources, including the Autoridades de la Biblioteca Nacional de España, Library of Congress Subject Headings, and the UNESCO Thesaurus. The annotations for each scene or event provide relevant historical, social, and cultural explanations as well as the institutional provenance of each particular video that places the material in context. End-user navigation in *Archivo Mesoamericano* is available in two modes: standard keyword searching and browsing by nine distinct categories, including event, geographical location, personal names, institutional provenance of the materials, and subject. Furthermore, each title in the digital video collection has been professionally cataloged and all of this content is discoverable via online library catalogs such as IU's IUCAT and WorldCat, the union catalog managed by OCLC. The assignment of a persistent uniform resource locator (PURL) to each video title ensures continuous access to it as online resources migrate and change location on the Internet.

In relation to permissions, *Archivo Mesoamericano* has adopted a very flexible policy for use and redistribution for research and educational purposes. Devised as an educational resource, the digital video portal adheres to the stipulations of a Creative Commons license by which users have free access to the content and can also share and redistribute the material in any medium or format for non-commercial purposes. Re-use or modification of the material is allowed but not the redistribution of modified material, a policy known as "no derivatives." In addition, users must give appropriate credit, or attribution, to the material.[52] For commercial use of any video material, the user must clear permissions directly with CIESAS, IHNCA, and MUPI, since partner institutions hold the copyrights to the materials.

Digital Archive of Latin American and Caribbean Ephemera

Subject specialists and area studies librarians have long been urged by scholars to document emerging social movements, cultural manifestations, political events, and other important developments around the world by collecting relevant ephemeral materials. Yet, they have been discouraged both by the arduousness of collecting ephemera and by the challenges inherent to making these kinds of materials available in large amounts in a cost-effective and timely manner.[53] The Princeton University Library has long distinguished itself through its persistent commitment to tackling these hurdles. Launched in early 2015, the *Digital Archive of Latin American and Caribbean Ephemera* represents the latest phase in this effort.[54] The project has been selected for discussion in this essay not only because of the exceptional research value of the content that it is making freely available in digital format, but also because it has put forward an unconventional and promising processing model that attempts to address the aforementioned challenges.

The origins of Princeton's Latin American Ephemera Collection go back to the mid-1970s when the library began to proactively acquire these types of primary sources in order to document the activities of political and social organizations and movements, as well as the broader political, socioeconomic and cultural developments of the region.[55] In time, the library developed an expansive capacity to collect ephemera generated throughout much of the region by building and nurturing an evolving network of agents and vendors who would seek the materials on its behalf. The goals of the effort have always been to represent a wide spectrum of perspectives and positions that would enrich and balance official statements and the establishment version of events, as well as enhance the generalizations of journalistic and scholarly accounts; and to ensure that the numerous voices and messages circulating outside or in the margins of mainstream communication channels are not lost. The product of this continuous effort is a vast and continuously expanding collection of ephemera that is unmatched in breadth and depth, and is widely recognized as an invaluable resource for researchers and students.[56]

Before the *Digital Archive of Latin American and Caribbean Ephemera* became available, Princeton University Library provided access to its thousands of pamphlets, flyers, leaflets, brochures, posters and other materials by processing them in a more or less traditional archival fashion. This involved painstakingly organizing materials into thematic sub-collections, cataloging, creating corresponding finding aids, and finally, microfilming them.[57] At the end of the process, which normally took several years, reproductions of the microfilm were commercially distributed to other research libraries and resulting royalties were reinvested to fund new acquisitions. This method of processing and offering access persisted until the middle of the last decade when it became unsustainable as research libraries increasingly shifted away from acquiring microfilm sets as a way of providing access to primary research materials.

Though microfilming was definitively halted in 2008, Princeton University Library continued acquiring ephemera uninterruptedly and storing it without any type of processing or description. An extensive backlog of print materials quickly accumulated and remained almost completely hidden even from local researchers. This backlog, which by 2013 was estimated to contain over twelve thousand items, would eventually become the backbone of the *Digital Archive of Latin American and Caribbean Ephemera*. Even though a significant number of items from earlier years formed part of this backlog, the bulk of the ephemera originated around the turn of the twentieth century and after. Some of the best represented topics within the collection are the politics of memory, human rights and activism in Argentina and Chile; public policies for development and social participation in Bolivia; arts and culture in Cuba; and political communication in Venezuela. More generally speaking, the subjects covered are very broad and, in addition to those already mentioned, include an array of aspects and issues related to children and youth, education, the environment, gender, health, race and ethnicity, religion, tourism and socioeconomic development in general. The vast majority of the ephemeral items are rare, hard-to-find primary sources unavailable elsewhere.

To understand how these materials differ from the content found in the three digital archives previously discussed, and also how they can complement each other, the categories presented by political scientist Louis Bickford in his examination of the documentary materials produced by the Chilean human rights movement that emerged as a reaction to the brutal repression that followed the military coup of 1973 can be helpful.[58] Bickford divided the large amounts of available documentation into three forms. First were the intake files of social service-oriented Human Rights Non-Governmental Organizations (HRNGOs), which include testimonies and documentation relating to specific violations as filed by the victims or their families as they sought legal, psychological, medical, economic, or logistical support. Second, the documents produced by those HRNGOs during the repression years such as reports and bulletins, including documents that might be considered social movement literature, such as clandestine newspapers, posters, meeting, notes and bulletins. And third, materials produced by civil society and by the state after the transition to democracy was initiated. These often presented new documentation and testimonies from victims and families, prioritized remembering the past, and reflected the increasing dedication of HRNGOs to educational activities.

Though by virtue of having been created by a repressive arm of the Guatemalan state, the *Archivo Histórico de la Policía Nacional de Guatemala* is in many ways the virtual opposite of an HRNGO archive. The documentation found in it, if thought about it in solely bureaucratic terms, can be appropriately characterized as belonging to the first category.[59] Items found in *Brasil: Nunca Mais digit@l* belong mostly to the first two categories. The content in *Archivo Mesoamericano* and the *Digital Archive of Latin American and Caribbean Ephemera,* though by no means limited to human rights issues, belongs to the last two.

The *Digital Archive of Latin American and Caribbean Ephemera* is a repository of digitally-reformatted ephemera with accompanying item-level metadata that is intended for indefinite future growth as Princeton University Library continues to acquire and add new content at a rate of several hundred items per month, and, as is projected, future project partners start contributing their own complementary collections to the database. All of its contents are freely and globally available to anyone with internet access through a discovery interface which includes faceted browsing and searching.

The administrative workflow tools underlying the database were developed locally by Princeton University Library staff using Hydra open-source software. A customized version of another open-source resource, Blacklight, was used for the public interface.[60] External funding sources were essential to the development of the project. The digitization of the ephemera, largely outsourced to an external commercial vendor, has been funded by the Latin Americanist Research Resources Project (LARRP). The substantial financial investment required for developing and deploying the new system for efficiently cataloging the ephemera and disclosing the newly digitized content was provided by a three-year starting grant from the Hidden Collections Program of the Council on Library and Information Resources (CLIR).[61]

After assessing potential legal risks and obtaining the approval of Princeton University's Office of the General Counsel, project managers decided to make the reformatted materials widely available on the web for educational and research purposes without clearing copyright permissions for individual items in advance, a task that would have been impossible to fulfill for a project of this scale which involves thousands of widely dispersed and often unidentified creators and publishers. It was determined that the purpose and character of the project constitutes fair use, and that because the materials were not produced by their copyright holders for commercial gain and were instead intended to disseminate their ideas and content as broadly as possible, the merits of having the library redistribute this content far outweighed the limited risks involved. Nevertheless, authorization was granted with these conditions: (a) public display of reformatted items includes appropriate language indicating that the content is intended for educational and research use only; (b) appropriate "take-down" provisions be displayed and implemented in case of any copyright dispute, and (c) any items representing greater risk would be evaluated and withdrawn from the project if necessary.

The system put in place for processing the ephemera represented a complete departure from the traditional archival organization model previously utilized. In the new workflow, item-level descriptive metadata is created by non-professional staff working directly from either the physical items or the images of previously digitized ephemeral materials. The metadata is created and processed without any preliminary sorting or topical grouping, and without requiring a decision by a subject librarian on how to present the items as a group. The resulting database of descriptive item-level metadata linked to digital objects makes the creation of pre-defined finding aids unnecessary as users employ the interface to browse, search and sort materials according to their selected categories. Users are now able to establish connections and make comparisons across the digital archive which would have been difficult or nearly impossible to accomplish under the previous model.

The system relies on simple data entry tools designed specifically for the project which require minimal technical expertise or training for the support staff and student assistants who conduct all metadata creation and file-ingest. The data entry mechanism has built-in linkages to Library of Congress Name Authority files and to a streamlined hierarchy of controlled vocabularies developed locally for ephemera collections of this type, that automatically generate LC subject heading equivalents, insuring that appropriate standards and quality control are attained without the need for dedicated professional original catalogers.

The new processing workflow that feeds the *Digital Archive of Latin American and Caribbean Ephemera* is vastly more efficient than the previous one on many levels. First, all materials can be processed and exposed to researchers in a much more timely manner. This is a very significant advantage considering the nature of research on current topics and emerging social movements. Moreover, numerous materials which in the past would have remained hidden for years because enough related items to build a topical collection had not been accumulated will no longer have to wait to be disclosed. The new model also allows the library to efficiently transfer newly-cataloged digital objects into the open-access discovery tool that makes them available worldwide to an exponentially larger number of users than was previously possible.

Although none of the technical components of this model are by themselves strikingly original, their integration into a new workflow that allows project curators to rapidly catalog and expose large quantities of primary sources in non-traditional formats with a high degree of efficiency does represents a significant innovation. The outcome has been the gradual turning of an exceptional collection from a practically inaccessible archive into a dynamic resource that can support present and future academic activities in interdisciplinary Latin American studies and in the broader social sciences and the humanities, and that will also be, at least potentially, available via the Internet to the countries and communities where the materials originated. Moreover, the expectation of project managers and developers is that the workflow and tools will be extendable and adaptable to other projects of a similar nature within Princeton University Library and to other repositories as well, thus opening the door for a future phase where other institutions can join the project in order to collaboratively develop a distributed database of analogous primary sources with integrated online discovery.

Digital Library of the Caribbean (dLOC)

A cooperative, multi-institutional, international digital library, the *Digital Library of the Caribbean*, better known as *dLOC*, provides centralized access to materials held in archives, libraries, and private collections across a broadly defined Caribbean and circum–Caribbean region.[62] Officially established in 2004 by nine founding partners, it contains nearly two million pages of content contributed by over forty partners that include newspapers, archives, official documents, ecological and economic data, maps, histories, travel accounts, literature, poetry, musical expressions, and artifacts.[63] Some notable examples of the more than twenty Special Collections that form part of *dLOC* are the *Caribbean Newspaper Digital Library*, the *Haitian Law Digital Collection*, the *19th Century Cuban Imprints Digital Collection*, the *Gay Freedom Movement* collection from Jamaica, and the *Vodou Archive*. Thousands of additional primary sources and research materials are grouped thematically and by format, discoverable through state-of-the-art search features. By bringing together these previously dispersed, hard-to-find and even endangered collections, *dLOC* is making a major contribution to both disseminating and preserving for future generations a vast and growing portion of the region's historical and cultural patrimony.

As much as for the significance and research value of its content, *dLOC* stands out as a model of international collaboration. Remarkably, this model has been implemented and sustained by partner institutions belonging to a geographically dispersed region of enormous cultural and linguistic diversity that also differ greatly from each other in terms of the financial, infrastructural and human resources available to them. To do so, they have collectively sought to build on the strengths of participating partners while simultaneously making a conscious effort to ameliorate disparities and resource limitations. This has been possible thanks to an unusually multi-layered program of collaboration that comprises all of the fundamental components of a complex digitization program including governance, the development of technical infrastructure and a support network, and fundraising. The encompassing scope of its collaborative model makes *dLOC* a unique and exemplary digital library project.

The *Digital Library of the Caribbean*'s institutional and governance structure is manifestly devised to maintain low-entry barriers, and to respond to the interests and needs of its seemingly disparate partners. Requirements for becoming a *dLOC* institutional partner are simple and attainable for most libraries or depositories wishing to join. They must have relevant Caribbean content, make corresponding digital surrogates freely available for the project, comply with common standards, and designate a representative to manage local participation. The program as a whole is governed by an executive committee with ample representation from among its partners. Managerial duties are provided by a program director employed by the Florida International University Libraries (FIU). Vital support and sustainability for *dLOC* are offered by an administrative host (FIU) and a technical host (the University of Florida Libraries Digital Library Center) (UF) that provide the system infrastructure and ongoing system development in support of the project.[64]

The democratic character of *dLOC*'s governance is viewed as critical to its success, as it balances the interests of U.S.-based research libraries that have comparatively ample financial and technological resources with those of Caribbean-based repositories that own valuable content, but in many cases operate under circumstances that limit their ability to widely distribute and preserve it. The first group seeks increased access to Caribbean collections for its students, faculty and the wider research community, as well as recognition of their leadership. The second is interested in wider accessibility and preservation, as well as in building their technological capacity, and in the networking and visibility that participation in the project brings.[65] The ability to adequately address both standpoints is surely partially the reason why *dLOC* has been able to quadruple the number of institutional partners since its establishment and, as a result, to make increasing amounts of primary sources widely available on the Internet.

All of *dLOC*'s digitized content is hosted and backed-up for preservation by a robust infrastructure at UF. It is made publicly available via a state-of-the-art trilingual discovery interface that offers enhanced search features including advanced, faceted, map, and full-text searching and browsing. This interface allows partners to present their contributions both as part of the joint *dLOC* digital collection or in system-integrated custom homepages that distinguish the original institutional source.

Reflecting the different types of content presented by the last two projects reviewed in this article, *dLOC* differs from the *Digital Archive of Latin American and Caribbean Ephemera* in its approach to copyright clearance in that its partners frequently work with publishers and copyright owners to request permissions prior to making materials digitally available. *dLOC* observes whichever copyright law affords the greatest protections: either the laws of the partner institution's home country or the laws of the country of origin.[66]

The availability to all participants of a common technical infrastructure and of a support network deliberately developed to facilitate multi-institutional collaboration have also been essential to *dLOC*'s growth and effectiveness. To aid the preliminary and underlying work that is required from all contributors at the local level in order to supply the database with new content, technical support is offered to partners in the form of high-level digitization training, ongoing technical assistance, and a standardized set of workflow tools for metadata creation, digital asset management, electronic submission and archiving.[67] This helps to guarantee that the system remains standards compliant and that all of its data can be migrated forward successfully as technology evolves. Equally crucial, the training and the sharing of technology among *dLOC* partners has contributed enormously to building technical capacity and expertise across the region. This is, of course, another factor that has attracted participants and an important reason for the growth and success of the program.

A project of such ambitious scope requires substantial financial resources to thrive. It is important to note that *dLOC*'s achievements would have been impossible to even remotely match through disconnected institutional efforts, not the least because the necessary financial resources would have been unavailable to most if not all of the partners individually. The collaborative character of the model has been essential to both securing local resources at member institutions, and to obtaining external financial support. This has been the case from the outset, when the project received two TICFIA grants from the U.S. Department of Education for 2005–2009 and 2009–2013 which, along with cost sharing from partner institutions, allowed *dLOC* to develop the technical infrastructure, training materials and network of active partners that are integral to its existence. Since then, current and ongoing support for the project has been provided directly and in-kind by partners, due-paying members, granting organizations such as the Latin Americanist Research Resources Project (LARRP) and the National Endowment for the Humanities (NEH) for specific projects, and other sources.[68]

The Digital Archive: Further Reflections

In the digital age, memory institutions, such as academic libraries, archives, and museums, have been active agents in the preservation and greater dissemination via online portals of unique, often endangered, and, at times, largely inaccessible, materials from Latin America and the Caribbean. As stewards of these invaluable cultural heritage collections, partnering institutions in the digitization projects reviewed in this article have not only preserved, digitized, and provided free online access to critical resources for research and historical interpretation but, perhaps most importantly, have broken new ground by seeking to engage the wider public in explorations of their own society and history, even supporting efforts to recover historical memory in countries torn by state repression and political turmoil. This is particularly significant in post-conflict societies such as Brazil, El Salvador, Guatemala, and Nicaragua.[69]

Digitization, however, is a complex endeavor. In pursuing digital creation—the creation of the digital archive—memory institutions often struggle with a multiplicity of issues including collaboration, funding, long-term sustainability, selection criteria, copyrights, privacy and the ethical politics of access.

Collaboration—a theme that runs across the five digitization projects—encompasses many dimensions. Consortial funding support has been a critical factor in the successful launching of these projects. Besides external grants from public and private sources, all institutions have made significant commitments of equipment, facilities, staffing and ongoing financial support necessary to maintain these projects beyond the initial grant allocations. Indiana University, for example, is committed to both hosting *Archivo Mesoamericano* and archiving digital master copies of the videos in perpetuity. Likewise, Florida International University and the University of Florida have agreed to serve as the administrative and technical hosts of the *Digital Library of the Caribbean*. A non-library institution, the Procuradoria Regional da República da 3ª Região (Federal Prosecutor's Service for São Paulo), has allocated resources to permanently host and maintain *Brasil: Nunca Mais digit@l*. This is also the case of the *AHPN: Archivo Digital del Archivo Histórico de la Policía Nacional de Guatemala*, supported by a combination of three administrative units within the University of Texas at Austin.

As most of these projects show, the commitment to build international partnerships among various library and non-library institutions is remarkable. This kind of coordinated collaboration has afforded organized access over the Internet to unique and, in some cases, culturally and politically sensitive content. Supporting courageous efforts by local organizations working under risky political conditions, international support has played a critical role in preserving and safeguarding the "archives of repression" in both Brazil and Guatemala. In both these cases, collaboration extended to critical partnerships with non-library entities, including the Procuradoria Regional da República da 3ª Região.

Even where international collaboration has not yet had any significant role, as in the case of the *Digital Archive of Latin American and Caribbean Ephemera*, project managers at Princeton University Library realize that collaborating and partnering with other institutions is the direction required in order to secure the relevance and sustainability of the ephemera digital archive. The goal is to initiate in the near future a new phase of the digital ephemera project where partner institutions—from North American peer research libraries to in-country specialized repositories in Latin America and the Caribbean—make coordinated contributions to collection development, digital reformatting, cataloging, online presentation, and preservation according to their local interests and resources. Developing stable partnerships has been identified as a strong indicator of long-term success in digitization of materials of scholarly interest.[70]

Considering the prevalent asymmetrical distribution of resources among international partners in most of these digitization projects—from diverse institutional missions to disparate operational budgets and technology infrastructure—the collaborative approach to digitization has allowed participants to pool resources, overcoming disparities to achieve mutual benefit. Many of these digitization projects have relied on cross-fertilization of expertise, bringing together scholars, activists, archivists, librarians, and information technology specialists to collaborate in project development. In most cases, the projects thrived as a result of long-standing institutional relationships between Latin American and North American partners. In the preservation field, LAMP has a solid track record working with Latin American and Caribbean institutions. Indiana University and the University of Texas at Austin have long histories of research activities in Central America and Mexico, whereas the University of Florida has traditionally had strengths in Caribbean studies. These institutional foundations point to the importance of dedicated leadership, one of the main requirements for building sustainable digital resources.[71] Furthermore, some digitization initiatives pursued deeper levels of collaboration in project development and management with the goal of ensuring the long-term sustainability of the digital archives. Research cooperation, technical training, software development, and introduction of workflows and best practices were all core components of the partnerships led by Indiana University, Florida International University, the University of Florida, and the University of Texas at Austin. The full-fledged governance system adopted by *dLOC* has strengthened this path-breaking initiative, becoming a model for newer initiatives in the Latin American and Caribbean studies field.[72]

Digitization can bring greater visibility and exposure to materials of research, cultural, and historical value. Still, the multiplicity of factors that influence digitization reinforces selection as a practice, contributing, perhaps unintentionally, to obscuring other kinds of records. In the digital archive, selection for digitization plays a role similar to appraisal in the conventional, physical archive, a curatorial process by which only certain kinds of materials are selected and permanently preserved by an institution.[73] Hence, users and researchers exploring the content accessible in some of these digital archives would be wise to heed historian Lara Putnam's warning about the risks presented by the systematic blind spots in the new landscape of digital information.[74]

Two of the digital archives reviewed in the article serve to illustrate this point. Neither *Archivo Mesoamericano* nor the *Digital Archive of Latin American and Caribbean Ephemera* is an organic archive in the sense that neither of them was created by an organization or government bureaucracy for its own administrative purposes. To a certain extent, this also applies to *dLOC*, a virtual library. As the curators of *Archivo Mesoamer-*

icano state, the main goal of the project was to "create a regional audio-visual archive where no other exists, even at the national level."[75] As noted, some content originated from CIESAS and MUPI affiliates, but a considerable volume of video materials selected and digitized for online delivery was not directly produced by the partner institutions themselves. Furthermore, the site does not provide access to the complete video holdings deposited in these institutions, but to a subset of these holdings, meaning that a selection process took place prior to digitization. Similarly, the *Digital Archive of Latin American and Caribbean Ephemera* is not a reformatted organic archive. The digital ephemera portal consists of materials gradually assembled by a U.S.-based repository through a network of individuals and vendors scattered throughout several Latin American urban centers. These agents acquire and supply the materials to the library according to guidelines established by the subject librarian responsible for the Latin American Studies collection. Although the stated goal of acquisition is to find materials that represent the voices of social groups on the margins of society, a number of factors influence the actual selection process that takes place on the ground, resulting at times in a collection that is imbalanced and inconsistent in terms of geographic, historical, and subject coverage. Although all of the ephemera collected by Princeton University is being digitized, it goes without saying that the materials that can be "discovered" online represent only a parcel of the extant ephemera produced in Latin America that is potentially collectable. It is incumbent for digitization project managers to make end-users aware of the broad parameters that make selection, not totality, a reality in the digital realm.

Significantly, the creation of digital resources entails more than the capture of images of text or non-text materials in intangible files composed of bits and bytes of data. Digital creation has a complex lifecycle of technical and non-technical processes and requirements. Digital data require curation, especially the creation of descriptive metadata, indexing, and web interfaces to make the content accessible, visible, meaningful, and intelligible by users. Digital surrogates can contribute to preservation, but by themselves surrogates have limited scholarly value if the materials are not searchable. In *Processing the Past*, Francis X. Blouin, Jr., and William G. Rosenberg make an eloquent plea for the application of metadata description to enhance digital assets: "How can preservation and access be ensured? Because digital documents are invisible until retrieved, any preservation system is useless without a corresponding access system that enables the display of its documents. Access and preservation are the two sides of the same coin."[76] From a technical perspective, the metadata and search functionality of digitization projects reviewed here stand out for their innovation and robustness. Ironically, the incessant drive to innovate in the information technology realm can have adverse effects. The open-source software supporting the digital video archive created by Indiana University is no longer actively maintained. The institution has instead been developing Avalon Media System, a new freely- available software for managing audio and video collections.[77] The downside of the new system is that it does not yet support annotations by video segment level, the key innovative tool that made *Archivo Mesoamericano* such a powerful resource for using video materials for educational and research applications. Project curators, therefore, face a dilemma. In the digital world, migration of content to newer technical systems is understood as a best practice, ensuring persistent preservation of digital resources. Migration to a new platform, however, may lead to the loss of functionality in the video portal, at least temporarily, until a new annotation tool is developed.

Interface design, particularly the language used for searching online, can create barriers for access to many users, particularly those in the countries where the materials
originated and especially to users outside academia.[78] In the *Digital Archive of Latin
American and Caribbean Ephemera*, the language of the interface, English only, works as
a limiting factor to users unfamiliar with the language. Similarly, linguistic boundaries
may potentially hamper use of *Archivo Mesoamericano, AHPN: Archivo Digital del Archivo
Histórico de la Policía Nacional de Guatemala*, and *Brasil: Nunca Mais digit@l* by the
international community of researchers and users who are not proficient either in Spanish
or Portuguese, since searching in these portals can only be performed in Spanish in the
case of the first two and in Portuguese in the third. The *Digital Library of the Caribbean*
has made a commendable effort to introduce not only a trilingual interface in English,
French, and Spanish, but has also implemented controlled vocabularies that enable
degrees of searching in the vernaculars across the collections.

Greater online access to digital resources has not only brought to the fore controversial issues relating to intellectual property rights but, most importantly, to the ethical
use of sensitive materials. As open-access initiatives led by university libraries and
research centers, but also by cultural heritage and official government organizations, the
five digitization projects discussed earlier have adopted very flexible policies permitting
unrestricted online access to and use of the digitized resources by essentially any person
who has a network connection. The implications of this policy are particularly significant
for two of these digital archives, the Guatemalan political police and the Brazilian military
court records collections, given their politically sensitive content. As previously discussed,
these official records show undeniable evidence of human rights violations undertaken
by the government authorities in Guatemala and Brazil. As such, prosecutors and advocacy groups have tapped these records to bring legal claims against perpetrators of violence in their respective countries. In both Brazil and Guatemala, these records have
been digitized and made deliberately accessible online as part of memory recovery projects. Internationally, the "archives of repression" have been known to contain gaps in the
records as well as factually incorrect information about individuals under state surveillance.[79] Cognizant of this problem, curators of *Brasil: Nunca Mais digit@l* have introduced
a warning that displays on the computer screen every time a search is initiated in the
portal: "Attention. A significant portion of the political prisoners' statements and other
information entered in court records was obtained with the use of torture and other
illegal means and cannot be considered as absolute truth of expression" (freely translated
by the authors). Potentially exposing traumatic and tragic experiences in the lives of contemporary Brazilian citizens, this sobering statement prompts users to treat the information retrieved from the portal not only critically, but judiciously and respectfully. This
is particularly relevant to individuals who were tried by the military courts and became
politically active after the restoration of democracy. Perhaps the most prominent case is
that of Dilma Rousseff who served as President of Brazil from 2011 until 2016.[80] Striking
a balance between providing greater access to sensitive information and protecting the
privacy of individuals is a pressing concern for institutions engaged in human rights
documentation digitization projects.[81]

Among memory institutions, digitization has also nurtured alternative approaches
and practices for managing and preserving international collections. Most notably among
these approaches is the post-custodial or non custodial model, as it is variously known.
The *AHPN: Archivo Digital del Archivo Histórico de la Policía Nacional de Guatemala* is

a case in point. This kind of collaboration departs from conventional collecting practices based on the acquisition, extraction, or transfer of physical collections from the original sites where they were created or located to repositories abroad. Although not couched in those same terms, *Archivo Mesoamericano* reflects core features of post-custodial digitization. The video source materials available on the portal have always remained in their home repositories, with digitization, indexing, and description performed onsite in collaboration with Indiana University. A variation on this theme is, of course, *Brasil: Nunca Mais digit@l*. The original physical collection of secretly copied military court records has always been deposited in a Brazilian repository. Deemed national patrimony, Brazilian authorities ceremoniously treated the transfer of the microfilm negative copy of the collection of court records from CRL's custody to the Federal Prosecutor's Service as an act of *repatriação*, or repatriation, of the collection. An official solemn ceremony organized by Brazilian authorities marked the occasion.[82]

From a preservation and access perspective, ensuring that record creators maintain physical and intellectual control over their own physical records and cultural heritage is the most significant contribution of the post-custodial digital archiving initiatives prominently pursued by the University of Texas at Austin. It is worth noting, however, that key features of the post-custodial model were manifestly present in earlier library cooperative preservation initiatives created and managed by North American library organizations. For years, LAMP has supported onsite microfilming projects in partnership with institutions throughout Latin America and the Caribbean.[83] Close collaboration between LAMP and Latin American repositories led to successful filming projects of rare books and ephemera, newspapers and serials, official publications, and archival collections. This critical work of institutional collaboration encompassed various arrangements, including negotiation of copyrights with publishers as well as supporting lab operations (from payment of technicians' salaries to providing supplies and equipment for the microfilming labs). Furthermore, institutional collaboration was based on principles of reciprocity: LAMP donated a copy of the complete microfilm set to the partnering institutions.[84]

The same principles lie beneath two important preservation initiatives: the Program for Latin American Libraries and Archives (PLALA), based at Harvard University's David Rockefeller Center for Latin American Studies, and the Endangered Archives Programme, managed by the British Library. For nearly two decades, the Program for Latin American Libraries and Archives (PLALA), founded and directed by the late Dan Hazen, Associate Librarian of Harvard College for Collection Development, funded close to 270 projects to improve access and preservation of library and archival collections in the countries of origin.[85] International in scope, the Endangered Archives Programme pursues digital preservation, keeping original materials in their country of origin. The program also provides master copies of the digitized collections to the partner institutions and makes digital copies accessible to users via the Internet.[86] Positive developments in post-custodial digitization build upon long-standing practices in Latin American and Caribbean studies librarianship that support preservation of and access to vulnerable or endangered scholarly and cultural source materials from countries in the hemisphere. As the digitization projects reviewed here denote, the application of the post-custodial approach, however promising, might not be universally feasible. As an emerging digitization model, post-custodial archiving can be very suitable, in certain situations, and its successful implementation may vary from case to case, depending on a wide range of factors related to institutional track records, the degree of trust among partner institutions, changing polit-ical climates, and the cultural sensitivity of the source materials themselves.

Perhaps the most important challenge facing many of the projects reviewed in this article is the long-term sustainability of a digital archive. Often interpreted as an issue mainly related to cost and financial aspects, project sustainability is much more complex and demanding. The creation and ongoing management of digitized collections requires a stable and permanent structure of technical expertise, leadership, institutional and financial support.[87]

The five digitization projects discussed here were originally funded by generous grants from sources external to the library institutions, including government and non-government entities as well as long-established cooperative initiatives in the Latin American and Caribbean Studies librarianship field. In the United States, one prominent example of government funding is the now-defunct TICFIA program from the U.S. Department of Education. Over the years, library-centered cooperative programs such as LAMP, LARRP, and CLIR, have strongly supported the creation of digital archives for the study of Latin America and the Caribbean. Digitization has been, and, to a certain extent, still is an activity that relies very heavily on external sources of funding, both to support initial development and new phases of a continuing project.[88] External funding, however, is typically available for creation, not for ongoing project management and curation. As a result, institutions must often commit their own budgets and resources to underwrite project costs and ensure the successful consolidation and future growth of a project after it has been launched. The collaborative funding approach based on membership adopted by the *Digital Library of the Caribbean* represents a promising model of long-term sustainability. Introduced in 2011, the membership system is based on the payment of annual dues by institutions and individuals.[89] Unsteady or insecure funding for digitization may prompt memory institutions to think creatively and strate-gically about the long-term financial sustainability of current and future endeavors in the digital archive realm.

It is generally agreed that archives and libraries as memory institutions mediate our relationship to a society's history.[90] The traces of the past contained in extant records of archives, libraries, and other repositories help both academic and non-academic users interrogate the past. For decades, Latin American and Caribbean studies librarians have striven to develop representative collections of the rich cultural and historical heritage of the countries from the hemisphere, preserving and increasing access to invaluable materials. No matter how comprehensive these collections aim to be, the collection devel-opment activities do not exist in a vacuum—often displaying gaps and silences in the coverage of cultural, social, and historical events. Embedded in the struggles for memory and power, memory institutions are not only the products of history, but also contribute to shaping understandings of history and identity. The creation of the digital archive is not exempt from these historical processes. Selection of content for digital preservation and access contributes to memorialization, the process through which remembering (and forgetting) certain voices and stories from the past is realized. Unintentionally or not, librarians curating the digital archive have fully inserted ourselves in the struggles for historical memory in Latin America and the Caribbean.

NOTES

1. Disclaimer: Both authors have been directly involved in some of the digitization projects reviewed in this article.

2. Rebecca L. Mugridge, *Managing Digitization Activities* (SPEC Kit 294) (Washington, D.C.: Association of Research Libraries, 2006), 11. For a concise overview of the growth of cultural heritage digitization projects in British and North American memory institutions, see Melissa Terras, "Digitisation and Digital Resources in the Humanities," in *Digital Humanities in Practice*, ed. Claire Warwick, Melissa Terras, and Julianne Nyhan (London: Facet Publishing, 2012), 51–53. For developments in Latin America and Spain, see Dan C. Hazen, *Preservation Priorities in Latin America: A Report from the Sixtieth IFLA Meeting, Havana, Cuba* (Washington, D.C.: Commission on Preservation and Access, 1995); Patricia A. McClung, *Digital Collections Inventory Report* (Washington, D.C.: Commission on Preservation and Access; Council on Library Resources, 1996); and Alfonso Quintero, "Project: Digitization of 19th Century Latin American Press (Digitization of the Great Colombia Press: 1820–1830), Final Report, May 30th, 2004," in *International Newspaper Librarianship for the 21st Century*, ed. Hartmut Walravens (München: K.G. Sauer, 2006), 139–145.

3. Nancy L. Maron and Sarah Pickle, *Searching for Sustainability: Strategies from Eight Digitized Special Collections* (New York: Ithaka S+R; Association of Research Libraries, 2013), 9–10, accessed October 17, 2016, http://www.arl.org/storage/documents/publications/searching-for-sustainability-report-nov2013.pdf.

4. Mugridge, *Managing Digitization Activities*, 11–12; Maron and Pickle, *Searching for Sustainability*, 10.

5. Founded in 1975 by the Seminar on the Acquisition of Latin American Library Materials (SALALM) in cooperation with the Center for Research Libraries (CRL), LAMP is a collaborative initiative charged with preservation of rare or unique Latin American and Caribbean primary source materials. LAMP is managed by CRL, a leading consortium of North American research libraries. Accounts of LAMP's early history and contributions appear in Carl W. Deal, "The Latin American Microform Project: The First Decade," *Microform Review* 15, no. 1 (1986): 22–27; and James Simon, "Area Studies Microform Projects at the Center for Research Libraries," *World Libraries* 15, no. 1 (2005), accessed October 17, 2016, http://worldlibraries.dom.edu/index.php/worldlib/article/view/126. LAMP's current mission and preservation initiatives are described in https://www.crl.edu/programs/lamp. SALALM's early history is covered in Mark L. Grover's "The Beginning of SALALM," in *Latin American Studies Research and Bibliography: Past, Present, and Future: Papers of the Fiftieth Annual Meeting of the Seminar on the Acquisition of Latin American Library Materials*, ed. Pamela F. Howard-Reguindin (New Orleans, LA: SALALM Secretariat, 2007), 16–42.

6. "Brazilian Government Documents," Center for Research Libraries, accessed October 17, 2016, http://www-apps.crl.edu/brazil.

7. For a comprehensive assessment of the project, see Scott Van Jacob, "Final Report: CRL/LAMP Brazilian Government Serials Digitization Project, December 2001," Center for Research Libraries, "About the Brazilian Government Documents Project," accessed October 17, 2016, http://www-apps.crl.edu/sites/default/files/attachments/pages/FinalReport.pdf.

8. "Presidential Messages," Center for Research Libraries, accessed October 17, 2016, https://www.crl.edu/grn/larrp/current-projects/presidential-messages.

9. The Latin Americanist Research Resources Project (LARRP) is a consortium of research libraries whose stated goal is to increase free and open access to information in support of learning and scholarship in Latin American Studies. For additional information, visit https://www.crl.edu/programs/larrp.

10. *Guatemala: memoria del silencio: informe de la Comisión para el Esclarecimiento Histórico* (Guatemala: Comisión para el Esclarecimiento Histórico, 1999), 71–73. An English translation is also available: *Memory of Silence: The Guatemalan Truth Commission Report* (New York: Palgrave McMillan, 2012).

11. AHPN's publication *Del silencio a la memoria: revelaciones del Archivo Histórico de la Policía Nacional* (Guatemala: Archivo Histórico de la Policía Nacional, 2011) describes in great detail the organizational structure and functions of the Policía Nacional. The English translation, *From Silence to Memory*, was published in 2013 by the University of Oregon. Documentation generated by the military, the police, and other government agencies in charge of surveillance and repression of civil society has come to be known as "archives of repression." For critical analyses of similar records in the Latin American context, see Ludmila da Silva Catela and Elizabeth Jelin, eds., *Los archivos de la represión: documentos, memoria y verdad* (Madrid and Buenos Aires: Siglo Veintiuno de España Editores; Siglo Veintiuno de Argentina Editores, 2002).

12. For a thoughtful account and reflection on the process by which justice activists in Guatemala worked to repurpose archives of state terror into instruments for the rule of law and tools of social change, see Kirsten Weld, *Paper Cadavers: The Archives of Dictatorship in Guatemala* (Durham, NC: Duke University Press, 2014).

13. For detailed information about all aspects of the project including research findings and reports see the official website of the AHPN at http://archivohistoricopn.org/.

14. "Once años por Guatemala," Archivo Histórico de la Policía Nacional, accessed October 17, 2016, http://archivohistoricopn.org/pages/inicio/actualidad/once-anos-de-trabajo-por-guatemala.php.

15. The open-access portal is available at https://ahpn.lib.utexas.edu/.

16. *Archivo Histórico de la Policía Nacional: siete años de trabajo* (Guatemala: Archivo Histórico de la Policía Nacional, Fondo Documental del Archivo General de Centro América, 2012), 10–11, accessed October 17, 2016, http://archivohistoricopn.org/media/Informe_de_Avances_AHPN%20o.%20Aniversario%20(1).pdf.

17. The AHPN Digital Archive is the core component of a broader collaboration agreement formalized in 2011 between the AHPN and the University of Texas at Austin, represented by three institutions within the university dedicated to human rights in Latin America: the Lozano Long Institute for Latin American Studies, the Rapoport Center for Human Rights and Justice, and the Benson Latin American Collection. Other components of the agreement included the exchange of technical expertise, cooperation in research, engaging in capacity-building for legal and academic networks, and organizing an academic conference around the AHPN.

18. Archivo Histórico de la Policía Nacional, *From Silence to Memory: Revelations of the AHPN* (Eugene: University of Oregon Libraries, 2013), accessed October 17, 2016, http://hdl.handle.net/1794/12928.

19. For details, see the Human Rights Documentation Initiative, University of Texas Libraries, accessed October 17, 2016, https://www.lib.utexas.edu/hrdi.

20. "From Custody to Collaboration: The Post-Custodial Archival Model at the University of Texas Libraries," 2, accessed October 17, 2016, https://library.stanford.edu/sites/default/files/Univ%20of%20Texas.pdf.

21. Theresa E. Polk, "Archiving Human Rights Documentation: The Promise of the Post-Custodial Approach in Latin America," *Portal: Web Magazine of LLILAS Benson Latin American Studies and Collections*, August 5, 2016, accessed October 17, 2016, http://llilasbensonmagazine.org/2016/08/05/archiving-human-rights-documentation-the-promise-of-the-post-custodial-approach-in-latin-america/.

22. For an informative discussion of the experience of the University of Texas' LLILAS Benson Latin American Studies and Collection, see "Identifying Post-Custodial Partners in Latin America: Lessons Learned in Mexico, Colombia, and Brazil with Special Considerations for Human Rights Archives," April 2016, accessed October 17, 2016, http://hdl.handle.net/2152/39032.

23. The open-access portal *Brasil: Nunca Mais digit@l* is available at http://bnmdigital.mpf.mp.br.

24. Anthony W. Pereira, *Political (In)Justice: Authoritarianism and the Rule of Law in Brazil, Chile, and Argentina* (Pittsburgh: University of Pittsburgh Press, 2005), 201–202.

25. The standard account in English of the creation of *Brasil: Nunca Mais* is Lawrence Weschler's *A Miracle, a Universe: Settling Accounts with Torturers* (New York: Penguin Books, 1991). A detailed book-length work in Portuguese is now available: Lucas Figueiredo, *Olho por olho: os livros secretos da ditadura* (Rio de Janeiro: Editora Record, 2009). See also "BNM—História (1979–1985)," *Brasil: Nunca Mais digit@l*, accessed September 7, 2016, http://bnmdigital.mpf.mp.br/#!/bnm-historia; and James T. Simon, "*Nunca Mais*: Human Rights Evidence Rediscovered," *Focus on Global Resources* 31, no. 2 (2012): 10–12, accessed September 7, 2016, https://www.crl.edu/focus/article/7500.

26. For overviews of the organization and contents of the report, see Weschler, *A Miracle, a Universe*, 50–55; and Ludmila da Silva Catela, "Territorios de memoria política: los archivos de la represión en Brasil," in *Los archivos de la represión: documentos, memoria y verdad*, ed. Ludmila da Silva Catela and Elizabeth Jelin (Madrid and Buenos Aires: Siglo Veintiuno de España Editores; Siglo Veintiuno de Argentina Editores, 2002), 34–36.

27. Catela, "Territorios de memoria política," 19; Janaína de Almeida Teles, "A constituição das memórias sobre a repressão da ditadura: o projeto *Brasil Nunca Mais* e a abertura da Vala de Perus," *Anos 90* (Porto Alegre) 19, no. 35 (2012): 265, accessed October 17, 2016, http://www.seer.ufrgs.br/index.php/anos90/article/view/29423/24263.

28. Rudolf von Sinner, Elias Wolff and Carlos Gilberto Bock, eds., *Vidas ecuménicas: testemunhas do ecumenismo no Brasil* (São Leopoldo; Porto Alegre: Sinodal: Padrereus, 2006), 185; Catela, "Territorios de memoria política," 39–40.

29. Archdiocese of São Paulo, *Torture in Brazil: A Report*, trans. Jaime Wright (New York: Vintage Books, 1986).

30. Catela, "Territorios de memoria política," 42–43. Part of the newly accessible content in *Brasil: Nunca Mais digit@l* consists of the correspondence related to the project that had been stored in the central offices of the World Council of Churches in Geneva. These materials shed light on the decision-making process that led to the donation of the microfilm set to LAMP in 1987. See documents in folder (*pasta*) 4290701_5_1 in the Acervo Conselho Mundial de Igrejas documents accessible in the online portal.

31. Simon, "*Nunca Mais*: Human Rights Evidence Rediscovered."

32. Additional information on the mission of the Federal Prosecutor's Service is available on its website http://www.prsp.mpf.mp.br/versao-ingles.

33. Key project development aspects of the broad-based collaboration are discussed in Marlon Alberto Weichert, "Brasil Nunca Mais Digital," Instituto Innovare, accessed October 17, 2016, http://www.premioinnovare.com.br/praticas/brasil-nunca-mais-digital-20140522152333975332; and "Projeto Brasil Nunca Mais," Projeto DHnet, accessed October 17, 2016, http://www.dhnet.org.br/memoria/nuncamais/bnm_digital.htm#apresentacao.

34. Some of these enhancements are discussed in Luiz Fernando Herbert Massoni et al., "Transparência

no acesso à informação e as memórias virtuais da ditadura militar no site 'Brasil: Nunca Mais digit@l,'" *Biblioline* (João Pessoa) 11, no. 1 (2015): 173–184, accessed October 17, 2016, http://periodicos.ufpb.br/ojs2/index.php/biblio/article/view/25643/14656.

35. Viviane Tessitore, "Projeto 'Brasil: nunca mais': história, metodologia e usos para a pesquisa" (paper presented at the XXVIII Simpósio Nacional de História, Florianópolis, Santa Catarina, Brasil, July 27–31, 2015), accessed October 17, 2016, http://www.snh2015.anpuh.org/resources/anais/39/1428344723_ARQUIVO_PesquisaBNMparaANPUHresumoextendido.pdf.

36. Sinner, Wolff, and Bock, eds., *Vidas ecuménicas*, 186; Catela, "Territorios de memoria política," 65–68; Luiz Sugimoto, "Brasil Nunca Mais revela história apreendida por militares," *Jornal da Unicamp*, 6 July 2003, accessed October 17, 2016, http://www.unicamp.br/unicamp/noticias/brasil-nunca-mais-revela-hist%C3%B3ria-apreendida-por-militares.

37. Catela, "Territorios de memoria política," 65–68.

38. Catela, "Territorios de memoria política," 58–59; Sugimoto, "Brasil Nunca Mais"; Weichert, "Brasil Nunca Mais Digital."

39. Sugimoto, "Brasil Nunca Mais."

40. The data were compiled using Google Analytics metrics and proprietary software. See Brasil, Ministério Público Federal, "Brasil: Nunca Mais digit@l: 3 primeiros anos. Relatório consolidado de acesso" São Paulo, Brasil, September 2016.

41. Weichert, "Brasil Nunca Mais Digital." The complete official report created by the National Truth Commission can be accessed on the organization's website at http://www.cnv.gov.br/.

42. "O que é o BNM," *Brasil: Nunca Mais digit@l*, accessed October 17, 2016, http://bnmdigital.mpf.mp.br/#!/o-que-e-o-bnm.

43. Personal communication with *Brasil: Nunca Mais digit@l* project administrators, September 21, 2016.

44. The online video archive can be accessed at http://archivomesoamericano.org.

45. For a summary of the objectives of these two media digitization projects, see "Mesoamerican Archive," Center for Latin American and Caribbean Studies, Indiana University, accessed October 17, 2016, http://www.indiana.edu/~clacs/resources/meso-archive/.

46. The purpose and mission of the TICFIA program are described on its website: http://www2.ed.gov/programs/iegpsticfia/index.html. Accessed September 7, 2016. Complete information on the actual amounts of funding awarded by TICFIA to both CAMVA (Award Number P337A050022) and CLAMA (Award Number P337A090016) from 2005 to 2010 is available at https://iris.ed.gov/iris/ieps/search.cfm?type=ADV&page=1&count=25&keywords=&keywordtype=0&scope=all&programs=8&years=0&languages=0&institutions=0&disciplines=0&regions=0&subjects=0&states=0&countries=0&unpublished=0&gofind=Go&sort=AwardNumber&sortorder=ASC&tab=BRW&COL=BeginDate. Accessed October 17, 2016.

47. From the oldest to the most recent, these TICFIA-funded projects were the *Latin Americanist Research Resources Project* (*LARRP*), the *Latin American Open Archives Portal* (*LAOPA*), the *Latin American Knowledge Harvester* (*LAKH*), the *Digital Library of the Caribbean* (*dLOC*), the *Central American and Mexican Video Archive* (*CAMVA*), the *Latin American Electronic Data Archive* (*LAEDA*), *LA-ENERGAIA*, the *Cultural and Linguistic Archive of Mesoamerica* (*CLAMA*), and the *Caribbean Newspaper Digital Library* (*CNDL*), which has since been folded into *dLOC*.

48. MUPI holds audiovisual materials originally created by Radio Venceremos, the official voice of the Salvadoran guerrilla. The two organizations are historically linked since the museum's founder and current director, Carlo Henríquez Consalvi, was a founding member of Radio Venceremos. On the history of these organizations, see Carlos Henríquez Consalvi, *Broadcasting the Civil War in El Salvador: A Memoir of Guerrilla Radio*, trans. Charles Leo Nagle V with A.L. (Bill) Prince (Austin: University of Texas Press, Teresa Lozano Long Institute of Latin American Studies, 2010), and Robin Maria DeLugan, *Reimagining National Belonging: Post–Civil War El Salvador in a Global Context* (Tucson: University of Arizona Press, 2012), 117–121.

49. For assessments of Radio Venceremos filmmaking, see Dennis West, "Revolution in Central America: A Survey of New Documentaries," *Cineaste*, January 1, 1986, 18–20; and Catherine Benamou, "Redefining Documentary in the Revolution," *Cineaste*, January 1, 1990, 11–13.

50. C. Gerald Fraser, "Julio Cortazar Dies in Paris; Argentine Writer of Fiction" *New York Times*, February 13, 1984, accessed October 17, 2016, http://www.nytimes.com/1984/02/13/obituaries/julio-cortazar-dies-in-paris-argentine-writer-of-fiction.html.

51. The project is described in http://www.eviada.org/.

52. "End User License Agreement," *Archivo Mesoamericano*, accessed October 17, 2016, http://archivomesoamericano.org/camvasb/login.jsp;jsessionid=A8EFE947BD86B4AE0249421E60D618E6. The complete stipulations of the Creative Commons license known as Attribution-NonCommercial-NoDerivs 3.0 Unported (CC BY-NC-ND 3.0) can be found on the Creative Commons site at https://creativecommons.org/licenses/by-nc-nd/3.0/.

53. Georgia B. Barnhill, "Why Not Ephemera?: The Emergence of Ephemera in Libraries," *RBM: A Journal of Rare Books, Manuscripts, and Cultural Heritage* 9, no. 1 (2008): 127–135, accessed October 17, 2016, http://rbm.acrl.org/content/9/1/127.full.pdf+html.

54. The digital ephemera archive can be accessed at http://lae.princeton.edu/.

55. Peter T. Johnson, "Latin American and Iberian Primary Sources," *Princeton University Library Chronicle* 57, no. 3 (1996): 465–67, 472–75.

56. Only the "Brazil's Popular Groups" initiative, based at the Library of Congress Field Office in Rio de Janeiro, Brazil, compares to Princeton's Latin American Ephemera Collection in the range of subject areas covered—though only with regard to Brazil. The contents of "Brazil's Popular Groups" collection remain available only in microfilm. For more information, visit https://www.loc.gov/acq/ovop/rio/bpg/.

57. A guide to the contents of Princeton's Latin American Ephemera Collections is available at http://libguides.princeton.edu/laec.

58. Louis Bickford, "The Archival Imperative: Human Rights and Historical Memory in Latin America's Southern Cone," *Human Rights Quarterly* 21, no. 4 (1999): 1104–1105.

59. Copious amounts of primary resource materials of the second and third types delineated by Bickford that complement the AHPN can be found in another archival collection located at Princeton University called *Civil War, Society and Political Transition in Guatemala: The Guatemala News and Information Bureau Archive (1963–2000)*. This archive was microfilmed for preservation purposes and a copy of the microfilm set donated in 2006 to the Centro de Investigaciones Regionales de Mesoamérica (CIRMA) in Guatemala. Thousands of digitized items from the ephemera section of the archive are freely available online at http://pudl.princeton.edu/collections/pudl0066.

60. For information about both open-source resources, see https://projecthydra.org/ and http://project-blacklight.org/

61. For information about this program, see https://www.clir.org/hiddencollections.

62. The digital library can be accessed at http://dloc.com/.

63. The original founding partners were Archives Nationales d'Haïti, Caribbean Community Secretariat (CARICOM), National Library of Jamaica, Fundación Global Democracia y Desarrollo (FUNGLODE), Universidad de Oriente Venezuela, University of the Virgin Islands, Florida International University, University of Central Florida, and University of Florida.

64. See "Digital Library of the Caribbean (dLOC) By-laws (Revision March 2012)," *dLOC*, accessed October 17, 2016, http://dloc.com/UF00095858/00004.

65. Shamin Renwick, "Caribbean Digital Library Initiatives in the Twenty-First Century: The Digital Library of the Caribbean (dLOC)," *Alexandria* 22, no. 1 (April 2011): 9.

66. See "Permissions: Rights and Responsibilities," *dLOC*, accessed October 17, 2016, http://www.dloc.com/dloc1/digit.

67. See http://dloc.com/dloc1/digit for details.

68. For more information on funding, see "About dLOC," *dLOC*, accessed October 17, 2016, http://dloc.com/info/about. A synopsis of the TICFIA grant awarded to this project (TICFIA Award Number P337A 050016) is available at https://iris.ed.gov/iris/ieps/grantshow.cfm?award_Number=P337A050016, accessed October 17, 2016.

69. Throughout Latin America and the Caribbean, library professionals see the emerging Open Government movement, demanding transparency in public affairs, and active citizenship as positive developments introduced by information technologies. See Dan Mount, "IFLA Trend Report 2016 Update," 11, accessed October 17, 2016, http://trends.ifla.org/files/trends/assets/trend-report-2016-update.pdf.

70. Maron and Pickle, *Searching for Sustainability*, 26–27.

71. Maron and Pickle, *Searching for Sustainability*, 21–22.

72. Modeled on *dLOC*, the *Jewish Diaspora Collection* (*JDoC*) (http://dloc.com/jdoc) is a collaborative digital library coordinated by the George A. Smathers Libraries at the University of Florida. *JDoC* seeks to preserve and provide access to Jewish heritage materials from Florida, Latin America and the Caribbean.

73. See the insightful piece by Ian Cooke and Marion Wallace, "African Studies in the Digital Age: Challenges for Research and National Libraries," in *African Studies in the Digital Age: Disconnects?*, ed. Terry Barringer and Marion Wallace (Leiden; Boston: Brill, 2014), 28. See also Marion Frank-Wilson, "Africana Personal Papers at Indiana University: Issues and Questions," *African Research & Documentation* 112 (2010): 15–24.

74. Lara Putnam, "The Transnational and the Text-Searchable: Digitized Sources and the Shadows They Cast," *American Historical Review* 121, no. 2 (April 2016): 377–402.

75. "Mesoamerican Archive," Center for Latin American and Caribbean Studies, Indiana University, accessed October 17, 2016, http://www.indiana.edu/~clacs/resources/meso-archive/.

76. Francis X. Blouin, Jr., and William G. Rosenberg, *Processing the Past: Contesting Authority in History and the Archives* (New York: Oxford University Press, 2011), 197.

77. Funded in part by grants from the Andrew W. Mellon Foundation, development of the Avalon Media System has been led by Indiana University and Northwestern University. For more information on this initative, go to http://www.avalonmediasystem.org/.

78. Katrine Mallan, "Is Digitization Sufficient for Collective Remembering?: Access to and Use of Cultural Heritage Collections," *Canadian Journal of Information and Library Science* 30, no. 3/4 (2006): 201–220.

79. Michelle Caswell, "Khmer Rouge Archives: Accountability, Truth, and Memory in Cambodia," *Archival Science* 10, no. 1 (2010): 25–44; Catela, "Territorios de memoria política," 70–72; Meirian Jump, "The Role of Archives in the Movement for the Recovery of Historical Memory in Spain. La Rioja: A Regional Case

Study," *Journal of the Society of Archivists* 33, no. 2 (2012): 149–166; A. James McAdams, *Judging the Past in Unified Germany* (Cambridge: Cambridge University Press, 2001), 67–68; and Weld, *Paper Cadavers*, 168–170, 247.

80. *Brasil: Nunca Mais digit@l* provides access to three military court cases related to President Dilma Rousseff: BNM 95, BNM 158, and BNM 186.

81. For thoughtful statements on the ethical issues of accessing human rights documentation for scholarly use, see LLILAS Benson Latin American Studies and Collection, "Identifying Post-Custodial Partners in Latin America," 6. See also Elena S. Danielson, "Privacy Rights and the Rights of Political Victims: Implications of the German Experience," *The American Archivist* 67, no. 2 (2004): 176–193; and Antonio González Quintana, *Archival Policies in the Protection of Human Rights* (Paris: International Council on Archives, 2009), accessed October 17, 2016, http://www.ica.org/sites/default/files/Report_Gonzalez-Quintana_EN.pdf.

82. Held on June 14, 2011, the solemn ceremony "Ato Público de Repatriação do Acervo do 'Brasil: Nunca Mais,'" received widespread coverage in the Brazilian press. Photographs and video clips of the ceremony are accessible on the *Brasil: Nunca Mais digit@l* site.

83. Deal, "Latin American Microform Project" 24; Simon, "Area Studies Microform Projects."

84. Deal, "The Latin American Microform Project," 24.

85. The mission and accomplishments of PLALA are discussed in Dan Hazen, "Archival Research and the Program for Latin American Libraries and Archives," *Hispanic American Historical Review* 83, no. 2 (2003): 345–354. The program has now officially concluded. A complete list of the projects funded through the program is available at http://drclas.harvard.edu/plala., accessed October 17, 2016.

86. For the program's objectives and accomplishments, go to http://eap.bl.uk/, accessed October 17, 2016.

87. This is aptly discussed in Maron and Pickle, *Searching for Sustainability*.

88. Mugridge, *Managing Digitization Activities*, 11, 13–14; Maron and Pickle, *Searching for Sustainability*, 26–27.

89. Complete information on *dLOC*'s membership program is available in "Institutional Members," *dLOC*, accessed October 3, 2016, http://dloc.com/dloc1/members.

90. The following works have informed our thinking on the interplay between libraries, historical memory, and power: Carlos Aguirre and Javier Villa-Flores, eds., *From the Ashes of History: Loss and Recovery of Archives and Libraries in Modern Latin America* (Raleigh, NC: A Contracorriente, 2015); Blouin and Rosenberg, *Processing the Past*; Catela and Jelin, eds., *Archivos de la represión*; Cooke and Wallace, "African Studies in the Digital Age"; Frank-Wilson, "Africana Personal Papers"; Eric Ketelaar, "Archival Temples, Archival Prisons: Modes of Power and Protection," *Archival Science* 2 (2002): 221–238; Joan M. Schwartz and Terry Cook, "Archives, Records, and Power: The Making of Modern Memory," *Archival Science* 2 (2002): 1–19; and Michel-Rolph Trouillot, *Silencing the Past: Power and the Production of History* (Boston: Beacon Press, 1995).

Archiving the
Latin American Web

A Call to Action

PAMELA M. GRAHAM *and*
KENT NORSWORTHY

Collection building in Latin American studies has often pursued two missions: support for immediate teaching and research needs, and future-looking stewardship of important scholarly resources. For many institutions it has been an ongoing challenge to collect comprehensively to meet the latter mission. Now, with more and more "publishing" shifting to an ever-expanding web in what we can call born-digital formats, the challenges of comprehensively capturing research and cultural outputs has become far more daunting.[1] At the same time, scholars are increasingly turning to the open web to incorporate a wider and wider range of sources and data into their work. While collecting of print and commercially distributed digital content will continue to be prevalent and important, we will be preserving less and less of the scholarly and cultural record of Latin America if we fail to increase our investments in born-digital collecting methods and practices. The great promise of the web as a publishing platform and site of cultural exchange is significantly compromised by the ephemerality and at-risk nature of many sources that live (and die) on the open internet. Web archiving represents one approach for capturing and preserving digital content that has research value today and in the future.

While we probably could not have said this just a few short years ago, today the technical challenges inherent to web archiving have been overcome to such an extent that we can assert that the primary obstacles to expanding these activities in libraries are less on the "technology" side and more on the "cultural" side. In brief the challenges for academic libraries lie at the intersection of several factors:

- The "taken for granted" imperative and rationale for collecting in print and other traditional formats has not carried over to born-digital or web-based content;
- Web archiving as an activity or a practice doesn't fit well within the typical organizational structures currently found in academic libraries;
- Web archiving is a collection activity that is greatly enhanced by cooperation

and collaboration among libraries, which is very difficult to achieve in practice.

This essay will explore a variety of conceptual issues and practical challenges involved in collecting the web. Our focus is not on the technical aspects of capture and preservation, which have been explored extensively elsewhere.[2] Instead, we seek to outline the value proposition involved in building a more robust capacity to collect born-digital content, and to explore the cultural and organizational challenges for web archiving programs.

We hope that this call to action will foster conversation and discussion about evolving collecting methodologies that we see as central to preserving the future of Latin American studies culture and scholarship and to transforming area studies librarianship in the digital age.

Background and Current State of Web Archiving

Web archiving is a digital preservation practice that seeks to gather, preserve and provide access to born-digital content from the World Wide Web. While mandates vary widely from country to country, and between different types of memory institutions, preservation of web content as a matter of practice has typically been conducted by institutions whose mission focuses on stewardship of cultural resources, including national libraries and archives, research libraries, state libraries, and museums. While examples of web archiving initiatives can be found throughout the world, the practice is largely rooted in the global north, particularly in Europe.[3]

In an organizational sense, web archiving has an important role to play both internally and externally. Internally, web archiving plays a vital role in the records management process of many organizations both large and small and in both the private and public sectors. Externally, web archive collections have a clear and demonstrated value vis-a-vis current and future research, similar to the role played by books and other artifacts of the cultural record in the pre-digital era. Like other forms of ephemeral content, web resources have value as evidence about what was happening at the time they were created or modified. Such evidence is valuable for research in many academic disciplines.

The basic steps, workflows, and processes involved in web archiving are summarized in the diagram of the "Web archiving life cycle model," developed by the Archive-It Team at the Internet Archive in 2013 (http://ait.blog.archive.org/files/2014/04/archiveit_life_cycle_model. pdf, p. 3). For conceptual clarity, this model breaks the web archiving workflow into individual steps or phases, but in practice each action is rarely discrete. There are typically close relationships, as well as high degrees of overlap, between activities. Likewise, the diagram is circular in shape to demonstrate the iterative nature of the web archiving process and the repetitive nature of the process.

Note that while many of the steps are broken out into specific segments, two instead consist of bands that are present throughout the life cycle—"policy" and "metadata/description"—since these are ever-present or are ongoing tasks conducted in conjunction with the other steps in the life cycle. The remaining steps are divided into the following two categories:

1. **High level decisions**: vision and objectives; resources and workflow; access/use/reuse; preservation; and risk management.
2. **Day to day tasks**: appraisal and selection; scoping; data capture; storage and organization; and quality assurance and analysis.

As we discuss below in regard to collection development, some of these decisions and tasks are similar to what we find in print collecting while others are unique to web archiving.

As an institutional practice, web archiving began in the late 1990s.[4] In 1996, Brewster Kahle launched the Internet Archive with the ambitious goal of creating a universally accessible digital library. That same year, the Internet Archive began archiving the web. While the Internet Archive has diversified its service offerings significantly since then, preserving web content remains at the core of their work. It was also in 1996 that the National Library of Australia and the National Library of Sweden launched what would become the first of many such efforts to capture part of their national domain, in this case the <.au> and <.se> domains.[5] Today many national libraries from around the world are engaged in such efforts.

In the United States, in the year 2000 the Library of Congress launched the Minerva Project, an ongoing program for collecting focused collections of web content in different areas of U.S. history, politics, and culture. Minerva was eventually renamed the Library of Congress Web Archives, a program that today sponsors many different web archiving initiatives focused on the United States and on collecting web content from throughout the world including Brazil.[6]

In 2003, a number of major players from the web archiving community joined forces to form the International Internet Preservation Consortium (IIPC). The IIPC, which currently has forty-four members, primarily national and major research libraries from twenty-five countries, is dedicated to "improving the tools, standards and best practices of web archiving while promoting international collaboration and the broad access and use of web archives for research and cultural heritage."[7]

The most widely deployed software platform for gathering content into a web archive is the Internet Archive's open source Heritrix crawler, first released in 2002. In 2009, the Heritrix file output format, the WARC file, was adopted as an ISO standard for web archiving. A robust community of developers has consolidated around the Heritrix core, expanding and extending the capabilities of the crawler and adapting many of its features to local community standards and practices.

In 2006, the Internet Archive launched the Archive-It web archiving service, a subscription based initiative that helps partner organizations to harvest, build, manage, and preserve born-digital collections. As of February 2016, the Archive-It subscriber based consisted of over 400 partners in forty-eight U.S. states and sixteen countries worldwide. To date, these partners have created over 3,000 public collections containing over 12 billion URLs using Archive-It.[8]

Within Latin America and the Caribbean, efforts to undertake web archiving have lagged behind those in other regions. Numerous factors have contributed to this lack of growth. For one, the absence of a preservation mandate for born digital materials, or in cases where such a mandate may exist, a lack of sufficient resources to carry out a robust web archiving program. Throughout the region, the legal deposit regime has historically been uneven in terms of compliance in published print formats; with the advent of digital publishing, the situation has only worsened both in terms of updating the legal framework and in terms of compliance. Beyond that, in more general terms, while the national library is the "natural home" for web archiving efforts in these countries, the reality is that throughout the region national libraries are woefully underfunded and understaffed and national bibliographic infrastructures remain weak and underdeveloped. In this context, new initiatives in the digital realm are typically overlaid on top of a very weak foundation.

Another factor is the prevailing cultural norm, particularly in official circles, of restricting access to information. A third factor is the legal and regulatory environment around copyright and intellectual property which has generally resulted in a risk-averse posture when it comes to archiving or providing access to digital content. To cite one example, the Dirección de Bibliotecas, Archivos y Museos (Direction of Libraries, Archives and Museums) (DIBAM) in Chile has had success building several large-scale web archives, including curated collections covering Chilean political parties and elections as well as ongoing harvests of Chilean media publications, among others.[9] However, due to restrictions in Chile's Law Number 17.336 on Intellectual Property, which is designed to protect the rights of copyright owners, the resulting web archived collections cannot be viewed by the public on the open Internet. Users who want to consult the collections must go in person to the Biblioteca Nacional de Chile (National Library of Chile) in Santiago or one of six regional libraries located in other parts of the country and use special computer terminals installed on their premises. This barrier to use and access has made it difficult for Chilean librarians and archivists to build support for expanding web archiving in the country.

Despite these and other impediments, the national libraries and archives in a few Latin American countries—most notably Chile, and to a lesser extent Colombia and Brazil—have been increasingly engaged in exploring or piloting web archiving programs and generally raising awareness in the region about web archiving. Nonetheless, for the most part, efforts in Latin America have yet to move beyond small exploratory or one-off projects. Chile seems to have made the most progress to date, having successfully piloted a number of different collections and approaches. DIBAM first started using Archive-It to harvest sites in the .cl domain in 2008 and has since built up significant expertise in born digital collecting among staff at the National Library using a variety of open source tools, including Heritrix, WGET, and OpenWayback. In 2014, Chile further solidified its regional leadership role in this area, becoming the first Latin American country to join the IIPC.[10] The Chilean National Library has laid out a convincing rationale for why web archiving is a vital activity for those responsible for stewarding national cultural patrimony:

> Today, the Internet is a major site for the creation and exchange of information and knowledge. For this reason, both today and in the future, websites, blogs, digital media, and other web-based platforms constitute an important source of information and documentation both for researchers and for the general public. With this in mind, the National Library of Chile has been focusing efforts on developing a system for the harvest, indexing, and playback of different collections of web-based content with the goal of raising awareness of our history as a country through new languages and digital platforms.[11]

These modest efforts to archive digital patrimony by institutions inside the region have been complemented by academic libraries elsewhere, particularly those that have a collecting mandate that covers, or includes parts of, Latin America and the Caribbean.

Some examples of large-scale and ongoing web archiving programs that have a significant, and in some cases exclusive, focus on the region are:

- Collections on regional energy policy, revolutionary art in Mexico, and comics and graphic novels in Chile at the University of New Mexico;
- Several Cuba and Cuban diaspora collections on politics, culture, and current events at the University of Miami;
- Human rights organizations collections at the University of Texas at Austin and Columbia University;
- Latin American Government Documents at the University of Texas at Austin;
- Brazilian 2010 and 2014 presidential elections and Brazilian cordel literature by the Rio Overseas Field Office, Library of Congress.[12]

Libraries and archives in the U.S. and Europe typically don't face the same legal constraints in conjunction with web archiving that their counterparts in Latin America do. For example, among public universities in North America web archives have typically been judged to fall within the purview of the fair use provisions of U.S. copyright law, opening the way for unrestricted access for research purposes. U.S. and European-based libraries interested in archiving parts of the Latin American web also have the advantage of more robust and advanced library information technology infrastructure locally. In addition, they benefit from operating in a context where web archiving is now viewed as a mature service offering with widely accepted standards and best practices and a marketplace characterized by multiple service providers and technology alternatives, both proprietary and open source.

Web Archiving as Collection Development

The maturing and emergence of widely accepted practices for the technical aspects of web archiving is enabling a shift of focus to collection development issues and to understanding the uses of web archives in research and teaching. Web archiving is essentially a technique and a method for building collections but for a number of reasons it has not yet been mainstreamed into more common collecting practices and workflows within academic libraries. In addition, the engagement and participation of subject librarians in web archiving has been limited in its nature and scope, and communities of practice around selection and collection building methods for web archives have not yet emerged to match those related to technical aspects of web archiving.[13]

Cultural and organizational barriers impede greater subject librarian engagement in the collection development potential of web archiving. Web archiving services such as Archive-It have made it easier for academic libraries to pursue web archiving without investing in extensive local information technology infrastructure, but some degree of institutional support is necessary in order for web collecting to occur. While there is consensus about the general value of digital preservation, the uptake by scholars using web archives as part of their research has been slow for a variety of reasons. Web archives typically lack the kinds of user demands and usage metrics that drive academic library decision-making on resource allocation. Organizationally, web archiving initiatives may be situated in digital library or digital preservation units, or within archives and special collections that approach web archiving through a different collecting paradigm than those who build general research collections. Subject specialist librarians may thus be less likely to be engaged in web archiving than other types of library staff.[14]

When involved, subject librarian participation is often limited to providing lists of websites that should be collected without further engagement in the life cycle of the web archiving process. Web collecting has a continuous, circular and self-referencing dynamic: collecting one website may lead to the discovery of other linked or referenced websites of relevance; the content of a website may continually change requiring ongoing selection decisions; and technical challenges inherent to collecting from the web may require ongoing quality assurance, review and revision of guidelines for collecting. While not all of these tasks may require the direct input of a subject librarian, some choices can have an impact on the overall nature of the web archive collection and warrant some level of engagement with a subject specialist.

Collecting the web requires a level of familiarity and conversance with technical issues related to the web's architecture and form as well as some understanding of the technical limits of web crawling technology. If subject librarians are the ones who actually use and manage crawling software, without assistance from other library staff, the technical aspects of web collecting can seem more demanding. Librarian support for downstream uses of web archives by researchers, still an emerging field, can require somewhat advanced technical skills. For subject librarians to select and build archives that are well aligned with researcher needs and uses, familiarity with digital research methods is also necessary.

Beyond these technical issues lies the problem of scale: the prospect of "saving the web" seems daunting and even impossible to accomplish with the degree of completeness (or at least somewhat known incompleteness) that we often apply to print or licensed digital collecting. Beyond concerns about the immense challenge of web collecting, legitimate and important questions exist regarding the appropriate role of academic libraries in the preservation of freely available born-digital content. In this area, academic libraries have mostly limited themselves to improving discovery and access to valuable content on the live web via cataloging and the development of directories, portals, and resource guides of various types. Long-term preservation of the web is not yet a widely accepted or embraced role across academic libraries, which grapple with a wide range of challenges in the digital realm that may compete with web archiving for resources and attention. A lack of clear standards and guidelines related to copyright, i.e., the right to capture sites, host archived sites, and provide for their reuse by researchers, presents an additional barrier to wider adoption of this collecting practice.

Despite these organizational and cultural barriers, we believe it is both possible and necessary to leverage the existing expertise and knowledge of subject librarians in the work of collecting the web. This need is especially important in Latin American Studies, where much digital publishing is not channeled or distributed through commercial publishers but is instead only taking place on the freely accessible web. Leveraging existing knowledge should be accompanied by re-conceptualizing the collection development process to fit the dynamic production and potential research uses of born-digital content. As we problematize and understand new conceptual frameworks for collecting, new kinds of skills must also be cultivated to help subject librarians navigate the publishing landscape that the live web represents.

Subject knowledge and existing skills are relevant to building web archives in Latin American studies. Deep expertise of regions, places, languages and cultures is central to identifying and evaluating content that should be captured and preserved. Knowledge of existing publishing streams (including print) forms a basis for understanding the broader cultural production landscape and traditional modes of dissemination; in turn we can identify publishing that sits outside the mainstream, i.e., gaps and silences that are not systematically documented. Examples include websites of marginalized social groups or movements, or emerging writers or artists who only disseminate their work online. Our existing collecting policies can guide and focus decisions about what to collect on the web. Indeed, some types of collecting translate with ease to the realm of web collecting—publishing that retains its analog shape and form such as government documents and reports, working papers, monographic essays and journals. For example, the Latin American Government Documents Archive, LAGDA, captures reports, statistics, and other government information that were commonly issued and collected in print formats in the past.[15] In these cases web archiving is deployed as a way to sustain collecting of material already identified as important and to carry existing print collections forward into the digital realm.

Sustaining traditional collecting is important but the most exciting potential of web archiving is the opportunity to transform collecting practices. For starters, the potential scope and scale of collecting is exponentially greater and more complex than is the case with print collecting. The web is not a static source but one that is continually changing, implying as referenced above, the need for ongoing and iterative re-selection. As Latin American studies librarians we may be able to collect new types of content, continuously, that has no analogous form in the pre-web environment. To cite one example, the "Earthquake in Haiti" collection archived by the Internet Archive's Global Events Collection includes archived copies of over 130 websites documenting humanitarian and crisis responses to the 2010 earthquake.[16] The collection provides a detailed trail of communications, social media posts and exchanges giving the user a unique window on the inner workings of this relief effort. In another example, the University of New Mexico's web archive of Chilean comics and graphic novels includes blogs and commentaries of artists that would have been difficult or impossible to capture prior to the existence of the web, which now offers a platform of cultural exchange that is both more dynamic and has far greater reach than published print versions of comics.[17] With such opportunities comes the need to carefully limit, focus and scope collecting projects to a greater degree than what may be necessary in print collecting.

Building web archives potentially transforms the role of the subject librarian from a collector of the fixed outputs of research to an active builder and creator of data sets. It also highlights the need for us to be attentive to emerging web research methodologies. Researchers are developing their own methods for how to work with web archived "data" and how to think about issues like scoping, sampling, representativeness of web data, and conceptualizations of networks and relationships as represented on the web.[18] Some have begun to use web archive collections in exciting new ways, including as corpora upon which to perform data mining, term frequency searching and topic modeling, link and network analyses, and to create various forms of data visualizations. More than was the case in print collecting, web archives can be greater than the sum of their parts.[19] Librarians may thus need to have an awareness of not only the individual sites they wish to preserve, but the coherence and value of the web archive at the collection level, as a singular entity that strives to represent a particular topic, event, or social dynamic.[20]

With such uses of web archives comes the need for a perhaps unprecedented level of transparency and accountability to researchers as we describe how websites were selected for inclusion, how we set up and scoped our crawls, the degree and nature of quality review of captured sites, and the impact of technical issues on the ability to effectively capture content.[21] In other words, in building collections of web content together with researchers we need to be better documentarians of our own practices and efforts. This would likely need to take the form both of explicit collection level statements and of metadata at different levels that provides information about collecting practices to end users.

Given the variety of opportunities, challenges and dynamics associated with web collecting, what kinds of conceptual frameworks should guide the development of web archive collections? Scholars of internet and web history offer conceptualizations of the web that may help us develop approaches to defining web collecting programs.[22] For example, Steven Schneider and Kirsten Foot have written about the concept of web spheres:

> We conceptualize a web sphere as not simply a collection of web sites, but as a set of dynamically defined digital resources spanning multiple web sites deemed relevant or related to a central event, concept or theme, and often connected by hyperlinks. The boundaries of a web sphere are delimited by a shared topical orientation and a temporal framework.[23]

This concept of a topical web recognizes the possibility of boundaries and thus the ability to set limits and develop manageable web collecting projects. At the same time, Schneider and Foot acknowledge the dynamic and organic nature of linking and connections among the set of websites within those boundaries. Are there discernible web spheres within Latin American studies that could guide our planning and efforts to preserve born-digital content? How do we make decisions grounded in user research needs and practices while also advancing the more general goal of preservation of cultural and scholarly production?

As we suggested above, one focus of web archiving is the effort to sustain collecting of materials that have migrated from print to web-based dissemination. Evaluating existing acquisitions arrangements for collecting government publishing, books and reports produced by scholarly societies, think tanks, and non-governmental organizations allows us to identify sources that could be collected via web archiving. An assessment of the "at-risk" nature of the websites, i.e., the possibility that they might disappear or be significantly altered, could help determine priorities for collecting. The degree of reliance on the open web as a publishing platform in certain fields and subjects might also be a useful criterion for evaluating the suitability of web archiving as a collecting method. This type of "sustaining collecting" can flow fairly directly from existing policies, practices and subject knowledge.

More challenging is the development of topical or thematic collections, which call for additional and novel strategies. It is essential to invest time in planning thematic collections—researching and understanding not only the topics we wish to collect and the practical development of lists of websites to include, but also the ways in which the web is being used as a platform and tool for communication in those topics and fields. How do researchers studying elections use and reference the freely available web in their work to monitor and track political parties, social groups and media? Are scholars of the history and use of the Internet in Latin America already scoping and defining web spheres that could form the basis for web collecting initiatives? For example, extensive work on the Cuban blogosphere has mapped individual and collective websites that represent social, political, and cultural commentary that will be invaluable for interpreting this critical period of Cuban history.[24] At the same time, anecdotal evidence suggests that researchers are creating their own personal archives of information saved, copied, or captured in some manner from the web.[25] How can those scholar-led archiving efforts inform more systematic and comprehensive collection building carried out by libraries?

There are ways we can leverage technology to help us identify and scope the boundaries of a web sphere. Scraping URLs or organizational names from research articles, bibliographies, social media, traditional media or other relevant sources enables us to identify websites that are being actively mentioned and cited in scholarship and broader cultural exchanges. This technique might be especially useful for current events-based collecting, or for topics that are broad, multi-disciplinary and multi-regional, defying easy categorization and scoping. Automated discovery of websites for potential inclusion, paired with vetting and review by subject specialists, can inform collecting approaches that maximize the research relevance of web archives. The dynamic and recursive nature of web collections means that we also have to listen to and learn from our web archives, reviewing linked or related websites that are picked up in our crawls to then determine how we might modify our scope going forward.

Ongoing evaluation and assessment of existing collections is also important, especially given the continually shifting nature of web publishing. It is increasingly possible to perform automated searching of existing web archives via application program interfaces; we can thus determine whether or not a given set of URLs have been captured. Even if a library may lack the capacity to grow the size of a web archive collection to include missing websites, well formulated assessments create a means of measuring and evaluating the scope and comprehensiveness of a collection. For example, if we were to compare the list of organizations included in the human rights category of the *Yearbook of International Organizations* with the list of organizations captured in the Human Rights Web Archive and the Human Rights Documentation Initiative web archive, we could indicate the percentage of the YBIO-listed websites are being captured and preserved as of a certain date.

This type of scoping exercise is one step in a key area that needs much attention: developing new metrics and measures for describing the quantity and quality of a web archive. More sophisticated tools, many in the early stages of development, will also enable assessment of such collections on a much larger scale. For example, graphical visualization techniques allow curators and researchers to evaluate large quantities of data, in this case web content, in summary and aggregate fashion. These could include things like tree maps, time clouds and timelines, or image plots.[26] Visualizations of link analyses allow librarians and curators to see the occurrence of websites from different domains and the pattern of linkages among sites.[27]

It is admittedly difficult at present for librarians to make full use of these assessment possibilities in the absence of easy to use toolkits and dashboards. It is possible, however, to create more robust conceptual frameworks for web archiving that align with needs and trends in scholarly research and with our ongoing mission to exercise stewardship over research and cultural outputs in Latin America. The development of analytical tools for the use of web archives should take into account the needs of librarians and curators so that they can serve both the development and the downstream use of web archives.

Vision and a Way Forward

What would a successful web archiving program for Latin American studies look like? We believe it is useful first to think about a "best case scenario," to describe the contours of a successful program if the usual constraints to this type of collecting were removed. We believe that the main elements of a successful approach would consist of a mix of collecting and crawl strategies along the following lines:

1. Periodic domain crawls, highly automated, for each country in Latin America and the Caribbean. These could be conducted perhaps once per year with the goal of providing a comprehensive snapshot of the web in each country.
2. A series of more focused, curated collections of a thematic or topical nature, typically ongoing over a period of many years. These collections, with crawl frequencies ranging from daily to quarterly depending on the nature of the content, would be largely driven by subject specialists and closely aligned with researcher needs.
3. Tightly scoped "one off" crawls of a relatively short duration linked to specific current or planned events, or to emerging developments likely to have enduring impact. In the political realm, for example, a political party campaign for elected office or a national election. As noted above, this will require a significant rethinking of collection development and the role of curators and subject specialists.

Given the scope and nature of these activities and collections, success will be closely linked to our ability to build strong collaborative relationships at several levels: within our libraries and on our campuses; among U.S.-based libraries; and between U.S.-based libraries and partners in Latin America and elsewhere in the world. We will need to consider which institutions are best placed to tackle different pieces of the web archiving puzzle. For born digital collecting, we can learn from, and build off of, existing experiences for traditional formats with cooperative collection development, shared service models, and other consortial and partnership arrangements.

We need to expand and to internationalize collaboration. When dealing with print and other traditional formats, collaboration among collecting libraries is an important strategy that allows individual institutions to expand the size and scope of their collections. And as area studies librarians, we have many successful existing experiences we can draw upon to help us structure collaborative arrangements around web archiving (for example, LAMP, LARRP, and the regional groups like LANE, LASER, CALAFIA, and MOLLAS).[28] However, it is important to note that collaboration for born digital collecting would likely look very different than for print and in some ways would be far easier to implement. The work of collecting, processing and preserving content would not have to be shared across all collaborators, as has been the case where print collecting has been divided among institutions. Instead, collaboration around web archiving could be more open and loosely structured. For example, a small college or university with a modest collecting program and budget, but with a knowledgeable area studies librarian, could contribute to the development of lists of websites to be crawled, description and metadata creation, and to evaluation and assessment. The only institutional commitment in this case would be the in-kind contribution of the librarian's time, and possible cost recovery to support the overall web archiving program. In the case of larger libraries, developers across numerous institutions could work jointly on the development of tools, application program interfaces, and extending the capabilities of existing open source core software applications for web archiving and access.

More challenging would be building collaborative ties among libraries and other institutions with a stake in web archiving across the Americas. A host of thorny issues would need to be worked out before such ties could be built between northern institutions and their counterparts among Latin American libraries, chief among them intellectual property and copyright concerns, cultural patrimony and "ownership" of digital data, and how best to secure funding and to split costs for this type of activity.

The context for these collaborative initiatives is the notion of striving for a "comprehensive collection." In the digital realm, the notion of collecting comprehensively needs to be thoroughly rethought and reexamined for a number of reasons. For starters, the very nature of the web as a dynamic medium, where content has fluid boundaries and is constantly changing, makes the notion of comprehensiveness very different than in a print collecting paradigm. What does it really mean to collect "everything" from the web? Furthermore, the concept of "duplication" is complex in web archiving. The variables of frequency of crawling and the "depth" or extent of content collected on a given site means that it may be acceptable or even necessary for more than one institution to collect a URL. Given differences in local researcher needs, our web collecting strategies may need to include overlaps in crawling.

While it is beyond the scope of this essay to try and map out a broad web collecting strategy for Latin American studies, we can identify some elements or characteristics that we feel would need to be present in any framework for robust and sustainable born digital collecting:

- **Close partnerships between librarians, technologists, and researchers throughout the entire the research lifecycle**. Born digital resources including web archives not only replace traditional bibliographic sources, they also change the nature of scholarly inquiry and underlying disciplinary methods. Librarians cannot work in isolation from the eventual uses of scholarly content but must work hand in hand with researchers to identify and steward resources, and with technologists to enable analysis and interpretation of such sources.
- **Collaborative arrangements that bring research libraries with Latin American collections together with organizations in Latin America that have a stake in born digital collecting.** Key needs and issues include supporting a shared technical infrastructure for crawling and preserving the web; coordinating collection, selection, and assessment policies and practices; developing necessary access and analytical tools for researchers; promoting standards and best practices in web design and hosting that can facilitate the work of web crawlers; and working through the issues surrounding the legal and intellectual property rights framework necessary to ensure broad access for researchers to web archives.
- **Development and/or adaptation of organizational structures and institutional commitments to born digital collection building.** Ongoing work should be done to develop best practices and approaches to situating web archiving activities within library organizations, recognizing the collection

development role of web archiving. Given the newness of this type of collecting and research practice, more purposeful exploration of existing and potential use cases of web archives will inform decision making over how to establish and support born digital collecting, whether it be through local programs or participation in collaborative networks.

Web archiving, and born-digital collecting, is a transformational process that extends far beyond a mere shift in format. Building capacity to identify and capture born-digital publishing is vitally important to the future of Latin American research collecting. New forms and types of cultural and scholarly outputs challenge us to re-conceptualize the practice and intentions of collection, curation and preservation and the role of the Latin American studies librarian in collecting for the twenty-first century.

NOTES

1. There are many different measures for the size and rate of growth of the Web and of Internet users in Latin America. Regardless of which measure is used, however, there is broad consensus that the Latin American Internet is large and is growing at a very rapid pace. For example, as of 2015 there were more Internet users in Latin America and the Caribbean than in the U.S. and Canada combined, see http://www.internetworldstats.com/stats2.htm. For an excellent measure for the rate of growth of the Internet in Latin America and the Caribbean between 2002 and the end of 2015, see http://www.lacnic.net/web/lacnic/estadisticas-asignacion.

2. For a detailed analysis and discussion of the main technical and workflow issues involved in web archiving, see Bragg, et.al. "The Web Archiving Life Cycle Model." For a broader guide to published sources on all aspects of web archiving, see Reyes Ayala "Web Archiving Bibliography 2013."

3. Evidence of this can been seen by looking at the current and founding membership list of the International Internet Preservation Consortium (IIPC), at http://www.netpreserve.org/about-us/members, as well as at the IIPC's timeline on the history of web archiving, at http://www.netpreserve.org/timeline.

4. For a good overview of the evolution of the Web and Web archiving, and the cultural and historical importance of preserving the Web, see Lepore, "The Cobweb: Can the Internet Be Archived?"

5. See Pandora, Australia's Web Archive, History and Achievements, http://pandora.nla.gov.au/historyachievements.html, and Kulturarw³, National Library of Sweden, http://www.kb.se/om/projekt/Svenska-webbsidor—-Kulturarw3/.

6. For a list of Library of Congress web archive collections, see http://loc.gov/webarchiving/collections.html. Public access to their collections is available at https://www.loc.gov/websites/collections/.

7. From "About IIPC," at http://www.netpreserve.org/about-us.

8. Up to date statistics can be found at http://www.archive-it.org/learn-more.

9. Information about Chile's web archiving program can be found on the "Archivo de la Web Chilena" website, at http://www.salasvirtuales.cl/.

10. For details, see "Adelante! Archiving Latin American Web Content," Natalie Baur, January 13, 2015, https://archive-it.org/blog/post/adelante-archiving-latin-american-web-content/.

11. From the "about" section of the "Archivando la Web Chilena" website, at: http://archivoweb.bibliotecanacionaldigital.cl/#que [translation by authors].

12. For more information, see the list of Web Archives Cited at the end of this essay.

13. Even a cursory glance at past programs from the IIPC General Assembly and from other library and archives conferences where web archives are included shows a dearth of collection development-related sessions in comparison to sessions related to technical aspects of web archiving.

14. In a literature review of web archiving, Jinfang Niu concludes, "none of the literature directly addresses the knowledge and skills required by the professionals in the field who perform the daily routine of selecting, acquiring and cataloging web archives." "An Overview of Web Archiving," *D-Lib Magazine*, 18(4), March/April 2012. http://www.dlib.org/dlib/march12/niu/03niu1.html. See also Peter Stirling and Jaanus Kõuts, "How to fit in? Integrating a web archiving program in your organization," IIPC-Sponsored Workshop, Bibliothèque Nationale de France, 26–30 November 2012. http://netpreserve.org/sites/default/files/resources/Report%20and%20Evaluation%20of%20BnF%20IIPC%20Workshop%20on%20Web%20Archiving.pdf.

15. See Latin American Government Documents Archive. http://lanic.utexas.edu/project/archives/lagda/.

16. See Internet Archive Global Events, Earthquake in Haiti, 2010. https://archive-it.org/collections/1784.

17. See University of New Mexico, Chilean Comics and Graphic Novels, April 2014–. https://archive-it.org/collections/4555.

18. Matthew S. Weber, "Observing the Web by Understanding the Past: Archival Internet Research."

WWW '14 Companion, Proceedings of the 23rd International Conference on the World Wide Web, April 7–11, 2014, Seoul, Korea, 1031–1036. http://wwwconference.org/proceedings/www2014/companion/p1031.pdf. Workshops and conferences held in 2014 and 2015 signal growing researcher interest in web archives. (WIRE Workshop at Harvard University in June 2014 and the Web Archives as Scholarly Sources conference hosted by a Research Infrastructure for the Study of the Archived Web, RESAW, in Aarhus, Denmark in June 2015.)

19. An individual researcher would be unable to engage in a close reading of a robust Latin American Studies print collection of 500,000 volumes, and at a human scale one is likely to value and benefit from discernable subsets of that whole. A researcher could easily datamine a 5 or 10 terabyte web archive, however, which arguably raises the need for a web archive to have coherence at scale that is not demanded of traditional library collections.

20. Numerous researchers and other users of web archives have described how, in a technical sense, a web archive does not capture or display a pure artefact or an exact replica of that which existed on the web at a given point in time. A more accurate description is that web archiving technology allows for the capture and playback of discrete content pieces allowing sites to be "born again" digitally. See, for example, the work of Niels Brügger, including "Web Historiography and Internet Studies."

21. A small study of potential use cases of the Human Rights Web Archive at Columbia University Libraries, consisting of in-depth interviews with researchers, confirms the high level of interest that researchers have in collection policies and methods. When completed, findings will be available at the Libraries' Web Resources Collection Program, https://library.columbia.edu/bts/web_resources_collection/collaboration.html.

22. Niels Brügger discusses conceptualizations of the web in "Web Historiography and Internet Studies," 2013.

23. Schneider and Foot, "Web Sphere Analysis," p. 158.

24. See the chapter "Cuba: Blogging away the Castro Blues" in Anthony Lowenstein's *The Blogging Revolution* (Carlton, Vic.: Melbourne University Press, 2008) 141–172, and Stefania Vicari, "Blogging POLITICS in Cuba: The Framing of Political Discourse in the Cuban Blogosphere," *Media Culture Society* 36 (7), October 2014, 998–1015.

25. See Columbia Libraries use case study, referenced in footnote #21.

26. See "Visualizing Digital Collections of Web Archives" https://library.columbia.edu/content/dam/librarywebsecure/behind_the_scenes/web_resource_collection/Kelly%20-%202015_columbiawac_thumbnails.pdf.

27. See the Visualizations page at the UK Web Archive for examples, http://www.webarchive.org.uk/ukwa/visualisation.

28. LAMP, Latin American Materials Project; LARRP, Latin Americanist Research Resources Project; LANE, Latin America North East Libraries Consortium; LASER, Latin American Studies Southeast Regional Libraries Consortium; CALAFIA, California Cooperative Latin American Collection Development Group; MOLLAS, Midwest Organization of Libraries for Latin American Studies.

Open Access in Latin America

Considerations for Collection
Development and Management

JENNIFER OSORIO

Latin America leads the world in its adoption of Open Access (OA) (scholarship that is "digital, online, free of charge, and free of most copyright and licensing restrictions"[1]) as a publication model for academic journals. Conflicting numbers abound, but a recent blog post by the Scholarly Publishing and Academic Resources Coalition (SPARC), made the following claims:

> In 2010, around 85% of academic publications in Latin America were publicly available through the Internet, however, about 35% satisfied Open Access journal standards of the Budapest Declaration. Currently, Scopus Journal catalogue points to the statistic that 72% of Latin American indexed journals are Open Access compared to about 13% of all journals.[2]

Several countries, Peru, Argentina, and Mexico, have passed legislation mandating Open Access for publicly funded research and others are discussing similar laws.[3] What this rapid evolution means for collection development in academic libraries has not been closely examined. I will discuss the Latin American research landscape and the reasons for the early and rapid adoption of OA in Latin America, current efforts throughout the region, and the factors that librarians should consider as they build Latin American research collections.

While worldwide adoption of OA is reported to be around 20 percent of all journals,[4] estimates for the percentage of journals that are Open Access in Latin America range anywhere from 51 percent to 95 percent.[5] Unlike the global north, where open access has been largely cost-driven and a response to rising subscription rates, the high rate of adoption in Latin America was born of a desire to raise the visibility of regional journals around the world and nurtured by the continued professionalization of graduate education and research throughout the hemisphere.

Lauded for their consistent high quality and rigid standards, OA databases such as *SciELO* and *RedALyC* now host to up to 72 percent percent of OA Latin American academic journals. These databases have worked hand in hand with government commissions to set standards of quality, leading to greater recognition for the region's scholarly output. At the same time, international indexes such as *Web of Science* and *SCOPUS* have increased their coverage of the region's academic output.

As strong supporters of Open Access, this is good news for academic libraries, as it frees them from the rapid increases in subscriptions prices common among for-profit publishers and provides consistent delivery of journal issues, a long-time issue with publications from the developing world. But Open Access publishing is not free; there are associated costs, both monetary and otherwise, which it would behoove librarians to keep in mind as they re-tool their collection development activities and strategies.

Without the subscription model to sustain journals, funding at the institutional or even individual researcher level becomes ever more important. This has the possibility of disenfranchising communities without strong funding models, an ever-present danger in the developing world. Additionally, standards for OA databases are set by national panels, creating an uneven playing field across the region. In some countries, politics intrude on the process, possibly affecting the research featured in repositories. Finally regional output is not evenly represented, with some parts of Latin American still invisible. This is particularly true of Central America and the Caribbean.

This essay will set the context for the Latin American Open Access model, explaining how it works on a regional and national level and pointing out factors librarians should be aware of as they build 21st century research collections.

The Latin American Research Landscape

Universities in Latin America go back over 400 years, to the twenty-five colonial institutions created on the model of the great Spanish universities in Salamanca and Alcalá.[6] Latin American independence meant a revamping of these academic ivory towers into institutions that would serve the dual functions of civic training and nation-building. The "Latin American University"[7] was large, publically funded, and aimed at training professionals, typically in useful areas such as medicine, law and engineering. Their mission was to build nations and civil society, and the faculty mostly consisted of part-time professionals, not researchers. The twentieth century brought growth in the areas of vocational training and private education, but the large, public institution remained the predominant model. As such, Latin American universities were often beholden to the whims of political regimes and uncertain funding.

In 1918, students in Argentina led a reform movement that came to be known as the Córdoba reforms,[8] which brought shared governance (between faculty, students, and non-academic staff). These reforms spread throughout the continent, decoupling most universities from state control of curriculum and budgets. The Córdoba reforms made universities more independent, but the nation-building function still predominated, with independent research on the model of America's great research universities rare. The Córdoba reforms also encouraged universities to take on a social reform role, and they largely heeded the call. Enrollment grew rapidly as the middle classes entered post-secondary education, lured by a free tuition in most countries. The education sector exploded, from 150 universities in the region in 1950 to over 700 in 1990. The 1.5 million students of 1950 became 14 million by 2003.[9] As public institutions grew, often in an unruly and highly politicized manner, private and religious education also grew in response. The mission of public universities—to build nations—became contested as they struggled to maintain quality and independence.

The answer, as seen by many, was to follow the U.S. model, where large public institutions serve as research centers, incubating ideas that become products to foster the economic growth of the nation. The American research university was an ideal model for the neo-liberalists that took over Latin American governments in the 1980s and 1990s. Universities could be the locus for economic development and globalization, and for this to happen, they needed to be educating researchers, not bureaucrats. In order to accomplish the goal of turning Latin American universities into research institutions, graduate programs expanded, increasing the production of MAs, MBAs and PhDs. Between 1993 and 2003, the number of doctoral degrees granted in Latin America and the Caribbean increased by 298 percent.[10] These new scholars increased the research output of the region and clearly, needed publication outlets.

Brazil, which later became a leader in adopting Open Access, also led the way in transforming its public institutions into research universities. In the 1960s and 1970s, they professionalized faculties, created smaller units and departments and boosted graduate programs, all reforms that grew the research sector. Unlike the rest of the region, where the messy process of democratization of universities also led to a loss of elite support, Brazilian universities continued to enjoy support from the nation's upper classes.

By the time the 1980s and neo-liberal reforms arrived, Brazilian universities were poised to join the world conversation, but infrastructure and language barriers remained. The academic publishing landscape was fraught with dangers. State funding still predominated (and does to this day) but was nowhere near the level of the developed world. Most Latin American countries devote only tiny percentages of their GDP (on the average of .5 percent[11]) to research activities. Political and social instability, an academic tradition that favored the book over serials, the lack of reliable distribution mechanisms, even the cost of printing all made publishing a journal in Latin America a difficult and unstable process. Print runs were vanishingly small, volumes appeared at irregular times if at all, and quality was extremely uneven. Researchers who published did so in international, English-language journals, bypassing local and regional publications that were seen as low quality backwaters. This was encouraged by government and institutional funders, who rewarded researchers for publishing in English-language, international journals that were seen as higher quality than local publications. National governments set up boards and programs to systematize research and reward certain kinds of research activity, especially that which focused on established research outlets, which more often than not, meant English-language journals in the United States and Europe. Many countries published "core" lists of acceptable journals for publication, a practice that continues to this day and which we will discuss further later in the essay.

Databases and indexes for academic journals largely ignored those from Latin America. Even where they were included, Latin American universities and libraries could not afford the high prices for such products. In his seminal article from 1995, "Lost Science in the Third World,"[12] W. Wayt Gibbs tells of a Mexican journal that managed to be included in *Science Citation Index* (*SCI*) in the 1980s, even paying the $10,000/year subscription fee, but lost its place when political and economic crisis forced a 6-month delay of publication. The *SCI's* editors would not bend their rules for them and dropped the journal from the index. Up to the point of Gibbs's article, the journal's editors had not been able to convince *SCI* to reinstate the publication.

It was into this landscape that Open Access arrived in Latin America.

How and Why Open Access Developed in Latin America

By the 1990s, academics in Latin America were realizing that something had to change. International indexes like *SCI* held to rigid standards that for one reason or another, excluded most publications from the developing world. Because there were no central standards imposed on them, journals throughout the region varied greatly in quality and had difficulty attracting the region's own researchers, who were often encouraged by their institutions to bypass local publications in favor of higher-profile international ones. Without interest from commercial publishers, who ignored regions without subscription possibilities, another model rose to the top.

In 1997, the Brazilian government by way of the Fundação de Amparo à Pesquisa do Estado de São Paulo (State of São Paulo Research Foundation) (FAPESP), funded a small pilot project that it hoped would help raise the visibility of Brazilian journals by moving them online. This project produced *SciELO* (Scientific Electronic Library Online) which eventually evolved into the behemoth it is today. *SciELO*, as of this writing, indexes 1,249 journals from fourteen countries,[13] along with e-books from Brazil. Its journals are divided into collections by country (and one thematic collection for Public Health). National portals are funded by public institutions exclusively, usually government agencies or universities, and work in tandem with the central *SciELO* unit to maintain standards. Each national portal requires a high degree of buy-in on a unified research policy and quality-control standards.[14] Because each portal set its own standards, this also means that what is required of journals varies from country to country.

SciELO (and numerous other open access projects born around the same time, including the *Biblioteca Virtual en Salud*) were both up and running long before the Budapest Open Access Initiative (2001), the Berlin Declaration on Open Access to Knowledge in the Sciences and Humanities (2003), and the Bethesda Statement on Open Access Publishing (2003), which are widely acknowledged as the documents that codified the worldwide Open Access movement.[15] Why is it, then, that Latin America was such an early adopter of OA?

By the 1990s, several issues had been identified, as far as Latin American research publications went:

1. Quality was uneven. There was no system of quality assurance along the peer-review model used in the United States. Participation in the local or regional publishing process, either as a writer, as a journal editor or as a reviewer, was not incentivized. The American tenure system, for all its faults, at least ensures that there is a ready pool of researchers to produce academic publications; without this system or one similar, Latin American journals had great difficulty maintaining quality. Those that could often preferred to publish in international, English-language journals.

2. Distribution was difficult. Mailing costs, small print runs, political instability and other factors all contributed to a system that made subscription-based publishing almost impossible. It is worth noting that even before Open Access, very few Latin American journals followed a pay subscription model. American libraries that tried to purchase these journals found delivery unreliable, often with long breaks in publication. Much of the distribu-

tion that did occur was through institution-to-institution exchanges, not through paid subscriptions.

3. Visibility of Latin American research was very low. A few elite researchers published in English-language, international journals but the vast majority of Latin American research appeared in local or regional publications with limited reach. Indexes such as the *Science Citation Index* (*SCI*) and *SCOPUS* were closed off to this research, making it practically invisible on a world level. A two-tier system was developing, where a few elite researchers could publish internationally and thus engage in the world-wide scholarly conversation and the rest were limited to low profile regional and local journals where their research had little visibility.

Open Access in Latin America thus has different roots from elsewhere in the world, especially the global north. In the United States, the main driver for Open Access initiatives has been cost. The rapid rise of journal subscription prices, the consolidation of the publishing industry and the shrinking of library budgets have all been major factors in the growing OA movement. The current subscription system is simply unsustainable. In Latin America, on the other hand, the main driver has been the desire to improve quality and raise the visibility of Latin American research. There was virtually no commercial production or distribution for Latin American research journals and only recently have commercial publishers shown any interest in the region.

Along with *SciELO*, several other projects from Latin America contribute to this effort. *LATINDEX*, a cooperative regional project started in 1997, is a directory for journals published in Latin America, the Caribbean, Spain and Portugal. It currently lists over 24,000 journals from the Americas and another 5,400+ from the Iberian Peninsula. As a directory, it does not provide full text, although it does rate journals according to a list of standards. Another prominent actor in the Open Access arena is the Consejo Latinoamericano de Ciencias Sociales (*CLACSO*). Its mission is to promote the dissemination of knowledge in the social sciences; one of the ways it does this is by maintaining a repository of publications from its 433 member institutions throughout the world. Other Open Access databases and indexes include:

- *CLASE* (*Citas Latinoamericanas en Ciencias Sociales y Humanidades*), a database maintained by Universidad Nacional Autónoma de México (National Autonomous University of Mexico) (UNAM) of over 350,000 journal articles, book reviews, essays, etc.
- *REDIB* (*Red Iberoamericana de Innovación y Conocimiento Científico*), a Spanish project that indexes some 1,500 publications. (REDIB was formerly known as CSIC)
- *Dialnet*, based at the University of Rioja, which specializes in the social sciences and humanities and offers some full text
- *HUMANINDEX*, (Base de Datos Bibliográfica de Humanidades y Ciencias Sociales) another UNAM product that is an institutional repository for UNAM's humanities researchers
- *América Latina Portal Europeo*, home to European research on Latin America through Red Europea de Información y Documentación sobre América Latina (REDIAL)and Consejo Europeo de Investigaciones Sociales de América Latina (CEISAL)

- *LA Referencia* (*Red Federada de Repositorios Institucionales de Publicaciones Científicas*), a network of national repository systems from nine countries: Argentina, Brazil, Chile, Colombia, Ecuador, El Salvador, México, Peru and Venezuela.

Portals dedicated to theses and dissertations include *Portal de Tesis Latinoamericanas* and the *Biblioteca Digital en Red de Tesis y Disertaciones*. There are also innumerable institutional repositories. In 2011, the Directory of Open Access Journals listed 233 Spanish-language repositories and 108 Portuguese-language ones.[16] (All of these sources are listed in an appendix at the end of this essay.)

But the most prominent counterpart to *SciELO*, is *RedALyC* (*Red de Revistas Científicas de América Latina y el Caribe, España y Portugal*) from the Facultad de Ciencias Políticas y Sociales (Faculty of Political and Social Sciences) at the Universidad Autónoma del Estado de México (Autonomous University of the State of Mexico) (UAEM). Established in 2003, *RedALyC* currently hosts 1, 079 journals from sixteen countries.[17] As *SciELO* was originally founded to highlight Latin American research in the sciences, *RedALyC* was founded to do the same for the social sciences and humanities. Both sites have expanded to include material across the spectrum of research, in all fields, but they do maintain an emphasis on their original focuses.

Successful Efforts

Open Access in general has been found to increase impact and the number of citations an article receives[18] and there is evidence to demonstrate that this is also the case for Latin American OA efforts. In 2006–2007, more than 85 percent of the journals in *SciELO* saw their impact factor increase. Journals that were indexed in both *SciELO* and *Web of Science* saw even larger increases.[19] In 2013, Web of Science added most of the *SciELO* index into its own citation database, further raising visibility for some Latin American journals. Today, *SCOPUS* also includes some 80 percent of *SciELO* journals in its index.

While *SciELO* and *RedALyC* still represent only a small portion of the publications produced in Latin America, they seem to have pushed the large international databases towards greater inclusion of the region's research output. As noted above, most of the *SciELO* index now appears in *Web of Science* and *SCOPUS*. In 2011, Sandra Miguel found that *SCOPUS* actually had a wider distribution of Latin American countries represented in its index, versus those of *SciELO* and *RedALyC*.[20] It also contained a greater volume of articles from the region, by a factor of 3 to 1 for *SciELO* and 6 to 1 for *RedALyC*.

Considerations for Collection Development

The benefits of Open Access to the Latin American scholarly publishing field seem clear: greater visibility, more consistence publication schedules, established standards for quality. These are all things that help librarians as they build collections focused on Latin America. But there are a few things that we should keep in mind as we develop our collections. To be clear, the topics discussed next are not meant to denigrate the strides made by OA or its proponents. Overall, Open Access has been very good to Latin American researchers; at the very least, they now have a place at the table in matters of visibility and access. But it behooves librarians to look at all the factors that affect scholarly publishing, especially if we want our collections to be accurate representations of Latin American culture, history and scholarship.

There's an old saying that if you want to know the truth, you should follow the money. In the case of research in Latin America, that trail will inevitably lead you to a university and from there, to some governmental funding agency. In many Latin American countries, the funding relationship between management of sites such as *SciELO* and *RedALyC* and the groups that decide which journals will be included in the "core" list of approved journals, is one and the same. In other words, the same councils that fund national portals in *SciELO* and *RedALyC* also decide in which journals researchers should publish.

While this is not necessarily problematic, it does create possible conflicts. In some countries, this close relationship extends to the core lists themselves; by inclusion in an OA portal, journals are automatically approved for the core list, or vice versa. This close relationship has the potential to exclude scholars or publications outside the mainstream or who come into conflict with government or institutional desires. No research has yet been done on how well portals cover marginalized peoples, such as indigenous groups, activists, anti-government groups, or others. The portals do not address research material in languages other than Spanish and Portuguese, either. Standards, by design and necessity, flatten the landscape, leaving outliers that may still be valuable for all that they are not predictable. Core journal lists vary by nation and these days, may be one and the same as the list of journals in either *SCI*, *SciELO* or *RedALyC*. They often privilege international or English language journals over native language ones (except for Venezuela, which prefers literature published in Latin American journals). To some critics, this preference for non-regional publications smacks of colonialism, as does the adoption of northern standards over local ones. As Fischman notes, "some argue that the definitions of 'quality' being applied by these groups are necessarily hegemonic in nature."[21] This feeling seems to be especially prevalent among younger faculty in the social sciences and humanities, who question why quantitative measures are being imposed on them from outside while qualitative measures—social impact or disciplinary relevance, for example—are not taken into account. Indexes also measure only the impact of journals, not articles,[22] presenting an incomplete picture of influence.

The standardization of quality controls, while certainly useful for helping Latin American journals break through into the international field, also has the potential to devalue local customs and traditions. Abel Packer, one of the founders of *SciELO*, calls for an "authoritative and international approach … for setting standards of operation … especially when these standards conflict with national traditions, habits, and costumes that can interfere with the quest for quality."[23] One hopes that "interferes" in that quote means that national standards and customs will be considered when setting standards, but it leaves open the possibility that international standards will subsume national ones. This adoption of international standards has been seen by some as a further colonization of Latin American research by the global north. In response, some researchers are deliberately choosing to stay "local," limiting their publications to national audiences.[24] If librarians rely on portals such as *SciELO* for their serials collections, they could miss out on this localized research.

These portals also tend to reflect the research output of the largest, most well-funded institutions. Smaller institutions without reliable funding for academic publishing or those that don't have institutional repositories of their own are left out, their research still out of sight. The majority of Latin America's academic journals are not indexed in either *SciELO* or *RedALyC*, nor are they represented in larger international non–Open Access portals, like *SCI* or *Web of Science*. Some areas, particularly Central America and the Caribbean see little representation in OA portals or repositories of any kind. Certain countries—Brazil, Mexico, Colombia, Argentina, Chile– are highly represented in *SciELO*, while others are not. The only Central American country with a *SciELO* portal is Costa Rica; it currently has twenty journals in *SciELO*. Only Cuba represents the Caribbean, with fifty-seven journals in its portal. No other publications from Central America or the Caribbean are indexed by *SciELO*. *RedALYC* is little better, although it does include Costa Rica, the Dominican Republic and Puerto Rico. It also includes Bolivia and Ecuador, better representing the Andean region, which has traditionally been underdeveloped.

The standards set by portals also mean that journals that fail to meet the standards through no fault of their own—publication delayed by faculty strikes, funding interruptions, political strife, all common occurrences in the region—will be dropped, just like that Mexican journal was dropped by the *Science Citation Index* back in the 1980s. Given that up to 40 percent of journals in one study[25] reported interruptions in publication for one of the above reasons, there is a high likelihood that a lot of quality research is not being included in the portals. Editors also report that they still have difficulty finding qualified reviewers, another requirement for inclusion in the OA portals we are discussing. Concentration on a small number of journals as the "approved" journals means that those reviewers that are available concentrate their efforts on those titles, leaving others begging for participation. A healthy peer review culture will account for a variety of types of journals, and there is a danger that the current situation does not allow that culture to develop. Without that development, improvement and innovation in Latin American research culture on a broad scale may stall.

Another issue is the sustainability of these initiatives. Open access, while free to the user, is not free to publishers. The technological infrastructure required to maintain massive portals is expensive. Even if writers and editors donate their time and efforts, *SciELO's* own estimates put the cost to produce each article in their database between $200 and $600.[26] Universities, which support up to 86 percent of titles,[27] may be subject to budgetary or political pressure. The cost for these initiatives has so far been borne by Latin American governments and universities, but will that always be the case? What happens if government funding disappears? Not to mention that now that overall quality has increased, commercial publishers are showing more interest in the region. The publishing landscape in Latin America may shift towards something more similar to what we see in North America and Europe, and the portals may find themselves competing with for-profit publishers that can offer added value, such as increased distribution and marketing services.

As librarians, we have the responsibility to seek out all voices for our collections. On the surface, the OA movement and its easy access to quality Latin American research makes that seem simpler than ever before, but the truth is that it makes it even more complicated. The issues that fomented the OA movement in Latin America still remain in many cases, meaning that we need to actively seek out publications from groups with variable or little funding in areas where market or political conditions may preclude steady and predictable publication. We need to look for publications from smaller institutions and seek out institutional repositories with little visibility. We need to be making a greater effort than ever before to build collections that will remain vital and relevant throughout the twenty-first century.

Appendix: Open Access Resources

America Latina Portal Europeo (REDIAL and CEISAL)
> http://www.red-redial.net/

Berlin Declaration on Open Access to Knowledge in the Sciences and Humanities
> http://openaccess.mpg.de/Berlin-Declaration

Bethesda Statement on Open Access Publishing
> http://legacy.earlham.edu/~peters/fos/bethesda.htm

Biblioteca Digital en Red de Tesis y Disertaciones
> http://www.teses.usp.br/index.php?option=com_content&view=article&id=49& Itemid=64&lang=es

Biblioteca Virtual en Salud
> http://regional.bvsalud.org/php/index.php?lang=es

Budapest Open Access Initiative
> http://www.budapestopenaccessinitiative.org/

CLASCO (the Consejo Latinoamericano de Ciencias Sociales)
> http://www.clacso.org.ar/

CLASE (Citas Latinoamericanas en Ciencias Sociales y Humanidades)
> http://clase.unam.mx/F?func=find-b-0&local_base=cla01

Dialnet
> https://dialnet.unirioja.es/

Directory of Open Access Journals
> https://doaj.org/

HUMANINDEX
> http://www.humanindex.unam.mx/humanindex/consultas/parametros.html

LA REFERENCIA (Red Federada de Repositorios Institucionales de Publicaciones Científicas)
> http://lareferencia.redclara.net/rfr/

Latindex
> http://www.latindex.org/

Portal de Tesis Latinoamericanas
> http://www.tesislatinoamericanas.info/

NOTES

1. Peter Suber, *Open Access Overview*, Accessed February 24, 2016. http://legacy.earlham.edu/~peters/fos/overview.htm.

2. Caralee Adams, "Open Access in Latin America: Embraces as Key to Visibility of Research Outputs," *SPARC* (*The Scholarly Publishing and Academic Resources Coalition*) Accessed February 2, 2016. http://www.sparc.arl.org/news/open-access-latin-america-embraced-key-visibility-research-output.

3. Dominique Babini and Juan D. Machin-Mastromatteo, "Latin American Science Is Meant to Be Open Access," *Information Development* 31, no. 5 (November 2015): 477–81.

4. Juan Pablo Alperin, Gustavo Fischman and John Willinsky, "Scholarly Communication Strategies in Latin America's Research Intensive Universities," 2012. Accessed Febraury 12, 2016. https://purl.stanford.edu/fj828hg2133.

5. Juan Pablo Alperin, Dominique Babini and Gustavo Fischman, eds., "Open Access Indicators and Scholarly Communications in Latin America [Consejo Latinoamericano de Ciencias Sociales]." Accessed February 2, 2016. http://biblioteca.clacso.edu.ar/clacso/se/20140917054406/OpenAccess.pdf.

6. Andrés Bernasconi, "Is There a Latin American Model of the University?" *Comparative Education Review* 52 (1) (2008) [University of Chicago Press, Comparative and International Education Society]: 27–52. doi:10.1086/524305.

7. Writ large, of course. There were differences from nation to nation, particularly in Brazil.

8. Daniel Levy, *Higher Education and the State in Latin America: Private Challenges to Public Dominance* (Chicago: The University of Chicago Press, 1986).

9. Bernasconi, p. 34.

10. Alperin, "Scholarly Communication Strategies in Latin America's Research-Intensive Universities," p. 4.

11. Nancy Gómez, Atilio Bustos-Gonzalez, Julio Santillan-Aldana and Olga Arias, "Open Access Indicators and Information Society: The Latin American Case." *OCLC Systems & Services* 25, no. 2 (May 2009): 82–92. doi:10.1108/10650750910961884.

12. W. Wayt Gibbs, "Lost Science in the Third World." *Scientific American* 273 (August 1995): 92–99.

13. Argentina, Bolivia, Brazil, Chile, Colombia, Costa Rica, Cuba, Spain, Mexico, Peru, Portugal, South Africa, Uruguay and Venezuela. Paraguay is in development.

14. Abel L. Packer, "The SciELO Open Access: A Gold Way from the South," *Canadian Journal of Higher Education*, 39.3, 2009, p. 111–126.

15. C. Bojo Canales, C. Fraga Medín, S. Hernández Villegas and E. Primo Peña, "SciELO: un proyecto cooperativo para la difusión de la ciencia [SciELO: A Cooperative Project for the Dissemination of Science]."*Revista española de sanidad penitenciaria* 11, no. 2 (October 2009): 49–56. doi:10.4321/S1575–06202009000200004.

16. Elías1Tzoc, tzoce@muohio.edu. "El Acceso Abierto En América Latina: Situación Actual Y Expectativas. (Spanish)." *Open Access in Latin America: Current Situation and Expectations. (English)* 35, no. 1 (January 2012): 83–95. http://search.ebscohost.com/login.aspx?direct=true&db=llf&AN=88995184&site=ehost-live.

17. Although RedALyC claims 22 countries on its website, it only lists the following: Argentina, Bolivia, Brazil, Chile, Colombia, Costa Rica, Cuba, Dominican Republic, Ecuador, Mexico, Peru, Portugal, Puerto Rico, Spain, Uruguay and Venezuela.

18. Johann Van Reenen, "Open Access and Connectedness: Stimulating Unexpected Innovation Through the Use of Institutional Open Archives [Acesso aberto e conexidade: estimulando inovações inesperadas Com O Uso de Arquivos Abertos Institucionais]," *Ciência da informação* 35, no. 2 (2006): 17–26. http://search.proquest.com/docview/57692966.

19. Packer, p. 112.

20. Sandra Miguel, "Revistas y producción científica de América Latina y el Caribe: su visibilidad en SciELO, RedALyC y SCOPUS." *Revista interamericana de bibliotecologia* 34, no. 2 (2011): 187–99. http://search.proquest.com/lisa/docview/1221405854/95308F724B89446CPQ/6.

21. Gustavo E. Fischman, Juan Pablo Alperin and John Willinsky. "Visibility and Quality in Spanish-Language Latin American Scholarly Publishing," *Information Technologies and International Development*. 6, no. 4 (Winter 2010): 1–21.

22. Molly Molloy, "The Internet in Latin America: Development and Reference Sources," *Journal of Library Administration* 43, no. 3/4 (November 2005): 129–47. doi:10.1300/J111v43n03•11.

23. Packer, p. 124.

24. Rogerio Meneghini, Rogerio Mugnaini and Abel L. Packer, "International Versus National Oriented Brazilian Scientific Journals. A Scientometric Analysis Based on SciELO and JCR-ISI Databases," *Scientometrics* 69, no. 3 (December 2006): 529–538. http://search.proquest.com/docview/57689830.

25. Fischman, p. 8.

26. Packer, p. 123.

27. Fischman, p. 7.

Nosotros

A Digitization Story Between a University Library and Its Latin American Community

Denis Lacroix

Collecting Latin American and Caribbean materials for a large Canadian university library in the twenty-first century now goes beyond the straight-forward acquisition of traditionally published information sources. The widespread use of approval plans allows academic librarians' attention to turn to born-digital resources and to the preservation of local ephemera. This is the case of the *Nosotros* digitization project described here that includes videocassettes documenting Latin American history and culture in Alberta, Canada. Subject and language knowledge remain essential abilities of liaison or subject librarians who need to interact with community members, whether they are researchers and/or content creators, in order to be seen as credible partners, and understand the subject and its information sources. In the case of the *Nosotros* digitization project, Denis Lacroix, subject librarian responsible for Spanish and Latin American studies at the University of Alberta, acted as the liaison between the University of Alberta Libraries' Digital Initiatives team and the *Nosotros* director and founder. The university library became the catalyst in digitizing the collection of almost thirty years' worth of audiovisual memory and in sensitizing all the partners in the importance of media preservation and long-term open accessibility and findability. The *Nosotros* project is much more than a digitization project: it is the story of a collaborative initiative spearheaded by a subject librarian.

A wealth of resources resides in North American university libraries, but more treasures remain untapped in the immediate communities surrounding them. The *Nosotros* project is one of these surprising hidden treasure troves. Who would have thought that Alberta's capital city, Edmonton, would have been home to a video collection recounting not only the history of the Latin American community in Edmonton and Alberta, but also the recent history of the Latin American countries from which immigrants originated? As statistics can only partially explain the presence of Albertans of Latin American origins, the *Nosotros* videos are an excellent primary source of historical and cultural information. They are a snapshot in time of the reality, concerns, and viewpoints of prominent community members and explore the socio-political issues that affect Latin America in general and the local Latino community specifically.

The project began when a student visited the Latin American studies librarian to request help finding a copy of an old episode of a local Latin American television program called *Nosotros* that had existed in Edmonton since 1981. This initial inquiry led subject librarian Denis Lacroix to contact the founder of the program and the program's current director in order to gain access to the episode. The librarian soon learned that all of the video tapes of the program dating back to the beginning of the program were stored in the founder's basement, which left the collection inaccessible to the general public, and at risk of disappearing or becoming unusable. At that point, the librarian began to discuss preservation and access issues with the Latin American community members.

Preliminary talks between the university library, the university's digitization technician and the *Nosotros* television program director revealed a willingness on all sides to find a lasting solution to preserve the videos and make them accessible to the world. Both academic partners were committed to making the project a success and to following the necessary protocols that would ensure the long-term viability of the content in digital format. The community connection was key, however, in securing the necessary buy-in from the owner of the videos who needed reassurance that all parties had the best interests of the videos and of the *Nosotros* program itself in mind. Having secured this trust, the university library became responsible for perpetuating the social collective memory of a local Latin American community and engaging faculty and students in contributing to the success of this digitization project with strong local ties and international content. This was partially achieved through formal academic partnerships and community service learning programs for the university's Latin American studies and library school students who assigned metadata to each video which allowed the digitized videos to be available online.

A Brief History of Edmonton's Latino Population and of Nosotros

Since 1971, Canada has proclaimed itself a multicultural nation based on cultural pluralism.[1] This is the context into which Latin American immigrants came to the country, and favored the birth of the *Nosotros* television program. The Hispanic-Canadian immigrant population grew from 4,780 immigrants before 1961 to 42,730 between 1971 and 1980, and almost doubled within the following ten years.[2] Furthermore, according to Statistics Canada's *2011 National Household Survey*, there are currently 544,380 people in Canada who recognize having Latin, Central and South American origins, 462,065 of whom ascribe to the Latin American visible minority category, which constitutes around 6.7 percent of the total immigrant population.[3] This is the immigration context into which *Nosotros* was born in 1981 and thrived for the next thirty-five years.

In Canada, the term "Latino" is "directly related to the U.S. reality"[4] and is therefore used sparingly in reference to the Canadian Latin American community and does not appear as an option in the Canadian census. Instead, the census asks respondents to consider whether they have Latin, Central, and South American origins, or belong to the Latin American visible minority. In the latter half of the twentieth century, the Canadian census asked about birthplace, country of last permanent residence, citizenship, and language spoken in addition to ethnic origin and visible minority. The question of origin reflects the multicultural official policy of recognizing diversity while still favoring unity.

For the purposes of this essay, therefore, the terms Latin American and Hispanic will be used interchangeably as we are only focusing on Latin Americans originating from Spanish-speaking countries.

Diversity also exists among the various provinces that welcome immigrants. For example, the reality of Latin American immigrants in the province of Quebec will be different from their counterparts in the province of Alberta. As Armony states, this reflects the "dual—by some definitions, bi-national—character of Canada."[5] It is probable that the thirty-five year existence of the *Nosotros* program may not have been possible in Quebec's "assimilationist"[6] context of the time, while Alberta presented fertile ground for it to thrive.[7]

When the Hispanic immigrant influx began in the early 1970s, Alberta was entering its boom decade.[8] The majority of immigrants settled in the large urban centers of Edmonton and Calgary, in which 10 percent of residents "belonged to one of the 'visible' minorities"[9] by the 1980s. Furthermore, in 1971 the Alberta Government introduced Heritage Day to celebrate ethnicity in the province. As a result, in 1976 "eleven ethno-cultural communities banded together in Edmonton's Hawrelak Park for a display of their cultures' traditional cuisine, entertainment, interpretive materials, and crafts"[10] in what is now known as Heritage Festival. Chilean immigrants were among these first ethnic communities that represented "Canada's cultural mosaic"[11] within Edmonton. Shortly afterwards, in 1982, one year after the creation of the *Nosotros* television program, Canada repatriated its Constitution and adopted a Charter of Rights and Freedoms, which includes "specific protection of multiculturalism throughout the country."[12]

Immigration waves correspond to the time of political and economic crises in various parts of the world. As Ginieniewicz and McKenzie point out, "until the 1990s most Latin Americans arrived in Canada as refugees."[13] This is seen in Alberta where a wave of Chilean immigration began after the 1973 coup in their country: within two years of this event the total number of immigrants from Chile increased almost tenfold. By the early 1990s, there were between 3,650[14] and 6000.[15]

In the 1980s, a wave of Salvadoreans escaped civil war in their country and immigrated to Canada and the province of Alberta. This new wave resulted in 3,665 Salvadoreans coming to Alberta, which represented 13 percent of the national total.[16] Guatemala also contributed immigrants to Alberta, but to a lesser extent than Chile and El Salvador. Most Guatemalan immigrants were, according to Kowalchuk,[17] *ladinos*, individuals of European descent.[18] All in all, by 2011, Alberta had welcomed 54,650 people with Latin Americans origins.[19]

Ginieniewicz and McKenzie recognized that the Latin American immigrant groups to Canada were "mainly composed of community organizers, intellectuals and professionals involved in politics, who also escaped political violence."[20] Palmer notes that the Chilean immigrants "faced a difficult period of adjustment because of their lack of English and limited job skills."[21] "Later, in the 1990s and 2000s, another large wave of skilled and well-educated Latin American immigrants arrived in Canada as a result of successive political and economic crises in the region."[22] Kowalchuk remarks that "political affinities make for friendlier relations between Salvadoreans and Guatemalan and Chilean immigrants, since all three fled right-wing dictatorships."[23] These common political affiliations and employment skill sets influenced the reasoning and way in which the *Nosotros* television program started.

Nosotros *Television Program Then and Now*

Even if there is not a published history of the Latin American communities in Alberta, the *Nosotros* program offers raw data to analyze, interpret, and apply in developing such a history. *Nosotros* displays a growing sense of "Latin American unity"[24] throughout its thirty-five year history and reflects the reality of the immigration patterns. The overarching theme of the hour-long *Nosotros* program is, as the current introduction announces, the Latin American communities in Edmonton and Alberta from Chile to Mexico, "desde Chile a México," and representing their memory, history, and sociopolitical worldviews. The founder, Medardo "Lito" Azócar, or Tío Lito,[25] recounted in the *Nosotros* November 4, 2013, episode that television, at the time of *Nosotros*' founding, was the best medium to communicate the message and stories told by Edmonton Hispanics, and, in his case, by Chileans who had escaped the Pinochet regime. This echoes Edmondson's assertion that "memory resides not just in things, but in people… [from] the creators […to] the archivists and [librarians]."[26] This is why the University of Alberta's *Nosotros* archiving project focuses on "guarding and sustaining [a] new kind of memory,"[27] making it, like Tío Lito's foundation of *Nosotros*, a sign of "effective democratization."[28]

When librarian Denis Lacroix heard about the *Nosotros* video collection in 2011, it consisted of original videos of every program aired on Shaw Television Channel from November 1981 until 2010 and was housed in Tío Lito's basement. After contacting Tío Lito and the current director of the program, Rod Loyola, the University of Alberta Libraries (UAL) was granted permission by *Nosotros*, the copyright owners, to begin digitizing the videos under a Creative Commons 3.0 license (**CC BY-NC-ND**) on a non-exclusive, worldwide, perpetual royalty free basis. This includes the right to publish, communicate, and make the videos available in a digitized format. The digitization process took place between 2012 and 2014 with the support of the Modern Languages and Cultural Studies (MLCS) Department and Dr. Victoria Ruétalo. Dr. Ruétalo, associate professor in the MLCS department, was instrumental in making her courses and students available to work on the project, as well as convincing the Arts Resource Centre (ARC), located in the basement of the University of Alberta's Old Arts building, to perform the digitization of the approximately 316 videos that arrived in two separate batches.

Digitization was a complex undertaking, for the original videos were in a range of formats: VHS, Super VHS, Betamax, and U-Matic. Thankfully the ARC had the expertise and equipment to manipulate, read, and digitize the diversity of materials. The ARC agreed to undertake the project because of the objective to integrate the videos in classroom teaching and as course content in some of the Spanish courses taught on campus. Thus, staff time was the only cost for digitizing the videos. However, student engagement with the video material became essential in order to assign metadata in the form of keywords and program summaries, but also, and perhaps more importantly, to begin sensitizing Edmonton Spanish and Latin American studies students to the Hispanic history and stories present in the city. The *Nosotros* collection allowed students to cast their intellectual gaze on their immediate surroundings in order to gain an understanding of Latin America.[29]

The University of Alberta Libraries (UAL) led the digitization project by ensuring that the videos were digitized, received complete metadata, and were uploaded to the Internet Archive. The project began as an initiative of Denis Lacroix, who secured the help from ARC and MLCS, and worked closely with Latin American community leaders to obtain and return the videocassette collection. Once the videos were digitized, Lacroix organized and supervised a curricular enrichment program called Community Service Learning (CSL) which allowed MLCS students to interact with the videos. The CSL program consisted of a group of students watching *Nosotros* videos and describing them using keywords and a brief program summary in a Google spreadsheet. A code book served as a reference for students in order to ensure standardization of the data (see Appendix at the end of this essay). The CSL projects also often involved students presenting information about the videos they watched to their classmates.

The large number of videos in the *Nosotros* collection required more time than CSL could provide, so the subject librarian engaged students from the University of Alberta School of Library and Information Studies (SLIS) and MacEwan University's library technician students to work on the project as part of their practicums. Library technician students helped digitize videos at the ARC, and SLIS students worked on the metadata aspect of the project. Once Sharon Farnel, the metadata coordinator, verified the consistency and accuracy of the metadata, the descriptive files[30] and videos were uploaded to the Internet Archive, whose mandate is "to prevent the Internet ... and other 'born digital' materials from disappearing into the past...[and to] maintain the accessibility of data."[31] An Internet Archive channel entitled *Nosotros*—Latin American Community Television Programme in Edmonton (Alberta) was created to house all of the uploaded digitized videos. Between July 2014 and January 2016, the Internet Archive *Nosotros* channel had 5,693 views.

The first *Nosotros* show to air in early 1982[32] discusses the reasons why the show was established. Various members of the Edmonton Latin American community talk about preserving their cultural heritage and language. Latin American unity "sin banderas ni fronteras" (beyond flags and borders) was the motivating factor for the views expressed on the show. It is clear, however, even before the host starts speaking, that a socialist worldview will inspire the programs since an image of a smiling dog bearing a red star opens the program. Based on the same socialist symbolism, this episode also features two performances by the musical group Los Jóvenes de Estrella Roja (Red Star Youth).

The third *Nosotros* show[33] interviews guests from the Salvadorean community in Edmonton and discusses the political and social turmoil and problems that are currently happening in El Salvador. The episode also features three traditional Salvadorean dances. This is the basic structure of a typical *Nosotros* program: a news story with an interview and/or a documentary, community announcements, and a concert of music or dance. While the first twenty years of the show were set in a television studio except for the taping of community events, the twenty-first century programs take place in situ with the host and participants located outside of any studio. They are, nonetheless, still associated with Shaw Television and broadcast on channel 10 five/six days a week. Current shows broadcast since 2012 are available on the Programa Nosotros YouTube channel.[34]

As a whole, the *Nosotros* shows have a pan-ethnic approach to representing the face of Hispanic Albertans. While an individual show usually focuses on the events or issues of one Latin American country, there is, in the sequence of shows, a fair representation of the origins of most Hispanics in Alberta; however, Chile and El Salvador are the countries most represented, but Peru, Nicaragua, and Guatemala are also featured regularly. As the local Mexican population is growing, it is likely that they will soon have a greater presence on *Nosotros*.

Nosotros reflects the concerns and reality of Hispanic Albertans, and contributes to building a memory and an identity, as Corina Andrea Norro would say, of what it means to be of Latin American origin and of its historical, social, political, and cultural roots.[35] In fact, Norro assigns a protagonist's role to audiovisual documents during dictatorships.[36] Similarly, Edmondson's description of audiovisual documents as being "populist"[37] is very much the case for *Nosotros*, which is a collection of artifacts of how the Hispanic community in Edmonton constructed its social memory at a given time. Through the digitization project, the videos can now have an impact on a new generation of Hispanic Canadians by providing them with a vision of their history that was heretofore remote or unknown.

The use of the Spanish language in the *Nosotros* shows contributes to the authenticity of the beliefs, values, and memories expressed. Beyond the cathartic effect of hearing their language, it allows viewers to experience a sense of belonging, or citizenship, to a community, for "[i]t is through the process of language socialization that children and other individuals acquire beliefs and values and form their identities."[38] The Wordle in Figure 1 portrays these values and beliefs as expressed through *Nosotros*. It is based on the metadata assigned to each of the shows: the larger the font the more common the theme over the years. Clearly the beliefs and values that viewers build when watching *Nosotros* are related to politics, history, and cultural activities.

Figure 1: Wordle Image Representing the Keywords Assigned to the *Nosotros* Shows (courtesy wordle.net).

Nosotros is first and foremost a social memory tool, to which its extensive thirty-five years' worth of historic material can attest. There is, nonetheless, a close relationship between *Nosotros*, the community television program, and a parent organization called Memoria Viva Society, whose mission it is "[t]o serve as an educational, artistic, and organizational hub for the Latin American community in diaspora in Edmonton."[39] The phrase *memoria viva* reflects the idea of keeping memory alive, and that is exactly what *Nosotros* achieves.

> Memory has an immense social role. It tells us who we are, embedding our present selves in our pasts, and thus underpinning every aspect of what historians often now call mentalités. For many groups, this means putting the puzzle back together: inventing the past to fit the present, or equally, the present to fit the past.[40]

The social role that *Nosotros* plays is one of solidarity, diversity, equity, peace with justice, ecological sustainability and indigenous knowledge, and democracy as stated in the program's values and principles.[41] These values are also compatible with the role of the University of Alberta Libraries which honor diversity, inclusivity, and intellectual freedom among other values.[42] Preserving memory by digitizing the *Nosotros* videos, uploading them to a safe storage facility like the Internet Archive, and facilitating world-wide access to them through metadata is a democratic act that helps bring the puzzle pieces of Hispanic Albertan history back together.

The predominant themes in *Nosotros* shows are by far democracy, solidarity, and justice. The definition of democracy that the founders of *Nosotros* had in mind relate to "people's power" and greater citizen participation in government.[43] This is closely tied to the values of justice and solidarity in terms of supporting socialist ideals and the rights of the poor in Latin America. Most of the shows from the first two decades address at least one of these values in one form or another. Not only do shows discuss the political turmoil in various Latin American countries, but they also address how to help the victims of persecution. *Nosotros* also mirrors local political organizations rooted in Latin America, e.g., Comunidad Eclesial de Base El Salvador (CEBES) and the Frente Farabundo Martí para la Liberación Nacional (FMLN),[44] and events, including the Víctor Jara Folk Festival, which honors the Chilean singer and activist. *Nosotros* has covered the Herramienta para la Paz (Tools for Peace) organization's support of Latin American artists, such as Luis Enrique Mejia Godoy in 1990, by bringing them to Edmonton to perform their music. Also, *Nosotros* covered an Edmonton Hispanic highlight in 1987: a concert by the exiled musical group Los Jaivas at the Jubilee Auditorium. Through cultural and political expressions the stories and memories of Hispanic refugees and immigrants to Alberta are revealed and in so doing become part of the historical fabric of the province itself.

There is an overwhelming presence of music and dance in the *Nosotros* shows, which makes it inextricable from social justice issues, for as Cobos and Sater point out, Chilean exiles wanted "to restore democracy to Chile usually through cultural expressions."[45] An example of this in *Nosotros* is the Mapuche support committee who shares the scene with other political groups, including a representative of the provincial New Democratic Party. Similarly, protest music with indigenous references, such as the Mapuche group Calafquen and the Venezuelan quartet Los Guaraguao[46] are given space to voice their concerns. One would think that with the diversity of political views, dissentions would become inevitable, but that does not appear to be the case for *Nosotros*, whose members "work well together" according to the first program director, Canadian-born Dave Trautman.[47] Rather *Nosotros* reflects Martin Guardado's conclusions on the cultural beliefs of an Hispanic Canadian couple he interviewed, which "reflected [its] understanding of Canadian multiculturalism, one in which all the different cultures ideally co-habit in the same geo-graphical and socio-politico-cultural space, without interfering with one another's cultural practices."[48]

Nosotros programming would not be complete without featuring local Hispanic school concerts from schools Gabriela Mistral, Salvador Allende, Jasper Place High, and Millcreek. Community outreach is essential to this type of program, which helps promote participatory democracy and "children's socialization into the cultural practices of their group [...] mediated by language."[49] Ava Becker's interviews of Edmonton Chileans high-light the potential for television to foster Spanish language preservation and "connecting with senior members of the community."[50] One can quickly see the possible interactions that exist when a *Nosotros* episode features Manuel Guerrero, town councilor of the Chilean municipality of Ñuñoa, discussing environmental protection and Chilean-

Canadian connections alongside local school representatives. The potential of such connections is tremendous and is a testament to the enriching possibilities of multiculturalism. The views expressed on the Nosotros program are meant to benefit Latin American unity, as the host of the initial show said. It is a grassroots initiative spearheaded by "obreros, doñas de casa, y estudiantes"[51] (laborers, housewives, and students) and is open to the entire Latin American community representing la "América morena" (the dark-skinned Americas) as the host of the first show explained.

Conclusion

In a September 2015 *Nosotros* documentary entitled "Monto Esperanza," an elderly Edmonton man shows documents from Latin American union organizations and political parties, a flag from the youth socialist party, copies of 1980 issues from the *Cuadernos de orientación socialista*, and a Frente Patriótico Manuel Rodríguez (FPMR) sign. He also recounts sending bikes, 86 school desks, and printing presses to Cuba in the 1980s. For a librarian these documents and these stories are sources of information to preserve for future generations. Such ephemeral and endangered documents along with the current *Nosotros* shows, which are only available through the program's YouTube channel,[52] may be future candidates for digitization, preservation, and long-term accessibility. However, for the long-term preservation of the first 30 years of *Nosotros* shows, in addition to the Internet Archive, the collection is also archived in the University of Alberta Libraries' digital media repository to ensure availability and access in the future. The repository, Umar Qasim[53] digital preservation officer at the UAL explains, will soon be integrated with the UAL's Blacklight Discovery Service, which will make the *Nosotros* videos discoverable to library patrons through a unified discovery system.

The *Nosotros* television archive is one of several community treasures waiting to be preserved and made accessible to researchers. Two such collections are the *Obispos y prebendas de Chiapa*[54] and *Obispados y prebendas en Guatemala*,[55] Latin American colonial-era manuscripts that were acquired by University of Alberta history professor Michael Polushin and whose deposit into UA's Dataverse[56] data repository was facilitated by the UAL. The *Obispos y prebendas de Chiapa* collection is currently one of the most downloaded in Dataverse. The unique structure of this data repository, which allows for file versioning, description, and sharing, allows the collections to grow as researchers interact with files and add new documents, such as manuscript transcriptions and translations. Library collections are therefore becoming organic, in the sense that patrons can add information to them, and taking on a life of their own. Similarly, the *Nosotros* collection, although static and not open to user-generated files, offers the potential for users to contribute their reviews of each episode on the Internet Archive channel, which may provide opportunities for experts to share their knowledge about the shows' content or context.

As the UAL moves forward with digital archiving, a future project will involve preserving websites and born-digital documents relating to Hispanic Albertans. This is possible using the Internet Archive's ArchiveIt web archiving service to which the UAL has contributed countless seeds in developing collections of historical value to Western Canada and University of Alberta researchers. From blogs and simple webpages to YouTube channels and Facebook and Twitter pages, ArchiveIt will be able to capture the history of the Latin American community in Alberta as it unfolds. The UAL reserves funds for building ArchiveIt collections, as it does for more traditional collection practices, because each seed added to ArchiveIt represents a cost and potentially a recurring cost depending on the frequency with which it is archived. Perhaps the *Nosotros* shows produced since 2012 and available only on YouTube can be preserved in such a way.

This UAL endeavour to preserve and ensure the long-term availability and findability of fragile and fleeting video and electronic documents has a direct impact on the communities it serves. The interests and expertise libraries have in providing access to information sources make them essential community partners. In the case of the *Nosotros* project, no one in the community but UAL was able and willing to find a home for all of Tío Lito's cherished videos. Now, because of its digitization, *Nosotros* can have a much broader impact than its original airings ever had. Furthermore, the process of creating digital surrogates of the videocassettes provided a learning opportunity for Spanish students to contribute to a real-life product and discover a piece of local and international history and culture they may never have encountered otherwise. For his part, the author of this essay and the librarian who undertook the initiative of digitizing the *Nosotros* video collection, experienced firsthand the discovery, preservation, and dissemination of a library collection that tells the story of a diverse and resilient community.

Appendix: Programa Nosotros— Metadata Guidelines

Below are brief instructions on entering descriptive information in the metadata template document (programa nosotros metadata template.xlsx).

For each episode (identified by the unique Item ID in column A), enter

- **Item ID**: corresponds to an approximate chronological order or the order in which the videos were received.
- **Tape #**: is the number the program director assigned to the tape
- **Format of original**: e.g. U–Matic, beta, super VHS, vhs, dvd
- **Episode recording date**: (separate items with a semicolon) is the date or dates indicated on the tape box. The date takes the form yyyy-mm-dd; e.g. 2010–12–05.
- **Episode play date**: (separate items with a semicolon) is the date or dates the program director indicates as the day(s) on which the program was aired. The date takes the form yyyy-mm-dd; e.g. 2010–12–05. N.B. check the play date given at the start of the film (on the colored bars), which should match the date given in the metadata spreadsheet. If it does not, change the metadata spreadsheet play date to reflect the information given on the film.
- **Episode title**: takes the form Programa Nosotros, dd—mm—yyyy, (Short Topic Title); e.g. Programa Nosotros, 13 de octubre de 1985, Rumbo al sur. N.B. use the first play date given at the start of the film on the color bars and find the short topic title at the start of the film or, in the absence of which, assign a short topic title based on your understanding of the film.
- **Program director**: (separate items with a semicolon) takes the form First name Last name and is taken from the tape box or from the film.

- **Program producer**: (separate items with a semicolon) takes the form First name Last name and is taken from the tape box or from the film.
- **Number of volunteers**: only indicate when known.
- **Persons interviewed and/or topics featured** (separate items with a semicolon); e.g. Spanish Bilingual School Father Leo Green; Victor Hugo Fernandez; University of Alberta SUB Theater 7pm 1989–11-19;
  - **Start time of each interview and/or feature** (separate items with a semicolon), e.g. 00:45; 15:01—NOTE: this information indicates the start time of each segment, interview or feature for each program.
  - **Keywords in English and Spanish**: (separate items with a semicolon) One to five words or phrases in English and Spanish that describe the general content of the episode, e.g. bilingual schools; Spanish language; fire fighters; Edmonton; St. Albert
  - **Program Summary**: this is one or more sentences in English describing each program and giving a general overview, e.g.
    - Tío Lito Azócar interviews two guests: Brad Palomo and Monica Chavez. Brad Palomo is a young Salvadorean-Canadian athlete who talks about how he joined two local soccer teams and his future career goals. Monica Chavez memorializes the life and work of Cardinal Raúl Silva Henriquez and his devotion to human rights in Chile. The show ends with a montage of Chilean culture.
- **Digitization Problems**: please describe briefly any problems in seeing or hearing the video. Please indicate the approximate film time when the problem occurred.

N.B. Only indicate the information for which you are certain. For example, if only the month and the year is given for the recording date and no other clues appear as to the day, you would only indicate the year and the month in the metadata for recording date.

NOTES

1. Harold Troper, "Multiculturalism," in *Encyclopedia of Canada's Peoples*, ed. Paul Robert Magocsi (Toronto: University of Toronto Press, 1999), 998.

2. Statistics Canada, "Immigrant Population by Place of Birth (260A) and Sex (3), Showing Period of Immigration (6) for Canada, Provinces, Territories and Census Metropolitan Areas 1996 Census (20% Sample Data)," Catalogue number 93F0023XDB96003.

3. Statistics Canada, "Citizenship (5), Place of Birth (236), Immigrant Status and Period of Immigration (11), Age Groups (10) and Sex (3) for the Population in Private Households of Canada, Provinces, Territories, Census Metropolitan Areas and Census Agglomerations, *2011 National Household Survey*, Catalogue number 99–010-X2011026, accessed January 2016, http://www12.statcan.ca/nhs-enm/2011/dp-pd/dt-td/Rp-eng. cfm?LANG=E&APATH=3&DETAIL=0&DIM=0&FL=A&FREE=0&GC=0&GID=0&GK=0&GRP=0&PID= 105411&PRID=0&PTYPE=105277&S=0&SHOWALL=0&SUB=0&Temporal=2013&THEME=95&VID= 0&VNAMEE=&VNAMEF=.

4. Victor Armony, "Introduction: Latin American Diasporas: Common Origins and Different Paths," *Canadian Ethnic Studies* 46, no. 3 (09, 2014): 1.

5. Victor Armony, "Latin American Communities in Canada: Trends in Diversity and Integration," *Canadian Ethnic Studies* 46, no. 3 (09, 2014): 8.

6. *Ibid.*, 8.

7. The cultural and linguistic situation of Hispanic-Quebecers may be changing. For the past nine years, the significant Hispanic population in Quebec and Ontario have had access to a Spanish language television channel, entitled *Nuevo Mundo Televisión* (NMTV), which offers a locally produced program called *Punto de Vista* that focuses on the city of Montreal. The objective of this new channel is to offer Canadian Spanish speakers the necessary tools to help them integrate into Canadian society. Ironically, this channel is not available outside of Ontario and Quebec.

8. Howard Palmer and Tamara Palmer, "Boom and Bust: The Lougheed Years and After," in *Alberta A New History* (Edmonton: Hurtig Publishers, 1990), 327.

9. *Ibid.*, 333.

10. Heritage Festival, "Heritage Festival History," accessed January 2016, http://www.heritage-festival.com/the-festival-history/.

11. Edmonton Journal, "Alberta Heritage Day Takes on a New Twist This Year," *Edmonton Journal,* Wednesday, July 21, 1976, 29.

12. David Erdos, "Canada and the Canadian Charter of Rights and Freedoms (1982)," Chap. 5.2.2, in *Delegating Rights Protection: The Rise of Bills of Rights in the Westminster World* (Oxford: Oxford University Press, 2010), 75.

13. Jorge Ginieniewicz and Kwame McKenzie, "Mental Health of Latin Americans in Canada: A Literature Review," *International Journal of Social Psychiatry* 60, no. 3 (05, 2014): 270.

14. Harry Diaz, "Chileans," in *Encyclopedia of Canada's Peoples,* ed. Paul Robert Magocsi (Toronto: University of Toronto Press, 1999), 350.

15. Howard Palmer and Tamara Palmer, "Boom and Bust: The Lougheed Years and After," in *Alberta A New History* (Edmonton: Hurtig Publishers, 1990), 333.

16. Lisa Kowalchuk, "Salvadoreans," in *Encyclopedia of Canada's Peoples,* ed. Paul Robert Magosci (Toronto: University of Toronto, 1999), 1111.

17. Lisa Kowalchuk, "Guatemalans," in *Encyclopedia of Canada's Peoples,* ed. Paul Robert Magosci (Toronto: University of Toronto, 1999), 627.

18. For further discussion of the use of the term ladino, see J. David Dressing, "Ladino," in *Encyclopedia of Latin American History and Culture,* eds. Jay Kinsbruner and Erick D. Langer. 2nd ed. vol. 4 (Detroit: Charles Scribner's Sons, 2008), 116.

19. Statistics Canada, "Ethnic Origin (264), Single and Multiple Ethnic Origin Responses (3), Generation Status (4), Age Groups (10) and Sex (3) for the Population in Private Households of Canada, Provinces, Territories, Census Metropolitan Areas and Census Agglomerations," *2011 National Household Survey,* Catalogue number 99–010-X2011028, accessed september 7, 2018, https://www12.statcan.gc.ca/nhs-enm/2011/dp-pd/dt-td/Rp-eng.cfm?LANG=E&APATH=3&DETAIL=0&DIM=0&FL=A&FREE=0&GC=0&GID=0&GK=0&GRP=1&PID=105396&PRID=0&PTYPE=105277&S=0&SHOWALL=0&SUB=0&Temporal=2013&THEME=95&VID=0&VNAMEE=&VNAMEF=.

20. Jorge Ginieniewicz and Kwame McKenzie, "Mental Health of Latin Americans in Canada: A Literature Review," *International Journal of Social Psychiatry* 60, no. 3 (05, 2014): 267.

21. Howard Palmer and Tamara Palmer, "Boom and Bust: The Lougheed Years and After," in *Alberta A New History* (Edmonton: Hurtig Publishers, 1990), 333.

22. Jorge Ginieniewicz and Kwame McKenzie, "Mental Health of Latin Americans in Canada: A Literature Review," *International Journal of Social Psychiatry* 60, no. 3 (05, 2014): 267.

23. Lisa Kowalchuk, "Salvadoreans," in *Encyclopedia of Canada's Peoples,* ed. Paul Robert Magosci (Toronto: University of Toronto, 1999), 1115.

24. Victor Armony, "Introduction: Latin American Diasporas: Common Origins and Different Paths." *Canadian Ethnic Studies* 46, no. 3 (09, 2014): 2.

25. Don Medardo Azócar passed away in Edmonton in February 2015.

26. Ray Edmondson, *Audiovisual Archiving: Philosophy and Principles (CI/2004/WS/2)* (Paris: UNESCO, 2004), 66.

27. *Ibid.*, 5.

28. *Ibid.*

29. Besides assigning metadata to the videos distributed to their groups, Latin American studies students were required to prepare a classroom presentation describing and reflecting on the topic of the videos. It is, for example, with great interest that students discovered an interview and a special children's program, which aired in 1984, with Chilean Luis Guzman, as Pippo the clown.

30. See *Nosotros* episode summaries at https://era.library.ualberta.ca/downloads/btb09j569j.

31. Internet Archive, "About the Internet Archive," accessed January 19, 2016, https://archive.org/about/.

32. See https://archive.org/details/programa-nosostros-1A.

33. See https://archive.org/details/programa-nosostros-1C.

34. See https://www.youtube.com/user/ProgramaNosotros.

35. Corina Andrea Norro, "Los Documentos Audiovisuales: Aportes Para La Memoria En Construcción," in *Preserving Memory : Documenting and Archiving Latin American Human Rights : Papers of the Fifty-Sixth Annual Meeting of the Seminar on the Acquisition of Latin American Library Materials, Philadelphia, Pennsylvania, May 28–June 1, 2011,* ed. Nerea A. Llamas, vol. 56, 36 (New Orleans, Louisiana: SALALM Secretariat, Tulane University, 2013), 34.

36. *Ibid.*, 37.

37. Ray Edmondson, *Audiovisual Archiving: Philosophy and Principles (CI/2004/WS/2)* (Paris: UNESCO, 2004), 7.

38. Martin Guardado, "Heritage Language Development: Preserving a Mythic Past or Envisioning the Future of Canadian Identity?" *Journal of Language, Identity, and Education* 9, no. 5 (01/01, 2010): 330–331.

39. Memoria Viva Society of Edmonton, "Memoria Viva Society of Edmonton," accessed January 2016, https://memoriavivaed.wordpress.com/.

40. James Fentress and Chris Wickham, *Social Memory* (Oxford: Blackwell, 1992), 201.

41. Nosotros Community Television Program, "About the Nosotros Community Television Program," accessed January 20, 2016, http://www.nosotros.ca/.

42. University of Alberta Libraries, "Vision—UofA Libraries," accessed January 2016, https://www.library.ualberta.ca/about-us/vision/.

43. Nosotros Community Television Program, "About the Nosotros Community Television Program," accessed January 20, 2016, http://www.nosotros.ca/.

44. The Edmonton branch of the FMLN still exists and even has Twitter and Facebook accounts.

45. Ana Maria Cobos and Ana Lya Sater, "Preserving the Memory of Chilean Exile, 1973–1989," in *Preserving Memory : Documenting and Archiving Latin American Human Rights : Papers of the Fifty-Sixth Annual Meeting of the Seminar on the Acquisition of Latin American Library Materials, Philadelphia, Pennsylvania, May 28¬–June 1, 2011* (New Orleans, Louisiana: SALALM Secretariat, Tulane University, 2013), 82.

46. Other musical groups featured on *Nosotros* from the beginning of the shows until 2010 are Inti-Illimani, Trigal, Rumbo al sur, Paulo Garrido, Isabel Aldunate, Amparo Ochoa, Tupac, B-Cuadro, Ramon Aguilera, Xuxa, Jauapiyajta, Grupo Amabana, Grupo Andino, Bafochi, Tepehuani, Los Iracundos, Amaury, and America Rosa among many others.

47. Dave Trautman, "Interview by *Nosotros* Host," *Nosotros: Fin de fase 1 y selección de episodios previos* (1982), section 8, 25:26, https://era-av.library.ualberta.ca/media_objects/avalon:39251

48. Martin Guardado, "Heritage Language Development: Preserving a Mythic Past or Envisioning the Future of Canadian Identity?" *Journal of Language, Identity, and Education* 9, no. 5 (01/01, 2010): 338.

49. *Ibid.*, 330.

50. Ava Becker, "Political Ideology and Heritage Language Development in a Chilean Exile Community: A Multiple Case Study," Master of Arts Thesis in Applied Linguistics (Edmonton: University of Alberta, 2013), 86–87.

51. See https://archive.org/details/programa-nosostros-1A.

52. See https://www.youtube.com/user/ProgramaNosotros.

53. Umar Qasim, e-mail message to author, February 8, 2016.

54. See http://dx.doi.org/10.7939/DVN/10160.

55. See http://dx.doi.org/10.7939/DVN/10150.

56. See https://dataverse.library.ualberta.ca/dvn/.

About the Contributors

Holly **Ackerman** is the Librarian for Latin American, Iberian and Latino Studies at Duke University and a member of Duke's graduate faculty in history. She holds a BA in sociology from Howard University, a MS in social work from Columbia University, a Ph.D. in International Studies from the University of Miami, and a postdoctoral certificate in Latin American librarianship from Duke University.

Fernando **Acosta-Rodríguez** has been the Librarian for Latin American, Iberian and Latino Studies at the Princeton University Library since 2003. Before that, he was the Latin American Bibliographer at The New York Public Library (1997–2003). At Princeton, in addition to being responsible for the development of its general library collections, he manages the Digital Archive of Latin American and Caribbean Ephemera and works closely with the Manuscripts Division.

S. Lief **Adleson** received an undergraduate degree in Latin American Studies (University of California, Santa Cruz, 1973) and a Ph.D. in history from El Colegio de México (1982). After six years of secure and tranquil employment at the Instituto Nacional de Antropología e Historia in Mexico City, he quit to seek full-time thrills as a specialized book vendor.

Judith Eckoff **Alspach** serves as Area Studies Program Manager at the Center for Research Libraries (CRL) and has coordinated its Area Studies Materials and Global Resources Projects since 2006. She has degrees in history from Northwestern University and Western Michigan University, and a Master's Degree in library and information science from Dominican University.

Peter **Altekrueger** is the Vice-Director and Library Director of the Ibero-American Institute (IAI), Prussian Cultural Heritage Foundation, in Berlin. He is also Bibliographer for Argentina and Paraguay. He holds an MA in Latin American Studies from Rostock University. He completed a training program for senior-level library service at the IAI and the Cologne University of Applied Sciences. He is a member of SALALM, and currently chairs its Subcommittee on Serials.

Sarah **Aponte** is the Chief Librarian of the CUNY Dominican Studies Institute at The City College of New York and an associate professor at The City College Libraries, teaching courses on Dominican Studies and bibliographical instruction. She founded the Dominican Library in 1994. She holds an M.L.S. from Queens College; an MSEd from Baruch College; a BA from the City College of New York; and an AA from Hostos Community College.

Sarah **Buck Kachaluba** is the Latin American Studies Librarian at U.C. San Diego. She holds a Ph.D. in history (Rutgers University) and an M.L.I.S. (University of North Texas). Her research focuses on women's and gender history and reproductive politics in Mexico and the research advantages, disadvantages, and possibilities offered by print vs. digital technologies (including ebooks).

Hortensia Calvo has been the Doris Stone Director of Tulane's Latin American Library since 2003. She holds a *Licenciatura* in philosophy from Universidad de Los Andes (Bogotá), an MA in Spanish and Spanish American literature from the University of Illinois at Urbana-Champaign, and a Ph.D.

259

in Spanish from Yale University. Her research includes the Spanish American Baroque, and the social history of print in Latin America. She also serves as Executive Director of SALALM.

Teresa **Chapa** is the librarian for Latin America, Iberia, Latina/o Studies and Indigenous Studies at the University of North Carolina at Chapel Hill. She was an associate professor of Spanish before receiving an Andrew P. Mellon fellowship in Latin American librarianship at Duke University's Perkins Library. After completing her fellowship, she began her position at Carolina.

Daisy **Domínguez** is the Information Literacy Librarian and an assistant professor at the City College of New York Libraries in CUNY. She received her BA in Latin American Studies from New York University, her MLS from Long Island University, and her MA in history from the City College of New York. Her primary library-related research interest is audiovisual collection development.

Julianne **Gilland** is the Deputy Director of the Colby College Museum of Art. She served as Director of the Nettie Lee Benson Latin American Collection and a member of the directors' team for LLILAS Benson Latin American Studies and Collections at the University of Texas at Austin from 2014 to 2017.

Luis A. **González** is the Librarian for Latin American, Spanish & Portuguese, Latino, and European Studies, and an adjunct associate professor in history at Indiana University. He holds a Ph.D. in history from the University of Minnesota, with a concentration in modern Brazil, and trained as a librarian at Duke University. In 2014–2015, he served as President of SALALM.

Pamela M. **Graham** is the Director of Global Studies and Director of the Center for Human Rights Documentation & Research at Columbia University Libraries/Information Services, where she also worked as the Latin American & Iberian Studies Librarian. Since 2008, she has served as a member of the steering committee for Columbia Libraries' Web Collection Program.

Julienne E. **Grant** is a Reference Librarian/Foreign and International Research Specialist at the Loyola University Chicago School of Law Library. She is also adjunct faculty at Loyola where she teaches a course on foreign, comparative, and international legal research. She received an MALS from Rosary College, and a J.D. from DePaul University. She is Chair of the American Association of Law Libraries' Latin American Law Interest Group.

Melissa **Guy** is the Director of the Nettie Lee Benson Latin American Collection University of Texas at Austin where she was Head Bibliographer from 2015 to 2017. She holds an MA in Latin American history from the University of Arizona and an MSIS from the iSchool at the University of Texas.

Sean Patrick **Knowlton** is the Research & Instruction Librarian for the Humanities at Tulane University. He has worked as a Latin Americanist and Iberianist librarian at the University of Colorado at Boulder, the Latin American Library at Tulane University, and as the first 2CUL Latin American and Iberian Studies Librarian at Columbia University and Cornell University. He earned an MA in Hispanic literature (2000) and an MSLS in library science (2002) from the University of North Carolina at Chapel Hill.

Jana Lee **Krentz** is the curator for the Latin American, Iberian and Latinx Collections at Yale University Library where she is a Fellow at Ezra Stiles College, and serves on the Executive Board of the Council on Latin American and Iberian Studies. She has Masters' degrees in Spanish and Portuguese literature and linguistics and library information from the University of Wisconsin–Madison. Her doctoral work was done at Indiana University in Bloomington in Hispanic literature.

Denis **Lacroix** has been a librarian for the past thirteen years at the University of Alberta Libraries in Edmonton. He has a BA and B.Ed. from the University of Saskatchewan and an MLIS from the University of Alberta. He is the chair of the Humanities and Social Sciences Library Scholarly Communication Team, a member of the University of Alberta's Research Ethics Board and Research Data Management Team, and liaison for Student Accessibility Services.

Lara **Lookabaugh** worked as a librarian in the University of Florida Latin American and Caribbean Collection from 2014 to 2016. She holds an MA in Latin American Studies, a graduate certificate in Gender and Development from the University of Florida (2015) and an MLIS from Florida State University (2011).

Paul S. **Losch** has served as Head Librarian and Bibliographer of the University of Florida Latin American and Caribbean Collection since 2014, and has worked in the collection since 2000. He holds an MA in Latin American Studies from the University of Florida (2002) and an MLS from Florida State University (2003).

Philip S. MacLeod serves as the Bibliographer for Latin American and Caribbean Studies, Romance languages and comparative literature for Emory University. He holds an interdisciplinary MA and Ph.D. in Latin American Studies from Tulane University and earned his MLIS from Southern Connecticut State University. He has previously worked as the Curator of Manuscripts for the Latin American Library at Tulane University.

Teresa M. **Miguel-Stearns** is a Law Librarian and Professor of Law at the Lillian Goldman Law Library, Yale Law School. She previously served as the Associate Director of Foreign and International Law at which time she was the Latin American and Iberian bibliographer and taught courses on law, politics, and society in Latin America, and legal research in foreign and international law. She received her MLIS from the University of Arizona and J.D. from the University of Richmond.

Ricarda **Musser** is the Director of the Acquisition and Cataloguing Department, and Bibliographer for Brazil, Chile, and Portugal in the Library of the Ibero-American Institute (IAI), Prussian Cultural Heritage Foundation, in Berlin. She holds a Ph.D. in Romance Cultural Studies and an MA in library and information science, Portuguese, and psychology from Humboldt University, Berlin. She is member of SALALM, and was elected as Member-at-Large for the term 2015–2018.

Guillermo **Náñez Falcón** received an MA and Ph.D. in Latin American history from Tulane University. He was the Manuscripts Librarian in Tulane Library's Special Collections until 1990 and served as Director of the Latin American Library at Tulane from 1990 to 2002. Since retirement from Tulane, he has been active as a volunteer working with a chamber music organization in New Orleans.

Kent **Norsworthy** is a consultant on born digital collecting and digital scholarship. He retired from the University of Texas at Austin in 2015, where he was the Digital Scholarship Coordinator at the LLILAS Benson Latin American Studies and Collections. Since 2005, he directed UT's web archiving program and was one of the founding directors of the Latin American Network Information Center, LANIC.

Jennifer **Osorio** is the Librarian for Latin American Studies, Spanish and Portuguese, Chicano/s Studies and American Indian Studies at the University of California, Los Angeles (UCLA). She holds an MLIS and an MA in Latin American Studies, both from UCLA. She is on the Council of the Scholarly Communications and Research Section of the Latin American Studies Association and chairs the Subcommittee on Marginalized People and Ideas in SALALM, along with serving on the Membership Committee.

Richard F. **Phillips** worked at the University of Florida as a cataloger of Latin American monographs from 1978 to 1986, and then as Head Librarian and Bibliographer of the University of Florida Latin American and Caribbean Collection from 1993 to 2014. He holds a MLS degree from Florida State University (1976), and an MA in Latin American Studies from the University of Florida (1981). In 1998/1999, he served as President of SALALM.

Theresa E. **Polk** is the Archivist for Post-Custodial and Digital Initiatives at the LLILAS Benson Latin American Studies and Collections at the University of Texas at Austin. She has a BA in Latin American Studies, and Masters degrees in library science and international peace studies. Prior to coming to the University of Texas, she worked on international human rights and development policy.

Nelson **Santana** is an assistant professor and Collection Development Librarian at Bronx Community College. He previously worked as Assistant Librarian/Assistant Archivist at the CUNY Dominican Studies Institute at The City College of New York. He holds an MA in the Study of the Americas from The City College of New York and a Master of Science in library and information science with a concentration in Archival Studies from Drexel University.

Laura D. **Shedenhelm** received her MLIS from UCLA, holds an MA in Spanish literature and is completing a Ph.D. in Romance languages at the University of Georgia. She serves as the Bibliographer for Latin America, Spain, and Portugal for the UGA Libraries, and as the Media Archives Cataloger in the Walter J. Brown Media Archives & Peabody Awards Collection in the Special Collections Libraries at UGA.

Lynn M. **Shirey** has held the position of Librarian for Latin America, Spain and Portugal at Widener Library, Harvard University, since 2004. In prior years she was Assistant, and then Acting Librarian for the same areas. She served as President of SALALM for 2011–2012. She has a BA from Boston College and an MLS from Simmons College.

Sócrates **Silva** graduated with a dual MA in Latin American Studies and Information Studies from the University of California, Los Angeles. Before becoming the 2CUL Latin American and Iberian Studies Librarian at Columbia and Cornell University Libraries, he was an associate editor at the *Hispanic American Periodicals Index (HAPI)* and Latin American and Iberian Studies Librarian at the University of California, Santa Barbara.

Gayle Ann **Williams** is the Latin American & Caribbean Information Services Librarian/dLOC Librarian at Florida International University. She received an MLS from the University of Texas at Austin and an MA in Latin American Studies from the University of New Mexico. She is a Past-President of SALALM (1997–1998) and serves as editor of SALALM's *Bibliography of Latin American and Caribbean Bibliographies.*

Index